IN THE TIME OF CANNIBALS

CHICAGO STUDIES IN ETHNOMUSICOLOGY

Edited by Philip Bohlman *and* Bruno Nettl

IN THE TIME OF CANNIBALS

The Word Music of South Africa's Basotho Migrants

DAVID B. COPLAN

The University of Chicago Press
Chicago and London

David B. Coplan is associate professor of social anthropology at the University of Cape Town. He is the author of *In Township Tonight: South Africa's Black City Music and Theatre.*

The University of Chicago Press, Chicago 60637
The University of Chicago Press, Ltd., London

Printed in the United States of America

03 02 01 00 99 98 97 96 95 94   5 4 3 2 1

ISBN (cloth): 0–226–11573–9
ISBN (paper): 0–226–11574–7

Library of Congress Cataloging-in-Publication Data

Coplan, David B. (David Bellin)
In the time of cannibals : the word music of South Africa's Basotho migrants / David B. Coplan.
p. cm. — (Chicago studies in ethnomusicology)
Includes bibliographical references and index.
ISBN 0-226-11573-9. — ISBN 0–226–11574–7 (pbk.)
1. Sotho (African people)—Music—History and criticism. 2. Music—Lesotho—History and criticism. 3. Sotho poetry—History and criticism. I. Title. II. Series.
ML3760.C66 1994
782.42162′963977—dc20   94-9093
CIP
MN

∞ The paper used in this publication meets the minimum requirements of the American National Standard for Information Sciences—Permanence of Paper for Printed Library Materials, ANSI Z39.48–1984.

In memory of

Burton Victor Coplan, 1918–1993
and
Seakhi Santho, 1963–1989

Contents

A gallery of photographs follows page 64.

Acknowledgments

An African scholar of my acquaintance suggested a novel, if typically African, way to spare oneself unnecessary reading in our print-surfeited profession. To absorb a new book most efficiently, he suggested, you need only read the acknowledgments. Well, as a Victorian lady commented upon hearing Darwin's news that humanity was descended from the apes, "Let us hope it is not true; or if it is, that it does not become generally known." As to my intellectual kith and kin, readers (truly an honorable title) will find them residing in the text. As to those without whom which . . . my everlasting gratitude goes to renowned Mosotho choral composer and my consultant and friend, the late J. P. Mohapeloa, who was the first to suggest to me that the migrants' songs were worthy of serious study; the Social Science Research Council and former Africa Staff Associates Martha Gephart and Tom Lodge; the National Endowment for the Humanities; the Council for the International Exchange of Scholars and Africa Director Linda Rhoad; Dr. Gwendolyn Malahleha and the staff and executive board of the Institute for Southern African Studies, National University of Lesotho; David Ambrose, Christopher Dunton, Tom Lynn, Sehoai Santho, and Makali Mokitimi of the National University of Lesotho; Dr. R. I. M. Moletsane, formerly of the University of the Transkei, now in Lesotho; Dr. Thoahlane Thoahlane, formerly of the National University of Lesotho, now Stellenbosch University; Mr. Gei Zantzinger and Ms. Lynne Gulezian of Constant Springs Productions; Professor Robert Edgar of Howard University; Mr. David Rycroft of the School of Oriental and African Studies, University of London; Professor Leroy Vail of Harvard University; Professor George Marcus of Rice University; Professors John and Jean Comaroff of the University of Chicago; Dr. Christopher Whann of Skidmore College and Dr. Paul Landau of the University of New Hampshire; Professor Stephen Blum of the City University of New York; Professor David Robinson of Michigan State University; Dr. Philip Bonner of the University of the Witwatersrand; Professor Jeffrey Guy and Professor Keyan Tomaselli of the University of Natal; Deputy Vice-Chancellor Martin West, Dr. Andrew Spiegel, and the entire staff of the Department of Social Anthropology at the University of Cape Town; Georgia McMillen; Solly Khoza of EMI Johannesburg; Armstrong Moqalepu, Morena Lerotholi oa Leshoboro of Likhoele; Ntate Nthebe Bulara and his family; Ntate Teboho Santho, 'Makhotso Santho, Khapametsi Santho, and Seakhi Santho; Joachim Ntebele, Cletus Sethunya, Pinky Monyake, M. K. Malefane, Edward Fobo, Potlako Ntsekhe; John Metzger and Adhiambo Ajulu; Makeka Likhojane, Molefi Motsoahae, Mphafu Mofolo, Hlalele Mabekanyane, Tieho Rakharebe; Samson Motolo, Thakane Mahlasi, Ntabiseng Nthako, Alinah Tsekoa, Sporty Mothibeli, 'Malitaba Sanaha, Puseletso Seema, Forere Motloheloa, David Motaung, Apolo Ntabinyane, Majara Majara, Phofolo Pitso, Rabonne Mariti. Above all, my wife Lydia, who worked hard on the Sesotho and kept the mundane world at bay while her husband assembled his tribute to her culture, and my long-suffering, unstintingly supportive parents, Burton and Ina Bellin Coplan.

Preface

What am I saying, eloquent poets of my home? . . .
. . . I am not an apprentice but a master healer—
I am the horned one;
I am no longer an owlet but a great horned owl.
What am I saying to you, my elders?
I'm the horned one who stays in the trees:
A little should I steal [reveal] for you.
Majara Majara

Among the many paradoxes that struck me during my first visit to South Africa in 1975, when apartheid was in bloated, parasitic flower, was the continuity and vitality of black popular culture and its almost total lack of documentation or recognition in South African public or intellectual life. Potted transplants like Alf Herbert's "African Jazz and Variety" shows or the "Dorkay Jazz" concert series, sudden blooms like the musical drama *King Kong*, international hit songs like "Skokiaan" (Louis Armstrong's "Happy Africa") and "Tom Hark," the success of exiled jazz virtuosos Miriam Makeba, Hugh Masekela, and Dollar Brand (Abdullah Ibrahim)—all seemed to the majority of the white public to have emerged out of nowhere. Having discarded African "tradition," these musical notables from the underground appeared as media-mediated products of Johannesburg's cultural hothouse. Inspired, I decided to discover from those who had created it the story of black Johannesburg, as enacted on the stages of its performing arts.

Ten years later, after the brutal repression of one rebellion (Soweto, 1976) and the outbreak of another (1984–90), not to mention seemingly endless procrastination by the publisher, this story appeared as *In Township Tonight!* (Coplan 1985). But by then some things, it seemed, were changing. Many voices had arisen to tell the South African story from within

South Africa itself, and they could do it in our language, in our idiom, in our classrooms, in our mass media. Nor were all the voices those of South Africa's small but powerfully eloquent black elite. A Zulu "garden boy" named Sipho Mchunu had left the servants' quarters of Harry Oppenheimer's mansion in Johannesburg's wealthy white suburbs to become an international music star with bicultural Johnny Clegg's Anglo-Zulu group "Juluka." Joseph Shabalala, leader of Ladysmith Black Mambazo, was rich and famous and profoundly respected by his people a decade before Paul Simon's *Graceland*, but now he spoke English as well as Zulu and you could interview him in New York instead of traveling to Clermont location, Pinetown, Natal. Mbongani Ngema and a crowd of school kids from Natal conquered New York in *Sarafina!* despite the puzzled incomprehension of the *New York Times*. In the summer of 1990, the aging originators of popular working class *mbaqanga* music, Simon "Mahlathini" Nkabinde and the Mahotella Queens with the Makgona Tshole Band, toured the United States alongside Nelson Mandela himself.

The origins of this volume go back to 1978, when my expulsion from South Africa led me to research the cultural continuities between rural and urban black performance in the neighboring countries of Botswana, Swaziland, and Lesotho. In Lesotho—entirely surrounded by South Africa and dependent on it for employment, resources, and supplies—I came across rich veins of cultural commentary, historical metaphor, and self-construction in the performances of some of the most unknown and least empowered participants in the southern African political economy. In the maw of the mines alone, guts of the South African economy, there were over half a million workers, more than a quarter of them Basotho. Man-eating work, but given the lack of alternatives, nice if you could get it. I spent time in the unlicensed house taverns called *shebeens* (from Gaelic, "little shop"; Coplan 1985, 92–98) or *lipoto* (sing.: *sepoto;* from English "spot"), where migrant mine and factory workers on leave, the retired, the unemployed, and their women gathered to drink and talk, sing and dance. Preliminary efforts to translate some of their song texts revealed a play of tropes so protean and inventive, so layered with history, so allusive that no ethnography of Basotho custom, no history of colonial invasion, no sociology of migrant labor, no political economic treatise on underdevelopment, no "oral literary" analysis could capture them. Their composers spoke no English. Social scientists and social workers had elicited some remarkable testimony from migrant workers and their wives by means of key informant interviews (Wilson 1972; Matsobane and Eggenhuizen 1976; Murray 1981; Spiegel 1980; Gay 1980a, 1980b, 1980c), but here were other voices, other rooms: a country not yet heard from in its own forms and contexts of self-representation.

Since then, the trades union movement, specifically, the National Union of Mineworkers (NUM), has emerged as a powerful medium for both the expression and pursuit of migrant workers' aspirations. But the methods of interpretive anthropology still offer the best access to the migrants' "local knowledge" (Geertz 1983). As the Comaroffs have observed:

> Culture always intervenes directly in consciousness and its expression. . . . History lies in its representation; for representation is as much the making of history as it is consciousness speaking out. . . . The poetry of representation, in short, is not an aesthetic embellishment of a "truth" that lies elsewhere. [It is] the stuff of everyday thought and action—of the human consciousness through which culture and history construct each other. (1987, 207)

My first fieldwork specifically concerned with the migrants' songs, known as *sefela sa* (pl.: *lifela tsa*) *litsamaea-naha*, "inveterate travelers' songs," was carried out between Christmas 1983 and August 1984 with the support of a postdoctoral grant from the Social Science Research Council. It included six weeks devoted to the shooting of the film *Songs of the Adventurers* (Constant Springs Productions 1986) with ethnographic filmmaker Gei Zantzinger. Under the auspices of the Institute of Southern African Studies at the National University of Lesotho, I conducted a survey of both male migrant and cognate women's genres, principally in the lowland border towns where labor recruitment offices are located and *shebeens* flourish. While the latter are the special performance arena of female composers, the most renowned male *likheleke*, "eloquent ones," preferred performing among their friends around town or at home in their villages, in front of the neighbors. And so we drove and walked over the rocky roads and the sledge and horse tracks of western Lesotho in search of eloquence and the experience and knowledge it expressed.

By this means I discovered who the performers were, where they were, and where they had been—which was all over the place. This would not be a community study in the residential sense, for the "performance community" was spread throughout Lesotho and the neighboring provinces of South Africa. The name "travelers' songs" was certainly apt, since performers were hardly ever found in the places I left them. Hiking the hills in hopes of making the acquaintance of a singer could make you feel like a Chicago G-man hunting Oklahoma for Pretty Boy Floyd. No one stayed home, but as the proverb teaches, *Tang-tang e betoa ke leroele*, "The one behind gets choked by dust" (Guma 1967, 85). *Lifela* performances are by convention unscheduled, impromptu, and competitive, so performance events were most often happened upon or inspired by the presence of the peculiar but amiable foreign "teacher," with his inexplicable but clearly serious interest in Sesotho, the language and culture of the Basotho. My poor command of the language at that point suggested there was little danger that I would actually understand the rapid, rhythmic bursts of figurative Sesotho I was recording. If I can be justifiably accused of initiating as opposed to merely witnessing performances, it cannot be said that they were created for my benefit. Looking over the texts after preliminary written transcription, I did occasionally find myself apostrophized, the singer praising himself with my name:

Lumela ntate David Coplan, *tsoeu ea kotase.*	Greetings Mr. David Coplan, the white one of the white miners quarters.
Nkabe ke sa cho, ntate, *"Lumela": o tlile ho' na.* *Lena o tlile ho tla mpona:* *Hoa ipaka kese ke le moholo.*	I ought not to say, sir, "Greetings": *you* have come to *me*. This day you have come to see me: It shows I am already one of the greats.

(Tieho Rakharebe, "Hulas Ralipotsotso")

Uncertainty about my competence and motives did not therefore vitiate the value and effect of my attendance, even if I was a cultural deaf-mute. But afterward, some performers got a rather nasty shock when I returned with their outpourings carefully written down, intent on the answers to a host of exegetical, biographical, and ethnographic queries: interview as interrogation, informant as informer, ethnography as espionage. Some of my colleagues, troubled by the patronizing (or worse) implications of terms such as "fieldwork" and "informant" have renamed these essential activities and roles. But in practice there seems to be little difference between yesterday's "fieldwork" and "informant" and today's research "dialogue" and "collaborator," and the historical connotations of the latter term are anything but savory. Perhaps another term now gaining popularity, "consultant," deserves to win the day, though the odor of contractuality that hangs about it should still make ethnographers uncomfortable.

Both the antagonism and the mutual dependency inherent in the relationship of artist and critic attach themselves to the ethnography of performance (and of all other aesthetic modes of representation) regardless of the physical, social, or cultural distances that might have been crossed to bring interpreter and subject together. The ethnographer, like the critic, seeks to categorize and comprehend; the performer to evade categorization and comprehension. As consultant, designated purveyor of local knowledge, the performer's discourse reveals, conceals, and manipulates cultural principles of aesthetic production. As creator of representations on some level distinctly his own, he is at once trickster, wizard, and hero—adding his personality to his collectivity, extending their vision uniquely. Yet there is clearly an important difference between the critic, foreign or domestic, who applies his or her own cultural standards to the explicit qualitative evaluation of performances and performers, and the ethnological analyst, who seeks to reveal and comprehend aspects and logics of cultural knowledge and meaning in performance that would never be voiced by their creators. "I don't know" is just as problematic a response to a previously unimagined question as the answer that is concocted to keep the interrogator happy. Or not so happy: respectfully inquiring whether my own "reading" of a certain line reflected one singer's intent, she replied, "So, instead of listening you want to put in words that I have not sung, say things I never said." It is here that interpretation and poststructuralism appear to collide and founder, though the problem is by no means confined to the subfield of performance anthropology.

So let me be clear rather than apologetic about the art of the possible in the methodology of studying Basotho aural art. I witnessed and recorded dozens of performances in every likely and unlikely setting—including my own house, when performers suggested, "Let's all go to your place," or when a little group of unknown eloquents showed up at the door explaining, "We hear you like *lifela?*" Interviews and discussions in Sesotho always followed performances, on the spot and whenever after. My assistants and I taped performances, transcribed texts into Sesotho, translated texts and testimony into English, hunted down performers and other knowledgeable people for exegesis and commentary, compared tapes, texts, and performance notes, reworked transcriptions and translations, read everything that seemed relevant, returned to the performers, interpreted, reworked, inquired, reinterpreted again.

What we could not do freely was conduct research in the environment of the mines. Mine police and officials were most unhappy to see us, and labor unrest and violence on the mine compounds were then, and are still, almost endemic. Performers there were frequently suspicious, worried, close-mouthed. In Lesotho, performers were in their own country, on their own ground, among their friends, and the difference in their confidence and sociability in relation to us was dramatic. The mines would have to wait. Only while shooting our film, when we had special permission from mine management, were we able to record performances in the compounds. Other performances, for example in Welkom in the Orange Free State, were recorded in the shadows and parking lots of the mine hostels and offices, but the setting was tense and unexpansive. No wonder: in 1991 eighty miners were killed at President Steyn mine in Welkom in a battle between militants seeking to enforce a union strike call and job-hungry migrants determined to work.

My initial premise was that what Basotho migrant singers had to say, and even the musicopoetic structures through which they spoke, could not be understood from the analysis of performance processes and products alone. In short, I had my own agenda, which the case of southern Africa had always seemed well suited to advance. This was to persuade social scientists and historians that performance was a rich, even indispensable, resource for understanding the role of consciousness and agency in the interplay of southern African forces, structures, processes, and events. By "consciousness" in I do not refer to an awareness of social class serving as a motivation for direct political action. Rather, I follow the Comaroffs, who have defined consciousness as "the active process—sometimes implicit, sometimes explicit—in which human actors deploy historically salient cultural categories to construct their self-awareness," and who recognize that "it is as crucial to explore the *forms* in which a people choose to speak and act as it is to examine the content of their messages" (Comaroff and Comaroff 1987, 207; italics mine). Conversely, it was also my purpose to demonstrate to students of performance that aesthetic expression is as rooted in the experience of historical and material forces as it is in the categories and qualities that structure the creative process. My methodology centers on this dynamic of reflexive influence and illumination between material, social, and representational processes, seeing them as mutually constitutive rather than discontinuous.

Between 1984 and 1988 I wrote several articles and delivered innumerable lectures on Basotho migrants' performances, analyses that became more and more difficult to present because of what had to be left out. In an article or lecture, the empirical data must be selected and focused in support of a comprehensibly narrow argument. This I did with increasing dissatisfaction. I couldn't discuss women performers without discussing men, life in Lesotho without life at the mines, experience without history, the structure of performance without the structure of social relations, musical poetics without political economy—any of them without all the others. So with an independent scholar's grant from the National Endowment for the Humanities and additional support from the Social Science Research Council, I headed back to Lesotho and the Institute of Southern African Studies to locate these performances in their total context. I collected fewer performances and more performance-related ethnography, went fewer places and worked more intensively with fewer performers, looked deeply into social relations and their representation, the symbolic practices of language, and the cultural construction of history. Courtesy of Anglo-American Corporation and Free State Geduld No. 2, I went down into the mine shafts. On the surface I conducted research and sponsored a singing competition. I filled in gaps and pursued new lines of ethnographic inquiry. I found, for example, that the men's texts are richly layered with allusions to Basotho traditional medicine and witchcraft beliefs, and that poets equate themselves metaphorically with the *ngaka*, the traditional healer and diviner. Deaf to admonition and disapproval (a Mosotho is not turned aside by nay-sayers), I embarked upon formal training as a *ngaka* in a small village just south of Mafeteng, in southwest Lesotho.

A broad contextual interpretation of texts and performances requires the application of analytical concepts and procedures not only from cultural anthropology, but from sociology, history, literary criticism, and ethnomusicology as well. Being no respecter of academic boundaries, it is unlikely that I have employed any of these techniques adequately by disciplinary standards. Perhaps this volume is one of those doomed to be praised by reviewers for its coverage of every area except that of their own specialization. If this were not problem enough, I discovered first hand the problematic empirical status of both textual and contextual data. No longer able, for any justifiable heuristic purpose, to exclude the essential dynamism and contingency of culture from its ethnographic representation, cultural anthropologists have had to abandon both the ethnographic tense and the collective informant. Local norms and knowledge are too differentially shared, personal responses to common situations too varied, to allow for broad characterizations. It is thus misleading to begin statements with such phrases as "The Basotho believe. . . ." or "Traditional healers agree . . ." Interview schedules in the local language, essential for establishing comparability of data and empirical grounds for consensus and generalization, can produce an even more diverse and conflicting record of ideation and practice than does participant observation. Furthermore, schedules can only be administered face to face in an unstructured manner, not only to open up unlooked-for avenues of information, but to allow questions and answers to be understood and engaged dialogically. Even so, such interviews are perhaps most useful as a starting point for a more revealing inquiry concerning the nature of and reasons for the contradiction between what people say and what they do.

My own *ngaka* often scoffed, perhaps disingenuously, at the notions and methods related to me by other healers or ordinary members of the community. We all have reputations to protect, politics to pursue. My task, of course, is to sort out the common concepts and convictions that underlie individual accounts, but this is of necessity my synthesis and not theirs. Therefore, I must bite my tongue when tempted to speak of "the Basotho." As a performance anthropologist, however, I am constrained to make statements about the shared experiences, perceptions, representations, and behaviors of these performers and audiences, who, because of their demographic background and position in the organization of production in southern Africa, comprise a specific social category of working-class Basotho. If culture were not by practice as well as by definition shared, there would be nothing of value to say about it, except to discuss why people think, speak, and act as if it were something they make together. People do, of course, share presuppositions as well as contest suppositions, embody and live Sesotho as well as create and manipulate a reified *Sesotho.* An account of both kinds of practices must reveal an ethnographic commitment: to describe what these certain people have made, and with what and by what means they have made it, as well as to demonstrate the significance and value it has for the rest of us, including those who have no material reason save curiosity to care about southern Africa or the Basotho.

An account that is as valid for one performer as for another, for those I never spoke to as well as for those I did, requires a synthesis that is by design more tailored to our needs than to theirs, since their understanding does not require one. This is accomplished by putting in place (perhaps too neatly?) the ill-assorted and ever-changing shapes of one's research puzzle, and then carting the pieces out of the field for "analysis"—inevitably a process of selection and abstraction in which data found to be opaque, ill-fitting, or contrary to the logic and thrust of the researcher's arguments are cut away so that the sculptural elegance of the account can be appreciated. Anthropologists no less than missionaries have their projects. But in the present case, I have included much that is puzzling because to me unencompassed otherness is endlessly fascinating for what it suggests of the world as I've not known it. It's not just another country heard from; without laughter (easy or uneasy), curiousness, and legerdemain, an ethnography of performance seems hardly worth the candle. The Basotho aurators—fence jumpers, honest thieves, eloquent revealers of true lies —enjoyed entertaining, educating, and having me on. I am here to let them have you on, and to have you on myself. My narrative is deliberately constructed to resemble the "concatenated" incrementation of a Sesotho *sefela*. To do this I dynamited the naturalistic ethnography of suspended disbelief. Gone are the empiricist (mis)representations of sociology, the unwarranted authority of synthesizing and synthetic positivist anthropology. I don't make it easy for readers with a particular disciplinary interest to pick out what they think they're looking for. I don't tell you where I'm going or where I've been. As Johannes Fabian says, "Parsimony is a supreme value for those who already know; ethnographers . . . are destined to tell baroque and tortuous tales" (1990, 15). And a ripping good tale I believe it is, this story my Basotho coauthors and I offer you, one told by ironists, full of sound and fury, signifying everything.

A FINAL NOTE. My researchers, a succession of texts, evidences, and ideas strung and handled like worry beads, were almost counted over when Seakhi Santho, my Sancho Panza and field assistant in 1984 as well as 1988–89, drowned in a swimming accident on the first of March, 1989. He was twenty-six. *Lefu ha le joetse*, "Death doesn't bother with introductions." After that I mostly went out alone, walking and talking in the presence of his absence, not quite believing that this giant of a man, who hefted heavy field equipment into the highlands without comment and ran performers and inquiries to ground with characteristic Basotho patience and tenacity, was now so suddenly among the ancestors. Much of this book is his, and I write it in his memory. And in memory, too, of my father, Burton Victor Coplan, who died on April 20, 1993, after a quarter century of supporting me in everything I attempted without ever disputing (at least out loud) why in heaven I was doing it. My superior in all things, including the grace not to mention it, this book is also his tribute.

Roma, Lesotho
January 1, 1994

Orthographic Note

In deference to Basotho sensibilities, I have followed the Lesotho national Sesotho orthography adopted in 1906, and not the South African orthography, except where a text in the South African orthography is directly quoted. The Lesotho orthography includes certain peculiarities of pronunciation, including the shift in which *l* is pronounced *d* when followed by an *i* or a *u*. Additionally, the vowel combination *ea* is pronounced *ya*, *oa* as *wa*, and *oe* as *way*. Hence *lifela tsa litsamaea-naha*, for example, is pronounced *difela tsa ditsamaya-naha*, and *ngoana'ka oe!* as *ngwana'ka way!* The several noun classes require separate prefixes added to root morphemes, and used in pairs to indicate singular and plural. Hence the land is Lesotho and a citizen is a Mosotho, while two or more of the people together are Basotho, and their language is Sesotho.

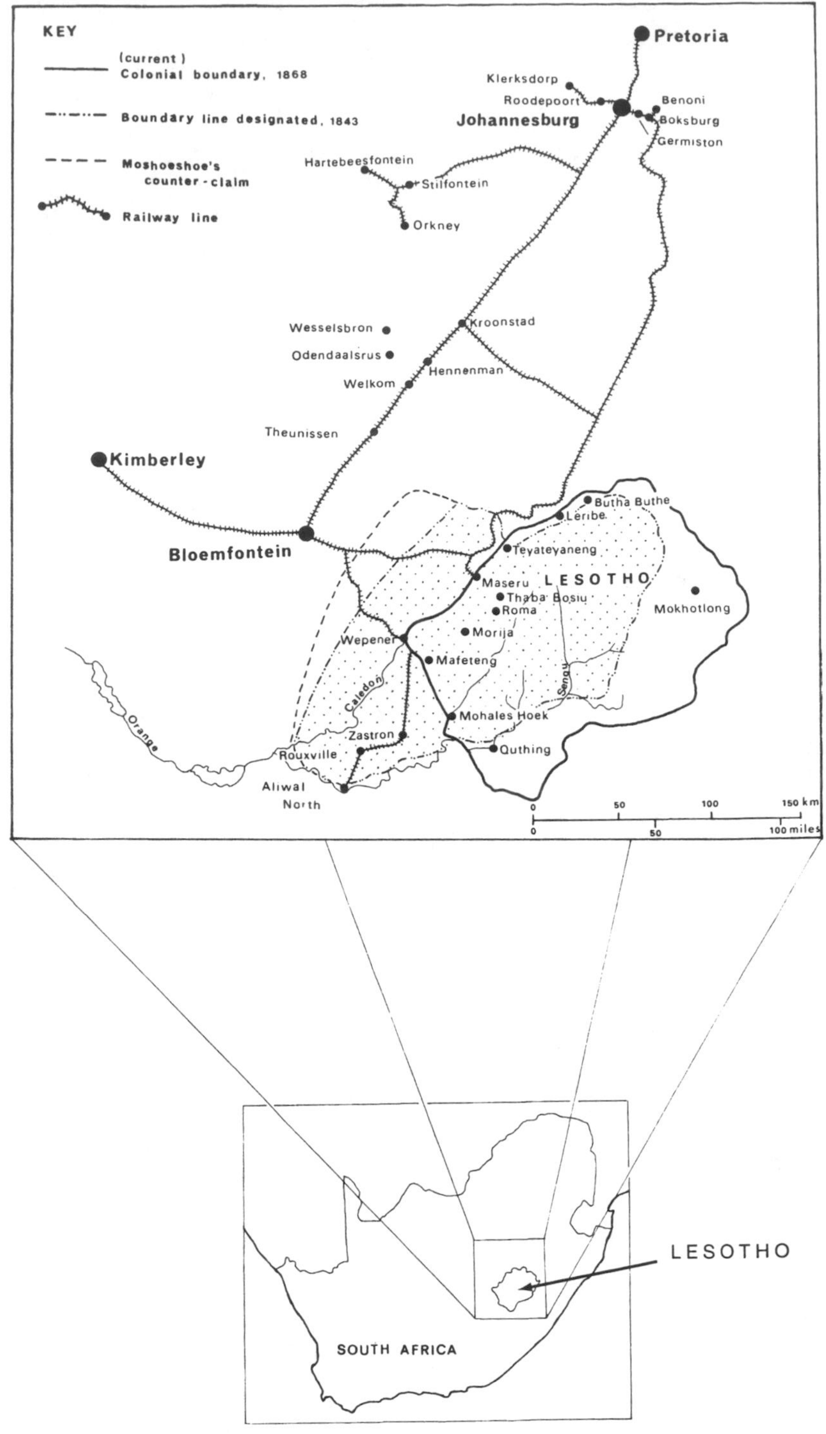

The Physical Geography of Basotho Migrancy

Chapter One

"Hyenas Do Not Sleep Together"

The Interpretation of Basotho Migrants' Auriture

It was in those times,
It was in those times when cannibals ate people.
Helele! Matsela!
In truth I am sure, I swear,
Me, I cannot simply be grasped!
The meerkat when it grazes keeps an eye out,
The antelope suckles [its young] at dawn,
Aware when hunters are coming—ee!
It was in those times when, it was in those times when cannibals ate people.

From "In the Times of Cannibals," mohobelo dance song by Letsema Matsela

The image of the cannibal, the human being who prospers by devourin his own kind in an ultimate zero-sum game, is a resonant and fearful sym bol in Basotho historical consciousness. The emergence of the Basoth kingdom in what in the late 1820s constituted the remote reaches of th Cape Colony's northeastern interior is framed in legends of grim defens against the predations of war, forced migration, starvation, and addictiv anthropophagy. The chiefs of militarized clans and incipient states wer much feared for their ravenous capacity to "eat up" external enemies, in- ternal rivals, and prosperous followers alike. Shaka Zulu, by far the mos famous, was seen by his unfortunate neighbors as a kind of Lord of Chaos consuming the chiefs and clans of the region and setting them to consum each other. Mohlomi (died c. 1815), a diviner-chief of the Bakoena clan tutored the young Moshoeshoe I (c. 1786–1870) in statecraft and gave him the medicine needed to found the Basotho kingdom. He is credited (ad- mittedly in the accounts of hardly unbiased missionaries) with the satur- nine deathbed prophecy: "After my decease a cloud of red dust . . . will come out of the east and devour our tribe. The father will eat his own child . . ." (Dornan 1908, 71). The "cloud of red dust" refers to the armies of

Shaka, whose approach could be spotted at a distance by the long clouds of red dust they raised against the clear southern African sky. The antiproductive powers of such heroes as viewed by their victims is summarized in the contemporary description of Shaka as "a determined, a systematic, and a practiced plunderer, raising no corn, breeding no cattle, and procreating no children" (*The Cape Colonist*, August 19, 1828). Killing one's agnates was considered understandable since they could as easily be rivals as supporters, but Shaka was baldly criticized, even by his own people in a praise stanza composed in his lifetime, for the shocking willingness to victimize even his own maternal kinsmen—the act of a witch:

> King, you are wrong because you do not discriminate,
> Because even those of your maternal uncle's family you kill,
> Because you killed Bhebhe, son of Ncumela of your maternal uncle's family.
> (Mbongeni Malaba, cited in Vail and White 1991, 68)

In the foothills and western reaches of the Drakensberg (the Maloti), fierce bands of refugees displaced by the Shaka's conquests (*lifaqane*) were said to have taken up hunting fellow humans as a preferred mode of subsistence. Cannibalism appears to have begun its sanguine career in the region as a metaphor for the dangerous untamed. Witness the Zulu term for South Africa: *Ningizimu*, "Cannibals' Africa." In African accounts, cannibalism arises as a by-product of war and social disruption. Among neighbors of the Zulu, cannibalism is said to have originated in Zulu-speaking areas of Natal. James Stuart's Zulu informants credit Shaka himself with both creating the conditions under which pastoralists became cannibals and with attacking and dispersing them (Webb and Wright 1979, 81), and Lagden cites Theophilous Shepstone's intriguing assertion that cannibals were a greater scourge to the Natal countryside than Shaka himself (Lagden 1909, 1:46–47). Perhaps Julian Cobbing (1988) is on to something, at least in arguing that Shaka was more of a spark than an engine of conflagration.[1] If the Shaka of conventional historical narrative is largely myth, however, it is a myth as much of African as European construction. Certainly for Basotho, Shaka is a symbolic foil for their own Bakoena aristocracy's efforts at state formation, a darkness against which to appreciate Moshoeshoe's light. There is no more powerful narrative of the Basotho vision of Shaka as both cannibal and king than Thomas Mofolo's novel

1. Thorough familiarity with the debate surrounding the work of Julian Cobbing and John Wright has not convinced me of the validity of the "Cobbing Thesis" to the effect that Shaka's state-building predations never took place and that the turmoil in the region was the result of European, specifically missionary slave trading.

Chaka, which he finished in 1909. Writing of the progress of Shaka's pillaging regiments, Mofolo abruptly editorializes:

> It was at that time that, on account of hunger, people began to eat each other as one eats the flesh of a slaughtered animal. . . . And then after a few years the persecutions and sufferings from the east climbed over the Maloti mountains and entered Lesotho, and there too cannibals came into being because of hunger. This is the worst of all the evil things of those days, and that too arose because of Chaka, originator-of-all-things-evil. (Mofolo [1925] 1981, 137)

Cannibalism thus has had a long career as an unsavory emblem of social pathology, parasitism, and disintegration in Sesotho. Moshoeshoe is said to have regarded the cannibals more as refugees than aggressors, and so it was said of the first of the legendary Basotho travelers, the revered Mohlomi, that he "visited the cannibal tribes who lived far to the north, and they not only did him no harm, but overcame their fears, and sacrificed an ox in his honor, saying that he was a man of peace" (Dornan 1908, 70). It is not at all fortuitous that among the achievements with which Moshoeshoe is credited (Ellenberger and MacGregor 1912, 218–24) is the reincorporation of cannibal bands into Basotho society. Among these were Rakotsoane's Bakhatla, who ate Moshoeshoe's grandfather Peete during the his emigration from Butha-Buthe south to the new redoubt at Thaba Bosiu in 1824. Contemporary accounts relate that when the culprits were dragged before the young monarch, he declined to defile the grave of his ancestor by their execution and instead purified them as living tombs, settling them upon the land with grants of land and cattle, which provide the food proper to socialized men:

> This song reminds me of the old days,
> When I was still a boy, I Letsema;
> I found places named with the names of cannibals,
> So when I asked the older people to tell me,
> Why in the end [they] are named in this way,
> They said, "There cannibals stayed."
> "So what finished them?"
> They said, "King Moshoeshoe slaughtered cattle,
> And collected them all.
> Then on arrival he gathered them at this home,
> He said, 'Look, men, the food to be eaten,
> it's these cattle—
> You shouldn't eat people,' and they understood."
> (Letsema Matsela, "In The Time of Cannibals")

Moshoeshoe's close friend, Thomas Arbousset, enhanced the legend in a letter from the mission field in 1846: "There is nothing more beautiful than a field of wheat or millet at the foot of a lair, the haunt of erstwhile cannibals; nothing is more gratifying to the soul than the sight of these men driving their flocks to the pastures. This is the spectacle which Rakotsoane and his people offers today" (Germond 1967, 146). Thus is the Basotho founder contrasted with Shaka, who sent expeditions to extirpate cannibals in his realm. It is possible that Moshoeshoe's inability to settle the marauding bands of Baroa (San, or "Bushmen") gatherer-hunters with gifts of cattle is indexed as wildness in the Sesotho term for South Africa: *Afrika Boroa*, "Bushman Africa" (Mabille, Dieterlen, and Paroz 1983, 443).

Since mountain areas were originally used only for summer pasture or as a place of temporary refuge, "Lesotho" formerly meant only the lowland areas, from most of which the Basotho were forced to retreat before the advance of settler colonialism. British Basutoland, since 1966 the independent Kingdom of Lesotho, includes the Maloti, their foothills, and what was left of Moshoeshoe's lowland domains. From the beginning, the campaigns and upheavals attending the rise of indigenous states were affected by the presence of white settlers and British colonial garrisons in the Cape of Good Hope. Male residents of what would become Lesotho were migrating to work on the farms and railways of the Cape as early as 1820 (Kimble 1982). The system of labor migrancy is thus coeval with the historical existence of the Basotho state.

During the middle years of the nineteenth century, Moshoeshoe's Basotho were subject to unrelenting attacks and depredations by African (Mzilikazi's Ndebele), mixed race or "Coloured" (Adam Kok's Griquas), and white (Free State Afrikaner) neighbors. It was the latter, however, who "ate up" Basotho lands with a rapaciousness beyond African comprehension. In disregard of universal indigenous legal norms, the Afrikaner intruders did not admit to becoming subjects of the rulers who granted them permission to till and herd within their realms. Nor did the whites' own practice of "annexation" retain its European application. In southern Africa, as a missionary noted in 1867, "It does not mean to bring a country and its people under a new Government but to expropriate the inhabitants in order to substitute oneself to them" (Germond 1967, 284). The settlers desperately required African labor, however, and so Moshoeshoe's subjects, if they were young, were coerced or cajoled to remain as servants and workers on white farms. Those who chose to take refuge in lands still under Basotho control were condemned for "*retreating before* civilization," but as the missionary Eugene Casalis complained in 1865, "It is the habit of our race when it establishes itself in the midst of primitive populations to embellish with the fair name of civilization that which would be termed otherwise under our European sun" (ibid., 267, 266; italics orig.).

Nevertheless, the Basotho took to commercial agriculture with alacrity, exporting wool, hides, grain, and livestock to the Free State and the new diamond-rush city of Kimberley. In 1874, despite the loss of lowland provinces and greatly increased migration, the 127,323 official inhabitants of Basutoland exported 100,000 bags of grain (ibid., 326). Temporary as opposed to permanent labor emigration centered on the diamond fields of Kimberley, where Basotho used their earnings principally to purchase rifles and ammunition. As Moshoeshoe had learned to his sorrow and his grandson, Prince Lerotholi, to his credit, "civilization" in practice meant that a people have precisely the rights they can defend.

During the late nineteenth century, Basutoland was a grain basket of South Africa (Murray 1980a), a situation that prompted white farmers in the Free State to protest that they were being out-produced and undersold by blacks to whose labor they regarded themselves as divinely entitled. By the turn of the century, the Cape railway that brought cheap Australian and American grain to Kimberley, drought, a herd-decimating rinderpest epidemic, and human-induced ecological degradation led to the irreversible decline of Basotho agriculture. British colonial policy responded to white farmers' complaints by restricting Basotho exports into South Africa, and with two-thirds of its arable lands now in the hands of the Free State, the kingdom was reduced to a rump, mostly mountainous "Basutoland," from which Basotho men and women ventured out to earn subsistence wages, pay colonial taxes, and subsidize another people's patrimony. As the Sechaba Consultants recently put it, "South Africa took the good land, took the produce of the land that remained to the Basotho, and took the labour of the dispossessed Basotho. What was left is poverty" (1991, 5).

After independence, Lesotho became increasingly dependent economically on the wages brought home from South Africa by migrant workers. An irony of this situation is that the massive retrenchment of mineworkers since 1987 has made the decade 1976–1986, when more than half of all working-age Basotho were absent as migrants at any given time, look like the good old days. There is little other work. Migration began as a source of ready cash to pay taxes, buy livestock, equipment, and seed, and supply consumer wants from rifles to concertinas. Labor migrancy still provides over half of Lesotho's gross domestic product and employs approximately 10 percent of the total population. Before it was made illegal in 1963, female migration made up a surprising 25 percent of the total. Even today women are estimated to constitute between 7 and 10 percent of the total migrant work force. Many others are working in South Africa illegally. But this does not include the thousands of women who, blocked from working in South Africa, have migrated internally to the capital, Maseru, and other burgeoning border towns (Wilkinson 1985). Lesotho is the only member of the United Nations Organization entirely surrounded by another state, and the only one whose chief export is listed by the UNO as "labor."

A worse and increasingly more prevalent fate awaiting unschooled Basotho boys than the necessity of leaving for the mines is the lack of any opportunity to do so. The mining companies blame massive retrenchments on mechanization, rising wages and benefits, declining production, and on uncertain gold and coal prices. In reality the reduced need for labor is being used to target union members, the highly paid, and foreign workers (all disproportionately Basotho) for dismissal. Under such conditions, those who still have jobs become the relatively fortunate, a kind of migrant "labor aristocracy" whose arrivals and departures are viewed with wistful envy by those condemned to home. Life is hard for most of the citizens of this labor reserve, and the risks of being "eaten up" by a host of social, economic, and political agents and forces are unremitting. When a black majority government comes to power in South Africa, the restrictions which forbid migrant workers from bringing their families nearer to their workplaces may be abolished. If Basotho workers are tolerated and not legally excluded as foreigners (a fond hope), it is likely that Lesotho will lose a large proportion of its working population and become more a political fiction than an independent state. But many will continue, by choice, to work as migrants. Lest this statement provide a note of cheer for those, Basotho or other, who see ingestion ("integration" is the currently fashionable term) by South Africa as Lesotho's only hope, there is no reason to suppose that an already overburdened New South Africa will willingly agree to accept its fully independent neighbor as a dependent region, or even its citizens as fellow workers. With the unavoidable reincorporation of the homeland "republics" and "national states," Lesotho could end up as the only effective Bantustan within South Africa, not a very just reward for one and a half centuries of stout resistance to colonialism and political cannibalization. Tragically, it is always the times of the cannibals for the Basotho, a perception expressed in the continuous reapplication of this metaphor in the emergent culture of migrancy. In October 1988 a youth from the village of Likokong in Mafeteng District, looking hopefully to a future as a migrant, declaimed the following self-praises (*lithoko*) upon completion of *lebollo*, the formal rites of initiation into manhood:

> Phuthiatsana [River], I can go and move there;
> I can take the red cow, leaving the calf.
> I once went traveling thoughtlessly—
> When I was above the gorge of the Caledon [River],
> I met them, the cannibals of war.
> I kept quiet and brought down my prayers.
> When I said, Let the earth swallow me up,
> They answered mercifully, the cannibals of war:
> "This day is your last."
> I heard, remembering evil times.
> It was the time blood almost choked me;
> It was right out in the unknown wilderness—
> There is a dam amidst the oceans yonder.

These praises begin with the initiate's assertion of an adventurous spirit, perhaps spurred by dissatisfaction with life at home. Hence the move across the Phuthiatsana River, a symbolic demarcation between rural and urban Lesotho, taking along only part of what belongs to him. Extending this theme, he imagines a poorly considered journey into South Africa. Bypassing the official job-seeking process requires a swim across the Caledon River, but no sooner does he descend to its waters then he is confronted by murderous "cannibals of war," waiting on the South African bank. At the mines, "cannibal" (*lelimo*) is a metaphor both for the earth itself, which consumes the miners in its belly, and for overeager black team leaders (boss boys) and white miners, who push black workers to the point of exhaustion in their gluttony for power and higher pay (see Coplan 1987a, 423). In the initiate's praises, "cannibals of war" conjures up in parallel the bloody chaos of Shakan times and the bloodsuckers who await the (illegal) migrant in South Africa. In addition, the image of war is invariably associated in contemporary styles of Sesotho song with the battles between fierce factions of Basotho *marashea*, "gangsters" (from English "Russian"), who formerly both defended and terrorized Basotho communities in South Africa's urban locations. No wonder the poet shuts up, praying silently that the earth, that oldest and most universal cannibal, will open and swallow him. The cannibals announce his death sentence in a citation from the famous depiction of the anticolonial Gun War of 1880–81 in the praises of Moshoeshoe's grandson, Chief Maama: *Bongata bo re ke letsatsi la bofelo*, "Many [men] they say it's [their] last day" (Mangoela [1921] 1984, 98). His imaginary life then passes before his eyes; times of hardship and suffering, images choking with blood, lost in South Africa's human wilderness. The poem concludes on a seemingly more hopeful note, that there is some kind of boundary or protected place amid the tempest-tossed oceans of life, or that one might like Hamlet take arms against a sea of troubles, and by opposing end them.

This book is an interpretation of a sample of such performances and genres, in which certain Basotho, migrant men and women, respond to their situation with complexly evocative word-music, creating a cultural shield against dependency, expropriation, and the dehumanizing relations of race and class in southern Africa. So in the passage I selected to open this chapter, Letsema Matsela, the renowned composer of men's *mohobelo* dance/songs, pictures himself in relation to rival composers and the world at large not as hunter but as hunted—an otherwise defenseless creature evading capture by instinct, experience, and wit. As with the Basotho performers, so with the performances: no hermeneutic boundary is here drawn around them, though they do serve as the nexus of the narrative.

I have devised the term "auriture" for these performances as a caution against the application of Western categories of literary analysis to African performance, categories inherent in the popular designation "oral literature" (see Finnegan 1970). Vail and White, in their recent volume on African performance as a historical source, cite the positive value of the term "oral literature" in forcing a consideration of these texts as *literature* and so preventing the separation of history from the aesthetic of its representation (1991, 26–30, 71). Karin Barber, in her monumental study of Yoruba *oriki* praise texts, argues similarly that the domains of literature and oral performance should be connected by the application of unified critical methods, rather than opposed as incongruent modes of expression and thought (1991, 36). African writers and critics, however, seem more concerned about the empirical misrepresentation of African compositional forms and processes that results when Western categories are adjusted for their analysis. Perhaps as a result, Ugandan critic Pio Zurimi's coinage "orature," a term popularized by Kenyan author Ngugi wa Thiong'o, is now widely accepted within the field of African literary studies and may soon become standard usage. What "orature" does not overcome, however, is the conceptual separation of verbal, sonic, and rhythmic elements of expression, a separation so uncharacteristic of African performance. Thus Opland (1983) could entitle a volume dedicated exclusively to "spoken" Cape Nguni aristocratic praises *Xhosa Oral Poetry*, unaccountably implying a formal recognition of Western categories of prose, poetry, and song in Xhosa ethnoaesthetics. Many authors, including Barber, pay lip service to the expressive inseparability of verbal, sonic, and visual media in constituting meaning in African genres, but do not address this unity in their analysis. Vail and White, who are historians, not literary critics, folklorists, or ethnomusicologists, deserve praise for demonstrating the importance of such musical features as repetition, rhythm, and sound shape in their analysis of texts ranging from the high register of Shaka's praises to the low but no less enduring satire of a Mozambican plantation workers' song (1991, 28–29, 206–11).

In discussing the European classical art songs of Schubert and Schumann, aestheticians and musicologists have argued without conclusion about whether song assimilates verbal text into a fundamentally musical mode of expression or whether the composer can be assumed to begin with the reading of a poetic text, which inspires and shapes its musical setting. The mutual constitution of literary and musical processes that so unsettles analysts of European songs is even more characteristic of songs composed in Bantu languages, with their semantic dependence on syllabic tone, alliterative and assonantal sonic parallelisms arising from nominative and verbal concords, ideophones (ideas in sound; see Kunene 1965), and rhythmic and reduplicative modes of delivery. To a Western observer like myself, the melodic declamation of literally hundreds of lines in a *sefela* performance made these songs appear powerfully text-driven. Yet in discussions and interviews, performers repeatedly advised me to focus on rhythm and melody as keys to the understanding of compositional creativity. As the singer-poet Makeka Likhojane—in Sesotho one of the *likheleke*, "eloquent ones"—explained firmly in deflecting the exegesis of an opaque metaphorical passage: "If you want to understand my song, mister, just listen to the music." However uncomfortable it makes historians working with African oral texts, such statements do seem to confirm Milman Parry's contention that word choice may be determined as much by rhythmic patterns as by semantic content. The term "auriture" (ironically, I admit, indistinguishable in pronunciation from "orature") makes no claim for the universality of intersense modalities in African performance but rather insists that empirical ethnoaesthetic categories be investigated rather than assumed. Additionally, "auriture" places the emphasis on the ears of the hearers, who include both performer and audience, and hence, properly, on the intended and experienced aesthetic transaction between all participants in a performance event, as pictured in a conceit found often in *sefela:*

Phakisang kapele batho,	Hurry quickly people,
Oa tseba, ba ha Mojela nkang mahlokoa:	You know, those of Mojela's should take dry grass stalks:
Joale le a menahanye,	Now you fold them double,
Joale u fate likonokono,	Now each one dig out the earwax,
U mamele mehlolo le meleko ea lefatse	And listen to the wonders and evils of the world

(Mabote Nkoebele, in Mokitimi 1982, 311)

As a term, auriture might seem well suited to the extension of "reader response" and other poststructuralist literary theories, but Karin Barber has perceptively observed that "at a deeper level post-structuralism is inimical to oral texts" (1991, 24). Aurality is a product of agency, and its performance has specific authors whose circumstances of interaction with their audiences are both identifiable and crucial to composition and interpretation. This is true for Basotho *sefela* songs, for example, even if the audience is migrant workers playing prerecorded cassettes in buses bound for the mines. To paraphrase Barber, aurators and auditors are always visibly and concretely present, and performances have no existence apart from them. "Auriture" does, however, encompass Bakhtin's crucial concept of the dialogic, in which utterances inhabit the space between a speaker and a hearer, a borderland in which social consciousness is constituted (Barber 1991, 36). This account is primarily about the pleasure, profit, creative occupation, and knowledge people derive from the ethnopoetic construction of experience, awareness, and social connection. The invocation of "auriture" both reminds us that performances attain meaning as part of a social process and recognizes that social reflection and historical commentary in performance are artistically constituted.

The interest of anthropology, though, is to reveal how the uses of meaning are rooted in operations articulating performance with consciousness and with the structure of social relations and material forces. The guiding medium of these operations in performance is language, and attached to language, the culturally patterned social production of meaning and sentiment in sound, movement, artifact, and design. With the collapse of modernism as a framework of intellectual life and the rejection of positivistic methods in cultural analysis, cultural anthropology has taken a much heralded linguistic turn. Inspired by a renewed appreciation of the language philosophy of Wittgenstein, new theories accord a fundamental role to language and conceptualizing processes in the explication of social life. Language and action are viewed as both mutually embedded and mutually constitutive (Giddens 1984, xx-xxi). The history, agency, and interaction that language both emerges from and structures ensure that metaphoric production is, as Kenneth Burke insisted, fundamentally *performative*. Images and their patterns of expression and interrelation are born and reborn from a collaboration of performer and audience. They make thought commensurate with common experience and action, exerting social gravitation. To paraphrase Bakhtin, they fill our mouths with the words of others. Beginning in the 1930s, Burke (1945) was among the first to describe precisely how language, and by extension all forms of culture, at once constrains and enables social action. In this description, both a person's understanding of a situation and his operation upon it are embedded in language. From this follows his view of the cultural categories of language as "terministic screens," linguistic glasses darkly, typologies that prefigure situations (Gusfield 1989, 12–13).

Language as culture, its categories and the way they are used in social process, shape the style of historical construction. So we are faced with the striking differences from Western narrative history of the aural forms and manners by which Africans represent history, power relations, and the preoccupations of licensed intellectuals. Drawing attention to these differences exposes one at best to the charge of following Milman Parry in conflating style with thought and at worst to the sin of revivifying discarded anthropological oppositions of self and other, Us and Them, based on Lévi-Bruhlian notions of prelogical primitive mentality. The dangers of opposing oral and written modes of representation and of confusing styles of history with thought about history have been pointed out by Vansina (1985) and are amply displayed in Vail and White's critique of the "invention of oral man" by Parry and his disciple Alfred Lord, by Marshall McLuhan and his disciple Walter Ong, and by the mercurial anthropologist Jack Goody (Vail and White 1991, 16–30). Aurality is indeed neither a cast of thought nor a mental condition. Yet we must still provide a structural description of the forms of African representation and an analysis of the social process in which culturally encoded modes of composition are embedded if we are to excavate the history, experience, and domains of contestation advanced in them.

A group of historians of black Africa, building on the insights and prescriptions of Vansina (1985), have turned from the narrative to the structural qualities of oral genres in seeking to mine oral sources for knowledge about the precolonial African past. In so doing, they have turned their methodology inside out. As one of their leading exponents, Joseph Miller, explains, these historians have responded to structural anthropology's critique of positivist historiography (de Heusch 1982) by arguing for the historicity of narrative traditions in ideological and social structural terms (Miller 1980, x–xi, 2–3). Oral narratives are no longer regarded as fragmentary documents, and they cannot be taken at face value or picked clean for "referential" content. As Harold Schueb observes, "Oral history is not the aligning of images in linear modes, but the fragmentation of lineal images and their recasting in new configurations and contexts" (1985, 4). Anthropologists John and Jean Comaroff have questioned further whether nonliterate peoples make the same distinction we do "between reality, the actual making of history, and representation, the terms in which its story is told and acted on" (1987, 193). As Robert Harms, Miller's collaborator, has written:

> Historians who work with oral traditions have recognized that many were symbolic statements of political or social ideology but have held that their symbolic formulation does not preclude their basis in historical events. Indeed, scholars have argued that, if the symbols and ideologies were themselves seen as historical phenomena, the oral traditions could be used to uncover aspects of social and intellectual history." (1983, 812)

Miller has pointed out the importance of social agency in the transmission of oral texts, arguing that unlike the archaeology of written documents, oral preservation is not accidental: "Nothing survives without someone's conscious decision that it should" (1980, 12). In this connection, Firth (1968, 181) suggests that extracting history from oral genres is not a problem of the process of memory, but of the social process that conditions the transmission of narratives. Western or Western-educated interlocutors intervene in these decisions when it comes to the production of written transcriptions or translations of oral texts, and our perspectives and projects become part of the process of transmission (Austen 1991) no matter how scrupulously we embed textual artifacts in contexts of performance. The questions of who records history and for what purpose the material is selected are as important in oral contexts as they are in literate ones (Ulin 1984, 155), and in many parts of the world, including settler-colonized southern Africa, it has been some time since these contexts have operated without mutual reference. As Vail and White explain (1991, 58), oral historians must somehow extract a history of events, a history of consciousness, and a history of expressive forms from a mix of actuality, ideology, and the changing perspectives and projects of research.

Aural styles of representation are forms of culture providing formal criteria for the historical production of performances as a social process. Miller states that "cultural emphases, little different from what has also been termed structuring, are perhaps the most powerful source of selectivity in oral traditions, because in the absence of literacy people preserve only matters that they regard as vital" (1980, 38). A problem with this formulation arises if one assumes that this "regard" is necessarily discursive or conscious. Oral traditions, by the very nature of their transmission, cause discursive history to become tacit knowledge. Over time, history as narrative becomes naturalized as cultural structure, manifested in lived experience (Bourdieu 1977, 78–79). It is not simply the social centrality of specific cultural themes, categories, or values, but their structuring of reality that makes them such powerful vehicles of selectivity. These are the conceptual emphases and symbolic forms that constrain as well as facilitate the representation of experience, creating a "Grammar of Motives" (Burke 1945), a system of meanings enabling social action. Rather than allowing history to simply "disappear" into the symbolic discourse of oral tradition, Cohen and Odhiambo provide the following gloss on the construction of texts among Luo elders in Kenya's Siaya District. Let me quote at length:

> If the production of history in Siaya constitutes an important force, it is also being reconstituted as texts through specific processes of stylization. . . . The rich commotion of the past, and the equally rich and commotional knowledge of history, escapes the oral narration as nomenclature and the simplified genealogical map gives structure to the oral text. . . .
>
> This is not to mean that large, important reservoirs of knowledge of the past "disappear into oral texts"; indeed there is no reason to assume that memory is depleted as individuals recite or compose texts. But a characteristic form of exposition is affirmed, reified. A method or methodology is implicated. And it is a method full of closures and silences. The process of articulation of historical knowledge as lineage chronicle is reminiscent of the process of producing a photographic record of a collective activity in Siaya in which the subjects quickly recompose position, posture, and gesture into a formal group portrait . . . remaking the effort of the photographer to record a "natural scene" into a conventional and, by routine, a naturalized portrait of kin and neighbors. (Cohen and Odhiambo 1989, 30–31)

Cohen takes a poststructuralist view of aural texts, arguing that the interests and thus the meanings imposed on representations of the past by the present erase any previous structure of significance. The painstaking but unavoidably speculative excavations of symbolic ideology by Vansina and successors such as Harms, Miller, Ralph Austen, Vail and White, and others thus appear to Cohen to be scaffolded very flimsily. Fortunately for me, the creators of the Sesotho aural texts with which I am primarily concerned are alive rather than long dead. My interrogations thus reveal that performative metaphors attain social authority precisely because they transport the salience of their previous applications into new contexts each time they are reapplied. The past gives meaning to the present as much as the present reconstitutes the nature of the past. In the much repeated words of William Faulkner, "The past is not dead; it is not even past." Further, the successive reapplications of established metaphors resonate with one another and with new metaphors juxtaposed to gain metonymic force from them, providing a "valuational comprehension of events that transcends history" (Vail and White 1991, 73). Master metaphors, at once historical and experiential, endure, wax, or wane depending upon their capacity to interpret the actual in terms of a more durable social and moral meaning. This is the value of Harold Scheub's notion of "cultural precipitates" (1985, 4), not as some fixed idea of "tradition," not history as code, but "history as drama, evaluation, and judgment: history with the metaphysics included" (Vail and White 1991, 73). Yoruba *oriki* praises, for example, are not an account of the past, they are symptoms of a state of being: "they capture and in some way sum up the essential nature of the person or lineage" (Barber 1991, 33).

Vail and White (1991, 40–83) propose "poetic license" as an aesthetic for oral poetry in which expressive competence confers interpretive authority on composer-performers who are the effective intellectuals of societies in which art and history are inseparable. At the center of the relationship between art and history is the shifting balance of power relations, and the "reciprocal determination of material forces and cultural forms" (Comaroff 1985, xii). The relationship between power and performance involves both contesting views and assessments encoded in the authoritative genres—what Raymond Williams calls the "selective tradition" of hegemonic social understandings—and competing genres composed in different linguistic, aesthetic registers by performers occupying varying social positions. This is one of the most significant dimensions in my own comparison of Sesotho aristocratic praise poetry and migrants' sung poetry. African literary scholars routinely object to the English gloss "praise poetry" because these texts so often include characterizations that are contradictory, inconvenient, even sharply critical. One might counter in defense of the term that the praises are not directed at the individual subject but at his or her historical achievements, assessed in terms of the social values attaching to the political identity that he or she embodies. For this reason it is not the performer but the performance that is licensed, and the form, not its exponent, legitimates the content (Vail and White 1991, 56). Let me illustrate with a story I was told by a praise poet in Jodhpur, Rahjasthan, in India.

The Maharajah of Jaipur and the Maharaja of Jodhpur both arrived with their entourages at a sacred lake at the same moment. A dispute ensued as to which monarch had the higher prestige and ritual status and was therefore entitled to perform his purifying ablutions first. To prevent a war of honor, the Maharaja of Jodhpur said to the Maharajah of Jaipur, "Let your praise poet decide." The man was brought but expressed extreme discomfiture at being thus put on the spot: "This is a sacred lake," he protested, "I shall have to speak the truth." Both kings enjoined him most sternly to do so without fear of reprisal. With a long face, the poet gave judgment: "The Maharajah of Jaipur and the Maharajah of Jodhpur are as two sides of a hand. The one killed his father to get his throne, the other his son to keep it." The unfortunate poet was of course summarily executed.

In the wake of colonial and capitalist intervention in local political economies of hierarchical reciprocity, so-called popular genres often arise, subverting authoritative genres that no longer express actual power relations and social structure as the people experience them. But whether authoritative or popular, aural poetry can be anything from an oppositional "voice of the people" to a sycophantic, hegemonic project of ideological mystification (Vail and White 1991, 56–57). More broadly, attempts like those of the Basotho to create forms that are qualitatively new yet invested with the authority of established cultural practices, a kind of cultural self-preservation through transformation, are widely characteristic of colonized societies both in Africa and elsewhere. The use of Sesotho performance by labor migrants to create an integrated, positive self-concept in the face of displacement and alienation represents simply the continued application of their preexisting cultural morality in the context of Basotho dependency in a "world system." Jean Comaroff (1985, 197–98) argues that syncretic reinterpretations of master metaphors as well as micro-level continuities in cultural practices can be explained essentially as forms of resistance to incorporation in a capitalist political economy. But as Christopher Waterman demonstrates in his recent study of Nigerian Yoruba popular *juju* music, cultural process is ideologically charged through productive mediation by social actors with particular values and experiences of power. So both continuity and syncretism can as easily mask empirical structural relations through the upholding of "selective tradition" as they can serve subversively the interests of the oppressed (Waterman 1990, 9). Such ambiguities raise unavoidably once again (see Coplan 1991) the issue of tradition in the study of aural genres.

As a conceptual vessel, tradition is listing badly and may soon sink into the history of ideas, torpedoed by scholars such as Hobsbawm and Ranger

(1984), who have shown how much of what passes for organic tradition has been deliberately invented to foster identity in the service of political interests. Cultural legacies are not, of course, self-reproducing, and the very fierceness with which the authority of tradition is defended or rejected reveals its tenuous empirical status and the contestation underlying its invocation. Indeed, whenever people's own categories of discourse refer to the past, they express a political instrumentality (Spiegel 1990, 35). Subordinate just as much as dominant sectors of society invent and reify tradition as ideology, and as Richard Bauman (1977) points out, folklore is always about the politics of culture. In Africa, colonialism fostered truly wretched excesses of invention as Europeans and Africans created their working misunderstanding of entitlement and appropriation, hierarchy and law, identity and social process. Groups who lost cases in "native" colonial courts because their customs were found repugnant to European cultural morality returned to court later with more acceptable customs (Wyatt McGaffey in Hobsbawm and Ranger 1984, 251). A more permanent and pervading result was often the creation of a new category in the minds of the colonized, the category of tradition. As the Comaroffs observe of the Batswana: "Tswana 'tradition' (Setswana) was to be fashioned during the course of the nineteenth century. If not wholly invented, . . . it was at least to be objectified; to be made into a heritage with imagined reference to the past but with its signs oriented toward the present" (1987, 194–95).

The codification of Basutoland's *Laws of Lerotholi* (1903) was an instance of the inevitable but unintended Foucaultian consequences of the British policy of indirect rule. Under the guise of preserving "age-old native law and custom" (with the parallel benefit of aborting the autonomous political development of the Basotho state), the *Laws of Lerotholi* appear to exemplify the colonial process identified by Hobsbawm and Ranger, in which resilient, adaptable oral custom is petrified as brittle, invariant tradition. Among the results was the institutionalization of autocratic powers for senior chiefs, already becoming an informal reality owing to their power over scarce land resources and the backing of the colonial authorities for whom they functioned as primary agents. Of possibly even greater social consequence is the confusion that reigns in Lesotho's legal system today, resulting from the ad hoc, personalistic manner in which judges sort out the relative status of Sesotho, Roman-Dutch, and English Common Law in specific appeal cases (see Poulter 1979).

In the field of African auriture, it is not at all coincidental that the genres most involved with the expression of dominant power relations, such as praise poetry, have lately become the embodiment of reified tradition. Once the institutional power of their subjects has been emasculated, authoriative genres can be appropriated by nationalist movements through nostalgic cultural reinvention, and their ideological values loudly honored only for being honored in the breach. As Anthony Giddens (1991) points out, today cultures cannot in any case be practiced without conscious self-identification by their inheritors. But we must also recognize the extent to which the instrumental and strategic aspects of identity are naturalized in the thoughts and feelings of those who express and act upon them. In this book, I have represented reflexive, self-conscious conceptions of Basotho culture in italics as *Sesotho*, and implicit, organic, socially emergent continuities of Basotho cultural practice simply as Sesotho. This distinction more than loses its usefulness, however, if it reinforces the construction of naturalized and rationalized dimensions of culture as a duality, rather than assisting the integration of culturally implicit and explicit sources of social action. So the indigenous concept of *Sesotho*, which designates not only the language but the entire self-conscious cultural practice of the Basotho, is an interested mix of implicit mores, historically embedded structural instrumentalities, and reinterpreted strategic inventions. Those who would see the controlling hand of colonizing capital in every African social and cultural form (see Wolpe 1972) have a tendency to see Africans as inhabitants of stereotypic social categories, exemplars of their class positions, rather than as conscious, often conflicted agents in the making of their own history.

The central contradiction of tradition revolves around its social and historical origins in opposition to its status in both native and scholarly discourse as something immutable, a structure of historical culture fundamentally immune to history. Harold Scheub expressed this paradox most clearly in defending the largely ahistorical nature of African folklore studies. Tradition, he proposes, is "the timeless in time," obviating history while depending on history for its images (1985, 4–19). We must not, however, confuse historical continuity and reinterpretation with timelessness, transcendence with reproduction. Nor must we normalize Western forms of narrative history by assuming that history vanishes in African symbolic modes of historical representation. Oral traditions are indeed essential to the symbolic construction of history and social experience, but we must recognize how consciously these traditions are often themselves constructed. The notion of immemorial traditions of performance, so popular with participants and folklorists alike, all too often evaporates under the scrutiny of historical research. Thus national traditional dances and ceremonies often turn out to have had conscious origins at a specific place and time. Further, performance traditions as reified forms of identity are rarely unitary, and their status is often a matter of by whom, under what conditions, and for what purposes they are claimed within the dynamics of internal and external relations of social power. Vail and White's (1991, 155–97) account of the reinvention after World War II of Swazi royal praise poetry, and of the Swazi monarchy itself, provides a salutary illustration. Seeing, but preferring to avoid, the analytical difficulties presented by these realities, most folklorists have shifted their focus from collective historical traditions to creative individuals and forms of extemporary composition in the study of performance as a mode of communicative action. This has led, unfortunately, to the neglect of both narrative and aesthetic history in folklore (White 1982, 10). Along with the study of the microdynamics of performance events, we must study the relation of performance to historical forces and the dynamics of form as history in performance (Joyner 1975). Opland's misinterpretation (1983, 175–80) of Chief S. M. Burns-Ncamashe's praises of Rhodes University chancellor Dr. Ian Mackenzie, mercilessly critiqued by Vail and White (1991, 30–32) is an object example.

Admittedly, daily life also consists of situations in which people experience no conscious impetus toward self-legitimation or self-defense. Their social practices, as well as the categories, tropes, and images they use to typify, integrate, and represent them, are drawn from culture and personal experience in a matrix of the familiar and the novel, the rationalized and the implicit. Anthony Giddens (1976) has formulated this as a distinction between what he calls discursive and practical consciousness: the difference between practices that serve active motivations at the level of rationalized discourse and those that enable people simply to carry on with life together but do not necessarily rise to the level of reflexive consciousness. This key concept in the work of Giddens, in addition to that of structuration, the mutual determination of social institutions and social practices, connects structure, process, agency, and event and bridges the gap between macro and micro levels of analysis (Spiegel 1990, 307).

Discussing the implications of Giddens's formulation for field ethnography, Spiegel divides practical consciousness itself into two kinds of practices, those without conscious instrumentality that nonetheless can be explained or at least discussed reflexively, and those that cannot. The ubiquitous sign of the latter is the reply "It is our custom" (Sesotho: *Ke tloaelo ea rona*), a statement that has exactly and only the value of "I wouldn't have thought about it except that you ask me" (Spiegel 1990, 9–

11). Hobsbawm though, has suggested that "custom" has particular value as a label for organic, situationally flexible cultural practices, as opposed to the invented, inflexible nature of "tradition" (Hobsbawm and Ranger 1984), an attempt to gloss the opposition expressed in my own distinction between Sesotho and *Sesotho*. In practice, however, this dichotomy between tradition as something consciously invented and hence invariant, inorganic, and inauthentic and custom as unconscious and creatively variable breaks down. At the most obvious level, many practices that are part of discursive consciousness have deeply historical, "authentic" roots in the whole life process of a social group, while others glossed as simply "our custom" (*whose* custom?) have more recent, exogenous origins. So "custom" must remain essentially synonymous with "tradition," even though the forms included range from the most purposively invented to the most thoughtlessly habitual.

The performance of aural genres is based on organic traditions of both discursive and practical consciousness, which provide what Joyner calls the "established structures of creativity" (1975, 262). Despite its problems, there is value in revivifying, if not entirely reinventing, a notion of tradition freed from the quarantine of italics and quotation marks. In this conception, tradition is not simply the reified emblems of authority but the immanence of the past in the cultural certainties of the present. It is what persists by virtue of both deliberate and undeliberate handing down, the metaphors of others with which our mouths are full. As E. P. Thompson explains, "Both the identity and meaning of a specific action or event, as well as its possible interpretations, are dependent upon a symbolically constituted past whose horizons extend into the present," upon a lived cultural past that limits and shapes the future (cited in Ulin 1984, 150). Oral genres are among the most capacious and continuous repositories of such symbolism. In this reflexive domain, tradition provides images, expressive principles, and aesthetic values by means of which performances are both fashioned and made sensible. Tradition consists more in the processual modes than in the products of action, forming a dynamic of persistence, a set of structures continuously emerging in history. Performance is the point of departure for the study of emergent culture: a nexus of tradition, practice, and emergence that "focuses on the very source of the empirical relations between art and society" (Bauman 1977, 40, 48). Methodologically, oral genres as emergent tradition have the status of internal meta-commentary, albeit mediated by the personal projects of translators and the compromises, idiosyncrasies, and misinterpretations of translation. The symbolic statements about common experiences and concerns made in oral genres reflect popular consciousness, giving us ethnography from within and history "from below" (Vail and White 1983, 887). In Fabian's metaphor (1990, 12–13), performance is the tip of an iceberg of culture floating in a sea of history and consciousness. The submerged ice carries the performance, which is part of, an instance of, metonymic with the block of ice, not a metaphor for it.

The dialectical, dialogic nature of tradition as practice, the question of whose tradition it is, cannot of course be ignored. The abandonment of the notion of societies as organic, functionally integrated wholes, even as a heuristic model, in the face of the empirically contested, fragmented nature of social reality has created a problem for anthropology. The negotiated quality of relationships and the culturally grounded yet improvised nature of social action undermines the empirical status of societal metaphors or totalizing symbols. Without disputing how deeply they are internalized, we must still discover rather than assume that symbols express a continuous set of meanings or interpretations. The ghost of Franz Boas is back, but he's in an ironic mood. The production and mobilization of collective metaphors are now regarded as essentially contingent processes, bricolages of meaning built upon the ramshackle foundations of opportunistic social networks.

That said, it must also be said that performance succeeds as communicative enactment by drawing upon a common reservoir of symbols, metaphors, and meanings, of values, rules, and criteria of production. Michel Foucault has proposed "archive" as a term for the level of cultural syntax that operates above the level of depository but below that of institutions of discourse. The archive is the generative level of textual practice, and thus

> it does not have the weight of tradition; and it does not constitute the library of all libraries, outside time and place; nor is it the welcoming oblivion that opens up to all new speech the operational field of its freedom; between tradition and oblivion, it reveals the rule of a practice that enables statements both to survive and to undergo regular modification. (Foucault 1976, 130)

An example of the manipulation of an archive in order to create expanded fields of shared discourse can be seen in the rise of the black popular theater of Gibson Kente in Johannesburg in the 1960s (see Coplan 1985, 207–12; Coplan 1986). Kente, like many literate Africans, had performed in plays and sketches at school and was thoroughly familiar with the comedic turns of the African musical variety companies of the 1940s and 1950s. The success of black performers working under white direction in the African musical drama *King Kong* in 1959 convinced him of the potential for an all-black "people's" theater capable of autonomous production under popular patronage (Coplan 1987b). He recognized that much of the difficulty of producing plays or musical theater in the Western sense in urban African communities was due to the absence of established ethnoaesthetic criteria and structures of creativity for theater among working-class Africans. Drawing on the multivocalic assemblages of African and Euro–South African expressive forms and practices current in both folk and professional performance, Kente generated an aesthetic within which formalized black popular theatrical productions could be created and appreciated. The heart of his method was an integrated complex of staging and performing techniques that related existing African values, principles, and modes of dramatization to the prestigious but novel context of British-American theater. Equally important was his ability to make "real life" larger than life, to enact urban African experience in the new setting in the language, sound, movement, and dress of that experience, not only as it is lived but as it is imagined and represented by those who live it. In so doing, he and kindred spirits like Sam Mhangwane created a new performance genre, a generation of trained performers, a set of model performances, and an audience eager to patronize them.

The archive of understandings that Kente both tapped and replenished is full of local knowledge, composed of forms that "inscribe a communal sensibility" (Geertz 1983, 12), what I understand to be "a people's conceptions and perceptions of themselves and of their situation in society and history, formulated in the terms and the occasions of their culture" (Coplan 1988, 337). It is by means of local knowledge, differentially transmitted and shared, that culture structures communication and social empathy. Local knowledge mediates and, as a set of practices, ultimately erases the heuristic distinction between semiotics and sociology.

Unfortunately, my description of local knowledge as an archive still begs the question of the logic by which meanings might be interconnected, signs associated, domains cross-referenced. Keesing (1989, 467) has warned that cultural texts, no matter how rich—perhaps even because they are so richly allusive—cannot in themselves serve as the basis for ethnographic interpretation. Insiders who perform them are just as likely as outsiders who study them to disagree among themselves. With key informants as with anthropologists, *'Thamahane ha li robale mmoho*, "Hyenas do not sleep together," or less literally, "Two of a trade seldom agree" (Guma 1967, 86). Evidence must be culled from folk practices as well as from folk exegesis, from what people do as well as from what they say to the ethnographer and to others. Monica Wilson's admonition that "the symbolism of another society must be translated systematically, not guessed at," still has force (cited in Murray 1975, 59), and as Spiegel and I have found in working with Basotho, people sometimes can't and sometimes won't comment usefully on their actions. In interpreting performance both within and beyond indigenous exegesis, the investigator must demonstrate the link between individual and collective understandings. This can be done, first, by explicating the actual meaning of performances with reference to oral testimony, the social position of the performers, the conventions of the genre, the context and contingencies of performance, and the importance of the genre and its performances in the expressive and practical culture of the people; second, through the identification and positioning of recurrent themes and images and the discovery of the process whereby metaphors bridge time, space, and experiential domains and are brought into relations of structure and meaning with one another (Vail and White 1983, 887).

Part of the legacy of structuralism in culture theory, whether of the British functional or the French symbolistic variety, is the presumption of the systematic qualities of collective representation. Structural analyses, however, as Giddens points out (1984, 283), tend to emphasize the "systemness" over the pragmatics of much social action, including the "pragmatics of metaphor" (Fernandez 1989, 470) in the everyday application of labels and categories. Jean Comaroff's analysis (1985) of the political economy of cultural signification among the Barolong of Botswana, for example, depends on "the notion that there are *systems* of signification with meaningful logics of their own" (Spiegel 1990, 48). Spiegel argues that until we have "thorough and systematic analyses of the historical construction of metaphor and the 'grammaticalization' of lexical forms in the region" (ibid., 306), we cannot locate these metaphors in putative symbolic systems or cohesive cosmologies of southern Bantu language speakers.

Spiegel acknowledges that the extensive literature on southern Bantu oral poetry has gone some way toward illuminating how metaphors of cosmology, society, and history are constructed and arranged. But he complains that these are expressions of extraordinary rather than ordinary speech contexts, aesthetically structured for rhetorical effect. Barber, however, sees a particular value in auriture on that account, arguing that its texts represent ideology more explicitly because of their "concentrated, 'worked-on' character." Further, performance texts are revealing because they are inherently discursive, lending themselves to verbal exegesis and articulating and giving form to "otherwise amorphous notions circulating in society" (Barber 1991, 3).

Additionally, my research into Sesotho genres has revealed that there is much continuity between performance and nonperformance, or better yet, between discursively and practically performative contexts. The taught texts of aristocratic praises may strive for "literary" effect in greater or simply different measure than the impromptu self-celebrations and "comic correctives" (Burke) of a migrant's sung soliloquy. Ordinary discourse is itself highly figurative, and can attain a "breakthrough into performance" (Hymes 1981) of aesthetic genres from proverbs to war anthems as easily as a migrant composer can launch into a singing challenge upon encountering a rival at the labor bureau. The songs of migrants and barflies buzz with the metaphors and syntax of everyday speech, while structured forms like the *hlonepho* respect/avoidance terminology practiced by Basotho wives toward their senior male affines make an art out of meaning what one may not say (Kunene 1958). It is my perception that processes of making and applying metaphors are to some extent continuous in Sesotho, and that the interpretation of migrants' performances within the context of Basotho speech genres will provide some understanding of their systems of representation. As Murray (1975) demonstrates in his analysis of sexual symbolism in Sesotho, the transference and transposition of cultural metaphors across categorial boundaries, bridging experiential domains, is based on a structured set of identifications rooted in representations of both cosmology and history. Rather more obviously, anthropologists still, as did ancestors such as Boas and Malinowski, find it necessary to pay particular attention to cosmological and other folkloric texts. This is not because they serve in some simplistic conception as charters for the present dispensation, but because in so many field situations the people we wish to understand employ versions of and references to such collective texts and metaphors both in daily discourse and in their dialogue with ethnographers to make themselves collectively understood. Further, it is these systematic relations of symbols both to material and social realities and to one another that enable the anthropologist to make explicit the implicit categories of the actors and "to do justice to the problem of translation" (Murray 1975, 60).

Some assistance in resolving the contradiction between contingency and structure, production and reproduction in culture has been given by Raymond Williams (1976, 1977). Williams attempted to dissolve the dichotomy between cultural and material interactions, between consciousness and existence, by developing a linguistic theory of social being. This theory follows Kenneth Burke in its hermeneutic emphasis on language. But Burke's emphasis on the dialogic nature of language as a set of limitations artificially ordering a multiperspectival reality made it seemingly impossible for him to link his insights to the determinant operations of power in social structure (Gusfield 1989, 42). As a cultural Marxist, Williams forthrightly explores the social and historical determinations of culture, "taking into account the power constraints to which they may be subject" (Ulin 1984, 165). E. P. Thompson (1978) contributed to the theory by demonstrating that social reality is created through the interpenetration of experience and self-understanding. The self—historically derived, structurally embedded, presentationally emergent—is therefore both a result and an active element of the process of social production. From this follows Williams's definition of culture: "The whole system of signification by which a society or a section of it understands itself and its relations with the world" (1977, 13).

While Williams's most valuable insights have been widely assimilated into cultural analysis, the problems that he and other contributors to the contemporary revitalization of Marxist approaches to culture have taken such pains to address may still be with us. They revolve around culture as an autonomous social force, not sui generis or superorganic, but the encompassing framework from within which human beings apprehend reality and attempt their life projects. In this area, Antonio Gramsci has been most responsible for giving culture the status of an independent variable in Marxist analysis, arguing that culture serves social structure implicitly, by patterning the perception of experience. Culture is thus "hegemonic," controlling social action through "the very terms and standards by which experience is interpreted and judged" (Gusfield 1989, 40–41). Despite this insight, Marxian cultural analysis has been unable to establish any overall congruence between class and culture without the admixture of contingent determinants of history, experience, value, and personal agency. Marx's assertion in *The German Ideology* that social being determines social consciousness is today conditioned by our understanding that social being itself is as much a matter of cultural values and cognitive structures as of empirical constraints and material needs (Thompson 1977, 261–62). Signification in fact encodes the social relations and contradictions of power as they arise in a particular history. These relations shape communicative interactions, just as their character is reflected in the constitution of symbols and meanings (Ulin, 1984, 118, 123).

As a rule, subsaharan African cultures do not compartmentalize spheres of social action, and the interpenetration of politics, religion, and art is regarded as normative as well as demonstrable. Where Western societies have tended to treat expressive forms as either independent of social and material forces on the one hand or epiphenominal to them on the other,

Africans historically have treated performance genres as legitimate, even necessary, modes of social action in political contexts. They exist as internal representations and analyses of power, empowered as art forms to record and shape the operation of social forces (Finnegan 1970, 142). Understanding the articulation of aural genres with the periods and structures of society that gave rise to them (White 1982, 10) requires a history of forms that integrates "the study of internal change within [the] tradition with the study of external change in the social context" (Joyner 1975, 264).

A good example is provided by Cope's summary (1968, 31–34) of the historical shift in values and images in Zulu royal praises (*izibongo*). During the eighteenth century, when the Zulu were a second-rank Nguni clan, praises resembled lyrical odes in which shrewdness, reciprocity, and diplomacy were emphasized. Animal metaphors portrayed chiefs as small species admired for cunning, quickness, and beauty. With the rise of Shaka and Zulu imperial power in the nineteenth century, these images were replaced by the lion, leopard, buffalo, and domestic bull, reflecting the strength, aggressiveness, authority, confidence, and social order of a monarchical state. A more nationalistic, epic style rooted in the heroic "Shakan stanza" became the stylistic signature of aristocratic *iimbongi* (praisers), developing into a "great tradition" throughout Zulu domains during the imperial period and wiping out district styles. With the defeat, dismemberment, and emasculation of the Zulu kingdom after 1879, the praises became more lyrical and nostalgic, with Shakan stanzas less numerous and significant. Cope thus traces changes in form as well as content in the symbolic construction of an oral genre over time. More recently, Vail and White's (1991) case studies of aural genres in southern Africa and Ralph Austen's (1991) investigations into an archaic Cameroonian epic have provided models and directions for understanding how genre development encodes social transformation.

In analyzing Basotho oral genres, I have not regarded performance contexts as either autonomous from or reducible to any set of external determinations, but have rather sought in them the articulation of relations of meaning with relations of power (Auge 1979, 107). These relations can be viewed in terms of a systematic sociology of social categories and classes, or more existentially as expressions of "cultures in fragments increasingly held together by their resistance and accommodation to penetrating impersonal systems of political economy" (Marcus and Fishcher 1986, 95). From either perspective, the concept of "cultural production" is perhaps the best vehicle for comprehending the interdependency of symbolic and material elements in the making and mobilizing of culture as performance.

The production (and reproduction) of culture (or other institutional practices) is accomplished by social actors from within a situational as well as structural confluence of material, social, and communicative factors (Giddens 1984; Coplan 1987b, 430). In the absence of normatively coherent social systems

> the social context of the cultural construction of meaning—the production of culture—becomes an integral part of interpretive analysis itself. . . . In social and cultural worlds of uncertain dimensions, the most certain and easily assumable social background for which a cultural performance has salience is that proximately involved with its production. This constitutes a means of sharply reconceptualizing social systems from the bottom up, since the sociological concepts with which ethnographers frame their cultural analysis become directly a matter of investigation. (Marcus and Fischer 1986, 184–85)

For a half century beginning in the 1920s, social anthropology, with its great tradition at South Africa's English universities, made indispensable contributions to the study of both social structure and social and cultural change. Since then, however, a new generation of South African anthropologists has recognized that the discipline must bear some responsibility for the white government's continuing obsession with ethnicity as a rigid marker of social identity, despite the historical fluidity of residence, social organization, political allegiance, language, and cultural practice in the region. Like colonial officials, functionalist anthropologists searched for the sources of stability in society, codifying African communities as models of hierarchical social equilibrium. By representing African polities as rigidly bounded, stationary sociocultural units, social anthropology created an artificial universe of tribes that would serve as an ethnographic basis for apartheid (Hobsbawm and Ranger 1984, 252). The theories of Malinowski, specifically, served in part as a basis for Native Administration policies in South Africa in the middle twentieth century. Distressed by the enforced squalor and social fragility of mid-twentieth-century African life first in urban and then in rural areas, social anthropologists tended to view the pragmatic dynamism of African social practice as merely the lamentable product of apartheid. Cultural inventions mothered but not determined by harsh historical necessity were deplored as expressions of deracination and analyzed as symptoms of social disintegration rather than as new vehicles of self-construction. Exceptions pointing to an eventual reorientation were Monica Hunter's *Reaction to Conquest* (1936), Godfrey Wilson's *The Economics of Detribalisation in Northern Rhodesia* (1941), and Max Gluckman's "Analysis of a Social Situation in Modern Zululand" (1942), which dealt directly with the ethnographic context of African motivation and agency within southern Africa's colonized and capitalized racial social structure.

More recently South African anthropology, inspired by major advances in regional historiography, has abandoned structural functionalism for a form of politicoeconomic historicism (see Mayer 1980). In view of the growing participation of members of all the country's "population groups" (an unfortunate phrase) in its central institutions, anthropology is also renewing its concern with culture, although "hesitating to leap forward to give cultural practice a momentum autonomous of political-economic processes" (Spiegel 1990, 294). As all sorts of South Africans are increasingly constrained to accommodate one another in shaping their future society, anthropology clearly has a potentially significant contribution to make, particularly in a country in which educators and professional intellectuals still have a major role in public discourse. In writing about African performance, it has been and still is my purpose to assist this mission. In so doing, I propose to follow Ortner's suggestion (1984) that we look at social practice on its own account, as agency and not just as response.

In the contemporary ethnography of southern Africa, the interpretation of oral genres in their contexts of production can reveal the cultural ground of agency, as well as people's modes of accommodation and resistance to the existing social order (Marcus and Fischer 1986, 133). For well over a century, if not longer, Basotho male migrants and their women have been composing and recomposing lengthy texts in musical performance, texts that serve as reflective, aesthetically intensified significations of experience. These songs are known as *lifela tsa litsamaea-naha le liparola-thota* (sing. and generic: *sefela sa setsamaea-naha le separloa-thota*), "songs of the inveterate travelers." Like all African auriture, they contain an inherent potential for social critique. As folklore, *sefela* "draws its life from its powers of adaptation to circumstances and changing environment, and its ability to reshape itself to fill a new need, like the shape changing wizards in the old tales" (Hilda Ellis Davidson 1978, ix; cited in Opland 1983, 271). Migrants' auriture provides commentary on changing structural relations in general and on the personal reality and effects of migrancy in particular. But it is also an irreducibly aesthetic construction of its creators' historical and social experience. We are thus engaged in an exploration of the ethnopoetics of the migrant experience of southern African political economy, revealed in performances rooted in the mastery of local knowledge.

As a socially recognized medium of expressive action, *sefela* appropriates and elaborates the complex symbolism of Basotho historical culture, establishing moral bonds with the past and future (Biesele 1986, 98). The songs relate theories of power to theories of the person, shaping motive and action by images and ideals of what constitutes goodness in people, relations, and conditions of life. As Beidelman observes, "To imagine another kind of world is always a judgment about this one" (1986, 204). In performance, such judgments are always made in reference to a process of rhetorical self-definition. Because culture is an essential constituent of the self, the operation of local knowledge in performance contexts depends upon the emotions attached to reflections about the nature of persons and social relations (Marcus and Fischer 1986, 46). As Harold Schueb puts it: "The drama of performance is an effort to capture the ritual, the graphic images of transformation, and, more importantly, the fierce focusing of venerable emotions on contemporary change" (1985, 5). Sentiment is therefore a primary constituent of performance as a social practice, a practice in which affect is essential to effect:

> You know, my fathers, my parents,
> Why should I steal [reveal secrets] in this way?
> I feel I want to shake the nation . . .
> . . . I say to you, gamblers [competitive poets],
> I am a person pierced [by pain]; I am still sick.
> I am a person with corns; I walk painfully.
> I am a person of the spirit;
> I desire the *hlope* dance:[2]
> I feel I want to dance this whole day.
> Witness the afternoon when the sun goes down,
> My heart feels pain.
> I feel I want to slaughter someone:
> You could order my father's younger brother, that I but slay him.
> What am I saying to you, gamblers?
>
> (Majara Majara, "Ngoana Rakhali")

This is why Raymond Williams's concept (1977) of the "structure of feeling," relating the articulation of experience to larger social forces and

2. The *hlope*, or "dance of the white beads," performed by diviners is essential to spirit mediumship and the curing of forms of spirit sickness (*lefu la moea* or *lefu la balimo*), and in particular the condition of ambulatory hysteria known as *motheketheke* (from *ho thekatheka*, "to wander about"). This affliction apparently first appeared during the 1930s, and was said to have been imported from the eastern Cape by Thembu people who form a significant minority community in southern Lesotho (Motlamelle 1938, 93). Considered a "modern" condition among Basotho, *motheketheke* is clearly a response to the intensified social and economic pressure upon rural Basotho households brought by colonial domination and the severe underdevelopment resulting from incorporation into the colonial political economy imposed by British and South African administrations in the region.

expressions of ideology, of emotions, perceptions, and reflections to the structure of reality, is so valuable in understanding the production of performance. The singer who desires to shake the nation with a song about his own experience must possess an intuitive seismograph, sensing the fault lines of feeling between social reality and social aspiration. Such aspirations, normatively oriented representations of a more balanced, less conflictual and contradictory social universe, are part of what Beidelman terms the "moral imagination: the art by which individuals struggle to transform their social baggage into gear that suits urgent situational needs in terms of meanings and moral judgments" (1986, 203). But like social reality itself, the structure of feeling is often ambivalent, multifaceted, a matter of mixed emotions. Our feet ache but the spirit demands an endless dance. Our hearts flood with pain, bringing to the surface the urge to murder a close relative who is also a rival claimant to our father's wealth and position. Tell me, my comrades in self-revelatory song, what am I saying? This book is based on the conviction that the more we are able to understand these travelers' songs through the ethnography of Basotho ethnopoetics, the more we can fathom culture as the diverse but universal human structure of feeling. To accomplish this we'd better keep traveling ourselves: *Bohlale ba bo hahe ntlo e le nngoe*, "Knowledge has erected many mansions."

Chapter Two

"The Mouth of a Commoner Is Not Listened To"

Power, Performance, and History

> We, the masters of the country, did drive you to live on human flesh, for men cannot eat stones. You ate my father, but before that I had eaten [dispossessed] yours. Oh, let it all be forgotten!
>
> *Moshoeshoe to the cannibal Rakotsoane, in Journal des Missions (1843)*

Among the rewards of the study of performance is the revelation of implicit, often-times unlooked for cultural knowledge (Fabian 1990, 6), a knowledge enacted in real time and not in an ethnographic present. The need to share the time of our subjects in our accounts as we do in our field research (ibid., 12) extends as well to the historical excavation of cultural categories and forms. Performance, after all, is not the product of a tradition but a social process through which traditions are elaborated and made perceptible (Vansina 1985, 33). Their historicity allows evanescent performances to leave their imprint on successive (re)enactments and discourses about them. As Harold Scheub puts it, "The oral arts, containing this sensory residue of past cultural life and the wisdom so engendered, constitute a medium for organizing, examining, and interpreting an audience's experiences of the images of the present" (1985, 1). So we must begin with a description of the principles and processes, genres and contexts, ideologies and realities out of which Basotho migrants' auriture emerged. Carried through time by the dynamism of social agency, we can then move to explore the changing communicative needs and questions to which this auriture has been an answer.

We cannot, unfortunately, observe long-past performances, or even consult nineteenth-century Basotho discourse concerning how performances were fashioned or evaluated or how they met the emotional, imaginative, or representational requirements of their creators and audiences. Such evidence survives only in the contingent continuities of production and reproduction, in the *habitus* of ethnoaesthetic principles, in the descendant embodiments of aural genres viewed as "cultural structures of cognition and experience" (Dorst 1983, 415). To start with, we do have an adventitious scattering of historical texts, many recorded in methodological circumstances that would impugn their usefulness if historians, linguists, folklorists, and literary analysts had not contextualized their provenance and made such coolly knowing between-the-lines readers of today's students of Africa's oral traditions. What we have secondarily are descriptive accounts by outside interlocutors, including missionaries, travelers, and amateurs of various kinds. Provided we have studied the mediator as well as the product of his mediation and understood the ideological transaction as well as the practical strategies involved in its production, we need not throw out the baby of primary evidence with the bath water of colonialism's willful or unwitting misconstruals. Indeed, which of us has not been surprised by the sympathetic perceptiveness of some of our less reflexive predecessors? Then, too, while there isn't any such thing as just the facts, those who in good faith tried to stick to them have often contributed a knowledge that may well survive the second-order, egocentric deconstructions of postmodern literary theorists and cultural anthropologists, including, of course, mine. So, to a selection of some facts, guided by the work of interpretation (Tedlock 1983) without which performances remain not merely misconstrued but opaque—history hardly more than one damn thing after another.

Like the Batswana chiefs in the north (from which his Bakoena had originally separated), Moshoeshoe I was not in fact the sovereign of a land, like the king of France, nor even of a people, like the king of the Franks, but of a range (Comaroff and Comaroff 1990, 204) on which he, his royal kinsmen, his vassals, and their followers alone had the right to plant crops and pasture their livestock. Moshoeshoe's people were bound to him by his ability to preserve and extend that range and to provide them with the cattle that embodied their fealty as a social contract (Sansom 1974, 163). As in the Praises of the Cow:

Khomo 'muu! se-lla-moreneng,	Cow moo! one crying at the chief's place,
Ha e lla metsanang ea ronana.	When it cries at the little villages, it is improper.

(Mapetla 1969, 4)

The moral equivalency admitted by Moshoeshoe in the epigraph for this chapter between the eating of his grandfather Peete by Rakotsoane and the "eating up" of Rakotsoane's fathers through the seizure of their herds is based upon the symbolic and social as well as the material convertibility of humans and cattle in precolonial southern African societies. Even today, the taboos against women slaughtering or milking cattle or going anywhere near a cattle enclosure reflect a complementary opposition between bovine and human reproduction (Gay 1980c, 60). Among Basotho, the pathways leading through every structural relationship and transaction were worn smooth by the hooves of cattle, called in their praises *molimo o nko e metsi*, "the god with a wet nose." Men slaughtered or sold cattle for sustenance only in the most extreme circumstances, since to diminish the family patrimony in this way constituted a form of social self-consumption. As the Sesotho *maele* (proverb) has it, *Ha ale fete khomo ale je motho*, "When you give up an ox to get food you are eating a person." Or as Mphafu Mofolo confessed satirically in his *sefela:*

Lebitso lebe e fela e le seromo—	A bad name is truly an omen[1]—
Litšoana ke tsa ka.	The dark beauties are mine.
Tsa ka ha Shale, li re ho 'na eang makhooeng:	Those at Ha-Shale, they say as I go to the mines:
"Le koana moo o eang, ngoana oa Mofolo?	"Even where you are going, child of Mofolo?
E ke o ka hola oa fetella."	Would that you grow shameless."
Ke 'nete ke fetelletse;	It is true I am shameless;
Ke jele likhomo ke le makhooeng—	I ate cattle while at the mines—
Seberekane ntata Thabang,	A hard-worker, father of Thabang,
Ka reka likhomo ke be ke li rekise	I buy cattle and even sell them

Equally if not more essential at the local level, of course, was women's work: the production and processing of cereals into the daily bread (porridge) and commensal beer of family and village life, the bearing and raising of sons to manage the family herd and daughters to add to it through bridewealth. The importance of cultivation, of women's work, is reflected in the comparatively high bridewealth that Basotho bridegrooms have historically given for their brides (Kuper 1987, 132).

Livestock, though, provided the means of capital accumulation and the currency of social exchange, convertible into clients and allies and thus military power, political influence, and expanded territorial resources. Cat-

1. This phrase is a very well known Sesotho proverb, roughly equivalent to the American adage "If it quacks like a duck . . . ," but according to some Basotho suggesting a literal link between one or several of a person's names and the behavior to be expected of them (see M. P. Guma 1993, 6). The poet's first name means "One Who Tells Things He Ought Not to Tell," from *ho phafunya*, "to tell unbecoming things."

tle were a source of constant conflict at and between all political levels. Cattle raiding was often both the immediate cause and ultimate object of war, and the test of courage, cleverness, and leadership for ambitious princes. Moshoeshoe himself was originally called Lepoqo (Dispute), but even before he became head of his own regiment—the Matlama (Binders), from his initiation name, Letlama—he conducted a successful cattle raid on a neighboring chief, Ramonaheng, and renamed himself Moshoeshoe (*Mo-shwe-shwe*), an onomatopoeic reference to the sound of a knife shearing a sheep. In praises that were later incorporated into his official praises (*lithoko*), the king proclaimed, with memorable phonetic parallelism:

Ke nna Moshoeshoe *Moshoeshoeila oa ha Kali.*	I am Moshoeshoe, the barber of Kali's.
Lebeola le beotseng Ramonaheng litelu;	The barber who shaved Ramonaheng's beard;
Le ho hola ha li eso hole, *Li ea sala li hola maisao.*	It has not even grown yet, It will remain growing in years to come.

(Guma 1967, 152)

But single-minded pursuit of expanded herds could lead just as easily to the ruin of a chief and the absorption of his followers. Again the Praises of the Cow:

Molimo o nko e metsi, *Oa ra-se-lohlanya-lichaba.* *Pshe'a ratso li linakanyana,*	God with a wet nose, That it's said drives mad the nations. Ostriches on a short leash, with little horns,
Li tsoha ka meso li ntse li lla! *Na li re mang a e'o lisa?* *A e'o tsosa likoebe matsaneng?*	That arise very early still lowing! Saying, who's going to herd us? Is that the one who awakens barbed stabbing spears from the lakes?
Khomo tsa lipholo, mehlolo selemo, *Ha li na le ngoan'a mong a lisitse,*	Oxen, miracles of spring, There is no one's child who has herded them;
Li mo tsoele pelo, li mo robokele!	They charge out in front of him, and they trample him!

(Mapetla 1969, 4; translation mine)

These feisty and fought-over wet-nosed gods, troublesome as ostriches, require their owner's attention from daybreak. The warlike pretender believes he can control them, but more likely they will lead him to destruction.

Sotho-Tswana chiefdoms were not based on any ritual or mystical ideology of cultural identity, any notion of ethnic *differànce*. The totemic clan (*seboko;* pl.: *liboko*) that formed the agnatic core of the chiefdom and its ruling family often did embody such an ideology but was not in itself a political unit or land- or cattle-holding corporation, and so in that sense was not a lineage system. Every chiefdom included people of other *liboko* who belonged by virtue of some form of contractual allegiance to the chief, and who often outnumbered people of the chief's own *seboko*. Hamnet (1965, 241) noted in 1965 that while the chiefs of Basutoland were largely of Moshoeshoe's Bakoena clan, they made up only about 30 percent of the total population. The essence of Sotho-Tswana chieftainship was negotiation and conciliation, reinforced by judicious applications of economic incentive and the threat rather than the peremptory application of force. Unlike his Nguni counterpart, the Sotho-Tswana chief ruled in constant watchfulness over the movements of his followers, lest in search of lusher pastures they wandered off to join a more attractive or persuasive rival (Sansom 1974). The idealized balance between hierarchy and reciprocity in these patron-client relationships is expressed in the Sesotho proverbs: *Morena ke batho*, "The chief is the people" (no people, no chief), and *Morena ke morena ka batho*, "A chief is a chief by the people."

When Shaka's expanding Zulu, along with forays by slave-trading Europeans, sent great clans and lesser refugees careening across southern Africa in the early nineteenth century, several formerly autonomous groups were welded into the emerging national amalgam of the Basotho. The term "Basuto" first appears in the written record in 1824, in an account of refugees from the attacks of Griqua (mixed race), Khoikhoi, and renegade white cattle thieves and kidnappers at Griquatown, west of Kimberley (Ambrose 1973, 60–64). Ellenberger and MacGregor (1912, 34) give the Nguni term shunta (*abashunto*, "knotted") as the origin of the root—*sotho*, referring to the *tseha*, a knotted loincloth worn by men whose descendants today speak Northern or Southern Sesotho or Setswana, which the Nguni men apparently found superfluous. Nguni low humor regarding the knotty or at least in their view curiously concealed physiognomy of Basotho privates is not without parallel in Sesotho, where the expression *tseha e ntšo*, "black loincloth," is a euphemism for male genitals.

Constrained to settle down under the protective but more autocratic rule of Moshoeshoe and his house, the precolonial Basotho retained the consultative political style, including the right to public argumentation and the expression of private opinion, that Moshoeshoe inherited from his forbearers and of which his court (*khotla*) and popular assemblies (*lipitso*) were the exemplars. Later, both Afrikaner settlers and British imperialists refused to recognize that Moshoeshoe's Tswana-style politics could not be like those of Shaka Zulu who, having united opposing Nguni clans by military and political incorporation, ruled absolutely by might-made right. Moshoeshoe's brothers were often headstrong and irresponsible, his subordinate allies restive, their followers transient. The treachery and cunning attributed to Moshoeshoe by indignant Europeans (and used to justify retaliation and expropriation) were largely the result of agreements he could not guarantee, intentions he could not fulfill, behavior he could not control.

Moshoeshoe must nonetheless, or perhaps even for those very reasons, be reckoned an exceptional political innovator who managed to build an increasingly unified national confederacy amid the chaos and depredations of the Shakan period and European encroachment. Based in the defensible and fertile western foothills of the Maloti, the Basotho state was both structurally incorporative and hierarchically centralized. Moshoeshoe's leadership, like his headquarters at Thaba Bosiu (Mountain of the Night), was a fortress under whose protection the four great clans of the Basotho—the invading Bakoena, the aboriginal Bafokeng, the vassal Bataung, and the conquered Batlokoa—could gather. Also counted among his subjects were numerous segments of Sotho-Tswana-speaking clans, including the Bakhatla, Lihoja, Basia, and others, as well as large communities of originally Nguni-speaking people such as the emigrant Thembu (Sesotho: Bathepu), Moorosi's Baphuthi of Zizi origin, and fractions of Swazi and Zulu clans known collectively as Matebele or Bakone—all of whom today speak Sesotho and regard themselves as fully Basotho. At the same time, they proudly refer to their distinctive origins and on occasion emphasize their distinctive cultural practices, especially those associated with the dance and with rituals of the life cycle.

The early French missionaries were initially unaware of any significant differences between Setswana (Sethlaping) and the dialect spoken by the people of Moshoeshoe, and were much guided in the initial transcription of Sesotho by London missionary Robert Moffat's Sethlaping vocabularies. Among the earliest recorded comments on Sesotho is a reflection offered by Moshoeshoe himself to the missionary Thomas Arbousset during an expedition to the northern reaches of his realm in 1840:

> "My language is nevertheless very beautiful!" said the chief unaffectedly. "We are only beginning to realize this since we have seen it written down. Thanks to the little books of the missionaries, it will not be altered; oh! your paper; that paper organizes everything well. . . . and then, I only see words that are being changed because they are Setlhaping words. My language re-

mains my language on paper. If that paper came from some remote corner of the Maloti, and if it arrived by itself at Thaba-Bosiu, it would be recognized as a Mosotho, and we would ask it if it had not been written by one of the subjects of Mokoteli." ([1840] 1991, 101–2)

The king's comments indicate his dissatisfaction with the missionaries' conflation of royal Sekoena with the Sethlaping dialect, and he refers to the process by which the transcribers were schooled to eliminate Sethlaping usages from their Sesotho vocabularies (ibid., 180). Sesotho as it later came to be written—Casalis's 1841 grammar is called *Études sur la langue sechuana,* "Studies on the Sechuana Language"—is most logically a blend of the Sekoena of the ruling clan, the Sefokeng of the aboriginal Bafokeng, whose female aristocrats the Bakoena chiefs deliberately married—we don't call our home language "mother tongue" for nothing—and the Sethlaping usages, both lexical and grammatical, injected by the missionaries (Ambrose, personal communication, December 1991). Moshoeshoe's approval of the apparent fixity which transcription would bring to Sesotho reflects his desire for a linguistic basis for the future political identity and irreducibility of his recently constructed monarchical state. Hence his satisfaction that missionaries' "papers" can be recognized as "written by one of the subjects of Mokoteli" (Moshoeshoe's great-granduncle and the eponymous ancestor of Moshoeshoe's section of the Bakoena clan, the Bakoena-Ba-Mokoteli). Even at this time, of course, Sesotho was dropping old terms and usages and picking up new ones, including numerous borrowings from the languages of the Dutch (Afrikaner) and British invaders (Germond 1967, 539).

The significance of the foregoing discussion is first that Sesotho is in essence a cultural style, a manner of doing things more than the things themselves, and thus requires no stable content and is not defined by its inventory at any particular time. Second, Sesotho taken in its more restrictive local sense as "Seshoeshoe," the cultural dialect of Moshoeshoe's Basotho, is the expressive counterpart of an essentially political construct with an internally acknowledged history, rather than an immemorial tradition embodying the inherent cultural "genius of a people," as the Germanic idealism of apartheid theory (and some self-appointed authorities on Sesotho) would have it. The diverse cultural and political origins of the Basotho are readily acknowledged among themselves, and the forging of allegiances through marriage, the attraction of noble vassals, the subjection of local rivals, and the incorporation of external refugees were the conscious cornerstones of Moshoeshoe's policies of state formation. At the same time, his royal sons and younger brothers were placed as rulers over the districts and vassals in his domains, demoting local, subject authorities and counteracting the fissionary tendencies of Sotho-Tswana chiefdoms as long as the first house of Moshoeshoe and his heir, Letsie I, could control the center.

Throughout the almost two centuries of Basotho history, the chieftancy has served as both the central symbol and vehicle of the defense of Basotho national identity. Nevertheless, as geographical mobility and the availability of new resources became limited, Basotho commoners became increasingly aware that it was not only foreign enemies who were capable of eating them up. In Sesotho, a cannibal is anyone who prospers by injuring, eclipsing, overtaxing, or expropriating the labor and substance of someone else, and by this standard the most voracious man-eaters have often been the Basotho chiefs themselves. Granted, the British made a mockery of the notion of official protection by routinely selling out Basotho interests to South African demands. But on the Basotho side, regional and district chiefs, relatives and putative vassals of Moshoeshoe, often played both sides against the middle, defied and betrayed the king, ignored the terms of the peace treaties he so painfully negotiated, and sent their followers out to die for the sake of chiefly wealth, power, and fractious advantage.

THE RHETORICAL ARTS, historically fundamental to communication and social process in mobile southern Bantu societies (Adams 1974, 128), flourished with the expansion of the Basotho kingdom and the increasing velocity of political conflict and transformation in the region. Auriture, the art of word music in motion, was as indispensable as ordinary speech to the settlement of disputes, the creation of social consensus, the promulgation of law, the legitimation of both command and dissent, and the practice of power. In substance, despite the framing of recognized categories and genres of performance, the difference between ordinary speech and aural art was one of degree rather than kind. In Sesotho rhetorical strategy, everyday speech employed many of auriture's devices, and conversation was interlarded with texts and textual fragments drawn directly from the corpus of aural genres, just as those genres drew freely upon one another. Casalis was made aware of the continuity of ordinary discourse with auriture through his own efforts to learn Sesotho: "The language, from its energetic precision, is admirably adapted to the sententious style, and the element of metaphor has entered so abundantly into its composition, that one can hardly speak it without unconsciously acquiring the habit of expressing one's thoughts in a figurative manner" (Casalis [1861] 1965, 307). Listening to praise poetry, Casalis wrote that in addition to its highly accentuated rhythm, it could be "distinguished from ordinary discourse by the elevation of sentiment, metaphors, the ellipse, and by turns now live and energetic, now melancholic and naive, which are proper to the language of the passions" (Casalis 1841, 52; translation mine). Writing later in the nineteenth century, the missionary Duvoisin, an unabashed paternalist who conflated race and culture with perfect confidence, nevertheless made memorable observations on the performative capacities of the Basuto (each and every one of them!):

> They have memory, imagination, sensibility, supple intellectual organs. They have no difficulty in memorizing, even that which least lends itself to this process; they have great facility in languages; they are born musicians and pick up most tunes on the spur of the moment; they have an incomparable gift of imagination coupled with perfect naturalness; they express themselves with ease and, on occasion, when well inspired, they can make speeches of artless and picturesque charm. (Germond 1967, 532)

Artless? Well, not if the good *berger* meant unstudied or uncomposed, and certainly not if he meant unconcerned with the pursuit of strategic social ends. As Casalis patronizingly put it:

> If art has not yet found her way to this primitive forum, eloquence is well known there; and this enchantress has spread over the wild simplicity of the *khotla* a prestige almost as great as that which surrounds our own Houses of Parliament. . . . A perfect sense of propriety, clear, cutting, picturesque, and at times noble language, seem natural to the Mochuana or the Caffre, called upon to defend himself. This kind of eloquence possesses a greater charm, form the accompaniment of action so natural and so perfect, that a person witnessing these debates is carried away in spite of himself. ([1861] 1965, 124, 229)

In the judicial system practiced at the chief's *khotla*, the advantages of seniority, position, and patronage were offset by the authority granted to eloquent disputation in its own right. It was the mediatory powers of rhetoric that gave some practical force to the judicial ideal enshrined in the proverb *Lekhotla ha le nameloe motho*, "The court is no respecter of persons," and that mitigated the realities of power relations expressed in the contradictory proverb *Molomo o mosehlanyana ha o mameloe*, "The mouth of a commoner is not listened to." Court cases were an entertainment and a "tournament of wits" (Ellenberger and MacGregor 1912, 266) in which rhetorical mastery, mounted upon moral persuasion, might marshal general opinion against authoritative political influence: *Mooa-khotla ha a tsekisoe*, "What is said at court is not blameworthy" (Guma 1967, 84). This morality was constructed so as to use the adjudication of individual claims to enhance structural stability, communal interests, and social "agreement" (*tumellano*). The core of litigation, therefore, was proverbial usage, strategic summaries imputed to a situation, based not on precedent but on principle as unwritten law.

I am reminded here of Johannes Fabian's opinion, expressed in his extended meditation upon the French Luba proverb *Le pouvoir se mange entier*, "Power is eaten whole," that "proverbs are neither legal rules nor philosophical maxims" (1990, 32–33). While Fabian is right that African proverbs need not carry such a structural burden, it is equally clear that there are contexts in which they are quite consciously made to do so. Perhaps mistaking European legal categories for African ones, Fabian bases his sweeping judgment upon the clear coexistence of mutually contradictory proverbs within the same corpus, and the possibility of multiple interpretations for a single maxim. For the Basotho, at least, neither of these conditions in any way vitiates the normative force of proverbs in specific adjudicative contexts. Axioms such as *Lintlo ha li jane*, "Houses do not eat each other," guaranteeing the material integrity of each of a man's polygynous "houses," have the use and validity of *molao*, the Law, a law inseparable from social philosophy. The principle *Lentsoe la morena le baheloa lesaka*, "The word of the chief must be stoutly defended," or even *Morena ha a tene moluopo*, "The chief can do no wrong," is not weakened by a concomitant recognition that *Mophongoa ha a na moholo*, "Even the great may be deceived" (Guma 1967, 83). If in many cases "the mouth of a commoner is not listened to," then equally, *Morena ke khetsi pea masepa*, "The chief is a shoulderbag of shit," and must "tolerate all his subjects, no matter how worthless they may be" (Damane and Sanders 1974, 241 n. 9). At variance with Fabian's suggestion (1990, 37), all of these are "crucial tenets of cultural knowledge," at least according to Basotho.

Law and social philosophy are not of course reproduced simply by reference to a corpus of sententious maxims. They are internalized by enculturative processes and media of various kinds, including performance, from the rhetorical turns of everyday speech to the secret, mythic compositions and enactments of the circumcision school (*lebollo*). Among the performances through which a Mosotho child is first exposed to the principles and contradictions of social philosophy and social behavior, even today, are those of folk narratives called *litsomo* (from *ho tsoma*, "to hunt, to take by surprise"). Intended, like auriterary metaphors, to roust startling meanings, these tales are full of surprises and attacks ranging from the uncanny to the fantastical, with mythical creatures, wild animals, and even wilder humans pursuing hyperbolic stratagems. At the core, as we might expect, are home truths about the nature of humanity and society, but adults seeking to surprise children with them do not let imagination linger near to home. In performance, *litsomo* are artistically and mnemonically enhanced by songs emphasizing key characters or episodes, structuring in audience participation and response.

Chiefs' praises make more direct use of episodes from *litsomo* than do migrants' auriture, but one character from the stories that does make an appearance in both is Kholumolumo (pronounced *Kodumodumo*), a great swallowing monster and cannibal archetype common in subsaharan African folk narrative, who engulfs the entire Basotho nation. The repentant nineteenth-century marauder Makonosoang, baptized a Christian in his old age, confessed thus to cannibalism: "I am *Kholumolumo*, the horrible beast of our ancient fable, who swallowed all mankind, and the beasts of the field" (Ellenberger and MacGregor 1912, 226). The ancient fable of which Makonosoang undoubtedly spoke is "Senkatana," one of the most widely known of all *litsomo*, and worth including here for the light it sheds on the representational structure of Basotho social philosophy. The tale has retained its influence and wide distribution. In 1952, for example, the outstanding Sesotho linguist, literary scholar, and author S. M. Mofokeng published a play entitled *Senkatana*, in which Kholumolumo embodies the white South African state, enveloping the black multitudes in bondage, while Senkatana represents their young liberator. As a folk narrative, the tale of Senkatana has as many versions as it has performances, and so as not to confuse the key elements of potential texts with any actual realization, I will summarize rather than recount it. The following synopsis accords with two versions translated by Guma (1967, 194–201) from originals transcribed by Jacottet (1908):

Kholumolumo appears and consumes the entire nation, along with all the domestic animals, with the exception of one pregnant woman who has rubbed herself with ashes and calf dung (in place of the ointment of fat and ocher favored by female initiates and pregnant women) so that the monster mistakes her for a soil-encrusted stone. Departing, Kholumolumo finds its girth is now too great to fit through the mountain pass and becomes stuck. Before long the woman gives birth and, having gone to the cattle kraal to collect dung,[2] returns to find her infant grown into a young man, fully accoutered with blanket, spears, and shield. When the woman asks of him

2. This is in violation of the strict Sesotho prohibition against women, during the years of their fertility, entering or even passing near a cattle kraal. In this case, with no one but her baby left alive, Senkatana's mother has little choice but to violate custom.

the whereabouts of her child, the youth replies that it is he, Senkantana (Ragged One), and he wants to know where the people, cattle, dogs, and chickens have gone. Informed by his mother about Kholumolumo, Senkatana proceeds to the pass, and finding the monster immobilized, he evades its maw and stabs it to death. The youth then attempts to cut open the beast to give birth to his people and their animals, but everywhere he jabs his knife a person within shouts "Don't cut me!" or a cow bellows "Muu!" or a dog growls "Koee!" until finally he hits a spot where it is only a fowl clucking, so he cuts open the corpse and the people and animals are freed. Returning to the village, the people grumble against Senkatana, complaining, "Can this small boy be our chief?" Soon they are plotting his death by various stratagems, but by foresight, cunning, and luck Senkatana always escapes and one of the plotters meets his demise instead.

In some versions the conspirators finally succeed, but in others Senkatana survives through the agency of a favorite head of cattle, Tololiphatsoa (Black and White-Spotted Gray), given him as a gift by another boy in gratitude for the rescue from the belly of Kholumolumo. As he herds it, Tololiphatsoa warns Senkatana of the plot, and when the plotters ask him for his cow he refuses, consenting only on threat of death. The plotters then attempt to drive, slaughter, flay, cut up, gather the meat, wash the pots, cook, and eat the animal. In each case Tololiphatsoa refuses, causing one of the plotters to be sacrificed in its stead, and they are able to succeed only when Senkatana is prevailed upon to talk to the beast (sing its praises) to gain its submission. The morning after the feast Senkatana pounds the hide of his cow, now pegged out on the ground, with his stick saying, "Tololiphatsoa, let us go home." The cow then regains its living flesh and bones, while all those who have eaten it die, together with their children and dogs. Returning home at last, Senkatana asks his mother for bread, but the cow warns him that it is poisoned. By mistake his father eats the bread and dies, and the cow has the last word: "You see, you would have died. Your mother does not like you."

This tale, which encodes with characteristic ambivalence the archetypes of both culture villain (Kholumolumo) and culture hero (Senkatana), plays around with a series of culturally sentient metaphoric tropes, bringing them into metonymic relationship and creating a dialogue between social ideology and practice. The terror of Kholumolumo is based upon the trope of consuming, eating up, or swallowing prevalent in figurative characterizations not only in Sesotho but in languages elsewhere in southern Africa and in black Africa in general. This trope has been analyzed by Kunene (1971, 102–8), who points out how fittingly the metaphor of swallowing is used in praises of the aristocratic Bakoena (Crocodile) clan of the Basotho. Royal praises of the Bakoena chiefs are populated with personified crocodiles, and by extension, the chiefs become mythical man-eaters who consume the enemies of the subject. Paramount Giffith (reigned 1912–39) is praised thus for his part in the defeat in battle of his father's (Letsie II) rebellious brother Masopha on January 12, 1898:

Kholumolumo pea e-ja batho,	Kholumolumo devoured the people,
Batho ba feletse mpeng ea selo!	The people have ended in the monster's stomach!

(Mangoela [1921] 1984, 186; translation from Damane and Sanders 1974, 228–29)

Letsie II's praises likewise begin:

'Mamaririele oa Lijabatho,	The hairy wild beast of the Man-eaters [regiment],
Seloana se maepho sa 'ma-ma-ts'ajoa-ke-batho, . . .	The long-haired monster which is feared by the people, . . .

(Mangoela [1921] 1989, 173; translation from Damane and Sanders 1974, 209)

The hero as vanquishing cannibal gives an intriguing Sesotho twist to Fabian's problematical proverb, *Le pouvoir se mange entier.* As Kunene points out though (1971, 106), the "Swallowing Thing" can as easily represent the chief's enemies, repelled by his supporters, as it can the valiant all-consuming ruler himself. In the folk tale the swallowing beast is the enemy, and the hero is the young Senkatana, born fully grown and conforming in this and other respects to the heroic model in black African auriture outlined and analyzed by Charles Bird and Martha Kendall (1981). Bird and Kendall point out that the saving and creative violence of the hero, while welcome in times of extreme crisis, becomes dangerous to the domestic social order once the danger is overcome. African social process as framed in the subcontinent's heroic texts is thus driven by a tension between role breaking, resource consumption, supra-social achievement, and structural innovation on the one hand, and personality assimilation, ordered collective action, and institutional reproduction on the other. "The hero is a loner, he has a vision only partly shared by the rest of his people. It is his task to use his special gifts to convince his fellows of the correctness of that vision, and to effect a transformation" (Scheub 1985, 20). Senkatana saves the nation but his precocity ("Can this boy be our chief?") and egoistic self-reliance (he herds his own cattle) upset the established ideology of male hereditary gerontocracy. Inevitably, the jealousy and condemnation Basotho characteristically express toward those who strive after "unwarranted" distinction ("When the cattle low in the little villages it is improper") turns murderous: thus always to heroes. In some versions of the story, Senkatana is called "Litaolane" (Divining Bones), after the string of divining bones found around his neck at birth, which suggest the prescience that enables him to escape each attempt against him. His charmed life is most clearly guaranteed however, by the advice of his gift cow, a prestation from his age-mate for killing Kholumolumo and the only expression of gratitude in this entire cautionary tale. Interestingly, the cow's unwilling cooperation with the plotters' demands on Senkatana is only secured by the singing of the cow's praises by the hero, including its hide-color name, in itself a form of bovine honorific in Sotho-Tswana languages. The youth, forward in cultural knowledge as well as leadership, revives his faithful savior by a magic that simultaneously destroys his gluttonous enemies. Returning to the supposed safety of home, his cow accomplishes the final stage of the young hero's coming of age, reflecting the association in black Africa of heroic and initiatory narrative themes. Senkatana is warned of his mother's treachery, the father dies as a result instead, and the young chief learns the indispensable lesson that a hero must not trust even a mother's love. So do Basotho comment on the power of perspicacity, the ways of the world, and human venality. Historically, the man of ordinary birth who attempts extraordinary achievements must do so in the face of social opposition as well as existential danger. Significantly, the oppositions between social value and social behavior are expressed in anthropophagous and gustatory metaphors, as if power—nay life itself—must, in the words of Fabian's Luba, be eaten whole. The last word on this issue is surely the Sesotho proverb *Phiri e jeoa moreneng*, "A hyena [scavenger, man-eater, devourer of its own kind] is eaten at the chief's place" (Guma 1967, 86), a political metaphor based on the *molao* requiring any dead predator to be given to the chief.

The irony fundamental to Basotho expression of such deeply held yet situationally deniable social truths in imaginative form was noted by Casalis in terms no less ironic:

> They love nothing better than to listen to story-telling, or to tell stories themselves and, as is generally the case with those whose imagination is greater than their concern for the truth, they are also very fond of inventing tales. With them, the most trifling incident often assumes unheard of proportions; a noise, a rumor, very soon becomes the text for endless commentaries and, as it were, a canvas on which they proceed to embroider in mutual

> emulation. Accounts thus retailed are known as *mashano* (lies), as if the language, that incorruptible witness of the ways and customs of a people, thereby meant to caution us to be on guard against them. ([1861] 1965, 533)

Indeed, the inherent capacity of narrative for creative misrepresentation is widely recognized by Sotho-Tswana speakers, among whom *U leshano!* (You lie!) is the mere equivalent of "No kidding!" *Leshano* also means "palate," and in the dialect of Sethlaping, *leshano*, "lie" can mean language itself (ibid., 534). Elsewhere in subsaharan Africa, Peek (1981, 26) has observed that the name "liar" is often used in praise of one's preoccupation with aesthetic rhetorical values, a speaker of words too good to be true. Bosko, who observed a keen awareness among Basotho villagers of the capacity of falsehood and truth, artfully managed, to preserve, shatter, and repair social relationships, suggests that creative deception is integral to Basotho social organization (1983, 97). Because villagers live close and are involved with each other in different social arenas, Bosko asserts, they have a "virtual obsession with lies," which can be used equally to keep overlapping spheres of relationship separate or *ho fapanya batho ba utloanang*, "to start a quarrel amongst those who understood one another" (ibid., 222–24).

The wide distribution of tales like those about Senkatana reflects the importance of grandmothers in the enculturation of children in rural communities, as it is from these ancestresses that most Basotho have heard *litsomo*. Children, of course, possess their own forms of auriture, consisting primarily of songs located at the structural heart of games, dances, satirical caricatures, and the public aspects of ceremonies of initiation, many of which survive in the common corpus of folk performance enjoyed by adults. But most significant for our purposes is the nonmusical verbal game *U tsoa Kae?* (Where are you from?), associated with the learning of family praises and the assertion of social identity, which children have begun to learn from their grandparents by the age of four or five. The game consists of two parts, a question and answer formula, concluded by an elaborate individual statement. I am deeply indebted to Charles Adams (personal communication, 1989) for the only collection of texts of which either of us is aware, and from which the following example is taken:

Q: *U tsoa kae?* [Where are you from?]
A: [*Ke tsoa*] *ha 'Mantilatilane.* [I'm from the "origin place of the people."]
Q: *Ua ja'ng?* [What do you eat?]
A: *Ka ja bohobe.* [I eat bread.]
Q: *Ua futsoela ka'ng?* [What do you mix it with?]
A: *Ka metsi ea pula.* [With rain water.]

Q: *Thelle he!* [A slip up! Explain yourself.]
A: *Ke thelleleng?* [What mistake? Explain what?]

When questioner or answerer can go no further, the one questioned concludes with the recitation of his or her *seboko* (totemic clan) segment praises, as far as he or she can go. A five-year-old may know the first fifteen words or so, while a fully grown man like myself ought to know the entire text. As an adopted member of the Bafokeng *seboko*, I should thus answer with as much of the following as possible whenever I am asked, especially by another Mofokeng, *Oa ha mang?* "A Mofokeng of whose place?" (which subclan):

> *Ke Mofokeng oa ha Pulungoana Pahla; ke motho oa mora Palo oa Masiea. Ke Letotoma, ke motho oa ha khomo he e tsoale bosiu. E tla meha ho tsoala motseare, banana ba e shebile. Hobane ha e tsoala bosiu e-ea hlola, ea bolaoa e bitsetsoe banana le bashanyana ba tlo eja. Re maila 'khoaba; khomo e 'khoaba ha e ruoe mona Phokeng. Re malepeletsa, manyela lilomong. Ha re nyela balimo ba thaba ba a khakeletsa ka liroto, ba re, "Joo! ba re fa lijo." Ha re rota ba thaba, ba re, "Joo! ba re fa metsi." Re batho ba ha mamohlamu oa ntoto; re batho ba ha manyoana, Bafokeng. Re batho ba ha Selimo sa mahlatsi a moloka.*
>
> I am a Mofokeng of November Pack-up; I am a person of a son of Palo of Masiea. I Letotoma, I am a person of the place where cows do not give birth at night. It should give birth in the afternoon so girls should see it. For when it gives birth at night, it is uncanny; it is killed, and girls and boys are called to come and eat it. We taboo the [white-necked] crow; the cow that is [white-necked like] a crow—it is not raised here in the place of the Bafokeng. We slide down, defecating off cliffs; when we defecate, the ancestors are happy. They collect it [feces] in rush [grain] baskets and say, "Joo! They gave us food." When we urinate, they are happy and say, "Joo! They gave us water." We are people of the place of rectums, of penises; we are people of the place of vaginas, the Bafokeng. We are people of Selimo of the vomiters of the moloka [plant].

As Matsela points out (1979, 169), aural performance is one of the few fields of nonliterate education, along with war, initiation, and herbal medicine, in which Basotho employ formal teachers. Games like *U tsoa Kae?* are a preparation for the memorization of clan praises, and of the secret archaic songs (*likoma*) and public songs (*macha*, *mangae*, and *bale*) taught at the circumcision schools where Basotho boys and girls are initiated into manhood and womanhood. This game has particular significance, however, in its emphasis on social identity and in particular on naming. In Sesotho practice, every level of personal development has a name-giving ritual, in which the new name symbolizes the achievement of a new state of social being. So if bridewealth has been adequately paid, the paternal and maternal kin each give a newborn Mosotho a *lebitso la nku*, a "sheep name," so called because of the sheep that is sacrificed at the ritual of their giving. The name given by maternal kin emphasizes the special relationship of the child to the mother's brother (Bosko 1983, 295). In addition, children may be called as namesakes of deceased grandparents, reinforcing the conceptual identification of alternate generations (Mohome 1972, 171). The Basotho, unlike neighboring Nguni-speaking peoples, practice clan endogamy, though this structural norm is freely ignored in practice, except among the Bakoena aristocracy. If the parents come from different clans, then adequacy of bridewealth payment determines the clan identity of the child, symbolized by the *khoetsa*. This is a string worn around the infant's neck with the body part of the animal that proclaims to whose people (*seboko*) the child belongs and which distinctive family customs (*leseko*) the child will be taught to practice, serving also as a magical protection against the enmity of certain ancestor spirits. (Bosko 1983, 74, 290).

Then come initiation names and Christian baptismal names if one is ritually circumcised or baptized. Because initiation confirms the transition to full human status, male initiates receive a number of names, recording their genealogical seniority, clan name and attendant status, personal characteristics, attributes, and praises. Some of these names are used only at the initiation lodge and are known only to other initiates, while a public name identifies the initiate in his praises, sometimes in the case of a prince, identifying his regiment as well (see M. P. Guma 1993, 13). A woman's initiation name may refer to personal attributes, but most often it consists of the prefix *ra* and her maternal uncle's name, identifying him as her "owner/father." She also must be renamed at marriage (*'ma* plus husband's family name) and motherhood (*'ma* plus the actual or prospective name of her first child), since it is insulting to refer to her as if she were still a maiden, though among some clans she will not receive the teknonym until she bears a boy. A man acquires praise names marking accession to chiefship or outstanding enterprises. Even the landscape of community attains personality as villages and neighborhoods are additionally named "So-and-So's-Place, after their current chief, or even for a local resident whose worldly success has given his home renown. Married women may not, according to the custom of *hlonepho* (respect/avoidance) pronounce the real names of their senior male affines or even use words that resemble them in sound. An aptly chosen *hlonepho* name may come to replace a man's original name in general usage. Throughout life one may acquire nicknames or "joking names," *lebitso la bosoasoi*, used as substitutes for sacred sheep names (Bosko 1983, 298) and to remark a person's special qualities. These include *noms de voix* for the attainment of a distinctive voice in poetic composition and performance (Matsela 1979, 146), hence *ho reneketsa,* "to call by a pet name, to name poetically or in a poem." In practical terms, Basotho cannot function within their social organization without multiple names and identities, and it is impossible to maintain a single identity where kinship is so bound up with bridewealth (Bosko 1983, 303). More broadly, Sesotho names express who one wishes to be or is defined as in a given context, and so they express and construct social relations (ibid., 312).

Naming is an idiom of personal progress that sets the parameters of biography, a process that begins with the citation and invocation of ancestors on both sides of family. The Bafokeng *seboko* praise-naming above provides an emphatic assertion of the commensal reciprocity at the heart of the relationship between present and past generations. If a chief is a chief by the people, then equally *Bomolimo ke bomolimo ka botho,* "Divinity is divinity through humanity." The necessary converse of this relationship is the harm that ancestors can cause their descendants through moral sanction, neglect, unpredictability, willfulness, and revenge. Indeed, a child born after the death of the mother's previous baby (*seqoma*) is most often given an evil or unattractive name to discourage the ancestors from taking it as well (ibid., 303). The *khoetsa* worn around the child's neck is a charm protecting it from the harmful designs of vindictive ancestors. This inherently dangerous aspect of hierarchical reciprocity in ancestor-descendant relationships is expressed ironically in the root, *limo* (spirit, above) common to *Molimo* (God), *balimo* (ancestors), *leholimo* (sky), and *lelimo, bolimo* (cannibal, cannibalism). In Basotho and Batswana folktales, Limo is a murderous giant. If the excretions of the living become the sustenance of the grateful dead, then the insatiability of the collective godhead (*balimo* is never used in the singular) can consume descendants in the antisocial manner of human man-eaters. Alternatively, Kuper (1987, 170–71) cites evidence provided by J. Tom Brown, a missionary to the Batswana, to show that cannibals are regarded as having an evil supernatural character of their own, identified with Satan or spirits of the evil dead in opposition to the "good" spirits of people's own ancestors. The association of cannibalism with the realm of spirits appears also in Sesotho (every cannibal must be the tomb of *someone's* ancestor), but the Manichean dichotomizing of good and evil is rather alien to African cosmology and is surely an infusion from mission Christianity.

If clan praises can be likened to an extended name, then the most "literary," authoritative, and honored Sesotho oral genre, *lithoko tsa marena a Basotho* (praises of the Basotho chiefs) are quite cogently described by Kunene (1971, 14) as a series of names of praise (eulogues), forming the core of noble genealogies. As the praises of Paramount Seeiso, who reigned only one year (1939–40), explain: "The chief dies, Lerotholi's son, but the name remains, The name remains and is given to descendants" (Damane and Sanders 1974, 251). These figurative identities are elaborated into a symbolic narrative on history and biography. It is not only chiefs and totemic clans who are thus praised, but also distinguished commoners, wild and domestic animals, birds, divining bones, locomotives, and other "animate" things. In the period of precolonial autonomy and active warfare, commoners composed their own praises (*lithoko tsa bafo*) and so provided a hierarchical continuity in the discourse of ideal personhood and achievement. As Damane and Sanders point out (1974, 18–21), even great chiefs did not rely entirely on their *liroki* (official poets) but often composed their own praises as well. During the nineteenth century, young Basotho could develop interest in and appreciation of such forms by witnessing the performance of praises by their elders. As Casalis observes in a now famous description:

> *Le heros de la piece en est presque toujours l'auteur. De retour des combats, il se purifie a la riviere voisine, puis il va deposer religieusement au fond de sa hutte, sa lance et son bouclier. Ses amis l'entourent et lui demandent le recit de ses exploits. Il les raconte avec emphase; la chaleur du sentiment l'entraine, son expression devient poetique. De jeunes memoires s'emparent des morceaux les plus frappants; on les repete a l'auteur enchante, qui les retravaille et les lie ensemble dans ses longues heures de loisir; au bout de deux ou trois lunes, ses enfants savent parfaitement le toko, qui sera desormais declame aux fetes solennelles de la tribu.*
>
> The hero of the piece is nearly always the author. Upon returning from combat, he purifies himself in a nearby river, then he goes to put down, religiously in the depths of his dwelling, his lance and his shield. His friends surround him and demand of him the recitation of his exploits. He recounts them with emphasis; the heat of sentiment leading him on, his expression becomes poetic. The memory of the young takes hold of the most striking parts: they are repeated to the delighted author, who ponders over them, and connects them in his mind during leisure hours; at the end of two or three months, these children know these praises perfectly, which are thereafter declaimed at the solemn celebrations of the tribe. (Casalis 1841, 53; translation mine, but see Damane and Sanders 1974, 18)

Aural genres—distinct, codified, culturally recognized modes of aesthetic expression—exist through performance in time, not in "timeless" tradition, and are therefore subject to the same kinds of historical transformation and interaction as other cultural forms and social institutions (cf. Coplan 1987a). Furthermore, there is nothing in their ethnoaesthetic definition or identity as "culture specific conceptions or domains of artful language" (Dorst 1983, 415) that requires them to exhibit standard patterns of prosody or versification (Rycroft and Ngcobo 1988), temporally stable formal or thematic requirements, specific contexts of performance, self-defining boundaries, or exclusive content. Such ideally defining qualities *do* of course characterize aural genres, both in specific periods and places of performance and in the aesthetic expectations and discourse of performers and participants, in the "theory" of generic realization distributed in local knowledge. Genres are oriented both to the social reality of performance and to the internal emergence of their structure (Dorst 1983, 415). As a result, the relationship between experience and auriture is an extremely complex process of mutual formulation, expressed in the categories, resources, and transformations of genre. So a delineation of these forms is needed if we are to understand the historical, performative, and ethnoaesthetic (theoretical) relationships among Sesotho texts.

These relationships are revealed in part through "intertextuality": the realization of one code in the terms of or in reference to another through the socially patterned interpenetration of performances. Second, the intertextual emergence of genres must be viewed as what Julia Kristeva has called a *productivité:* the transformation of experience into verbal art for social purposes through the incorporative capabilities of genres (Sherzer 1977, 143). These capabilities enable performers to project a particular vision of social reality into the production of social structure in specific contexts of contestation. It is in these terms that we must explore the emergence of *sefela.*

In his efforts to historicize the analysis of genres, Raymond Williams (1977) disaggregated the notion of cultural tradition by articulating categories of verbal art with relations of power. Since cultural reality is both continuous and dialogic, the reification of such categories at once undermines their usefulness. The Zeno's Paradox of analytical modeling can be mediated to some degree in this case by seeing Williams's categories as a continuum, arranged along a progression from what Bakhtin described as "epic" time to "novelistic" (contemporary) time (Holquist 1981, 13–18). The far end of the continuum, epic time, represents an immemorial, valorized past inaccessible to performer and audience. This is a world "constructed in the zone of an absolute distanced image, beyond the sphere of possible contact with the developing, incomplete and therefore rethinking and reevaluating present" (ibid., 17). European epic literature, and in Africa, aural epics such as the *Sunjata* of Mali, display this epic distance; there is no South African parallel. The epic distance from the present in the *Sunjata* is far less extreme than in Homeric, Virgilian, or Norse epic, since the *Sunjata* is still performed with great compositional variety by and for the direct descendants of its characters, in the original territory and language. Even so, the essential episodes and narrative progression of the *Sunjata* are fixed and appear in virtually any competent performance. The text is not presently malleable or incorporative, and unlike southern African praise poetry, the *Sunjata* is neither intertextual nor a *productivité*.

Austen (1991) has ingeniously suggested that African epics actually begin as praise poetry during a period of state formation and dynastic consolidation. During this period, they remain elliptical, allusive, and plotless, retaining their incorporative capacities as records of existing power relations. The "story" and its underlying ethos are provided, not in the text, but in the environmental transmission of local knowledge. Hence the *Sunjata* as we know it most likely did not exist during the time when anyone alive could remember Sunjata Konté as a living man. It was only later, as the Mande state of Mali became a historical memory, that the bards transformed the praise songs of the heroes into an epic, replacing lost local knowledge with explicit, fixed textual narrative. In accord with this reasoning, indigenous South African states would still have been in the praise poetic phase of epic time when European colonial intervention and historiography aborted any movement by composers toward heroic narratives recited in epic time.

Unquestionably, the decline in the political prestige and power of chieftaincy during the late colonial and independence periods has been accompanied by a reduction in composition and performance among praise poets. For many members of the Basotho professional, bureaucratic, and commercial elite, as well as for some members of the urban proletariat, *lithoko tsa marena a Basotho* may today represent national cultural identity more than they do relations of social structure or power. Chiefs still possess some de facto control over the allocation of land and other social resources, and there is great overlap between the chieftaincy and the commercial, professional, and bureaucratic elite. But the ability of Major General Lekhanya, head of the ruling Military Council but a commoner, to remove King Moshoeshoe II and force him into exile in 1990, promulgating a legal decree replacing him with his son, Letsie III, demonstrates the aristocracy's lack of autonomous structural power. The only formal occasion on which the performance of a chief's praises is required is his installation, and even Moshoeshoe II maintained no praiser-in-residence at the royal capital at Matsieng. I would argue, however, that reports of the death of praise poetry in Lesotho (Damane and Sanders 1974, 25,33; Opland 1983, 142) are misleading. The composite texts published in Mangoela's *Lithoko tsa Marena a Basotho* ([1921] 1984) are studied in Lesotho schools, and rural boys with no formal schooling still learn large portions of their district chief's praises, especially if they undergo circumcision (*lebollo*) at the initiation lodge (*mophato*). MaMpho Chopo, a village chieftainess, first learned *lithoko* out of Mangoela in primary school, and has since become one of the country's most renowned *liroki* (sing: *seroki*, "chiefly praisers"), brought to Maseru at government expense to perform before crowds on the King's Birthday. She composed splendid praises for Moshoeshoe II, for the late chief of her own district, Leshoboro Leroala, and composed and performed new praises for Leshoboro's successor, Lerotholi, at his installation in 1988. MaMpho is not alone in having secured the chiefship for herself upon her husband's death (20 percent of village chiefs in Lesotho are now women), but she is virtually unique in having become a *seroki*, as women do not as a rule have, let alone compose or perform, praises (Damane and Sanders 1974, 22). In any event, one may still hear the praises of chiefly ancestors recited at public occasions, and new poems are still being composed for reigning aristocrats. More important, historical and social conditions may as easily shift to bring about a resurgence of praise poetry (as has been the case with male and female initiation schools) as to bring about its fossilization or death, depending on the changing role of the chieftaincy and how this role is ideologically framed by various categories of Basotho.

During the nineteenth century and into the twentieth, spanning the transformation from political and economic autonomy to colonization and dependence, chiefs' praises displayed some qualities of what Williams calls "emergent" culture, referring "not only to existing expectations, values and interactions, but also to the process through which new meanings and relationships are continually created" (Ulin 1984, 164). But unlike the emergent culture of migrants' auriture, chiefs' praises are also an expression of Williams's "selective tradition," genres that appear to represent the whole of social life, "but are in fact partial to the legitimation of the existing social order" (ibid.) As selective tradition, Basotho aristocratic praises are closer to epic time than migrants' songs, because "in a patriarchal social structure the ruling class does, in a certain sense, belong to the world of 'fathers' and is thus separated from other classes by a distance that is almost epic" (Holquist 1981, 15). The space between the idealized, "official" epic time of the Basotho royal heroes (however recent) and the conceptually present, novelistic time of migrants' songs is filled with artifacts of national tradition (ibid., 14). In a similar process, Moshoeshoe I and his councillors selected and reified the horse, the fighting stick (*molamu*) and knobkerrie (*koto*), the wearing blanket (*kobo*), and the conical straw hat (*molia-nyeoe, mokorotlo*) as universal and continuing symbols of Basotho national culture.[3]

The *seroki*, the praiser of chiefs, is responsible for the symbolic constitution of authoritative discourse, and so for the representation of social reality as selective tradition. His genre, however, entails a social charter for the expression of conflict between the hero (*mohale*) and his adversaries, between conflicting centers and wielders of power. Additionally, the praise form legitimates, even enjoins, the insertion of popular sentiment on issues of contention in the subject's career, framed in the terms of authoritative political values. High genres like chiefs' praises evaluate their subjects in relation to dominant ideological values, while reinforcing the validity of the institutional structure itself. Thus overt criticism can be offered as "praise." Even the hyperbolic lauding of royal ancestors in their descendant's public praises can in practice diminish the "hero" by implicitly invidious comparison. The art of praising is an exercise in moral imagination as well as political communication. Moshoeshoe I himself, for example, is obliquely criticized in the important final lines of his praises for failing to rescue his restive, cattle-hungry brother, Makhabane, who was surrounded and killed during a campaign against the Thembu in 1835. The suspicion was that Moshoeshoe wished to be rid of his uncontrollable sibling, to augment his own resources, and to avoid the challenge to his power that might have resulted had Makhabane survived to retain the cattle he had captured from the enemy:

Khoali [Moshoeshoe], *le hoja u tlile ka monate,* *Empa u tlile ka bohloko,* *U tlile ka pohomel'a lillo,*	Black white-spotted ox though you come with gladness, Yet you have come with grief, You have come with cries of lamentation,

3. The straw hat was originally a symbol of aristocratic status and did not attain general popularity in Lesotho until after the Second World War. It's name, *molia-nyeoe*, "thing of the councillors," also means a court case, and it may be that chiefs wore them when settling disputes in earlier times, as it is still the custom to take off one's hat when a decision is delivered at a local chief's court in Lesotho. Its other name, *mokorotlo*, is also applied to the highly

U tlile basali ballitšoara lihloho,	You have come as the women hold their heads,
Ba ntse ba ikakatlela melala!	And continually tear their cheeks.
Le e thibeleng e se kene ho tsa me,	Keep it [the captured herd] from entering my herds:
Le ho tsoala, e tsoalle mohlabeng,	Even in calving, let it calve in the veld.
E tsoalle Qoaling le Koro-Koro.	Let it calve at Qoaling and Korokoro.
Ho tsena tsa heso e tlisa tlokotsi,	To these cattle of our village it brings distress,
E tlile ka koli, paka-mahlomola	It has come with a dirge, a cause of sadness.
Na, Thesele, e mong o mo siea kae?	Thesele [Moshoeshoe], the other one [Makhabane], where have you left him?

(Mangoela [1921] 1984; translation from Damane and Sanders 1974, 31)

Other authoritative genres were less idealizing than chiefs' praises, often stressing the reciprocal rather than the hierarchical dimensions of the Basotho political ethos. The *mokorotlo* (from *ho korotla,* "to make grumbling sounds") genre of war anthem, named after the deep, rumbling vocal timbre in which it is sung, was described by Adams's informants as "a song by which Basotho remind themselves of [reflect on] very great matters [and] distinguish/differentiate themselves from other peoples" (1974, 172–73). The prestige *mokorotlo* enjoys, greater even than that of chiefs' praises, derives not from this collective reflection and differentiation by itself but from its expression through the harmonious integration (*tumellano,* "agreement") of text, music, and movement. In Sesotho, auriture is more aesthetically prestigious than orature. Even so, *mekorotlo* are replete with characteristic Sesotho grumbling about the durance suffered in the service of chiefs. The following *mokorotlo* was recorded in Basutoland by the late Hugh Tracey in 1959 (ILAM TR-102 N2B-9):

Hee! Lekhotleng la Mosiuoa Masupha,	Hee! At the court of [Chief] Mosiuoa Masupha,
Hee! Matholoana, o re fepe re none!	Hee! Matholoana [chief's wife], feed us so we grow fat!
Hee! Koali Mots'eoa hlaka la Masupha,	Hee! Koali Motseoa, reed [foundation] of Masupha,
Hee! Morena oa bobeli ho Motlalentoa—	Hee! The chief second to Motlalentoa—

prestigious genre of Basotho war anthems that in itself is a distinctive marker of national identity.

Hele helele! Marumo!	Hele helele! Spears! [praise name of the chief]
Hee! Marumo Oo! oo! oo! *Hee! O ea kae—ooe?*	Hee! Spears! Oo oo oo! Hee! Where are you going—ooe?
Hee! Rona ba ha Makoali, rea lla.	Hee! We of Koali's mother, we are crying.
Hele helele hee! Marumo!	Hele helele hee! Spears!
Hee! Rona ba ha Makoali, rea lapa	Hee! We of Koali's mother, we are hungry!
Hele helele he! Marumo!	Hele helele he! Spears!
Hee! Habofane, re fepe re none,	Hee! Habofane, feed us so we grow fat,
Hee! Re Bakone, re ntše re le ba hao!	Hee! We of Nguni origin we are still your people!
Hele helele hee! Marumo!	Hele helele hee! Spears!

Because of his military legend, Masupha is a popular subject of *mekorotlo*, but the praise name "Spears" here is more than faintly ironic. Masupha, it seems, is ready enough to lead his followers off to war, but slow to provide the hospitality and patronage that are the due of loyal followers. Though we, the singers, are just Matebele immigrants, and therefore of low clan-totemic status and a shield for your spear, we are nevertheless your people.[4]

Conversely, to the degree that high genres universalize selective tradition, they exclude the novelistic time of contemporary reality. "Contemporaneity, flowing and transitory," as Bakhtin observes, is the basic subject matter "only in the low genres. . . . in that broadest and richest of realms, the common people's creative culture of laughter" (Holquist 1981, 20):

> Laughter has the remarkable power of making an object come up close, of drawing it into a zone of crude contact where one can finger it familiarly on all sides, turn it upside down, inside out, peer at it from above and below, break open its external shell, look into its center, doubt it, take it apart, dismember it, lay it bare and expose it, examine it freely and experiment with it. . . . Laughter is a vital factor in laying down that prerequisite for fearlessness without which it would be impossible to approach the world realistically. As it draws an object into the fearless hands of investigative experiment—both scientific and artistic—and into the hands of free experimental fantasy. (ibid., 23)

As culture of laughter, popular and ironic forms such as *sefela* not only appeal to but also contest the underlying values of the dominant ideology:

4. Ashton (1967) notes that a *letebele* boy was customarily the first in line to undergo trials at the initiation lodge, symbolizing the status of the sons of Nguni Matebele clans as "shields" for the sons of chiefs.

Kerefisi o shoele a nkhethile;	[Paramount] Griffith died having chosen me;
Morena a rata o nketsa ramo,	The chief wanted to make me [his] ram,
Ke tle ke tsoala likonyana tsa pele:	So I should beget the first lambs:
Le ho boea, ke etsa likhokoloana,	Even the wool, I make balls of it,
Hoba ke le lekoele-koele la motho,	Because I am a sneaky Pete,
Seea nyatsing, se koetlile lesapo.	A master adulterer, concealing a bone [under my blanket].
	(Mphafu Mofolo, "Ngoan'abo Mokhoati")

In this passage from his *sefela*, retired migrant Mphafu Mofolo boasts that Paramount Chief Griffith (reigned 1913–39), chose him as his "ram," as genitor for his royal heirs and inheritor of his wives. Mphafu's virility is confirmed by the condition of his wool, and by his cleverness at adultery. When sneaking around houses at night on amorous adventures, he takes care to carry a bone beneath his blanket, to distract the snapping dog of his lover's absent husband. The double entendres in "balls" and "bone" will not have escaped the reader. Very funny, but not the end of it. Griffith was the younger brother of Paramount Letsie II, but he refused to govern as regent for the latter's infant son, saying he would "sit on the throne 'with both buttocks' and that his own children should succeed him" (Damane and Sanders 1974, 214). But Griffith fathered no children with his senior and second wives, and only a single son with each of his remaining two junior wives. Griffith attempted to deny the succession to Seeiso, son of his third wife, because of his strong but legally irrelevant conviction that the boy was not his natural child (ibid., 243). The poet appears ready to confirm Griffith's suspicions by suggesting that this third wife, Sebueng, having been sent back to her father's home but not divorced, had availed herself of Mphafu's superior procreative powers in conceiving Seeiso. In the praises of Paramount Seeiso (died 1940)—the British never allowed African monarchs the English title "king"—the matter is handled thus:

> The child of the bulls of the Beoana, Seeiso,
> Was begotten by hardy bulls,
> He was begotten by Griffith and Letsie,
> And so it was that he became a leopard . . . (lines 1–4)
> . . . Ts'oana, staff of Mokhachane, Seeiso!
> The chief is the chair of Lerotholi,
> The nations will sit there in time of war.
> Pay cattle, son of Lerotholi,

To wash out the impurity of a woman, of
Sebueng,
Of a woman rejected by her husband. (lines 329–34)
(Damane and Sanders 1974, 244–45, 258)

Seeiso's *seroki*, George Lerotholi (1905–63) here establishes, in the opening lines of the poem, the virile connection of Griffith's heir with the Basotho royal line: the Beoana were the personal regiment of Moshoeshoe's earliest recorded ancestor, Kali; Mokhachane was Moshoeshoe's father; the Letsies (I and II), Lerotholi, and, most important, Griffith complete the list of Moshoeshoe's successors and begetters of Seeiso. In the very last lines, however, the poet does mention the problems in the chief's mother's marriage, even referring to her by her maiden name, Sebueng, rather than by a normative honorific like 'MaSeeiso or "[Chief] Nkoebe's daughter," urging the "son of Lerotholi" (actually the grandson), to do everything possible to redeem her good name (Damane and Sanders 1974, 258). Although both praise poetry and *sefela* are full of hyperbole and flights of imaginative fancy, the praise poet seldom employs reflexive humor or satire to criticize, while mockery, burlesque, and belly-thumping comedy are the stock in trade of the *sefela* entertainer.

In view of Bakhtin's and Williams's reflections contrasting authoritative and popular genres, the comparative treatment of common themes in *lithoko* and *sefela* reveals the productive relationships between these genres. In many compositional dimensions, clear contrast is evident; elsewhere, comparable devices are embedded in divergent generic structures. Where *lithoko* and *sefela* employ similar devices, themes, and metaphoric tropes, they often do so in ways that derive from divergent social perspectives and that place poetic subject and audience in contrasting temporal planes and relationships (see Kunene 1967).

Daniel Kunene, the foremost Sesotho literary scholar, has responded to the potential for critique inherent in *lithoko* by abandoning the English gloss "praises" in favor of "heroic poetry" (see Kunene 1971), a term that encompasses the ambivalence with which extraordinary personal powers are viewed. While I have attempted to give the notion of praise a broader ethical significance, Kunene's heroic concept has manifold uses, giving it reference beyond the single genre of chiefly *lithoko.* So although migrants' *lifela*, pace Ruth Finnegan (1970, 146), cannot be called praises, they both articulate and expand the ambit of the heroic in Sesotho, extending it to the socially constructive exploits of men of common birth possessed of uncommon cultural knowledge and productive and expressive powers. The chiefly *seroki* does nothing but (in one sense or another) praise, and his subject is never himself unless he is himself a chief. When *sefela* composers praise in the *seroki's* manner, they themselves are most often the subject, almost always as courageous, tireless miners or as masters of cultural knowledge and aural performance. By this means, they reinforce the license of poetry and the right to an audience by the power of individual productivity and metapoetic displays of talent.

To begin with beginnings, praise poets do not greet or address the audience, but in effect greet the subject hero himself by his actual name and a variety of metaphoric or associative praise names. The praiser heightens the dramatic quality of his performance by changing voice, by turns describing the hero in the third person, then switching to direct, hortatory address in the second person, then speaking in the first person as if he were himself the hero. "In these movements in and out of the hero, the poet manipulates the distance the audience feels from the action, as well as their empathy with the hero and the event that has occasioned the poem" (Kunene 1979, 67). The poet may even create an audience *within* the poetic drama, but if he wishes to address the actual audience directly, he must take time out and break the frame of the narration if not of the performance (ibid., 64–67). *Lifela,* on the other hand, tend to begin with direct salutations to the audience, followed immediately by metaphors and place names serving as apostrophic self-identifications of the singer. Nor is it uncommon for performers to greet or salute the audience in the midst of a *sefela.* The late Mphafu Mofolo, a famous *kheleke,* even took his "singing name" (Ngoan'abo Mokhoati) from his habit of using a salutation as a formula punctuating transitions in the episodic flow of his texts: *Banna! Likhomo! ngoan'abo Mokhoati!* "Men! Cattle! [salutations!] [I] brother of Mokhoati!" The word "Cattle!" here is shorthand for the common greeting, bespeaking mutual prosperity through patron-clientage, that Basotho yeomen give to chiefs and wealthy men: *Likhomo tseo!* (Those cattle!), to which is answered, *Le manamane a tsona!* (And their calves!). By explicitly recognizing their listeners, *lifela* singers put themselves, the subject of the song, into an equal and coeval relationship with them. They cannot manipulate narrative distance very much because it is always "up close and personal."[5]

Speaking of (in) names, Kunene (1979) points out that a metaphoric praise name can become so closely identified with a chief that it replaces his actual name in ordinary discourse, as was the case with Lerotholi

5. For a different but parallel interpretation of polyvocality in African auriture, see Barber (1991, 37) on Yoruba *oriki* praises.

(1836–1905), who was universally addressed as "Lekena" (Enterer), referring to "the way in which Lerotholi used to enter the ranks of his enemies in battle" (Damane and Sanders 1974, 138 n. 1). Any personal quality or talent, including performance, may generate a name, as in *mokorotlo*, where the leader and soloist has a special "dancing name" (Ashton 1967, 95). As my frustrations in asking after familiar performers by the "actual" names recorded in my log attest, *sefela* singers may be best known by their singing names, and no law prevents a performer from changing or having more than one singing name. These may confirm social identity through kinship affiliations—as with Ngoan'abo Mokhoathi above and another veteran singer, Makeka Likhojane, "Ngoana Mokhalo" (Mokhalo's Child)—but more often refer to qualities of the singer either as a person or a performer, using multiple meanings as a metaphorical device, and frequently taking an ironic tone. "Raleqoele," for example, comes from *seqoele-qoele*, and means both the sound of iron on iron and deviousness or cunning (Mokitimi 1982, 180). The singer known in his songs as "Raleqoele" was celebrated both for his ringing voice and for his ability to appropriate the verses of fellow poets into his own performances. Good singers don't borrow; they steal. One singer is called "Sebili" (Wheels) because of his rollingly rhythmic, highly musical style of delivery; another, "Raliekhe" (Mr. Worldly), a cunning linguist who could compose in several African languages plus a bit of English, and who included snatches of international news in his *lifela*. Also known as Mopapa (the Pope) Molise, this performer said he was abandoning the singing name Raliekhe since "small boys [novices] are now using it in *lifela* and pretending to be me!" Among the most ironically celebratory singing names is that of Tieho Rakharebe, whose last name means "Owner of a Virgin." His singing name used to be Hulas "Ralipotsotso" (Owner-of-Tight-Trousers) because of the flashy town girls he favored. Married Basotho women and conservative girls wear skirts or blankets. This was later changed (by his public) to "Ralipopelo" (Owner-of-Wombs), perhaps in reference to the reputation of "modern" girls for doffing their trousers and getting pregnant.

Personification is a favorite means of qualifying the hero in both *sefela* and *lithoko*. Chiefs tend to be personified as forces of nature or as powerful, dangerous animals, either wild or domestic. This is reflective of southern African concepts of normative chiefly character, not as tolerant or even reasonable, but as adamant, combative, shrewd, dangerous, and unpredictable. A chief who is easy to persuade, manage, or figure out is easily ignored, deceived, or dispensed with. *Sefela* singers, in contrast, delight in inverted praise, personifying themselves as tricksters: shifty, deviant, cunning, destructive, bitter to the taste (and thus hard to consume or overcome), and as creatures monstrous, fabulous, uncanny, and antisocial. It follows that in the image of the cannibal these qualities overlap. Chiefs, we recall, are portrayed as swallowing enemy hosts and enemy cattle or as preventing enemies from swallowing their people. Power is eaten whole. During the nineteenth century, great chiefs often held competitions during which renowned poets rivaled each other in praising their noble sponsors. The performance of praises was most closely associated, as Casalis suggests, with a hero's return from battle. On such occasions, the performer challenges his comrades to surpass his exploits and consume his reputation by subsuming them within their own. As the missionary Jacottet recalled:

> After a battle, each warrior praises his exploits and then dances, beating the ground with his assegai. The assembly responds. When he finishes, the one who has been singing of his battles says: "Hi! Eat me, comrades." They respond, "Hi! We are eating you! We are cannibals, we eat Men!" If he hasn't yet finished his war praises, he responds to them: "How will you eat me?" and continues to sing. (1896–97, 151)

Renowned *sefela* singers, the *likheleke*, organize competitions among themselves, as a result of which they may call one another *lelimo*, referring to the relish with which they ingest the words and renown of a rival, transforming and encompassing his art in theirs. This sobriquet may also be applied as a self-description, implying a traveler beyond the boundaries and constraints of civil society, a man who by his wild character and wilder auriture consumes people and sets social authorities against one another in a self-destructive excess of reflexivity:

Lelimo le bua le lona, litsamaea-naha	The cannibal speaks to you, travelers
Joale lelimo ho puruma, *la habo Mosenyehi;*	Now the cannibal roars, the one of Mosenyehi's;
Joale ke ena e puruma, nong-thoboro,	Now it's this one roaring, the black vulture,
Lena ke lehipi, ngoana Makoloane . . .	This one, the "hippy," child of Makoloane . . .

(Moletsane 1982, 42)

Chieftaincy is handled by praise poets as the structural locus of leadership and authority, embodied in narratives of history: war and heroic exploits, chiefly rivalry and dispute. Aristocrats are described as warriors even if they have never raised a weapon in anger, and to those who have, no faintheartedness or defeat is ever attributed. *Sefela* singers view chieftaincy dialogically, within a conscious moral economy (Scott 1976) of hierarchical reciprocity. So in the travelers' songs, the ideology of chieftaincy is applied in the practical assessment and ironic summation of an actual person—the chief:

Morena o'a fana khotsong ea me:	The chief is dispensing harmony at my village:
O fana likhomo; o fana lipere;	He gives out cattle; he gives out horses;
Monongoaha, o fana le masimo.	This year, he even gives out fields.
Feela ha a eja, oa nketha.	But when he distributes, he discriminates [against] me.
Ke bone ha a khetha macholo-cholo,	I saw when he favored the swindlers,
Batho ba jakang ka lipere,	People who settle by [giving] their horses,
Batho ba jakang ka basali.	People who settle by [giving] their wives.
Naha ha e sena tjako u tlohe;	A place where you cannot dwell you should leave;
U eo jaka ho a mang makhosana.	You should settle among those who are [real] chiefs.
	(Tsokolo Lecheko)

Here the poet reflects upon proletarianization, through which a quarter of married Basotho men have become landless (17 percent have neither land nor livestock) despite traditional land allocation rights and the legal principle enshrined in the maxim *Lefatshe le la sechaba*, "The land belongs to the nation." The rich and the powerful prosper by corruption, while the migrant must move on. Conversely, a chief who upholds Sesotho notions of hierarchical reciprocity, even at the mines, is worthy of praise:

Ke sebelitse esale Morena Patsoana,	I've worked since Chief Patsoana's time,
Induna e mona ea Butha-Buthe,	The overseer here from Butha-Buthe,
Morena a sa khetheng tsobotsi.	The chief who doesn't discriminate.
Ha re ho mofo, "Mofo tooe!"	He doesn't say to a commoner, "Hey, you commoner!"
Ho Moqhotsa, "Moqhotsa tooe!"	To a Xhosa, "Hey, you Xhosa!"
Ngoana o re entse ba eena.	He has made us all his younger brothers.
	(Makeka Likhojane)

Because the land itself is governed and allocated by chiefs, the recitation of their names in *lifela* is also a naming of places. The political and historical geography of *lithoko*, depicted through legendary exploits and epic contests, is traveled in *sefela* as a social landscape and a literal "map of experience" (Vail and White 1991, 40–83). These "songs of the country travelers" are metaphors for the migrant pilgrim's personal progress in the context of the toponymic establishment of identity through the eloquent display of cultural knowledge (Coplan 1987a). Such knowledge is displayed by quoting the *lithoko* of one's high chiefs as well, demonstrating a command of the more prestigious genre as well as the social identity that such expressions of allegiance confirm. On one occasion when I asked the poet Makeka Likhojane (Ngoana Mokhalo) to comment upon the difference between *lithoko* and *lifela*, he answered, "There's no difference." Leading the witness, I frowned. "Well I mean," he added hastily, "you can recite the *lithoko* right in *lifela*." The following couplet, for example, appears in the praises of the Mafeteng District chief Lerotholi Mojela (1895–1961):

Ntsoareleng, Marena, ke fositse,	Forgive me, Chiefs, I've erred,
Ke fahlile 'Muso ka lehlabathe!	I've stung the Government's eyes with sand!

(Mangoela [1921] 1984; translation from Damane and Sanders 1974, 236)

I discovered the same couplet in the *lifela* of two reciters from that area, T. Moleme (Separola) and Molefi Motsoahae (Ngoana Sebili). Further, at the end of his *sefela* Motsoahae, on an emotional high, burst into a *mokorotlo* anthem (his companions supplied the chorus without missing a beat) into which he transferred the couplet as well, achieving both intertextuality and a "breakthrough into performance" (Hymes 1981) of one genre from that of another.

Such displays, which give authority to the performer and legitimation to the performance of a genre of relatively low social status, are themselves illustrative of contrasting generic contexts. Basotho practices and lore, *mekhoa le meetlo ea Sesotho*, including herbal and divinatory medicine, witchcraft, initiation, plant and animal lore, the ancestor cult, and performance genres themselves, are subjects in which the *sefela* singer and his audience take prideful pleasure. In chiefs' *lithoko*, such domains of "custom" are almost never mentioned explicitly but contribute implicitly to the poet's artistry, to his ability to delineate his subject's heroic stature in profoundly cultural terms. To gain renown in the performance of their respective genres, both praise poet and *sefela* singer must "know Sesotho," but in *sefela* the *kheleke* must *show* he knows Sesotho.

RELATED DIMENSIONS OF CONTRAST can be shown in comparing the formal qualities of heroic praise poetry and heroic migrants' hymns. This comparison, like the thematic summary above, is greatly assisted by that of Professor R. I. M. Moletsane in his doctoral thesis on *lifela tsa litsamaea-naha* (1982, 30–55). Since *lithoko* set the standard for poetic composition in Sesotho, it is not surprising that migrants' songs employ many of the same devices. Both *seroki* and *kheleke* use intensive, multiple forms of parallelism, idiom, and alliteration and assonance in strongly rhythmic, twelve-syllable (plus or minus one syllable) lines. In common with everyday discourse, both genres change and mix verb tense for dramatic effect without regard to narrative sequence, and episodes do not follow chronologically. Structurally, *lithoko*, which are putative recreations of "fixed" texts, are more refined, architectonic, and intensive, while *lifela* are tangential, concatenated, and expansive. The classic Parry-Lord formula of repeated verbal phrases appears far more often in *lithoko.*

With regard to language, the historical continuity and higher register of *lithoko* includes numerous archaic words, while archaisms are rare in *sefela.* The latter, like Basotho recreational songs in general, is far richer in localized, folk, and slang usages, including expressions and words considered too rude or blunt for use in polite discourse, never mind the exalted plane of chiefly praises. Where a polite elder might say, *Ke qaphaletsa leihlo la mokotatsie*, "I'm splashing the eye of the stork" (I'm going to urinate), a *sefela* will simply say, *Kea rota*, "I've got to piss," and *lithoko* contain very few references at all to such bodily functions. *Sefela* also frequently and quite deliberately deploys Sesothoized foreign words, especially from the Afrikaans, English, and African languages heard in South African workplaces. By this means, the conceptual challenge of the non-Sesotho world is domesticated. Generations of European linguists and missionaries have imagined that these Sesothoized versions of European words—scant attention has been paid to African loan words—represent an inability to pronounce them properly. My research, however, strongly supports Bosko's point (1983, 295) that Basotho have no problem with foreign words except for their foreignness. Sesothoization is a process that extends into virtually every domain of activity and expression, transforming the alien and dangerous into the familiar and comprehensible, encompassing *Sekhooa* (European ways) and importing contemporary formulations into the heart of Sesotho. Interestingly, *sefela* employs the complex tenses and auxiliary verbs so common in ordinary speech, while *lithoko* exhibits the simple, direct tense construction that results from the conscious refinement of oft-repeated praise passages.

In the domain of performance, *lithoko* are classified as "speech" (*ho bua*), while *sefela* are "singing" (*ho bina*). Although the pitches of *sefela* are indeed more stabilized and the shape of phrases more melodic than those of *lithoko*, *sefela* sound rather more like rhythmic speech than true song to most Western ears. For Basotho, the distinguishing characteristic of song is rhythm (*morethetho*), which is clearly more varied and pronounced in *sefela*, though both genres are performed solo, without instrumental accompaniment. *Seroki* do not move much while actually praising, but breaks in the recitation provide the opportunity for strongly athletic movement patterns known as *ho tlala*, "to dance praises." Additionally, the poet's words may excite his comrades to accompany him with choruses and sequences of *mekorotlo* songs and dancing. *Lifela* singers do not move, except for the occasional gesture of the hands or face, and songs focus entirely on the performative creation of an aural pattern of sound and text. *Lifela* are classified as *lipina tse binoang ho nngoe*, "songs sung standing [still]," characterized by the meditative concentration of both performer and audience. They may be accompanied by *mangae* initiation songs, also sung standing still, and occasionally by *mohobelo*, a male dance song genre that similarly emphasizes male comradeship and cooperative sociability, in contrast to the individualistic, militaristic, prestige-seeking *mokorotlo*, a *pina ea binoang ka maoto*, "song sung with the feet" (Adams 1974, 134).

Overall, the handling of thematic domains, metaphoric images, cultural knowledge, and formal devices and techniques in the two genres reveals the dialogic, decentered, reflexive quality of *sefela*, and its greater, explicit focus on composition in performance. *Lithoko* present a single, representative model subject from many angles in the successive reworkings of essentially fixed materials. As the poet B. W. Vilakazi said of Zulu praises:

> Stanzas in primitive Zulu poetry are like lights shed on a sculptured work from different angles. These lights operate independently of one another, but yet bring into relief the whole picture which the artist presents in carving. Lights are generally hidden from the onlookers, but their effect to the eye and mind bring perfect unity in their very difference. . . . The piece of sculpture and the lights are one configuration indivisible as a mental setting which induces an aesthetic sense. Analysis can only be reached when one knows where every light (outlining the sculpture) has been placed. (1945, 112–13)

In *sefela* the singer himself is the central source of light, shooting beams in a compass of directions, illuminating a contemporary landscape of personality, experience, and commentary. Chiefs praises are authoritative—a repository of cultural prestige and history, a record of the exercise of leadership and power—individuated but structurally embedded emblems of collective destiny that create a sense of historically continuous community: the chief is the people. Migrants' songs are multivocal representations of actual, differentially shared experience, metonyms of contemporary laughter created from valorized historical symbols by trickster heroes: the chief is a shoulderbag of shit.

A miner waves good-bye to Lesotho. Maseru Bridge, Christmas 1983.

Girls undergoing *bale* initiation dance during their middle, "white" phase. Mafeteng District, 1988.

". . . I was playing an organ at the location." Mohale's Hoek, 1988.

Thakane Mahlasi. Motolo's *shebeen*, Hlotse, 1984.

’Malitaba singing. Ha-Mafefoane, Roma District, 1984.

Litolobonya dancers. Pontseng Ha-Lebeta, Mafeteng District, 1988.

Phoofolo Pitso, in competition with Mphafu Mofolo. Ha-Mafefoane, Roma District, 1984.

Herdboys. Motse Mocha, Mafeteng District, 1988.

Young initiates recite their graduation praises. Roma District, 1989.

Apolo Ntabanyane. Maseru, 1988.

Puseletso Seema. Soweto, 1989.

The *mohobelo* dance. Berea District, 1984.

Letsema Matsela. Ha-Ramamapepe, Mapoteng District, 1988.

Hlalele Mabekanyane, "Kanono Nthako," performing at President Brand Mine, Shaft 3, Welkom, Orange Free State, February 1989.

A traditional healer. Maseru market, 1988.

Women dance the *mokhibo*. Berea District, 1984.

Chapter Three

"Greetings, Child of God!"

Generations of Travelers and Their Songs

"Why are you sad, Lethetsa of Malimatle?"
"I am going into the wilderness in the Republic [of South Africa],
There where people live through unceasing work."
She said, "What takes you among [those] evils yonder?"
I said, "Your relatives disgust me girl;
They want cattle for your brideprice."
Lethetsa Malimatle

The plotting of relationships among aural genres in political time and space, following Williams and Bakhtin, provides a basis for analyzing the intertextual emergence of Basotho migrants' auriture in the context of the social forces at work in nineteenth-century southern Africa. More challenging even than the attacks of "Coloured" (mixed race) Griquas under Adam Kok or African rivals like the Batlokoa chief Sekonyela (defeated 1853) were the advancing Europeans, for while the whites destabilized local polities and expropriated land and labor, they also offered new material and ideological resources. From the beginnings of Moshoeshoe's kingdom in the 1820s, Basotho were migrating to work on the railways and in the growing towns of the eastern Cape. Largely owing to this shrewd monarch's injunction to his departing followers not to return without the indispensable tools of political survival—rifles and horses—the Basotho retained their independence from both the Orange Free State and the Cape until his death in 1870. By that time, more than 15,000 Basotho were working outside his domains, with 5,000 on the Kimberley diamond mines alone. Indeed, the desire for guns was the most compelling reason for Basotho migration at this time. Establishing a legendary stubbornness where the defense of their personal interests is concerned, Basotho miners led a walkout in response to the announcement of lower wages in 1876 that brought the diggings to a standstill and forced the payment of higher wages instead (Kimble 1982).

This movement into temporary contract wage labor was only partly due to the "pull" exerted by European manufactured goods. Despite Moshoeshoe's courage and resourcefulness, the Basotho had lost two-thirds of their arable land in the Seqiti Wars with the Free State (1865–68).[1] Even so, Basutoland's agricultural economy continued to flourish on the demand for its products created by the diamond rush. During the following decades, however, the railway line from the Cape reached Kimberley, bringing huge amounts of cheap Australian and American grain. A regional rinderpest epidemic in 1896 wiped out a significant portion of Basotho cattle and drove many Basotho pastoralists to work on white farms. In 1913, the notorious Land Act dispossessed many Basotho farmers in the Free State, leading to a major immigration into Basutoland as an effective "native reserve," not dissimilar to those that later formed the basis for South Africa's "bantustans" in the 1960s. In Basutoland, drought, cattle disease, soil exhaustion and erosion, and a British colonial policy that discriminated against Basotho suppliers in favor of uncompetitive Afrikaner farms in the neighboring Free State all conspired to transform the colony from a breadbasket into a labor reserve (Murray 1980a).

Also on the "push" side of the equation was the squeeze on Basotho commoners created by the expanding numbers and resource accumulation of the Bakoena aristocracy. Moshoeshoe's placing system (Hamnet 1965) operated to solidify his family's rule over the nation and to keep both incorporated non-Bakoena clans and Bakoena collateral nobility from rebelling against royal primogeniture. Royal sons and junior brothers were placed as district chiefs, degrading the rank of existing title holders and of the local chiefs beneath them. By this process, new districts came under royal control and the potential for conflict over succession was at least theoretically reduced, but it also meant that senior regional chiefs became junior, and junior ones became commoners. The system worked while the population was small and the land plentiful, but increasingly there were too many chiefs for too few places, and new placings were resented and resisted both by commoners and by the minor chiefs who were thus displaced (Jones 1951, 7–8). As *sefela* composer Mphafu Mofolo puts it in describing a neighboring district: *Thaba-Chitja e 'ngoe; marena a leshome,*

1. *Seqiti* refers to the noise of cannon, but by virtue of its use as a term for the longest and last of a series of armed conflicts with the Free State the word has come to mean "endless affair" in Sesotho as well.

"Thaba-Chitja is one; chiefs are ten." Additionally, the intensifying land shortage served to increase the power of those senior chiefs who allocated it (Dutton 1923, 58). As the *maele* observes, however, at the chief's court, "the mouth of a commoner is not listened to." During the colonial period, chiefs were responsible, not to their people, but to the chief above them and to the British administration above him, which allowed no rebellion or secession or shifting allegiance. Minor chiefs who appealed to their people against their superior chief were suppressed as peacebreakers with the backing of the colonial authorities (Jones 1951, 33, 69).

Labor migrancy only gradually replaced mixed pastoralism as the foundation of Basotho economic life. Quite apart from South African policies that solidified migrancy as a system of labor supply, African farming was organized around female labor, nonalienable land, and seasonal demands on men, which lent themselves to the migrant pattern. Most migrants took only occasional contracts of short duration. These "target workers" returned as soon as they had the cash necessary to pay colonial taxes and to purchase livestock or manufactured goods. Men from the lowlands of Basutoland went home for November-December to plow, those from the highlands in February for sheep shearing. At the turn of the century, mine wages were unattractively low and conditions in the compounds so bad that one migrant in ten could expect to die there of disease, exposure, or injury. Paramount Lerotholi (died 1905) was so shocked by the treatment he witnessed on a visit to Johannesburg that he attempted to withdraw Basotho labor from the mines.

Basutoland was by then, however, already integrated into the South African economy as a labor reserve (Van Der Weil 1977, 13). Increasingly, Basotho men could no longer expect to make a living at home and were both urged and constrained to seek one across the Caledon. So originated the enduring social contradiction by which the landless moves off to support his land, the fiancé or family head sets off for the resources to found or preserve his family, the traveler endures homelessness to defend his home. Today, indeed, it is migrant earnings and not cattle that drive the whole redistributive process in rural communities, flowing through kinship, marriage, friendship, and residence networks of reciprocation and patronage (Heap 1989, 68).

The inexorable decline in Lesotho's domestic economy and the opportunities in the Transvaal and Free State towns led to an increasing degree of permanent emigration as well, creating the *lechepha* (from English "cheap") who moves from one mine and contract to another without coming home; the *lekholoa* (from *ho kholoa*, "to be satisfied"), the deserter to

South Africa; and even the *sebono morao* (buttocks to the rear), contemptuous of his homeland, who shows only his behind to Lesotho. In many cases a mine contract was only an expedient to better-paying, less arduous work in the growing manufacturing and commercial sectors. Given economic and social conditions in Lesotho, it is hardly surprising that large numbers of isolated, deserted, and destitute Basotho women followed their men to the Witwatersrand despite the coordinated efforts of chiefs, the colonial administration, and the South African authorities to prevent it. The auriture the migrant men and women created expressed social transformation more than social structure. As John and Jean Comaroff, following Marx, remind us, "The transformation of any society should be revealed by the changing relations of persons to objects within it" (Comaroff and Comaroff 1990, 196). These relationships, both normative and actual, between persons and both the movable and immovable portions of their estates have all along underlain the changing structures of power and authority, identity and entitlement, in Moshoeshoe's partly territorial, partly ideological kingdom.

There was no railway service to Basutoland until 1906, and migrants commonly hopped aboard transport wagons hauling agricultural produce to the diamond fields. Migrants traveling on foot were often assaulted, robbed, or dragooned into service by white farmers. For this reason, fairly large companies of young age-mates and homeboys set off on the more-than-200-mile journey to the diamond fields together, using the resources of Sesotho auriture to beguile the time, boost their courage, and seek a common understanding of the changes in Basotho life of which they were both the subjects and the instruments. In time they created a new, partly narrative, partly lyrical genre, artistically encoding their experience. The importance of Kimberley in the emergence of the *sefela* genre is reflected in textual references even today to the immoral atmosphere of the city's early years, and its name is still emblematic of the rural Basotho perspective on urban life:

Ke reng ho lona, likempolara?	What do I say to you, gamblers [veteran poets]?
Ke buoe ka mokhoa ona:	I speak this way:
Oa tseba, ke buoa ka Gemele,	You know, I speak of Kimberley;
Ke buoa ka Sotoma . . .	I speak of Sodom . . .
	(Majara Majara)

Though currently only an insignificant number of Basotho actually work at the Kimberley diamond mines, *Libere*, "DeBeers," as they are called, after the company that has operated them for more than a century, seems to have left an indelible imprint upon *sefela:*

Ke ne ke e ea ho 'me' ke ntše ke thotse:	I was going to my mother quietly:
"'Me' nkukele lengolo; ke ee Libere.	"Mother, take a letter for me; I am going to DeBeers.
O tlo mphatse ka qetella pele	Scarify me with *qetella pele* [medicine of leadership]
Lichaba tsena li ntsale morao."	So that these multitudes should follow me."

(Majara Majara)

And follow him they have. The question immediately arises as to why Basotho migrants felt compelled to create for their specific use a new genre of sung poetry, while their Xhosa comrades, for example, simply adapted praise poetry (Xhosa: *izibongo*) to express their reaction to conditions at the mines (Wainwright 1979). Certainly Basotho praises could demonstrate the same incorporative capacity, as in the following lines from the *lithoko* of Chief Joel Molapo (1842–1919). Part of a passage referring to the Gun War against the Cape in 1880–81, they warn those who prefer living or siding with the British that it is the whiteman's razor-sharp, hippopotamus-hide whip, the sjambok, that awaits the migrant in South Africa, rather than the anticipated wealth to buy cattle. Admirers of word music will enjoy the way the verb *ho jaka,* "to emigrate," is chosen from among alternatives here so as to incorporate the Afrikaans word *sjambok* in the alliterative and assonantal parallelism of the verse:

Bajaki ba jakang Makhooeng	Migrants who migrate to the Whites,
Ha le jake khomo, le jaka sjambok,	You don't migrate to cattle, you migrate to a sjambok,
Le jaka tlalo la mo-lala-metsing!	You migrate to the hide of the sleeper in the water!

(Mangoela [1921] 1984, 127; translation from Damane and Sanders 1974, 204)

The praises of Moshoeshoe's younger brother Posholi (1795–1868) comment on the lack of any values of reciprocity to complement those of hierarchy among Free State Afrikaners:

Ba basoeu, ha le na le setsoalle,	You whites, you haven't any friendship
Le tsoe le hloka selekane, Mabasa . . .	You're lacking the spirit of alliance, Bosses . . .

(Mangoela [1921] 1984, 17; translation from Damane and Sanders 1974, 93)

How then to explain the migrants' creation of a genre of Basotho auriture in self-conscious opposition to, or at least distinction from, the dominant genre in which relations of power had customarily been expressed (White 1982)? From the perspective of one and one-quarter centuries later, there can be no sure answer. While some illumination may be provided by considering the conjunction between changing social structure, genre definition, and ethnoaesthetic values, there is no simple correspondence, and the comparative situation in relation to migrant labor and the chieftaincy is extremely complex.

In contact with white settlers as early as the mid-1700s, the Xhosa-speaking peoples of the eastern Cape fought and lost nine fiercely contested "frontier wars" over the following 130 years. The famous "Cattle Killing" incident (Peires 1989) of 1856–57 seriously depopulated the Ciskei and Transkei and drove tens of thousands of Xhosa to work for whites in the eastern Cape Colony. A number of Xhosa chiefdoms were threatened by disintegration, owing to labor migrancy, permanent emigration, and the subsequent rise of an independent Xhosa Christian peasantry (Crais 1992, 76–77, 212–20). By the time the diamond fields were in full operation in the 1870s, Xhosa chiefs had long been incorporated into the colonial administrative system, while Basotho chiefs had not. The Basotho were brought in only after the onerous extension of the Cape government's "protection" over Lesotho in 1870 and more extensively under direct British administration after 1881. The Xhosa by then were long adapted to working for whites, but not on the mines, considered the lowest paid and least desirable form of migrant employment. But after Xhosa began to work on the mines in significant numbers around the turn of the century, "singing the praises" of Xhosa chiefs became qualitatively no different from praising anyone else in authority, including African mine clerks, compound overseers (some of whom were chiefs), and white compound managers. All of these "officials" were—as they are now—in a position to do the miners good or ill under the terms of a unified bureaucratic structure and were therefore flattered, cajoled, or satirized in their praises as the situation suggested.

The Basotho retained greater political independence, albeit under considerable duress. Victory over Cape forces in the Gun War of 1880–81 ensured that Basutoland would not be incorporated into the Orange Free State or Natal. The country's status as a direct protectorate of the British crown (and not of the Cape Colony) reinforced the powers of the chiefs over local affairs, spared the resident population some of the direct injustices of apartheid, and led not only to the emergence of Lesotho as an independent constitutional monarchy in 1966, but to the independence of Bechuanaland (Botswana) and Swaziland as well. The important point is the Basotho's very different sense of themselves as a polity and a people, an imagined community if you will, to some extent constructed in direct contradistinction to Africans ruled by the Cape authorities, regardless of empirical similarities in the nature of the colonial chieftaincies and their role in labor recruitment.

The development of *sefela* was in part a response to the increasing autocracy and self-aggrandizement of the Basotho chiefly class under British colonial "protection." *Lifela* were composed, not in praise or protest of bureaucrats, but in support of the migrants' own identity and status as citizens of a an autonomous polity, in which commoners might still attempt to hold their leaders socially accountable. Under colonialism the subgenre of commoners' praises appears to have gone into decline, while heroic praise poetry became exclusively associated with chiefs, who came to symbolize the nation's tenacious resistance to political dissolution and external domination.[2] *Lithoko* came to be recited most often either at commandeered work parties (*matsema*) on chiefs' lands or at open district meetings (*lipitso*) sponsored by chiefs. At the same time, the growing numbers of Basotho migrants were increasingly critical of the collaboration of the chiefs with the mining companies, South African authorities, and British colonial officials in the system that pushed them off their land and into the mines. According to *lefatse le la sechaba*, the legal maxim enshrining inalienable ancestral trusteeship of the land, every married man had a right to fields. In a country of which only 13 percent is arable, however, many of the fields allocated had little economic value. So sings Hlalele Mabekanyane, renowned as "Kanono Nthako" in *sefela:*

Banna! Koana haeso, haho falleloe.	Men! Yonder at my home, people cannot settle there.
Tjako e teng, masimo ha eo.	Refuge there is, but no fields.
Lea teng a batla, a khetha.	What fields there are, are selectively allocated people.
A nka banna ba basali ba batle.	Those who receive are men with pretty wives.

2. This contradiction was evident among Basutoland's nascent commercial and Christian educated class as well. The Lekhotla la Bafo, "Assembly of Commoners," an anticolonial forerunner of the pan-Africanist Basutoland Congress Party, active in the nineteen twenties, thirties, and forties, condemned reigning chiefs in the name of restoring the chieftancy to its idealized precolonial moral and political accountability. The more accommodationist Basutoland Progressive Association, which included the mission-trained author of *Chaka*, Thomas Mofolo, proposed to abolish the chieftaincy, and yet its leaders often sought support through cooperation with chiefs (Edgar 1986, 25–29).

Ha u nyetse mosali ea mobenyana,	When you are married to an ugly wife,
U tla fuoa 'simo lerallaneng,	You are given a field on the hillside,
Likara li hlole li robehile	So that your ploughshare breaks
Le mabili a hlole a pshatlehile.	And its wheels are smashed.
Bo, Kanono, re lema manyeke-nyekeng	I, Kanono, am given a field on the infertile soil
Koung mona ka tlasa motse.	Where the river turns below the village.
Lehlabatheng lena la Mantsonyane,	In this sandy soil of Mantsonyane,
Masimo rea qetetse ka Morena Sephehi.	We last saw good farmland from Chief Sephehi.
Mojalefa ha eso re nehe.	His successors have never given us [land].
Re se bile re phela ha Motanyane,	We have just been living at Chief Motanyane's,
Re se bile re phela ka liahlolo . . .	We have just been living by sharecropping . . .

Of course, as Mphafu Mofolo observes, even having a pretty wife isn't all bliss:

Ha-Maama ke ea falla.	At Maama's I pack and go away.
Ha ke tlohe hobaneng ke hloka tjako teng;	I don't go just because I need a place to live;
Teng ke batla ke se ke nyatsa masimo a teng.	I dislike the fields at that place.
Ke bona a khetha—	I see them chosen—
A nehoa banna ba basali ba batle ba banana.	Fields are given to husbands of pretty young wives.
O nyale ngoanana o ikhethele;	You should marry such a girl and stand out;
O nyale a mosifa o motenya	You should marry a muscular [nubile] one
E tle ere ha morena a o chaketse,	So that when a chief visits you,
O nke leqala o ee lipereng.	You take a walking stick and go to herd horses.

More important, under the same maxim commonage for pasture was a free good, but ownership of livestock was becoming increasingly more concentrated than rights to land per se, a small percentage of households in any community owning a large majority of draft animals and cattle. To secure a future in their communities and retain effective access to domestic means of production and reproduction, men had to go out to earn the cash needed for wives, cattle, and horses. The migrants' experience no longer conformed to the outmoded identity of chiefly clients. *Lifela* songs emerged from migrants' awareness of their dependent position in both a changing system of local relationships and in the political economy of South Africa, in which they often felt more like livestock themselves than like livestock farmers. Riding the train back to the mines, the poet Makeka Likhojane sings:

Li fapana, li na le kutse.	They crossed one another, ours and a freight train.
Kutse eena e apere matata:	That freight wore karosses [skin capes, a chiefly prerogative]:
E nkile likhomo, le furu'a lesere,	It carried cattle, feeding on fodder,
Lipholo li tloha ho Verwoerd	Oxen given by Verwoerd[3]
Tse tlang ho tona kholo.	To the prime minister [of Lesotho].

Crossing paths with a freight train while on the way to the mines, the poet reflects that the freight, dressed in the cattle-hide robes of nobility rather than the wool blankets of migrants, is a vehicle of social dominance. As the quintessential social currency of Basotho pastoral life, cattle are not only the symbol but the calculus of reciprocity in patron-client relationships. Here Lesotho's prime minister (1966–86), the late Chief Leabua Jonathan, has sent his subjects to labor for his counterpart in South Africa in return for gifts of cattle. Victims of this exchange, the migrants see themselves as having more in common with the cattle than with chiefly clients. They are a cargo who, in the their own phrase, are "driven like oxen" to the mines, rather than followers sharing in the redistributive beneficence of an autonomous stratified state.

In *sefela* we have the emergence of a clear divergence of interests between chiefs and their erstwhile followers. Class analysis in the Marxian sense is not readily applicable to Basotho political economy before the extension of colonial "protection" in 1868. Prior to the expropriation and forced enclosure of Basotho territory, a system of hierarchical reciprocity obtained in which common people owed allegiance, service, and some tribute and labor to the chief of the lands they occupied in return for leadership, protection, dispute resolution, and an allocation of productive resources. This system was both symbolized and embodied in the institution of *letsema*, obligatory communal work parties on lands specially designated for the purpose by the chiefs, whose produce was used to feed visitors, the poor, and the chief's followers in general in times of scarcity (Eldredge 1986). If a chief failed to deliver or was (sometimes for that reason) over-

3. Hendrik Verwoerd was prime minister of South Africa from 1959 to 1966 and chief architect of the policy of racial separation known as apartheid.

come by a more powerful or generous rival, people could migrate and their allegiance could shift. The same was true of the loyalty of junior chiefs to senior ones. Not for nothing was Moshoeshoe the state-builder (tutored by Mohlomi) said to be the most hospitable of regional chiefs. Indeed, when urged to embrace Protestantism by French missionaries, Moshoeshoe inquired as to how he would feed his scores of visitors without his many wives to cook for them. Moshoeshoe is a common surname in Lesotho, but its bearers are not aristocrats. The generous monarch is said to have paid brideprice on behalf of many of his ordinary subjects during a time of drought and pestilence, entitling the children of these unions to the name Moshoeshoe, since social fatherhood and naming "follows the cattle." Once the boundaries of Basutoland were fixed, chiefs became salaried officials, and the allegiance and immobility of their followers (locally at least) were enforced by colonial authority. From this point, an analysis based on more stereotyped notions of social differentiation becomes more feasible. Even the produce from *matsema* work parties was appropriated by chiefs for personal rather than communal use, and the British magistrates, viewing it as a form of forced labor, protected people who refused to participate (ibid.).

It is characteristic of popular culture that it does not originate "merely as a response to questions and conditions; it asks questions and creates conditions (Fabian 1978, 316). The origin of the generic name *sefela* encodes such a reflexive awareness. The word *sefela* is most commonly used to mean a Christian hymn, as in the famous volume published in Sesotho in 1854, *Lifela tsa Sione*, the "Hymns of Zion," but the word itself was borrowed from rather than loaned to Sesotho by the missionaries. The legendary London missionary Robert Moffat, ever seeking to steal the heathen's thunder, first appropriated the term from the Bathlaping Tswana, among whom *sehela* was a term for sacred initiation songs similar to those known as *likoma* among Basotho. Moffat brought the term with him when he came to work in Basutoland in the late 1830s, where it was given the local form *sefela* (Wells 1994). This perhaps accounts for the otherwise curious association, in the minds of some of Guma's informants (1967, 117), between the sacred secrecy of *likoma* and the profane publicity of *lifela*. The linking quality that attracted Moffat was a moral emotionality, by turns spiritually or materially animated, for according to Basotho commentators, both the songs of the travelers and the songs of Zion are "cries of the heart." *Sefela* often express sincere religiosity as well as satire of Christian institutions and doctrine, explicitly mirroring the emotional catharsis of hymnody:

E tlo bona katekisemane ea lona likheleke:	It's evident I'm the catechist of you poets:
Buka Bebele, ngoan'abo Makhoathi,	A Bible book, brother of Makhoathi,
Hobaneng e koatile, e tla ipala.	Because it is grieved, it will read itself.
	(Mphafu Mofolo)

Moletsane (1982, 2) suggests that *sefela* originally referred to the self-praises performed by initiates against a background of *mangae* choral songs on the day of their graduation. In the 1940s, Ashton reported, "The most talented [new initiates] are allowed to sing *mangae*, which are *lithoko* with a chorus. . . . The onlookers follow these songs and choruses with keen interest and applaud at the end of each. Many of them are witty, some salacious, and a few are beautiful and moving. At the end of a good recital people may be seen wiping tears from their eyes and, as often as not, the parents and friends of the boy concerned, overcome with pride and emotion, weep unashamedly" (1967, 26). If *lifela* was indeed a term for initiates' praises performed in the musical contexts of graduation, then perhaps it was this fervent quality that led early missionaries to appropriate it for their hymns.

Conversely, the use of the term *sefela* for their songs suggests the migrants' resistance to the message of heavenly hymns. The monarchy has always been strongly influenced by the Christian mission churches, first by the French Protestants and, after the conversion of Paramount Griffith to Roman Catholicism in 1912, the Catholic Church. Chiefs' praises, such as those of Paramount Seeiso (died 1940), themselves, express criticism of the Christian missions for interfering in aristocratic politics. In the secret songs and graduation choruses of male initiation schools, which were never controlled by the monarchy, the behavior of Basotho Christians is often deprecated and satirized. In migrants' *sefela*, this critique is satirically extended, right alongside sincere expressions of Christian spirituality, for virtually all Basotho are at least nominally Christian. As we shall see, however, miners regard themselves as co-workers of Satan, even as devils, spending their workdays in the hellish depths of the earth. This identity is reflected in the educated African mine clerks' slang term for underground miners, *lisatane tsa makhisa*, "long-haired devils." The sobriquet is not without ambiguity, however, since in Lesotho the display of extraordinary or uncanny ability in performance or on the playing field will lead onlookers to shake their heads and exclaim, "Ay, Satane!" At home, miners who have apparently lost their courtly Sesotho manners are often called *likoata*, "uncivilized ruffians" (from English "squatter" or "squad," or more likely Afrikaans *kwaad*, "to sulk or be angry"). So migrants' songs are named as a rhetorical irony, encompassing reflexivity and spirituality in a structure of feeling: the hymns of Zion for those bound for heaven, the hymns of the travelers for those bound for hell.

Migrants' songs appear to derive from *lithoko tsa bafo*, the praises of male commoners, and from *lithoko tsa makoloane*, the male initiates' praises out of which those commoners' praises are later developed. Commoners' and initiates' praises are less constrained by preexisting cultural images of appropriate form and content—the need to "get it right"—than are the praises of chiefs (Adams 1974, 120–21, 197). So they share with *sefela*, and with popular culture in general, a greater potential for expressive innovation. As I mentioned above, the alienation of Basotho migrants from their land and from an abused colonial chieftaincy led not only to the emergence of migrants' *sefela*, but to the decline of commoners' praises. I was unable to record a text of this subgenre in Lesotho, but my colleague, the eminent Mosotho educationist R. I. M. Moletsane assures me that he has heard them performed. By chance, one of the items documented simply as *lithoko*, "praises," by Hugh Tracey during his recording tour of Basutoland in 1959 turns out on closer inspection to be the self-praises of one commoner, Kola Khoali:

Tholang lerata le utloe mokhosi,	Be quiet and listen to celebration,
O kopaneng le seboko.	Mixed with cries of weeping.
Bahlankana, le ithehe mabitso,	Young men, you should give yourselves names,
Ha le chaha sehlankana:	When you harvest lustily in the way of young men:
La ka, ke sentse ke ithehile.	Mine, I have already named myself.
Ke Kola Khoali, moshemane oa Kubung,	I am Kola Khoali, the boy from Kubung,
Kola, e ka re ke tsoere hantle.	Kola, when I am working hard.
Ea qhoma ea kena lihala-haleng.	It [I] burst and entered through applauding crowds.
Ke matiisetsa oa ntho tse thata.	I can withstand difficulties.
Ke sema-marela, ke tsoa Joalesoetsa.	I am the sticker, I am from Joalesoetsa.
Ke moromelloa, ke phatšo'a ea Linare.	I am the messenger, the black and white ox of the Buffalo regiment.[4]
Haeso ke koana ha Rantolo.	My native home is there at Rantolo's.
Khomo li hlajoa ha mafube a hlaha.	The cattle are slaughtered as the red of dawn appears.

4. *Phatsoa*, meaning black and white, is a play on *khoali*, a term for a white-speckled black ox and a well-known praise name used in the *lithoko* of Moshoeshoe and other great chiefs (see Damane and Sanders 1974, 25).

Selemo se akana le lehlabula.	When Spring and Summer embrace,
Pele-pele li le teng lithupeng.	There is sorghum scattered on bending stalks.
Banna ba ea reha, ba ha Mohale,	Men that can [truly] name it [me?], those of Mohale's,
Ba ka reha ngoana lebitso le sele.	They can give a child the wrong names.
Ba re: Namoneiti, metsi ea Sekhooa, chenche biri.	They can say: Lemonade, the European water, ginger beer.
Se otle batho, Morena; hase liphoofolo.	Do not beat the people, Chief; they are not animals.
Ha ba ke ba bolaoa.	They are not supposed to be killed.
Ke bona mali, kea khabutlella.	When I see blood, I grind my teeth.
Ha nke ke re, "Ichu, ke robehile."	I never say, "Ouch, I have broken [a bone]."
Ke re, "Nkotlelleng, bahlankana ba heso."	I just say, "Beat me up, my young companions."
Ke poli ea makhooa.	I am the white people's goat.
Ke lla mesifa.	I cry [about] a pulled tendon.
Ke bone ha kelle, litjotjela.	I saw when I was crying, [you] *litjotjela* regiment.
Khomong tsa heso, ha o bapalloe.	Among the cattle of my home, you do not play around.
Ke hana ho etsoa mokhatlo teng.	I do not even let a gathering to be held there.
Ho tla thijoa ntšonyane,	They will stop the dark-faced one from fighting,
E bitsoang Bataung.	That one called Bataung.
Ke otla motho ka lere lehetleng,	I hit a person on the spine with a stick,
Mali a motho a mothapo oa hlooho.	Blood of a person from vein in his head.
Mochana, tloho le senotlolo,	Nephew, bring the key,
Sa motse oa ha Rantolo.	The one of Rantolo's village.
Hobane ke mokhoenyana oa moreneng,	Because I am the son-in-law of the chief's residence,
Morena oa Kerefisi le Letsie.	The chief of Griffiths and Letsie,
Oa Api le Makhaola,	Of Api and Makhaola,
Oa Nkoebe le Lerotholi,	Of Nkoebe and Lerotholi,
Oa Peete le Makhobane,	Of Peete and Makhobane,
Oa Mafa le Ramabilikoa,	Of Mafa and Ramabilikoa,
Chapo le Ramachalea.	Chapo and Ramachalea.
Leqai ka hara Maama,	Uninitiated boy in Maama's village,
Thaka ngoana Maseqobela,	Age-mate of Maseqobela's child,
Ke utloa bohloko—hobane?	I feel very sad—why?
Ke lesole le mona, la bo-Ntolo.	I am the soldier here, Ntolo's brother.

Ha senna oa ho laoa.	I am not the one who was disciplined.
Melaolo ea basali, ea methamahane.	In the fashion of women, [who drink] weak sorghum beer,
Ea ntšoareleng-botlolo,	Of the hold-the-bottle-for-me types,
Ke ea thekesela.	I am staggering [drunk].
Ke ne ke laoa ke banna ba baholo feela.	I was reprimanded only by prominent men.
Ba nea nama ka theko ea lerumo.	They gave me meat on the end of the spear.
Ba re ke, e lome ke tšoele fatše.	They told me, bite it and spit it on the ground.
Nama ea likhohlela hase ho mpolaea.	The meat slimy with spittle doesn't kill me.
Ke ena; e ntutse pelong.	Here it is; it is settled on my heart.
Ke phamolane, phamola!	I am the snatcher, [I] snatch!
Motho oa ha Rantolo.	The person of Rantolo's.
O phamole motho a sa nkha letsuka,	You should snatch a man while his body still smells,
A sa nkha 'tsuka la mosali oa hae.	While he still smells his wife's body odor.
Haeso ha Mako, mahlalela.	My native home [is] at Mako's, [I] the unemployed person.
Haabo Karabo le Lepolesa,	At the village of Karabo and Lepolesa,
Haabo Mafosa le Ralitšepe.	At the village of Mafosa and Ralitsepe.
Amen!	Amen!

Because I did not witness this performance or have any chance to discuss it with its recorder, creator, or audience, no defensible interpretation is possible. Nevertheless, its rarity and illustrative quality makes it worthy of transcription and an attempt at textual analysis. Here we have the common people's contemporary culture of laughter framed in the terms of *lithoko*'s poetry of names. Both praises and *sefela* often begin with *Tholang lerata* (Damane and Sanders 1974, 46), and here the praiser develops the formula to note the mixture of emotional extremes that his praising excites in his listeners. Characteristic of *lithoko*, the poet begins by naming himself while challenging his comrades to do likewise if they can. The following lines (5–17), up to "ginger beer," offer an extended exercise in what Kunene (1971, 20) might call a "locative eulogue," a self-description framed in images of native landscape, but satirizing the naming abilities of others. A single couplet criticizing the cruelty of the chief is followed by a lengthy (lines 20–31) boast of the poet's own stoutness in the just defense of his family's cattle. This stoutness is then rooted in "associative eulogues" (Kunene 1971, 35–36, 47–52), in which the poet claims affinal kinship with both central and collateral lines of Basotho royalty (lines 32–40).

From these sublime heights he descends quickly to the ridiculous, claiming that he is not one of those hold-the-bottle-while-I-take-my-time tipplers, but a staggering drunkard so incorrigible that the elders must be called to scold him. In a passage remarkable for its direct exposure of the "secrets" of the initiation school (lines 49–52), the poet recounts his endurance of one of its quintessential tests of fortitude. During these rites, initiates are made to stand with their hands behind their backs and to snatch a piece of roasted meat off the point of a spear with their teeth. Far from being a delectable morsel, this meat is covered with the saliva of his teachers and comrades, who spat upon it after it was affixed to the spear. The lesson of this experience having been taken to heart, the poet remains "the snatcher," seizing his antagonists fresh from their wives' embraces, before their morning bath, which I can say from experience is about the only time other than the dead of night that one is likely to find a Mosotho villager at home. Identifying his village again for good measure, this time by reference to his ordinary neighbors and friends, the poet ends with the Christian coda frequently used in *lifela* as well, "Amen!"

These common man's praises share many stylistic qualities and a generally dialogic perspective, at once self-promotional and ironic, with initiates' praises, an old genre that like the initiation rites themselves is still very much alive in Lesotho. Initiation songs and the composition of self-praises are taught to the initiates at the lodge by an elder instructor called a *mosuoe*, who may even give an initiate his initiation name. At the graduation ceremonies, these instructors lead the initiates in the choral *mangae*, during which each initiate in turn stands to recite his self-composed praises to his village. His personal verses provide the initiate with a new name and consist of "a combination of farewells to the past, self-praises, and the construction of a poetic image of one's identity" (Adams 1974, 135). As such they are a sort of preexperiential counterpart to the postexperiential composition of the travelers' hymns. An example of a contemporary initiate's *lithoko* was given in the last chapter, and we shall enjoy more of them when we come to consider initiation as a theme in *sefela*. The only written texts that predate my own field collection are those published in a small pamphlet at Morija by the Mosotho Evangelical Church elder H. E. Jankie in 1939. While the contents and early date of the texts offer a fascinating comparison, it is uncertain what to compare them to. While the pamphlet is entitled in the plural, *Lithoko tsa Makoloane*, "Initiates' Praises," all the texts employ the same praise name, "Lefeta." It is the custom for initiates, upon graduation, to walk the countryside together performing their praises at the various homes of their number, and these texts might represent successive performances by the same initiate. Perhaps different initiates using the same initiation name composed them. Equally likely is that Jankie, though already sixty-three and a pillar of a church that condemned Sesotho initiation in the most energetic terms, composed all the texts himself as poetry in the style of young initiates. Writing in Sesotho about Jankie and his pamphlet, M. D. Mohapeloa (1950, 27–31) observes that the book could have used an introduction explaining the poems, and one can only concur. The late Professor S. M. Guma, who has tortured countless Basotho students with his unassimilable grammatical texts on Sesotho (1971), bases an extended discussion of initiates' praises entirely on passages from Jankie's texts, which he reproduces and translates without citation as if they were unmediated field transcriptions (1967, 139). In the one instance where Guma refers to Jankie's book, he calls it a "collection." Since only those short passages have ever before been translated, I offer the following item in order to expose Jankie's contribution to a wider, non-Basotho audience:

Ngoahang ola ka ntoa ea Seqiti,	During the years of the Seqiti war
Hoja Lefeta o n'a s'a le moholo	If Lefeta had already grown up,
A ka be a kile a hlabana ntoa,	He could have fought a battle,
A ka be a kile a tšoaela motho!	He could even have been a champion!
Motho mosesanyane oa ha Ntoi,	The thin man of Ntoi's place,
Le ba babasesanyane ba e loana.	Even the thin ones can fight.
Kanono ea khabola lehoatateng,	A cannon is bellowing in the desert,
Kanono ea khabola thunya li lla,	A cannon is bellowing, and the guns are thundering,
Mahlobi ea e tabolela litjobo.	It tore apart the Mahlubi's thongs.
Mokone ea mo tlosa qooma thekeng!	It tore a Mokone's [Nguni's] penis cover from his waist!
Lekhoaba la tlaka le sa tsoa tlaka,	The crow shrieked praises at us continously,
Banna ea ba etsa matsekelana.	The men divided severally into the ranks of the defeated.
Ngoan'a monna ea mo suha lehata,	A man's child, it cracked his skull,
E mong ea roba mokokotloana,	The other one, it broke his spinal cord,
Mofana ea mo senya sefahlehoana,	Mofana, it destroyed his face,
E mong ea mo suhlahanya lirope,	Another, it crushed his thighs,
Likhomo ea li etsa mefela-fela,	Cattle it killed in countless numbers,
Nku le poli tsona hake li bolele!	Sheep and goats beyond estimation!

Ba ka ba babeli bana ba monna, *E mong a otla, e mong a, tšoaela;*	They can be two, a man's children, Another, it hit him, another was hit again;
Rona le 'nake rea etsisana: *A hape tšoeu, ke hape tšooana,*	I and my pal imitate each other: He captures the white one, I capture the little white one,
Li e'o ts'oana ka'mala sakeng.	When they are in the kraal they have the same colors.
Ka lala Bokone, ka lala thakeng,	I slept at the Bakone's place, I slept with my companions.
Ka lala ke kukunoa ke makukuno. *Tlhare tsa Bokone ka li tseba tsohle:*	I didn't sleep comfortably at all. The Bakone's medicines, I became familiar with them all:
Ka tseba sepaqa, ka tseba sefehle,	I became familiar with *sepaga*, I became familiar with *sefehle*,
Ka ba ka tseba le more oa liphieo.	I even became familiar with *more oa liphieo.*
Lefeta ore le mo sehele thebe,	Lefeta is saying you must make him a shield,
Le mo sehele e tšoeu, e khubelu,	You should make him the white and red one,
Enore h'a tlola, a be a hlanake,	So that when he charges, he can hit the ground rolling,
E be eka a ka abeloa mofoli.	So he can be rewarded with a large hare [*lepus saxatilis*].
Lekiti-kiti la lipere ke leo, *Tlohang bana tlhakong tsa lipere.*	There is the sound of galloping horses, Take the children away from the horse's hoofs.
Pere e loana ka oto la morao, *Oto la pele ke ho etsa mokhabo.* *Ke fumane 'Mammoki a tšola,*	The horse fights with a back foot, The foreleg is used for dancing. I found 'Mammoki finishing her cooking.
Ke itse ke re ho eena: 'Ngoathele! *A nka pitsa a ribeha hlama.* *Ka otla poli e phatšoa phororong,*	I pestered her: dish out some for me! She took a pot, hit the dough. I hit a black and white goat at the waterfall,
Ka e o tla, ka e hlanamisa 'mala, *Ka re e tla jeoa ke manong selemo.*	I hit it, and burst its entrails, I said it will be eaten by the vultures in spring.
Kapoko ka mahlong e pulutsoana,	I have snowflakes in the eyes, the bluish one,
E pulutsoana ke boea ba litšepe.	The one which is bluish because of the springbok's hair.
Tšepe e ka shoa 'Mammalane;	Mammalane the springbok can die;

Molau oa 'mamashapa-tšooana, *Ha o khitle molepe, o'a reteletsa.*	Molau, "beater-of-a-white-one," It doesn't knock out the widow-bird, it beats it about.
Baseli ba il'o sela molapong,	Those wanting grain are going to buy it from the brook,
Ho sela ba banyane le ba baholo.	The grain is bought by the young and by [their] elders.
Ho sela Mabenyane le Seeqela.	It is bought by Mabenyane and Seeqela.
Ramosoeu oa leoatle o kae? *O sa ile tlase bophirimela,*	Where is Ramosoeu of the Ocean? He has already gone down in the West,
Mohla a khutlang o tla tla busa. *Banna ba heso khoeli ee ke mang?*	The day he returns he'll rule. Men of my home, which month is this?
Pherekhong ke tlhakola-molula. *Banana ba e khetla lilopotsiea,* *Ba bang ba a khetla a e-s'o butsoe,*	January, as in its praises. The girls are scraping the first fruits, The other ones are even scraping those not yet ripe,
A le tšoere, a le khahlela molula.	She is holding one, severely scraping it.
Letjeke-tjeke la pitsi e khunong, *Le tsoang tlase, Mahalimane,*	The dance of the roan horse, The one that comes from down in Mahalimane,
Bashanyana ba le hlabetse mokhosi. *Banana ba 'mamokolokonyane,* *Ba kolokile ka mora' likhamane.*	The boys are shouting at it. The girls have formed a line, They are lining up behind roaring flames.
Moshanyan'a lenakana pelong, *A ka ntšosa, ka re tho letsoalo.*	The boy with a horn on the heart, He can frighten me, in the fibre of my human being.
U n'u tsoa lisa kae, thak'a me?	Where have you been herding, my companion?
Ke ne ke tsoa lisa ka sehlabeng.	I have been herding on top of the plateau.
Lefeta, tlola-tlola u ee holimo, *U e'o bona ha e khiba methepa.*	Lefeta, jump and go up, To go and see the maidens performing their knee dance.
Ba kentse ngoanana e mosehlana.	They have a light-skinned girl among them.
Bahlankana ba mo hloele sehlopha, *Ekare a bua a be a leletse!*	All the boys are staring at her, When she speaks; she bats her eyes coquettishly!
Mokhosi ha o lla, rea phalla,	When the command is shouted, we jump to it,

Re hopoletse ha kanono li lla.	Remembering when the cannons were thundering.
Re sa ea koana Mollo-oa-Tuka;	We are going yonder at Mollo-oa- Tuka [Fire-Is-Burning];
Ha o tuka ha o qhoauoe mashala.	When it is burning, you don't have to fuel it with coal.
Khomo tsa teng li tsoile kaofela,	All the cows have gone out,
Ho tsoile Tsoana, ho tsoile Pulutsoana.	Tsoana has gone out, Pulutsoana has gone out.
Khom'a sekhoahla, 'Makhoalipana,	The swift cow, 'Makhoalipana,
Ha e re hae tloha, santa-santa,	When it leaves, it walks firmly,
E hopotse Mohohong, thabeng.	Remembering Mohohong, at the mountain.
Lefeta, khurumala, thebe e hlajoe,	Lefeta, crouch down, so only the shield can be pierced,
Hata, mar'a fihle thebeng ea hao;	Step quickly, so that the troops can reach your shield;
Ngoan'a marumo a maphatšoa, Lefeta.	The child of the blue spear, Lefeta.
Lefeta ka 'ona ha a ke a betsa,	Lefeta with them he never throws,
Ka 'ona o khantša ho nanabela.	With them he is boastful of grasping the spears.
Ere a hlaba Mokone, a mename!	When he pricks a Mokone, he bends!
Se-bala-buka, se-bala-lesaoana.	The bookworm, the reader of empty vanities.
Qai ekare le tšaba ho bolla,	The uninitiated boy when he fears circumcision,
La re: Ha le mpone ke halaletsoe,	He says: Can't you see that I am holy [a Christian],
Ke halaletsoe ke moea oa sekolo!	I've been seized with the spirit of education.
Thisa ekare le tšaba ho bolla.	The uninitiated girl when she fears circumcision,
La kuta hloho, la kuta lekoroana,	She shaved her head, she shaved herself bald,
Motutla la o mena malobo-lobo!	The blanket she folded it so clumsily![5]
Qai le eme ka lepae thabeng,	The uninitiated boy is on the mountain in a short blanket,
Thisa le eme ka fokona thoteng.	The uninitiated girl is standing with a *fokona* in the wilderness.

(Jankie 1939, 13–17; translated by Edward Fobo)

These praises are remarkable for their use of historical narrative as a metaphor for personal prowess. The subject is the fierce Seqiti Wars, along

5. Cf. Guma 1967, 141.

with mention of the arrest of the fleeing Hlubi chief Langalibalele in 1873 (Damane and Sanders 1974, 6–7). Projecting his boasts of bravery back into history, the composer personifies himself as a cannon, piling up images of his fearsome destructive capacity like so many shells lobbed onto the heads of helpless enemies. Though but a slender youth, the performer is aware of the Sesotho proverb: *Ntoa ha e etsetsoe likhoka*, "War is not simply a matter of muscles." As his hearty appetite for battle consumes the enemies of the Basotho, so his explosive talents dismember the praises of rival poets. Other episodes anticipate a combative worldliness, as the composer travels among the Bakone ("Nguni," i.e., Xhosa, Zulu, or Swazi) peoples and learns their powerful, dangerous medicines. Personifying himself as a dancing horse (for which Lesotho is famed) whose cavorting endangers children, he demands food from a woman who appears less than compliant. He responds by killing a black and white goat, an adherence to custom in that goats that are not shiny white are always killed in Lesotho. The shining coats of goats are symbols of both the light of ancestral wisdom and the openness and clarity of mind necessary to receive it. For this reason a billy goat is sacrificed at the initiation (*lefehlo*) of new diviners, who eat goat but are enjoined from consuming sheep, a comparatively stupid, muddy-colored animal. This is followed by some allusive praises describing his neighbors and home village, and an absent heir to the chieftship. Included is a boast that he is so accurate with a stick he can even beat the male *molepe* bird, which because of its long tail flies low, with a slow, jerky motion during the mating season. As the village girls are processing the harvest, they are attracted by the composer in the form of a dancing roan horse. In a curious interlude he asks the whereabouts of a fellow herdboy, "the boy with a horn on his heart." This description suggests a deep knowledge of medicine and charms, since horns are the symbols and containers of the diviner's potions. Then it's back to courting the girls, including a fair one whose coquettish voice and glances suggest she is well aware of her attractions. After that, its war once again, with an interlude praising the family cows, and a line about grasping a spear that echoes the famous *mokorotlo* lyric, "Death is called when spears are grasped." As a counterpoise to Lefeta's bravery, he mocks the Christian youth of his community for their fear of circumcision; and as a fresh initiation graduate, he urges uninitiated children to come out of the wilderness of social isolation and undergo these rites of incorporation. Incredible that a man of Jankie's faith and commitment would write such things, yet equally incredible that he would make the effort to follow heathen initiates around to transcribe them! Guma, after all, perhaps the leading authority on Sesotho language and auriture, apparently never troubled himself to collect a single performed text of this genre.

These praises, like commoners' praises, employ the historical perspective of chiefs' praises as a metaphor for, rather than a record of, heroic exploits and personality. In their evocation of the horses and maidens who dance in the poet's village, they are clearly closer than chiefs' praises to the dialogic evocations of common experience characteristic of the culture of laughter. Yet Jankie's text, like *sefela* and the initiates' praises I recorded, is composed through the intertextual mobilization of the symbolic and expressive resources and cultural prestige of chiefs' praises. Metaphors in these other genres that incorporate and rework the images of chiefs' praises or *mekorotlo* anthems cloak both the performer and his words in the symbolic authority of "tradition" and the precolonial Basotho state. In performance, these metaphors are a means for displaying the deep cultural knowledge considered indispensable to "eloquence" (*bokheleke*) in Sesotho. The right to his audience's attention is confirmed through the performer's eloquent display of knowledge and the metapoetic knowledge of eloquence. As a generic medium of self-praise, the examples of a commoner's praises and Jankie's text above may be revealingly compared to a *sefela* by the veteran *lebollo* initiation and *sefela* composition instructor Hlalele Mabekanyane. Aged fifty-six in 1989 when this song was recorded, Hlalele is too young to have fought in any wars despite his singing name, "Kanono," so prominently featured in our Jankie text. Yet he imagines himself a Second World War veteran and a British military recruiter in Maseru in the following passage:

Mohale, oa koebela, Maphopholetsa,	Kanono, swaggering hero, Maphopholetsa,
Tjemptjete ke phuthi ke hloaele.	The heron is an antelope when I am on top.
Moshanyana, ke maname tseleng,	The young lad, I am hiding on the road,
Ke mametse ha tsa khosi li lla.	I am listening when the ones of Queen 'Mantsebo are crying.[6]
Phala e lla, masole a lumetse.	When the whistle is blown, soldiers should be ready.

6. This is a story of the recruitment of Basotho to serve in the Second World War by the British at the time of Queen Regent 'Mantsebo. The singer heard this from the war veterans.

Masole ha tloha ha Ratjomose,	When the soldiers leave from Ratjomose's,
A tloha Maseru teropong koana.	They leave from Maseru in town yonder.
Banna! Ka la pele Mphalane,	Men! On the first of August,
ke nkile libuka tsa mabitso a batho.	I was carrying books of men's names.
Ka buoa le lisajene ka li bitsa	I called and talked to the sergeants
Joale le tsona ka phetha melao.	Now with them and obeyed the law.
Qetellong ka laola maqosa,	Finally I ordered the messengers,
Ofisiri tsa bona li lutse thokoana.	Their officers were standing far away.
Ke re li joetse morali oa Nkoebe hantle,	I said they should tell Nkoebe's daughter properly,
Likompone li batla li sa fella.	Those from the mine compounds are not enough.
Ho arajoa ke, "'Matšaba."	She replied, "'Mantsaba."
Motlatsi oa 'musisi ke utloile,	I heard the assistant colonial governor saying,
"U ee ka Fokothi u ilo ba bona;	"You should go to the Lerotholi Technical Institute;
Batho ba teng ba ntseng ba fihla.	There are some newcomers who are still coming.[7]
U nke babang ho tlatsa lenane,	You should take some to add to your number list,
Le N.R.C., u qotse."	Even at the N.R.C. Labour Bureau, you should take some."
Ho Maburu, hone hosa busa Rapiti;	As for the Boers, Retief was still the ruler;
Poulo e ne e sale moshanyana;	Paul was still a boy;[8]
Lesotho koana, ho sa busa Ntsane.	Lesotho yonder, the ruler was Ntsane.
E ne e sale ha mohlomi Sefikeng,	It was Mohlomi's place in Sefikeng,
Liherefe li ne li sale ka Bethani.	*Liherefe* were still in Bethany.
Ke mohale ea hlotseng balichaba,	I am the worrior who had defeated foreigners,
Ke tsoa hlola Benkase, tlase,	I had defeated them at Bengu's, below,
Pakeng tsa Cairo le Ekhepeta.	Between Cairo and Egypt.
Moo hoa eshoa ngoana oa mo Italy;	There died the child of an Italian;
Mussolini u shoele a le mafura,	Mussolini died very fat,
Mahlong a beng baka, hae ba mo talimme.	In front of the eyes of his elders, as they watched him.

7. Recruits taken directly from the mine compounds are not sufficient; therefore, men newly arriving for mine contracts should be diverted into military service under the British.

8. Here the singer imagines that, during the events of the 1940s of which he sings, Piet Retief, murdered by the Zulu king Dingana in 1838, was still an Afrikaner leader, and Paul Kruger, the famous president of the Transvaal Republic who died in 1904, was "still a boy."

Loana u tiee mokone u Kanono.
Molimo u ntumeletse ho loana,
Le koana moo ke tsoang, ke tsoa ntoeng,

Ke tsoa khabong ea masumu e tuka,

Khabo eka chesa bahale matsoho.
Ke tsoa chesa Hitlelara lieatla,
Ke hapile likhomo, ha kea li bona,

Ka bea ka tsona ho morena e moholo,
Ho mofu Mahali, 'me'Matšaba,
Ke utloa ba re u li file matona,

Batho ba lulang lekhotleng.
E ne ele bo Molise oa Molingoana,
Matona, re ile ntoeng, masole,

Ba bat'so ba mona ba habo Ntšebo

Sebetsang le sa fihla baeti,
Tsela tsa mokhathala ha li tsejoe.

Fight fiercely, Kanono, you Nguni.[9]
God had given me permission to fight,
Even yonder where I come from,
I am coming from a war,
I am a flame that comes from
blades of spears,
The flame can burn warriors' hands.
I had burned Hitler's hands,
I have captured cattle, but I haven't
seen them,
I offered them to the queen,
To the late Mahali, mother of Tšaba,
I heard that she had given them
to her councilors,
People who sit at the court.
It was Molise and Molingoana,
Her councilors, while we had gone to
the war, we soldiers,
The dark-complexioned ones
of [Queen] Ntšebo's family
Make hay while the sun shines,
Because you will never know
you will become tired.

My PURPOSE, once again, is not simply to tell the story of Basotho migrancy through performance or to interpret performance by reference to migrant experience, but to articulate social forces and processes with cultural principles, practices, and forms. A narrative directed toward this end might take any one or, in these postmodern, "hypertextual" days, more than one of a set of alternative, parallel courses. The particular shape of my account is arguably better only because it is partly mine, written in the academic voice now natural to me, and partly theirs, the Basotho poets', influenced by the forms in which their experiences and reflections were composed. Because it is the foundation of these performances, I will describe Basotho labor migration, not as some synthesized entirety but as a set of conditions and impacts crystallized in social arrangements and action. Certainly there is no purpose served by merely repeating the extensive, superbly detailed sociological analyses on migrant labor in South Africa already available, to which books by Crush, Jeeves, and Yudelman (1991), James (1992), and Crush, James, and Jeeves (1992) are recent fine

9. The singer belongs to one of the many segments of clans of Nguni origin that reside in Lesotho. The Nguni-speaking clans have a warlike reputation.

additions. Instead we will consider those features of migrancy that are salient in migrants' cultural productions, not to presume to know what it is like to be them, but to see how their consciousness is socially constituted through cultural forms.

Over the past century, labor migration became the pervasive reality of Basotho life, with 80 percent of men and an unknown but significant minority of women involved in it for some period of their working lives. Just as important, the degree and qualities of Basotho participation in the migrant labor system have changed as the sheer numbers of migrants steadily grew and, most recently, steeply declined. Legislation and management policies regarding foreign migrant workers have changed, favored mines and categories of employment have shifted, pay and working conditions improved (since 1974), unionization progressed, and the relationship between Lesotho's domestic economy and migrant earnings has been transformed. This narrative, however, will not proceed historically, both because the earnest collection of migrants' songs only begins with Mapele in 1975 (Mapele 1976), and because the purpose of *sefela* is not to recount history or reflect its transformations as Western readers understand it. A *sefela* is a poetic autobiography composed in social context, a personal odyssey of common travails and travels, summarized in the old fashioned salutation to a migrant that entitles this chapter, *Lumela, ngoana oa Molimo!* "Greetings, child of [only] God! Our texts and talk will map the experience of migrant life as the singers have lived and sung it, in images as evocative, indelible, and shifting as memory itself:

Ke hahile Quthing Sebapala—	I reside at Quthing Sebapala—
Ke tsoaletsoe teng; ke khafela teng.	I was born there; I pay tax there.
Khaitseli ea bo 'Mamphasa le 'Mamoitheri,	The brother of 'Mamphasa and 'Mamoitheri,
Ke lesole la habo 'Mamokhesuoe.	I am the soldier of 'Mamokhesuoe's village.
Ha ke ne ke tloha ke eea makhooeng,	When I was leaving to go to the whites' place [mines],
Ka bua le pelo ra ba ra qeta,	I spoke to my heart and we finished,
Le moea, ra ba ra utloana.	And my soul, we understood each other.
Mahlo a ka a lla ke sa fahluoa;	My eyes cry though nothing has got into them;
Pelo e nyeka ke sa ja letho. . . .	I felt like vomiting [though/because] I've eaten nothing. . . .
. . . Bo-ntate, banna ba makhooeng,	. . . Fathers, men of the mines,

Ke sebelitse la malimo a batho,	I have worked with cannibal men [slavedrivers],
Liphakoe, banna ba Matelile.	Hawks, men of Matelile.
Ha ke ntse ke nepa,	If I'm still correct,
Ke tseba batho ba mino ba kae:	I know the whereabouts of men of song:
Ke tseba ngoana Rahlothu,	I know Rahlothu's child,
Ke tseba Teboho Mothae,	I know Teboho Mothae,
Motsoalle, Raleqhoele, molotsana,	A friend, Raleqhoele, the cunning one,
Kapa ngoana Nkaeana, ha ese ngoana Masiu.	Or Nkaeana's child, not the child of Masiu.
Ke re'eng, litsamaea-naha?	What do I say, inveterate travelers?
Likepechele, batho ba makhooeng.	The Knobkerrie poets, men of the mines.

(Makeka Likhojane, "Ngoana Mokhalo")

Chapter Four

"An Initiation Secret Is Not Told at Home"

The Making of a Country Traveler

I'm the chief herdboy [leader], country travelers,
The prophet of God, Mahase.
Me, I'm not born but issued:
I descended from God on a Thursday;
Friday found me on the way;
On earth I arrived on a Saturday.
When I arrived in my village of 'Muso,
There are the aged women in that village;
These include Grandmother 'Mamokoto
And the good-hearted woman 'Makoloi.
I heard and saw ululations [of joy]:
"By this warrior we are saved!—
He is born, the eloquent one, in the village of 'Muso.
The roller [fluent one] of the Bafokeng [clan] cries!"
Tsokolo Lecheko

Along with countless other African genres, *sefela* defies the attempts by Parry and Lord and their successors to classify "oral poetry" as by definition "composed in performance" (see Vail and White 1991, 30). Basotho migrants' *lifela* are composed and recomposed incrementally both in rehearsal and in public. Starting as a rank amateur (at *sefela*) and a novice (at mine labor), the future *kheleke* starts with a few snatches picked up from older relatives and reciters, works into them passages of his own, appropriates and reworks with increasing skill the memorable material of superior competitors, and ultimately fashions an aural work in a style and substance peculiarly his own. So as he has a single life, a composer may be thought of as creating only one *sefela*, forty years or more in the making. Yet it is never performed in the same way twice, nor in its (nonexistent) entirety once. Every performance is a novel interweaving of well-worn, freshly phrased favorite passages, stolen verses old and new, and newly composed, often extemporaneous extensions, elaborations, transitions, and digressions inspired by experience, vision, and the demands of the performance event. A performer who offers to sing first one and then another *sefela* is most often extemporizing hypertextual recompositions drawn from the corpus of his aural autobiography. Lest anyone identify this with the discrete "oral mentality" described by Father Ong (1982), note that these performers are to varying degrees both nonliterate and illiterate, some partly literate in Sesotho only—imaging without writing a world saturated with the power and structure of literacy. During a series of takes for Gei Zantzinger's documentary film about *sefela* singers, *Songs of the Adventurers* (Constant Springs Productions 1986), I asked Tieho Rakharebe (Hulas Ralipotsotso) if he could "sing the song exactly the same way again." He shook his head and explained that he understood what I meant by "exactly the same" (verbatim), but that, sorry, he couldn't do it.

Neither sequence nor chronology is preserved either within or between renditions of these raconteured rather than recounted narrations of the migrant life. As often as not, they begin with a current or central vision, and proceed or even end with an evocation of a boyhood that is father to the man. So we shall not start where the eloquent ones themselves usually do: calling for the attention of their comrades, creating a sense of occasion, and proclaiming their identity by origin, association, personality, and accomplishment. Seizing on the notion of socially resonant poetic autobiography—*sefela* as the composed expression of a migrant life—we shall begin, as in the epigraphic passage, with the traveler's birth. If as the eloquent ones insist, *Bophelo ke mathata feela*, "Life is just troubles," then that indeed is where the trouble starts:

Khele! 'Na, ha kea tsoaloa.	Khele! Me, I am not dropped.
Ha kea tsoaloa; ke emotsoe feela.	I am not dropped [beastlike]; I'm properly delivered.
Ke hlahetse lefielong thabeng.	I was born in the broom grass on the mountain.
'Me' a hloloa ke Letsoetla, ka hlaha.	My mother, divorced by Letsoetla, so was I born,
Hoa tsoaloa sehole sa motho.	So was born an incorrigible man.
Banna, hoa rongoeloa heso lapeng.	Men, news was sent to my home.
Khele! Ho ka rongoeloa Makhalaneng,	Khele! It was sent [as far as] Makhaleng,
Koana ho Nkhono Mpati.	Yonder to Grandmother Mpati.
Hoa tsebisoa sechaba sa motse oo	It was made known to people of that village
Oa ntate, oa Morena Matjoba.	Of my father, of Chief Matjoba.

Ho tsebisoe banana le bashanyana.
Le banna, ba tsebisoa,
Banna le ka basali—oe!
Batho ba no joale,
Bashanyana, ba 'ngala;
Ba ka 'ngala ba bulela marole.

Banana joale, ba e ea merohong.
Basali, ba 'ngala ba e ea patsing.

Banna joale, ba etsa mokorotlo.

Maqheku a na a maholo ke ana;
Ba fihla ho, 'na bo Nkhono Mpati

Ba mphutha ka mose oa khongoana:
"Ha re tsamaea, ngoana oa ngoanaka—
oe!"
Ha ke fihla haeso lapeng—oe!
Jo! Ka potoa-potoa banna
ka hara seotloana
Bongata bo qalang ho mpona—oe!
Ba ntsuna le marameng oe.
Litelu tseo le li bonang tsena,
Li ne li sobe teng mehleng ea joale.
Ekaba le sa tseba ho sheba batho—
Khele! Le nchebe lifotong mona:
Ke papatlele ea naha.
Le tle le mamele, litsamaea-naha:
Ke beuoe moetaneng; ka raha.
Ka raha metoho;
Ka raha meseme.
Meiteli, ke hlola ke e rahile—oe!
Seboko seo ke reng—ke se lla!
Sa 'mokotsana le tsebe—oe!
Ho ronngoe mosali a le moholo;
E leng 'maea Edward Mokoena;

Mosali enoa ke mohatsa Seeta.
"Oena, mosali! Tooe o ke o utloe.
Phakisa kapele, monna—
O e khotla batho, ke bao ba lutse."

Le hle le tsebe ha re fihla ho bona.

It was made known to girls and boys.
Even men, they were informed,
Men as well as women—oe!
Those people now,
The boys, they forsook me;
They forsook me to graze one-
year calves.
Girls now, they went for wild greens.
Women, they deserted to gather
firewood.
Men now, they performed
a war anthem.
The old notables were there;
They came to me, those of
Grandmother Mpati.
They wrapped me in a calfskin skirt:
"Let's go, my grandchild—oe!"

When I arrived at my home—oe!
Jo! I was surrounded by men
in a reed courtyard enclosure.
Many who first saw me—oe!
They kissed me on the cheeks.
These beard hairs that you see,
They hadn't grown in those days.
If you know how to look at people—
Khele! You look at my photos:
I'm a wanderer of the country.
You should listen, travelers:
I was put in a pot; I kicked.
I kicked [over] the porridges;
I kicked the grass mats.
Cow dung, I always kicked it—oe!
That yowling I say—I cried!
A muted cry you should know—oe!
An elder woman was sent;
She was the mother of
Edward Mokoena;
That woman was Seth's wife.
"You, woman! You should hear.
Hurry now, man—
You should go to the court, people are
sitting."
You should know when we
came to them.

A fihla ho bona a hle a ba joetse:

"Ntate, Morena Matjoba,
Monna ea tsoetseng moshanyana."
Ka ha le molato leea ikahlola,
O ne a sa bitsa bana le lebitso la motho.

Ntate ke eo a etla—oe!
Le tle le mamele, litsamaea-naha:
O sare, "O reng, mosali?"
"Ngoana enoa o mo tsoetseng enoa,
O tsoetse ea joang ngoana?
Ngoana ke enoa a re tsietsa—oe!
Le letsoele lena, o ea le hana.
Le ka meso, banna, o ea re tena—oe!"
Ntate ke enoa a etla;
O sare ho eena mosali enoa oa motho,
"Oena, mosali, tooe!
Ekaba ke hobaneng le le lihole—oe?
A se letsoejana, ntho ena;
Ho sa bonahala moshanyana
enoa o llet se khoetsa.
Ho tloha mona, o lletse lebitso."
Hoa qaluba joale manyofo-nyofo:
Hoa bitsoa, banana le bashanyana—oe!

Banna ba nang le basali ba bitsoa—oe!

Maqheku a na a maholo ke ao;
Hoa fihla ha re shatata moreneng,

Ha ntate, ba Morena Matjoba.
Ho ne ho thoe ba nthehe lebitso—oe!

Hoa qaluoa ka theko ea banana:
Ba re, "Ho betere ngoana enoa
e mpe e be Raseea—oe!

E nore ha re ea merohong koana,

Re ee le eena, ngoana oa Mariti."
'Me' le ntate habae lumele:
"Ngoana, oa ka a ka shoela merohong;

She came to them and indeed
told them:
"Father, Chief Matjoba,
The man who begot the boy."
Because the guilty one judges himself,
She hadn't called the children
and the name of the person.
Here is my father coming—oe!
You should listen, travelers:
He says, "What do you say, woman?"
"This child you have fathered,
How did you beget [such a] child?
This child is giving us trouble—oe!
Even this breast, he refuses it.
Even at dawn, men, he tires us—oe!"
Here is my father coming;
He says to that female of a person,
"You, woman, you!
Why are you such fools—oe?
It's not a growing pain, this thing;
It reveals this boy's been
crying for his birth charm.
Leaving here, he cried for a name."
That now started the disorder:
They were called, the girls and
the boys—oe!
The men and the women were
called—oe!
The great elders are there;
A multitude assembled
at the chief's place,
At father's, those of Chief Matjoba.
It was said they should give me
a name—oe!
It began with the side of the girls:
They said, "It's better this child
be called 'Raseea' [Ready-to-Go]—
oe!
So that when we go among
wild greens yonder,
We go with him, Mariti's child."
Mother and father do not accept it:
"My child, he can die among
wild greens;

A ka shoa ke beng ba banana.

Kea tsaba ka 'nete, le ntsoarele."
Le tle le mamele, litsamaea-naha.
Joale hoa kena theko ea bafana:
Ho betere ngoana enoa e be Chesetsi

E nore ha rele masimong koana,
A chesetsa batho."
'Me' le ntate ha a le lumele
Mmm! Hoa Kena theko ea basali,
Ho betere ngoana enoa e mpe e be
Moshathi
Hobana ha kene ke le balimong,

Ke ne ke ba shatela, maqhekoana."
Ke ne ke bile ke le bohlale, Mariti.
E re ke bona basali ke bao,
Ke kalama mokulubete ke tebe
ka ona ke lebe fatše.
Ke fulutse le metsi, sekeleme sena,
Ke re basali ba na ba seke ba mpona.
Ka Jehova oa leholimo,
Bo-'me le ntate ha a le lumele.

Hoa kena theko ea banna,
"Ho betere ngoana enoa e be Sematli,

E nore ha a le makhooeng koana,
A nke majoe a maholo haholo
A lihele ka hara kokopane."
"Ngoana rona a tle a tsebe ho phomola,
A setise Ramokoro ho bulela,

A tlanne a fasi lipeseng koana."

'Me' le ntate ha ba le lumele.
Joale hoa kena theko e kholo; banna,
Le tle le mamele.
E re e le basali ba le baholo,
Ba kang ba re ho Nkhono Mpati—oe!
"Ho betere ngoana enoa e be Thabang,

Hoba ke ne ke tsoale ka
letsatsi la thabang."

He can die by [the hands of]
the husbands of the girls.
I am afraid truly, pardon me."
You should listen, travelers.
Now came the side of the boys:
"It's better this child be
Chesetsi [Burner],
So when we are in the fields yonder,
He burns [to fight] people."
Mother and father do not accept it.
Mmm! Comes the side of the women,
"It's better this child should be
'Moshati' [Insolent],
Because when I was among my
ancestors,
I was insolent to them, the elders."
I was becoming clever, [I] Mariti.
When I saw those women,
I mounted a tadpole and
sank with it to the bottom.
I roiled the water, [I] the rascal,
I say so the women could not see me.
By Jehova of Heaven,
My mothers and father don't
agree to it.
Came the side of the men,
"It's better this child be
'Sematli' [Strongman],
So when he's there at the mines,
He should take huge stones
And throw them in the ore-cars."
"Our child should know repose,
He should make Ramokoro chip off
[pieces] to open [the way],
While he's stuck fast in the
mineshaft stope holes there."
Mother and father do not accept it.
Now comes the side of a notable; men,
You should listen.
When it's the notable women,
Those like Grandmother Mpati—oe!
"It's better this child be
Thabang [Happiness],
Because I bore him on a day
that was happy."

Ka tsoala; ka keresemese ka hlaha	I was born; on Christmas I appeared,
25 khoeling ea Tsitsoe.	The 25th of the month of December.
Lichaba tsena li thabile haholo;	Those people were very happy;
Lirurubele tsena li ntse li fofa.	Those butterflies were still flying.
Linonyana li fofa, li shebile 'moho.	Birds flew, facing in one direction.
Khomo li botha, li shebile 'moho;	Cattle were sitting, facing in one direction;
Li shebile ha Molapo, bochabela.	They were looking to Molapo's, east [Leribe District].
Ke tsoteletseng, setsamaea-naha?	What do I care for, [I] the traveler?
Nkahe ke re, "Amen, ke phethile."	I should say, "Amen, I've finished."
Ha hona 'mino o fetang ona,	There's no music surpassing this,
Hona ke hosa kapa ho kekela.	So will [the wild fire] burn out or spread.

(Rabonne Mariti)

Paradoxically, but not unusually, the forgoing passage concludes rather than opens the *sefela.* The singer, Rabonne Mariti, begins by explaining with some irritation (*Khele!*) that, while his mother's expulsion led to his birth out on a mountainside, he was not "dropped" (*tsoaloa*) in the fashion of an animal, but properly born or delivered (*hloloa, emotsoe*) as a human child, with a social identity. Even so, in the next line he reverts to the ruder verb *tsoaloa* and calls himself incorrigible, the quality of a born traveler. Though the news of his birth is widely announced, boys, girls, and women sulkily desert him. The adult men, however, sensing the arrival of a future warrior, perform the war-dance anthem in praise of this little "incorrigible." The paternal grandmother, as is the custom with a firstborn boy, takes charge and brings him to his father's village. There, the senior men of the kindred gather in the enclosed homestead courtyard and kiss him on his not yet bearded cheeks. But the boy is truly an *enfant terrible,* foreshadowing his migrant disposition. Unable to deal with his bawling recalcitrance, the grandmother goes to the extremity of summoning his father from the chief's council. The father arrives and proclaims the cause of his son's protestations: a hunger for social identity. The *khoetsa* charm identifying his membership in his father's *seboko* and placing him in a healthy relationship to his ancestors has not, possibly owing to his mother's rejected status, been tied around his neck. That resolved, a palaver begins among the assembled villagers over the naming of the child. Each group by age and gender proposes a name, but in each case it bespeaks their own selfish ambitions for the boy and not the care of those who love him. Finally his grandmother settles the issue by naming him Happiness, since she—meaning her daughter—bore him on Christmas Day. This solution makes everyone happy, even the butterflies. Birds and cattle, though, gaze portentously toward his family's ancestral home, north and east in Leribe District. The poet concludes his song of more than 400 lines with the common ending formula, "Amen, I have finished." He adds another couplet praising the song metapoetically and inquiring whether other singers will come forward to spread the brushfire of eloquence he has lit or let it smolder and burn out in silence.

As soon as they can run, Basotho boys are taken from their mothers and put among other boys, some already in their teens, and put to the task of herding livestock, at first on the outskirts of the village, later in the remote highland cattle posts. From about the age of six, virtually every rural and some urban youths make an economic contribution to the homestead through stewardship of goats, sheep, and (ideally) cattle. Herding is considered by Basotho definitive of their society, shaping a collective male character through common experience in youth. Grazing is a free good under the rule of *lefatse le la sechaba*, but villages and networks of stock owners and caretakers jealously guard their allocated pastures and assigned cattle posts. Pasture is a scarce resource in a severely eroded country the size of Belgium, of which two-thirds is covered by mountains. In average elevation, Lesotho is among the highest countries in the world, and herding is practiced under harsh conditions of wind and rain, heat and cold. Herdboys fortunate enough to be working near their villages will get two plain meals of corn porridge and greens each day, but out on the remote upland pastures and cattle posts, they must provide themselves with food and fire. It is not uncommon for herdboys to freeze to death when sudden early winter snowstorms blanket mountain districts. Older boys school the younger in rugged self-reliance, stoic endurance, one-upmanship in securing the best grazing spots, hunting for wild rodents and edible plants, locating lost (and stolen) animals, and overall animal husbandry (Dobb 1984).

Their sport is the ancient martial art of stick fighting, beginning with dry corn stalks but graduating to the heavy hardwood *molamu*. It is with the latter that one's grazing rights are defended against the encroachments of boys from neighboring villages. As adults, Basotho countrymen characteristically carry some sort of *molamu* whenever they are away from their homesteads. They are much favored among migrant workers, who pay significant sums for sticks made of the best regional hardwoods and elaborately decorated with rings of plastic-coated multicolored telephone wire. Many of these stick-types have names, such as my own, called *o motso o monotala* (the black one from Natal) after the imported black hardwood from which it is made. Knowing the injury these lethal weapons can inflict and wishing to avoid the social complications that inevitably follow their use in quarrels among neighbors, Basotho who live away from the rough and tumble of the capital, Maseru, and other lowland border towns are entitled to call themselves peaceable people. But this peaceableness also recognizes the need for deterrence, and there is a formidable fighting spirit, developed through herding, that is quickly ignited in defense of a man's name, ancestry, wife and children, livestock, comrades, or community at large. Wholesale cattle raiding, until recently quite common in rural areas, has died off in favor of more furtive, individual stock thefts now that shotguns and handguns, brought from South Africa, have become so common in rural areas. The sentinels set to watch for (and occasionally carry out) misappropriation and sound the alarm are, of course, the fearless little herdboys.

Ho lisa, "herding," a verb that signifies watchfulness, caretaking, and leadership, is a core institution among every Bantu-speaking people in southern Africa. In Lesotho, the task attained particular significance both because of Moshoeshoe I's emphasis upon large herds rather than military might as a political tool and repository of national strength and because of the grueling conditions under which it was practiced. Herding is regarded as a fundamental experience in the process of male socialization, inculcating comradeship and self-reliance, stoicism and aggressiveness, responsibility and independence, cooperation and wildness. Herding both shapes and symbolizes what Basotho (yes, virtually all of them!) regard as their male national character. Though among Basotho migrants the claim "We opened the mines" is regarded as a satisfactory answer to "We built a mighty empire" from the Zulu, Basotho themselves never mention migrancy as a necessary experience in the construction of their identity as a people. In aristocratic praises, the chief is depicted as the legendary Basotho herdboy (*molisana*), safe-guarding and guiding the cattle of the nation, be they actual bovines or his metaphorical herd of human followers, as in these lines from the *lithoko* of Mopeli Mokhachane:

Rona badisa ba mor'a 'Mamakhabane	We herdboys of the son of 'Mamakhabane
Re eme ka lithunya le ka dilepe	Stood armed with guns and axes
Ra re: "Tsena tseso	And said: "These of our village
ke ditjhitjana, ha di tshware,	are round and smooth, they cannot be caught,
Ke ditjhitjana, di thella diatleng."	They are round and smooth, they slip out of one's hands."

(Kunene 1971, 109)

A sacred *koma* text taught to boys during their initiation rites puts it less metaphorically:

Ho se be modisana	Let there be no herdboy
Ya dumellang tsabo di hapuwe	Who allows his cattle to be captured
A eso hlajwe	Before he is stabbed
A phunngwa ka kwebe	And ripped open with a barbed spear
Madi a keleketla.	And blood trickles down.
	(Guma 1967, 121)

In *sefela* we encounter images and narrations of herding at once realistic and metaphorical. It is the raising of personal experience to the level of a more general significance that perhaps accounts for the placement of episodes of herding near the conclusion of many *lifela*. Here, from one of the greats, Makeka Likhojane (Ngoana Mokhalo):

Le utloe, ka tloha heso lapeng—	Listen, I left my place at home—
Ke khanna likhomo, Ngoana Mokhalo;	I drive cattle, [I] Child of Mokhalo;
Ke ea koana Maluting.	I go yonder to the Maluti.
Ke ilo li lisa; ke ne ke lisa likhomo tsa malome.	I went to herd them; I was herding my uncle's cattle.
Ke lisetsa Mantšonyane, pela motebo oa morena,	I herded at Mantsonyane, near the cattle post of the king,
Ke e Moholo motebo, bolela oa 'Matsaba.	The cattle post of Moholo, I mean of 'Matsaba.
'Khomo ke li emetse,	The cattle I was looking after,
Tsona li tsa tsoha li lahlehile—	Those which on rising were found missing—
Athe lehloa le nele Kolone	Since snow had fallen in the Cape
Bosiu ke lutse, oa hatsetsa litorobela,	At night as I sat, freezing the stouthearted ones,
Lipholo tsa tsoha, li thobile bosiu.	The oxen on rising, they stole off in the night.
Moea o hlaba lipholo, liloteng mona.	The wind pierced the oxen, here through the hump.
Ke ne ke re ba ne ba li utsoitse;	I was thinking they had stolen them;
Masholu, a ne a li nkile.	Thieves, they had taken them.
Ke tlolaka ka holim'a sehlaba,	I was chasing over the highlands,
Ke tlolaka ke sa li bone.	Chasing though I failed to sight them.
Ha ke se ke palama Qholontso,	As I'm riding on Qholontso,
Ke theohile ka Noka-ntšo,	Getting down along Black River,
Ha ke fihla ha Rankomo,	As I arrived at Rankomo's,
'Khomo, monna, ha ke sa li bona.	Cattle, man, I don't see them.
Kea fumana moo maqaphaqapha!	I found from there a trail!

'Khomo, tse nang le e tsehlana,

E namane e ntso joale e tsebe li lisholo,
Ebile e letsoele le le tonanahali.

Ke tla mona ha Rankomo.
Ha habo Morena Mongali,
Ke fumane banna ba lutse khoaling.

Ba lesakaneng, monna;
Ke tseba manamane ka sakaneng,
'Khomo tseso, li khethetsoe Sesotho.

Tsona li ka holim'a sehlaba,
E ne le, hona li tla hangoa.
"Bo-ntate, banna, le ntholle?

Na, ke molisana ke emetse."
Ba re, "Likhomo, monna, li
senya mabele a batho;
Nts'a chelete o li patalle."
Ba joetsa 'Masefabatho, mosali,
eo ke mong'a motse oo;
O tsoa moo a s'a loana,
Bashanyana ba li thiba.
Likhomo li fihla patlellong—
Utloa lerata har'a motse oo!
Bashanyana ba hlabile mokhosi,
Ba bona lipoho li ntse li loana.
Khoalibe li thulana le Terebere;
E hlile li thulana ho tla ntlong,
Ntlong moo ho lulang 'Mabatho,
Mosali eo ke mong'a motse oo.
Molika-liko ke oa'ng sakaneng?
Tlohellang moraba-raba!
Ebile a se likhomo tsa lebese,
Tsena ke khomo tsa Maburu,
Ba ntse ba etsa melato ho tsoela pela.

E reng ho bona ba li khanne."
Ba re ho 'na ke li khanne;
Ke kena ka hare ka tsoka lepae.
Ka li bitsa, tsa ntsala morao;

The cattle, including the
tan colored one,
The black calf now with short ears,
Then the one with the ponderous
udder.
I came here at Rankomo's.
At the home of Chief Mongali,
I found men sitting at the hut
in the court.
They were by a small kraal, man;
I knew the calves in the kraal,
Cattle of my family, sorted out
in the Sotho way.
Those that were up on the highlands,
It was they, going to be milked.
"Fathers, men, have you picked [them]
out for me?
Me, I am the herdboy who watched."
They said, "The cattle, man, they
have spoiled people's sorghum;
Take out money to pay for them."
They told 'Masefabatho, that woman,
owner of that village;
Where she came out fighting mad,
The boys prevented the cattle.
The cattle arrived on the common—
Hear the noise in that village!
Boys are shouting the alarm,
As they see the bulls go on fighting.
Khoalibe contends with Terebere;
They fight mightily toward the house,
The house where stays 'Mabatho,
That woman who owns that village.
What's the commotion at the kraal?
"Stop [playing] moraba-raba!
Since they aren't even milk cows,
These cattle of the Boers,
Those men are doing ever more
damage [by playing on].
Tell them to drive them [off]."
They say I [must] drive them;
I got right in waving a little blanket.
I called them [cattle], they followed
after;

A nkapara, makanyane,	They ganged up on me, the hyenas [cattle],
Tse ntšo tse mona tsa ka ha-Long.	[As did] those black ones here at Long's.
Utloa ha ke letsa moqhollelo—	Hear as I sound the long stresses—
Lesiba ke le letsa ka mokhoa ona;	The *lesiba* I play in this manner;
Ke le letsa le 'mametse:	I play it that you listen:
"Bu be nke-ke nke-ke ke ke,	"Bu be nke-ke nke-ke ke ke,
Bu be nke-ke nke-ke ke ke."	Bu be nke-ke nke-ke ke ke."
Li theosa Mantsonyane;	They came down Mantsonyane;
Li tla mona ha-Choko,	They came here to Choko's,
Choko ha-Mohlakoana.	Choko's at Mohlakoana's.
'Khomo, monna, ke li lisitse.	Cattle, man, I herded them.
Ke mohlang li tsohang li fihlile,	By the time they arose and arrived,
Batho ba ile masimong.	People had gone to the fields.
Ha li fihla heso lapeng,	When they reached my home,
Ho hlajoe linku, Ngoana Mokhalo,	Sheep were slaughtered, Child of Mokhalo,
Ho hlajoe linku lapeng heso.	Sheep were slaughtered at my home.
Ho hlajoe linku, ho nooe joala ba Sesotho.	Sheep were slaughtered, and Sesotho beer drunk.
Joale ba re 'khomo li tlohile luting koana pele ha nako—	Now they said cattle have left the mountain yonder too soon—
Athe ke'na, Ngoana Mokhalo,	Whereas it was I, Child of Mokhalo,
Molisana oa likhomo tse khunong,	Herdboy of red-brown cattle,
Mohlankana oa molisa bosiu!	Lad who watches in the night!

Makeka Likhojane's passage is a straightforward narrative episode needing little exegesis. Looking after his uncle's cattle at a highland cattle post, the singer as herdboy arises one morning to find some of them missing. Such incidents are common enough, and herdboys spend endless hours searching upland valleys for lost animals. In this case, frigid air created by snow to the south has blown into Lesotho's Maluti, forcing even the stoutest of his herd to seek refuge lower down. Fearing that stock thieves have made off with them, he finally picks up their trail and traces them to a village where he inquires of a group of men whether his lost cattle have been put aside in anticipation of his arrival. The men respond that he'll have to pay for the damage his beasts have done to crops before they are returned to him, and it transpires that these village *kibitzers* are too engrossed in a game of *morabaraba* (Basotho draughts) to corral the animals, having left this task to inexperienced boys. The result is that two bulls have gotten into a fight and are rampaging through the settlement, much to the annoyance of the local chieftainess. *Morabaraba*, after all, is a game more properly played by herdboys during listless hours than by grown men who, she feels, might at least break off long enough to prevent the village from being destroyed. Perhaps they are migrants on leave, averse to work at home after months of punishing labor in the mines. In any event, the comic effect of the image of these players mesmerized over a game board while bulls knock down houses around them is not lost on *sefela* audiences. The chieftainess demands that our young hero simply clear off with these unruly cattle, scorning them as the sort of scrawny milkless creatures that Afrikaners in the Free State pawn off on bargain-hungry Basotho, and he is only too happy to oblige. His ragged blanket flapping as he hops joyfully over the hills followed by his loyal herd ("those hyenas"), he takes out his *lesiba* and sounds a few high, pulsating breaks. The *lesiba* is an instrument once widespread in southern Africa that is now virtually unique to rural Lesotho. It consists of a single string fixed along a straight stick, bound and bridged at one end with a braided cord. At the other end, a short section of quill feather is attached to the string and fixed to the stick by bending and wedging the point of the quill into a split plug. The quill end of the stick is held to the mouth with cupped hands, and haunting, vibratory tones are produced by forcibly inhaling and exhaling over the quill (see Kirby [1934] 1965, 181–91, plates 50, 52). Studies of the *lesiba*, like those of Adams (1986), should be classified as zoomusicology, since the instrument is used primarily to develop and express a herdboy's relationship to his cattle, as well as to soothe and cajole the animals as he pastures and herds them in the uplands: "Whenever they hear him play [they easily recognize his mode of playing and distinguish him from other performers], they exhibit their appreciation of the music by clustering and huddling around him" (A. G. Mokhali, cited in Adams 1986, 6). Heading straight home rather than to his cattle post, the singer finds a feast in progress at his homestead, and some among those filling their mugs and stuffing their faces criticize him for bringing the cattle home before dusk. What do you know of it, he retorts, for "It is I, Child of Mokhalo,/ Herdboy of red-brown cattle,/ Lad who watches in the night!"

Herding is at base an economic practice, of course, and changes in domestic strategies, resource allocation, and social experience have affected it as well. The need for adolescent male labor produced a situation in which basic literacy and extended primary education were more common among Basotho girls than boys. More recently, education has come to compare favorably with cattle as a form of investment, and an increase in schooling has both helped to raise the literacy of herdboys and to reduce their number. Herdboys tend now to be the sons of very poor, perhaps female-headed families who can afford neither school fees nor livestock, so the boys are hired out to wealthier households that can. Alternatively, they are senior sons in those 7 percent of families owning significant numbers of stock and possessing their own cattle posts, and the boys are looking after their inheritance while less fortunate age-mates head for the mines. Not all stories of the herding life end as happily as that of "Ngoana Mokhalo." On the day his name was called at the Maseru labor bureau to leave for the mines, Tsokolo Lecheko performed a *sefela* that concluded with a narrative passage of more than eighty lines in which he searches for the lost cattle of his wealthy father. At each settlement, he explains worriedly, *Ke lahlehetsoe ke khomo tsa morui*, literally, "I've been lost in the cattle of a rich man," only to be told that they have been seen heading elsewhere. When he finds them at last, he is unable to pay the fine for the crop damage they have caused, and the song ends. While we might assume that their owner will redeem them, an atmosphere of loss pervades the end of the performance, as if the singer himself, despite his persistence, has somehow squandered a patrimony: Tsokolo heads for the labor bureau. This atmosphere corresponds with the sense of shame felt by some migrants that their land, so much of it lost by their forbearers to the Europeans, can no longer provide an independent living for Basotho men, who are driven off like stray cattle to the mines. Worse yet, among the many Basotho aged eighteen to twenty-five, herdboys are often those who, in today's reduced labor market, have been unable to find jobs as migrants and must eke out an existence herding for more fortunate kith or kin. Many urban boys barely herd in any case. For instance, my research assistant, Seakhi Santho, son of a high school vice principal, explained, "I herded, but I was not a real herdboy because I came home for lunch."

Herding is good preparation for another institution, the rites of initiation into manhood called *lebollo* (from *ho bolla*, "to circumcise"). Initiates, like herdboys, spend a great deal of time running barefoot and ill-clothed over the mountains undergoing various physical ordeals. As the *maele* has it, *Bonna bo thata bo tjekoa majoeng*, "Manhood is hard; it is dug out from the rocks" (Guma 1985, 30). Though at various times almost driven to extinction by missionary Christianity and chiefly politics, ideologically *lebollo* is located even closer to the heartland of Sesotho than *bolisana* (herding). This is because initiation, through all of its historical evolutions and manipulations, has remained at least symbolically a repository of Sesotho as cultural knowledge, the essence of particularity and opacity in Basotho self-definition. As a means to display cultural knowledge, *lebollo* is a popular theme among the eloquent ones in *sefela*.

Prior to the establishment of the Basotho state, initiation was a cornerstone of clan identity and of the hierarchy sustaining the authority of clan chiefs. The ritual formalities of *lebollo*, which centered upon circumcision, collective hardships and responsibilities, and the mastery of an arcane auriture, varied from clan to clan. Senior chiefs convened the initiation schools, usually when one of their own sons was ready to undergo the rites. Though an ideology of equality and corporateness pervades the activities at the *mophato* (mountain initiation lodge) where, as the ancient *koma* (song of initiation) puts it, *Ha ho ngoana motle*, "There is no beautiful [favored] child" (Guma 1967, 118), this young prince would become the leader of a regiment formed from the age-mates initiated with him, who were thus bound to him (and to each other) in service for life. Constantly struggling to secure his authority over a composite polity and to counter fissionary tendencies, Moshoeshoe I sought to gain control of *lebollo*, which provided the foundations of the existing educational and military systems. In 1860, the aging king tried to convene *lebollo* at Thaba Bosiu for two of his grandsons, the children of his second son, Chief Molapo, but in the end only persuaded them to come to fetch ritual medicine from his chiefly *lenaka* (medicine horn) (Mothibe 1988, 10).

Conversely, the astute monarch sought to hedge his bets (a fundamental principle of Tswana-Sotho politics) by deliberately inviting Christian missionaries to work in his territory in 1833. This, he foresaw, would enhance external recognition of his new state, help standardize Sesotho, and provide both diplomatic and ideological defenses against the new invaders in the region who considered that "heathen" chiefdoms could with justice be dismembered and absorbed into "civilization." At times Moshoeshoe employed the backing of his French Protestant missionaries in attempts to have *lebollo* abolished altogether. Ultimately Mohammed went to the mountain by sending his sons to be initiated with those of his noble vassals, where they would become comrades-in-arms treated with medicines from the same medicine horns (Guma 1965, 243). Further, even today every initiate is given a *koto* (knobbed stick) to hold while reciting his self-praises at graduation, representing the *molamu oa tšukulu*, the rhinoceros-horn scepter that Moshoeshoe carried as a symbol of his sovereignty and that he reputedly bequeathed to his successors (Machobane 1990, 7–8).

Nevertheless, initiation continued to symbolize the tension between clan and regional identity and national unity. The succeeding, Christian paramounts of Matsieng, the capital established by Moshoeshoe's successor, Letsie I, abandoned *lebollo*, leaving the mantle of traditionalism to the northern chiefs and to Moshoeshoe's third son, Masupha, at Thaba Bosiu.

In combination with general missionization, this led to the general decline of *lebollo* and to the unfortunate running of initiation schools, not by chiefs, but by entrepreneurs for cash, still a common practice. With the explicit alliance of Church and chieftaincy that emerged from the conversion of Paramount Griffith to Roman Catholicism in 1912, many prominent chiefs, for example, Maama, second son of Letsie I, no longer underwent initiation themselves. While there are no figures, observers like anthropologist Colin Murray (personal communication 1984) suggest that overall attendance at the initiation lodges was in decline until at least the end of the Second World War. But by 1950 *lebollo* was making a comeback (Jones 1951, 25), a trend that has strengthened since Lesotho's independence in 1966. The last quarter century has seen the steady reemergence of Basotho nationalism, the decline of the political influence of the Catholic Church, and an increasing mistrust and deprecation of people and things foreign in the face of South Africa's exploitative dominance. Along with this has come a renewed prestige and defense of things Sesotho, including *lebollo*, so that today initiates both male and female are commonly seen in large groups in villages and even major towns throughout Lesotho. Uneducated Basotho, grist for the mill of migrant labor, regard initiation as vital to the restoration of *Sesotho*, in resistance to missionary disapproval and pervasive European cultural and political dominance (ibid., 26). The institution is now at least verbally honored by most chiefs and even by members of the urban bureaucratic, professional, and commercial elite, but this does not in general impress the "peasantarian" migrants who perform *sefela*. The texts assert a nonliterate cultural authority derived from their composers' attendance at *lebollo*, and chiefs or Christians who do not support it may be bitterly criticized:

> I am ruled by a chieftain;
> I am ruled by this Chief Lebenya:
> Unfortunately for the boy, this dog has not gone to the initiation school.
> He is just a coward, who feared to carry people on the mountain.
> Further, he's a fornicator.
>
> (T. Moleme, "Separola")

Here, one Chief Lebenya is called at once a "boy" and a "dog" because he did not attend initiation (where the initiates on occasion are made to carry one another). Yet as the singer complained to me, the chief wants to be associated with initiated men, despite his refusal to receive the initiates formally at their graduation as he should. Oh yeah, and he's a womanizer. To initiates, the chieftaincy, unlike initiation, has no a priori status as a repository of tradition.

These days, as Mothobeli Guma (no relation to the linguist S. M. Guma) pointedly observes, *lebollo* "is a scene of competition and factional power struggle" (Guma 1985, 3). Like other institutions, initiation is a context for social action, sensitive to the realities of local power and patterns of interaction, not some functional building block of a "traditional village social structure." Those chiefs who support the institution still convene it, and in other cases powerful and successful men, even those of common birth, organize the rites when their own sons come of age. The cost to the parents can be considerable, as organizers, instructors, and attending herbalist-diviners must be paid, a grown bull must be ritually sacrificed, and the graduation ceremonies require a huge feast and new blankets and other accoutrements for the initiates. Not surprisingly, many a proud parent is a successful migrant: in their own absence as fathers (and mothers), and skeptical of the costly benefits of Western schooling, migrants are often eager to see their sons and daughters initiated into *Sesotho.* Despite the increase in attendance, it is likely that only a small proportion of Basotho children presently undergo these lengthy secluded rites. This does not, however, prevent *lebollo* from constituting one of the most powerful symbolic complexes of *Sesotho.* Among our reasons to be concerned with *lebollo* is its function as a social context in which the cultural prestige of auriture and respect for the mastery of composition and performance are inculcated. Out of respect for the insistence of initiated and even most uninitiated Basotho that the rituals of male *lebollo* be kept secret, I shall restrict my discussion to information either already published in English or freely offered, bearing upon initiation auriture and its relationship to *sefela.*

Those appointed to instruct the cultural neophytes in all aspects of manly accomplishment and cultural knowledge, including auriture, are the *mesuoe.* This term derives from *ho sua,* "to make [skins] supple, to tan," and indeed these taskmasters readily tan the hides of their charges, not merely the one who may have committed an infraction, but frequently all of them, for they bear collective responsibility for each other. The most important auriture that the *mesuoe* must teach the initiates are the memorized, sacred *likoma,* a term with several meanings but here referring to secret archaic texts held to contain the esoteric essence of Sesotho as a culture. As one *koma* puts it:

> The corral of the ancestors
> Has no door:
> It is simply round.
> Call traditional healers
> To come and circle [doctor] it.

While they circled it,
Having circled [it] once,
Inside it
There arose a foal
Of the hidden head.
It [foal] turned itself into a mountain,
A mountain of settlement,
Of the settlement of villages,
Those many villages
That belong to our uncles;
They do not belong to our forefathers.[1]
(Guma 1967, 124; with my revisions)

Other specific meanings of the term *koma* include "snuffbox" and "male genitals" (Guma 1985, 30), referring symbolically to the procreative power of the ancestors, which clears the head and stimulates the body like a pinch of snuff drawn sharply up the nostrils. This explains the use of the word *koae*, "tobacco, a smoke," as a euphemism for sexual intercourse; *tsubi*, "smoked thing," for a boy's penis; and the little game in which a grandmother puts one index finger on her infant grandson's member and the other to her nose, inhaling sharply with the exclamation *Koae!* said to promote future virility (see Murray 1975). Snuff, a favorite with the elderly, is often called "the tobacco of the ancestors." More broadly and more profoundly, *koma* means any guarded, exclusionary cultural knowledge, any sacred "secret truth." As Mothobeli Guma, an anthropologist and trained herbalist-diviner who has officiated at initiation schools in South Africa explains, the *likoma* songs themselves unite these meanings. Their texts touch upon "truths" (core images) about sexuality as reproduction and origin, including the origin of the initiate's social identity in his family, district, chiefs, culture, and nation. The intent is to turn a prehuman into a man, a fully formed social and procreative being, one able to create a family and to accept extreme hardships in order to defend and maintain it. All *likoma* are said to have been composed by a legendary great-granduncle of Moshoeshoe, Ratlali, and in respect of this contribution the initiation school is often spoken of as Ha-Ratlali, "Ratlali's Place." The terse six-syllable lines of *likoma*, impacted with repetitive linking and allusions lost

1. These final lines apparently refer to the Bafokeng clan, the aboriginal inhabitants of the Caledon valley into which Moshoeshoe led his conquering Bakoena. Moshoeshoe deliberately took his senior wife, Kholu, from the Bafokeng, urging other Bakoena chiefs to do likewise, so that the Bafokeng would become mother's brothers, "uncles" to Bakoena royalty, creating a strong affinal bond between the Bakoena and their more numerous Bafokeng subjects.

and found, would seem to bear little relation to the florid, prolix popularisms of the travelers' songs. Yet like herdboys and migrants, initiates are taught traveling as a discipline and are "forced to march long distances at a time throughout their country, to familiarize them with its topography" (Machobane 1990, 16). A few *likoma* seem as well to prefigure the enforced wanderings of the migrant life:

Wanderer
Of the homeless,
Wander on and let us go,
Let us go there to bondage,
To bondage where we go
Not to stay;
But to tarry for a while
Praising little meercats,
Meercats, the rat and others,
Rats who have placed themselves in high places.
(Guma 1967:125)

Ancient songs called *macha* were once, and in some places may still be, performed on the first day of initiation, when the initiates depart for the mountain *mophato*, but I was unable to ascertain in what respect they might differ from *likoma*. From within a postconversion consciousness, S. M. Guma responds to Robert Moffat's intuition to replace *likoma* with the hymns (*lifela*) of Zion by seeking to discover pre-Christian intimations of the Revelation in these texts. Some Christian Basotho intellectuals, disturbed that Sesotho should be identified with "heathen superstition" and "primitive" beliefs and institutions, have sought to incorporate the Christian archetypes into Sesotho tradition, interpreting our folk tale hero Senkatana, for example, as a prefiguration of Christ.

This discussion brings us back to the issues of knowledge and secrecy, identity and exclusion, but now in the more profound context of the reflexive construction and meaning of *Sesotho* as a culture.[2] As I have explained, the domain *Sesotho* includes not only the language but the entire self-identified culture of the Basotho nation both as theory and as practice. Broadly, *Sesotho* is Basotho "local knowledge," but in specific usages, *Sesotho* is localized types and qualities of things and local styles of enactment. So home-brewed sorghum beer is *'joala bo Sesotho*, as distinct from *'joala bo Sekhoa*, European-style industrially brewed and packaged beer and liquor.

2. The following discussion draws heavily upon two of my recent articles, "The Meaning of Sesotho" (Coplan 1992) and "Fictions that Save: Migrants' Performance and Basotho National Culture," (Coplan 1991).

Tubers originally imported by the French missionary Eugene Casalis but now gathered wild in the fields like greens are called *litapole tsa Sesotho*, Sesotho potatoes, though the word itself comes from Afrikaans *aartappel* (earth apple). Here *Sesotho* is a provenance rather than an item of cultural inventory, linking Sesotho as noun and adjective to its more fundamental, adverbial essence, *ka Sesotho*, a Sesotho way or manner of doing things. The most common means of referring reflexively to *Sesotho* as "tradition" is *mekhoa le meetlo ea Sesotho*, "ways and ideas," but most simply by using Sesotho as a qualifier for any relevant noun, as in *'mino oa Sesotho*, "traditional music." In southern Africa's politics of culture, however, *Sesotho* has had more forceful and wide-ranging uses and implications. In discursive, self-conscious definition, *Sesotho* is anything that Basotho regard as purely of their own devising, unadulterated by "external" influences. Of course there are no identifiable historical boundaries or contents of *Sesotho* in this sense, but this is not the point. In its emergence, *Sesotho* achieved its self-reference specifically in terms of Moshoeshoe's political project, as distinct from and opposed to the politicians, projects, and identities that threatened it. As a concept, *Sesotho* has long served as a cognitive and behavioral defense against the loss of Basotho national identity and the misappropriation of the resources to which this identity gives title. From varying and sometimes conflicting perspectives, *Sesotho* is spoken of by all classes of Basotho as vital to both social and "national" survival.

Certain ceremonies of the initiation, such as graduation, take place in public, but most are guarded with the most extreme secrecy. Hiking in remote areas, one encounters initiates and their lodge at one's peril. Such secrecy is embodied and symbolized in the sacred, esoteric *likoma* songs. An initiate who reveals or performs any song, and by extension, any of the procedures or secrets of *lebollo* to noninitiates is subject to severe physical punishment. Thus *koma e sa binoe hae*, "a *koma* is not sung at home," and its converse, *ho bina koma hae*, "to sing a *koma* at home," the *maele* applied to any talk considered indiscreet, that inappropriately or needlessly reveals personal or family business in public. As colonized social and economic relations have increasingly shaped the structure of Basotho village life, everything regarded as properly, autonomously *Sesotho* (*Sesotho 'nete 'nete*) has come to be walled behind an ideology of secrecy, and this is explicitly the case with male (but not female) *lebollo*. Nowadays virtually everything associated with *lebollo* is regarded as secret, and the identification of these ceremonies as the essence of *Sesotho* as ritual practice and cultural knowledge has intensified to the point where in the minds of many, *Sesotho* itself is all *likoma*, knowledge both to be kept from outsiders and free of outside influences.

Christian clergy have unceasingly attempted to undermine *lebollo* as the sustaining epitome of the "superstitions" (meaning the entirety of *Sesotho* apart from the language itself) to which Basotho are attached. To this end Father Leydevant (1978) published an account of initiation in Sesotho that does contain some accurate descriptions, but in an unbalanced, prejudicial discourse. With possibly the same end in view, an initiated Mosotho calling himself "L. T." published in 1963 what purported to be a full account, entitled *Lebollo*. The Lesotho government responded to the resulting scandal by seizing every copy it could get its hands on. Another anonymous Mosotho meanwhile wrote a reply to the defamations allegedly contained in the apostate's now unavailable pamphlet, entitled *Baa R'eng Batho ha Buka ea "Lebollo"* (What the People Say about the Book "Lebollo"). Still later, the indefatigable Professor S. M. Guma (neither an initiate nor a Lesotho citizen) retailed most of the contents of *Lebollo* in his article, "Some Aspects of Circumcision in Basutoland," in the Witwatersrand University journal *African Studies* (1965), and issued a small collection of sacred texts called *Likoma* (1966). L. T.'s account has been excoriated by Bosko (1983, 109–10), among others, as simply another Christian attack on Sesotho, and he seems principally upset by its claim (popularly accepted) that initiates are given medicine from a chief's medicine horn containing elements of cooked human flesh. That is why, *ho thoe*, "it is said," that those beginning their initiation are dubbed *malingoana*, "little cannibals." This, and the assertion that they also consume preparations containing pieces of their own foreskins perpetuates what in Bosko's opinion is the misconception that the Basotho engage in *liretlo*, "medicine murder." This practice putatively involves the mutilation of a kinsman or neighbor so that the perpetrators' can advance personal ambitions strengthened by medicines made from tissue removed prior to the victim's agonized death. Accusations of medicine murder have been no trifling matter, since in 1949 three of the highest chiefs in the land (one a woman) were convicted of *liretlo* by the British administration and hanged. The published results of a subsequent investigation by G. I. Jones of the Colonial Office (Jones 1951) strongly argue that such murders did in fact occur. Bosko is not the only foreign scholar who regards Jones's report as a smear and argues that medicine murder is simply a political tool or a red herring used to conceal the motivations of more materially motivated homicides, and that the 1949 executions were a frame-up meant to repress opposition to colonial regulation of the chieftaincy.[3] As with witchcraft, there are also Basotho who scoff at the idea of *liretlo*, despite widespread belief that it is practiced, not only by ambitious junior chiefs but even by Indian shopkeepers and white officials at the mines. Bosko (1983, 108–18) states categorically that initiates are not doctored from a chief's medicine horn, that such horns do not contain burnt human flesh, that *malingoana* means something else, and that medicine murder is a myth. I have no wish to involve myself in this controversy except to assert the one thing I am sure of, which is that neither Bosko nor any other outsider is in any position to know. These things are *likoma*, secrets, and we have no reason to believe that the post hoc testimony of Bosko's informants was any more veracious than that offered to Jones. I say this, I suppose, out of a reluctance to dismiss the writings of Leydevant, who was, to be fair, a serious ethnographer much respected in Lesotho, and of the distinguished Professor Guma, no matter how tainted by personal bias. It is Father Leydevant, after all, who draws suggestive connections between five subjects dear to the hearts of *sefela* composers: cannibalism, ancestors, medicine, performance, and manhood. In discussing *leshoma* (*Boopane toxicaria/disticha*), a poisonous plant whose bulb is mixed with other medicines and with pieces of "the flesh of enemies killed in war" in a concoction given to initiates, Leydevant explains:

> The initiates are taught that such a remedy will imbue them with the qualities of their ancestors and will tend to make men of them. When the signs of intoxication produced by the mixture are apparent, they are accepted as a token that the spirit of manhood has entered the youth's body. . . .
>
> . . . This remedy is also considered as a cup or draught of inspiration for the initiates at the circumcision lodge. During the initiation period, every boy has to compose a piece of poetry or praises, which he will recite publicly when he is liberated, and the medicine which is given them is supposed to communicate the gifts of poetry and eloquence. (1932, 65–66)

The choral accompaniment to initiates' praises and the most well-known, publicly performed genre that the boys must learn are the short songs called *mangae* (from *ho ngaea*, "to howl like an infant"), many of which the teachers or their most inspired and talented charges compose fresh for the occasion. These will be remembered and performed by local age-mates at get-togethers throughout life. When our film crew arrived at a *shebeen* (unlicensed tavern) in one of the rougher sections of old Maseru,

3. G. I. Jones's private papers, stored at Cambridge, strongly suggest that the British did wrongly convict at least one of the executed chiefs, and that they did so to protect their client Paramount Chieftainess 'Mantsebo (regent 1940–60), who was in fact guilty of medicine murder.

a group of unemployed age-mates sang us the following *lengae*. It appears in our film *Songs of the Adventurers:*

'Na, ke bonya le basali ba batho ba bang.	Me, I can flirt with the wives of other men.
'Na, khutlela ho 'na!	Me, come to me again!
He-hoae-hom!	He-hoae-hom!
'Na, ke bonya le basali ba batho ba bang.	Me, I can flirt with the wives of other men.
'Na, khutlela ho 'na	Me, come to me again!
He-hoae-hom!	He-hoae-hom!
Le hoja ba bonya le 'na libeseng mona,	When they flirt with me at the bus station here,
'Na nka kena, he-hoae-hom!	I can get in, he-hoae-hom!
Le hoja ba bonya, le basali ba batho ba bang,	When they flirt, the wives of other men,
Nka kena, khutlela.	I can get in, come back for more.
'Na,ke bonya le basali ba batho ba bang.	Me, I can flirt with the wives of other men.
Nka kena, khutlela, he-hoae-hom!	I can get in, come back for more, he-hoae-hom!
Ke bonya le li nkile, he-hoae-hom!	I have flirted with those indeed, he-hoae-hom!
Le bonya le linku le 'Matsepo,	Even flirting with sheep and Tsepo's mother,
[Melilietsane!]	[Women in crowd ululate]
'Na, nka kena le bonya le basali ba 'batho ba bang, he-hoae-hom!	Me, I can flirt with the wives of other men, he-hoae-hom!

When an initiate becomes a migrant and tries his hand at performing *sefela*, it seems likely that material from his initiation praises might be used to fill in a *sefela*. The only clear indication of such intertextuality would be the discussion of initiation itself within a *sefela*, extremely rare in my collection. In a text collected about a decade ago by Mrs. Makali Mokitimi of the National University of Lesotho (Mokitimi (1982, 263, 382–83), Holomo Tsauli, aged twenty-eight, only gets through fifty lines of his *sefela* before calling it quits with the standard ending formula (never used in mid-performance), *Nka be ke re "Amen, ke phethile?* "Shall I say "Amen," I have finished?" Perhaps embarrassed by this poor effort and faced with Mrs. Mokitimi and her tape recorder, not to mention whoever else was listening, he launched into a new text that seem unmistakably to be his initiation praises, though I have never spoken to either the performer or Mrs. Mokitimi about it.

I, the head leader peer of the Lijabatho ["Men-Eaters," a *morija* regiment].
He praises himself, the uncircumcised new-ground-breaker of Ramapepe's.
He praises himself, the uncircumcised black-new-ground-breaker of Ntsebeng.
I, as a child when I was first given instructions,
I was given instructions at Khotla hut.
I could tell from the faces of my village men of Tsepe;
I could read news from Pitso Rasepanyama's face,
As well as Ramatsoai of Masiu's.
They were together with Sentso of Matsoso's village.
They gave me raw bull flesh;
They pierced it with a spear,
Saying, child, eat this meat and finish it.
A child as I was, I ate it all up;
I did not share it with anyone.
But this meat makes my heart uneasy;
This meat makes me quick whenever I hear an alarm. . . .
. . . One day on the occasion when we boys had to sleep outdoors,
When we boys had to sleep in the open air,
That was as pleasant as a pleasant game.
There was a woman ululating on the hill side.
Later I heard her weeping,
Complaining as to what had befallen her son;
Her son had suffered.
As for me, the peer of Raboqha's son, I took off my blanket,
And the boys stared at my hollow flank.
Khele! Gentlemen, I always say whoever says I am a coward is a liar.
Whoever says I am a coward is a liar.
Whoever says I am a coward is talking nonsense.
I am not a coward.
I have not shut the door of his house.
I, the child, when I am dead,
I shall require that all Ramapepe's men be called before me,
Especially Pitso Rasepanya, be called for me,
That Sentso of Matsoso be called before me.
That all the uninitiated and the uncircumcised may see me in the late afternoon,
As the sun gradually goes down to set.
Amen.

In this text or passage, Holomo heaps praise on himself as an intrepid initiate and scorn on those who lacked the courage to endure *lebollo*'s ritualized ordeals. We have heard of the ordeal of the spittal-drenched morsel before, in the commoner's praises of Kola Khoali in chapter 3. Kola, well past initiation, is forced to repeat the ritual as punishment for his abuse of alcohol (like walking a straight line, it's more difficult if you're drunk). Judging from the final line, the treatment works:

Ke ea thekesela.	I am staggering [drunk].
Ke ne ke laoa ke banna ba baholo feela:	I was reprimanded only by prominent men:
Ba nea nama ka theko ea lerumo.	They gave me meat on the end of the spear.
Ba re ke, e lome ke tšoele fatše.	They told me, bite it and spit it on the ground.
Nama ea likhohlela hase ho mpolaea:	The meat slimy with spittle doesn't kill me:
Ke ena; e ntutse pelong.	Here it is; it is settled on my heart.

Holomo, though, swallows the morsel and ingests the proper fighting spirit. Further on, he shrugs off the hardships of sleeping in the open but sympathizes with a comrade's mother, who at first sang in praise of her son, then wept at his sufferings, shared by the stoic Holomo, who reveals his "hollow flank." *Ngoan'a moshemane ke kabeloa-manong*, "A boy-child is vulture feed," warns the *maele* (Matsela 1979, 186). So Holomo makes liars of those who call him a coward, and he vows on his death to leave an exemplary corpse. The entire passage is pervaded by the "future perfect" attitude of initiates' praises, rather than the completed present and past perfect Sesotho tenses of *sefela*.

I asked Hlalele Mabekanyane (Kanono Nthako), a renowned *ngaka ea lifela*, a teacher of composition to aspiring *sefela* performers, as well as a *mosuoe* at local initiation schools, whether he ever taught any of the boys *sefela* at the *mophato*. There is time, he replied, so those who show talent in composing their praises, if they have interest, may ask him to teach them *sefela*. Some *sefela* performers noted that while they had not learned about the genre at initiation, the compositional skills taught there were of value when they began to compose *sefela* as migrants. Hlalele agreed with Moletsane's (1982, 2) suggestion that *sefela* originally emerged from the solos of *mangae* in the context of migrancy. In my field collection of initiates' praises (as we saw in Jankie's texts), severe criticism, even insult of Christian youth and other uncircumcised Basotho boys and girls is expressed. *Sefela* performers, however, appear in the main to practice or at least respect sincere Christian spirituality, reserving satire or criticism for hypocritical laymen and venal clerics, and for interdenominational rivalry.

Comparing the *lifela* and initiate's praises of T. Moleme (Separola), one performer from whom I was able to collect both categories of texts, one finds more difference in content that in poetic language or style. Many of the same subjects are touched upon, including social criticism, the dangers of witchcraft, and personal prowess. The praises, however, contain direct self-praise of the initiate as a stout-hearted lad who has overcome obstacles and doubters. The subject of initiation itself (but not the secrets of the *mophato* lodge) and the objects, customs, and adventures related to it take up a good portion of the text. Separola's *sefela* mentions initiation only by way of criticizing the chief for not undergoing it, in the passage quoted above, and includes self-praise as a poet, not as an initiate. Most of the song is devoted to the mines, the witchcraft with which he believes his in-laws have ruined his migrant career, and the hardships, frustrations, venalities, and folklore of village life.

In brief, initiation contributes to *sefela* in training the future performer in *Sesotho* as language and culture, in the emotionally rewarding expression of eloquent knowledge. Moeketsi Christopher Tieli (Mokotla) a literate performer, offered this comment during a discussion of the qualities that make a good *sefela:*

> You must use the whole language; proverbs, local phrases, the language that covers the names or places where events happen. That language, we call it *limomonyane* [literally: "nectars"; from *ho momonya*, "to suck up"], all the very nice things in language, that you must learn from the old people, praises and so on from the *lebollo*, where you learn them. This is different from the *koma*, which are secret songs or language. . . . When your *sefela* is good and contains the real Sesotho you feel very nice, inside yourself; when you play with the language, you are getting pleasure by sharing your feelings.

Language play for its own sake, not a noticeable feature of aristocratic praises, is associated with the low register of poetic discourse, not only in *sefela* but in other contemporary song forms, providing performance space for the common people's creative culture of laughter. We should not be surprised, then, to discover that the *mangae* songs composed at *lebollo* today reveal the influence of South African popular culture. The following *lengae* was recorded at an initiation graduation at the village of Sephokong, Mafeteng District, in March 1989, and was performed in two choral parts by younger and older initiates. Part one is the refrain of a popular "barroom" (*famo*) song by recording star Apollo Ntabanyane:

He! He! Oa le bona, khomosha lena?	Hey! Hey! Do you see him, that foreign-speaking vagabond [criminal]?
"Somoria napau, napau napau." [habeli]	*"Somoria napau, napau napau."* [twice]

The second line is not Sesotho, but replicates the slang that street gangsters use so they cannot be overheard by others. The whole notion of slang here expresses the double meaning of *lekhomosha,* a word referring to one who has abandoned his people and home and become comfortable with foreign ways of speaking, including the outlandish Sesotho slang of the South African townships, but with the additional connotation of shady character, someone with something to hide. The original lines come from one of the cops-and-robbers dramas frequently broadcast over Radio Sesotho, the South African government service from Johannesburg. Part two of the *lengae,* the response, continues:

Na mabele a butsuoe?	Has the sorghum ripened?
A bolilana se ka maeba.	It is distasteful to the rock doves.
Selemo se lekana le hlabula;	Spring is followed by summer;
Loetse e lekana le Mphalane.	September is followed by October.
Le Mafeteng ka fetella,	And Mafeteng compounds its vices,
Le ha Mojela ba ntjella.	And at [Chief] Mojela's they live off others' harvest.
Le Ntate, Molimo oa khotso,	And Father, God of peace,
Le rona, likhutsana, rapeleha.	And we, orphans, are moved to prayer.
Le rona, litsamaea-naha,	And we, inveterate travelers,
Le manyeloi a matsoho.	And angels of hands [bless us].

I have included the Sesotho text here so that readers of this clever, sardonic *lengae* may note the typical homophonic word play on *Mafeteng/fetella* and *Mojela/ntjella.* The answer to the opening query is that it must be May, for this is the month when the sorghum grains are so hard that birds cannot eat them, thus the Sesotho name for May: *Motsehanong,* "Laughing-at-Birds." As one season or month follows another, the wrongs committed by Mafeteng people mount up, the people of Chief Mojela (to the south of Mafeteng town and the area where the song was recorded) still live off the labors of others, in particular the "orphans" and "travelers," who must go to the mines and look only to God for assistance.

Among the most interesting composers of Sesotho popular songs today is David Sello Motaung, leader of the band Tau ea Linare. In 1986 Motaung, at the age of thirty-eight, decided for the first time to attend *lebollo* and become an initiate. The reasons for this, he stated, were to immerse himself in *Sesotho* and to learn more deeply the variety of performance genres taught at the circumcision lodge. This would provide him with skills, techniques, and inspiration for composition, and enable him to relate the latter more directly to his own strong feelings of identity as a Mosotho. On his 1988 album, *Litaba Motaung* (CCP L4 RAIN [EO]

4062294), there are two songs that he says are direct results of his experience at *lebollo*. On one, "Makhooa" (Whites) the chorus is performed by four male singers in the style of a *lengae* initiation song, though backed by the usual accordion, drum, and bass. The solo takes the place of an initiate's praises:

CHORUS:

Whites, whites, hey! whites—
Hey, jo! Whites are of no use. [twice]
They don't appreciate a man who knows his work:
Whites are of no use. [twice]
Hela! Whites, whites, whites—
Hey! Those are whites; they have no use. [twice]
Pretoria is the final court, hey!
Those are whites; they have no use. [several repeats]

SOLO:

Pretoria is the final court. [twice]
You, man, Seshoba,
Hee! You, my child, drive; we are leaving.
So we go to the place of Europeanism [the mines].
  Hey you—ee!
Hee! We should take our tax receipts.
President Brand, President Steyn [Mines],
  mine compounds are the same.
The child who slips away to join [the mines]
  does not complete [the contract],
Se jo'na! [alas!] Hardships!
Many men, we fear *moqhasheoa* [heat-tolerance test],
Jo! Man-child across [the river] in
  Johannesburg [the mines],
He oele! oelele! oelele! oelelele, man!
  [after the opening formula of female *famo* songs]
Pretoria, the far away lands,
Jo! My child, jo! My child, bo!

This blend of initiation song and praises and popular neotraditional accordion and drum songs from the mines and migrant beer bars (*sepoto*, from English "spot") appears to mix categories and put the meaning of *Sesotho* in question. But it is clear that the postinitiation experience of migration to the hostile world of the mines, where indolent white mine team captains lord it over real workers (Basotho), backed up by the distant but inescapable authority of Pretoria, has crept into Sesotho.

Once an initiate, it is time to become a traveler, crossing borders and rivers to a world turned upside down. Having spent his first eighteen years or so 6,000 feet up, herding, stick fighting, and becoming a man on an upland range under wide heavens, the Basotho lad heads down to the plains, enters the harsh new liminality of the labor recruitment system, and descends 6,000 more feet to the sweltering hell of the mines. It is for this journey, and for the return, that the songs of the inveterate travelers are created.

Chapter Five

"These Mine Compounds, I Have Long Worked Them"

Auriture and Migrants' Labors

I left home at night
When the cocks were crowing;
Further, crowing the first cocks,
The second crew while on the way,
The third ones as I was passing the Phuthiatsana [River];
I entered Maseru, in town yonder
When the sun touched the mountains,
B. A. Maseru at Mejametalana.
Me, at seven in the morning I was hired,
Then at eight cows were milked.
At nine schools were in [session],
At ten I was taken to the doctor:
It was "'Mokose," my companions.
He put a metal [stethoscope] on the chest here,
I breathed twice he was satisfied:
"Alright! Child of Malimatle,
There is nothing my brother,
Go and drive them at the mines yonder."
Masimphane is a man, he works
Lethetsa Malimatle

Challenged by the demands of his prospective in-laws for bridewealth, the *sefela* poet, a proud Mokoena clansman, depicts his unavoidable departure for the mines. The singer pictures himself leaving his village before dawn, reaching Maseru at sunrise, and hired by seven A.M., something of a bureaucratic miracle.[1] By ten he is undergoing the preliminary medical exam,

1. The poet refers to B. A. Maseru: standing for "Basutoland" and its capital, the letters "B.A." formerly appeared on every automobile registered in Maseru prior to independence, when the letters were changed to "L.A." Currently, Maseru liscence plates display the Basotho hat, the *mokorotlo,* followed by A and a number.

where the doctor, one well known to him and his comrades, is imagined praising the singer's fitness and industry. So is another kind of rite of passage accomplished, and the young herdboy becomes a migrant. Not all *lifela* accounts of departure for "the wilderness of South Africa" are as sanguine. Many recount slipping away in the predawn hours without any farewell, lest envious neighbors or kin use the occasion to bewitch the migrant and curse his journey, which like success at the mines, is an uncertain prospect in any case:

Mohlankana mohlang ke tsohang ke palama	Lad, the time I'm going and ride away,
Mosali ea loeang ha se ho sokola.	A woman of witchcraft was already hard at work.
Ke bone a tsohella, ho ea mabitleng.	I saw her rise early, going to the graveyard.
O thethana ea mafitoane o ntse a e fasa;	A knotted string skirt she fastens on;
O phaka sa mofu o ntse a foka;	She the arm of a corpse is waving;
O mothamo oa mali o ntsa a khoefa sebakeng.	A mouthful of blood she spits into the air.
O re, "Banna ba eang ka Libere,	She says, "Men going to DeBeers,
Ba ka tla ba shoeletse tlelemeng."	They can come home dead from the mines."
Ho 'na, Ngoana Rakhali,	To me, Rakhali's Child,
Ha kea shoa; leha joale ke ntse ke phela,	I am not dead; even now I still live,
Leha ke phela mahlomoleng.	Though I live in difficulties. . . .
	(Majara Majara)

Home is familiar and secure; to stay there is ruinous and cowardly. Work in the mines destroys body and soul, but to go there is not only necessary, but manly, heroic. Here, too, Majara introduces the theme of traveling, a concept at the heart of the experience of migrancy as a "whole life process," to paraphrase Raymond Williams's definition of culture itself. In Sesotho, traveling is linked to cultural and empirical knowledge, to the wisdom of worldly experience, in ways that transcend and ultimately transform the mundane but encompassing reality of the migrant labor system. As the *maele* puts it: *Ho tseba naha ke ho hata mohlaba,* "To know the world one must walk the country." Mohlomi, original culture hero and philosopher king, was a legendary traveler. Diviner-herbalist healers (*lingaka*), including Mohlomi, are said to have always traveled about seeking new medicines, healing texts, and cures; hence the *maele: Ngaka e shoa e etile,* "A doctor dies abroad" (Guma 1967, 82). Diviners even more than poets are persons of cultural knowledge, partly explaining why *sefela* singers so often metaphorize themselves as *lingaka* whether they have such training or not.

Moshoeshoe I is not, interestingly, actually praised as a traveler, though he certainly could be considered one. In addition to his admittedly reluctant journeys to Bloemfontein and Aliwal North to negotiate unfavorable treaties with Free State and British authorities, Moshoeshoe went on voluntary inspections of the far reaches of his realms. In particular, there was an arduous expedition to Mont-au-Sources in the northern Drakensberg with the missionary Arbousset in 1840, undertaken when the monarch was already in his mid-fifties (Arbousset 1991).

The theme of travel is of course made emblematic in the generic name for migrants' songs, *sefela sa litsamaea-naha le liparola-thota*. While the best English gloss for this phrase might be "songs of the country ramblers," one informant tried helpfully to explain it as the songs of "those who have seen the places and the spaces in between the places." Structure is extemporaneous and concatenated in *sefela*, and since no sequential or chronological relationship between episodes is required, traveling becomes the main experiential and thematic principle of textual progression. The poet crosses and recrosses boundaries in space, time, and narrative structure as the migrant transcends and restructures the boundaries of Basotho social organization (Babcock-Abrahams 1975, 166–67). Customarily, *lifela* begin with some lines of self-identification and praise, mixed with exhortations to the listeners to listen, followed by a leave-taking for the mines. Implicit in the symbolism of travel is the acquisition of knowledge through experience, whether on the horsetracks of Lesotho or the highroads of South Africa's social wilderness.

A migrant's traveling does not, literally or figuratively, begin with crossing the Mohokare River. Much of the traveling in *sefela* is done on foot in Lesotho, where the solitary migrant, strangely without comrades, establishes identity and status through knowledge of his country and its inhabitants while remaining critically apart, a homeboy with a homeless mind. Most migrants take buses and taxi vans (in some cases commuter flights or even their own cars) from their villages to the labor depots and mining centers, but in *sefela* these modes of transport hardly exist. Instead, the migrant pictures himself in a Brechtian theatrical metaphor, lean and penniless, walking through the mountains and river valleys on his way to or from the western border towns. As he long-legs it through the country, the poet identifies in a few telling details each village: its natural features, its social character, its poets and medicinal specialists, the name and personal qualities of its chief, memorable occurrences, scenes of his crimes and the crimes of others. Discovering a similar penchant among migrant workers in Bolivia, Taussig noted succinctly that "natural iconography is popular historiography" (1980, 186). Poetic travel in Lesotho is a picture of the political as well as physical landscape, a social geography providing opportunities for commentary and satire as well as praise on a wealth of characteristic behaviors. A man of knowledge ought to know his own country, and none can truly be called *kheleke*, "eloquent," without displaying a word-painter's eye and a homeboy's love for its features and creatures. Thus Majara Majara, a young poet from Ha-Abia near Maseru:

Linonyana tsena ka 'mala li ntle:	These birds are beautiful in color:
Litsomila le letle lehlabana;	Red-winged starling is beautiful brown and black;
Letsoanafike le lephatsoana lipheeo;	Mountain Chat has black and white wings;
Seroebele 'mathe a bolile.	Sparrow [of] the high, sour whistle;
Motintinyane se le konki;	Neddicky is not a large bird;
Lekolikotoana khaka 'malane.	Quail finch is bar-breasted [black and white].
Kokolofitoe, ea malula o futahane:	Heron, sitting doubled up:
"O futantseng, mokota naheng?"	"Why are you folded up, country breeder?"
"Ke lahlehetsoe ke lenaka la meleko—	"I have lost my medicine horn of sorcery—
Ea le thotseng, a mpe a ntholise."	Whoever has picked it up, please give it [to me]."

Or an evocative couplet from a *sefela* by the renowned veteran, the late Mphafu Mofolo of Ha-Shale in Chief Maama's district (Roma):

Maru ke ana a pepile mafube;	These clouds cradle on their shoulders the dawn;
Khoeli ke eane e pepile naleli.	This moon cradles on its shoulders the stars.

Human nature is an even more prevalent subject of commentary, providing the opportunity for the poet to entertain his audience with some juicy asides while establishing his own moral authority:

Mphafu, ke qala ho etsa thapelo	Mphafu, I begin to make a prayer
Oho Jehova oa Maholimo	To Jehova of the Heavens:
Batho bona, re ntse re le ba hao.	These people, we are still yours.
Sebe se ka re hlola re se lekile;	Sin can overcome once we've tried it;

Esita le ngoana lejakane a emara,	Even a child of a Christian becomes pregnant,
Le 'ma'e a tsamaea a phuthile.	Regardless of whether her mother attends revivals.
	(Mphafu Mofolo, "Nogan'abo Mokhoathi")
Ke kopane le banana ba le bararo ba ronngoe ka masimong;	I met three girls who'd been sent to the spring;
Ba il'o tsosa lithaha.	They'd gone to scare the bishop birds.
"Nkhono, koana re tsoang,	"Grandmother, yonder where we're from,
Nonyana lia jele lia qetile."	Birds have eaten and finished [all the grain]."
Hoa llua ke mohats'a Emile:	Thus cried Emile's wife:
"Ra-Emile, sesiu seo u hle u se tlohele.	"Father Emile, please leave that grainbasket.
Bana ba sentse pereisi ea lenyalo.	Children have ruined the price of marriage.
Ba hopotse kobo tsa mafitori;	They think [only] of Victoria blankets;
Ba hopotse Khauteng Kopanong.	They think of the Union of South Africa.
Ba hopotse 'Thoa-Thoa,' Billone. . . ."	They think of 'Thoa-Thoa,' Benoni. . . ."
. . . Bo-ntate, ba shoele ba iketlile.	. . . Our [fore] fathers, they died in peace.
Maqheku a khale-khale, ba ne ba roala lieta tsa lifatla;	The elders of long ago, they wore shoes homemade of oxhide;
Ba tena tšeha tsa likonyana.	They wore lambskin loincloths.
Ha ba boka, ba re ke sekhotsing.	When they fornicated, they said they were in-laws.
Bacha banna, le hlanoletse;	Young men, you have gone astray;
Ha le rata basali ba batho,	When you love people's wives,
O 'mitsa hampe joaleng mona;	You call for her rudely here at the shebeen;
Ntlong ea joala tameneng mona,	At the beer house canteen here,
O s'a mo hula-hula bathong.	You pull her this way and that among people.
N'qe ngoe, o mo robele leihlo,	Once again, you wink at her [boldly],
Ha o tsebe le haeba monna oa hae oa 'mona.	When you don't even know if her husband's around.
	(Makeka Likhojane, "Ngoana Mokhalo")

Mphafu's passage, on the face of it a straightforward prayer for Christian exculpation, contains a defensive aside reminding his fellow Christians that they are as susceptible to temptation and sin as the "heathen" Basotho they affect to pity and despise. Makeka first depicts an elder lamenting (as parents of all nations have done since time everlasting) the dissolute ways of youth—girls who, rather than attend to the tedious and exhausting duty of scaring birds away from the ripening grain, think only of expensive blankets they might get across the border in South Africa. Because of their laziness and wanton behavior, no bridewealth can be gotten for them. In this case, there is strong historical substantiation, since as Philip Bonner (1988) has documented, Benoni township near Johannesburg (called "Thoa-Thoa" by Basotho in imitation of the sound of gunshots heard there during the white miners' strike of 1922) was until the early 1960s notorious for the illicit brewing (and sex) trade carried on by Basotho women fleeing rural poverty in Basutoland. Later Makeka calls upon tradition in the persons of the ancestors to support his condemnation of contemporary behavior in Lesotho's border towns. If you took a woman in the old days, he asserts, you treated her relatives like the affines they had indeed become. Today men meet married women at the back-street bars and, abandoning the ancients' discretion in matters of adultery, drag them about, not caring who notices, thoughtlessly risking fights with outraged husbands. Significantly, moral commentary is almost always focused on behavior in Lesotho, rather than on experiences in South Africa. The latter provide *sefela* listeners with plenty of lubricious fun, but observance of Sesotho custom or morality can hardly be expected in the ethnic and social chaos of the black townships.

The deeper tragedy at the root of social distortion, of course, is the rural poverty of Lesotho and the necessity of labor migration. Mphafu, too poor even to buy food for the journey, calls his comrades to hunt mongoose as provisions, despite the freezing winds:

Ke hona re sa tla tsamaea naha;	It is now that we shall really travel the country;
Banna ba heso, re hle re tasole.	Men of my home we're in for a forced march.
Lipabala, re tsamaea sehlotsoana;	Distinguished sirs, we travel in a troop;
Bofutsana bo re qhalile lapeng.	Poverty has dispersed us from our homes.
Ke bitsa lintja ke ilo tsoma;	I call dogs to go hunting;
Litsumi li tsoere ke tlala polasing.	The hunters are caught by hunger in the farms.
Polane ea banna ba batsamai:	The plan of traveling men:
Betlang melamu; re etse makhate.	Sharpen your sticks; we'll make spears.
Chekang matoli; re batleng mofao.	Dig out the little mongoose; we need provisions.

Moea oa makhapu oa re bolaea;	Wind from the bushes is piercing us;
O foka lithabeng tse telele.	It is blowing in the high mountains.

Not everyone is a migrant, however, and even in rural areas the traveler will pass the homesteads of wealthy men as he contemplates the deprivation of himself and his family. The image of the migrant as a homeless proletarian is symbolized in singers' frequent use of the terms *molele* (vagabond), *papatlele* (aimless wanderer), and *khutsana* (orphan) to refer to themselves in *lifela:*

Ngoana Rakhali, e ke ke khutsana ha kena beso.	Child of Rakhali, it's as if I were an orphan without family.
Ke re, bo-ntate, likempolara,	I say fathers, gamblers [poets],
Ke hloma, o hlomole.	I am a cut sprout, ever resprouting.
Mofutsana ha a na setsa naheng. . . .	A poor man has no place in the country. . . .
Bafutsana, re maoto matelele;	Poor men, we are long-legged;
Oa tseba re tla shoela hole.	You know we shall die far away.
Oa tseba matlong a likhorane ha ho kenoe.	You know rich men's houses are not entered.
Oa tseba, bafutsana, bo-ntate, batsoali ba me,	You know, poor men, fathers, my parents,
Ke bone ka ngoan'eso Khotso:	I saw my brother Khotso:
Motho, ke bona ke 'mala likhopo.	Man, I saw I could count his ribs.
Lefu ha le khethe; tlala oa khetha.	Death does not choose; famine chooses.

Yet those who accept the necessity of labor migrancy with courage maintain self-respect and moral superiority in the face of hardships and contempt:

Ke e ea le lithota, koete;	I was going over the fields, [I,] a handsome fellow;
Ke be ke feta ha Phohleli motseng.	I then passed through Phohleli's village.
Banana ba teng, ba ka ntseha kobo lesoba;	The girls there, they laughed at my tattered blanket;
Ke re ha ho na taba, ke kobo ke apere.	I say it's no matter, [at least] a blanket I'm wearing.
Utloang, ke moo ke fihlang Masenodo hantle,	Listen, when I reached Mazenod,
Ke be ke utloe molilietsane.	It's then I heard ululating [women cheering].
Oa tseba, ke nahana joale ho hlahile sephankha sa mohlankana,	You know, I thought now a stout young champion had appeared,

Kathe ke mosali ea bitsoang 'Maliengoane—	But it was a woman called 'Maliengoane [a barkeeper and "madam"]—
Joale o se a fihlile.	Now *that's* who had arrived.
Oa tseba, le joala, ha ke bo noe, Ngoana Moroba;	You know, even beer, I don't drink it, Moroba's Child;
Ke feta ntlo ea joala ke soenya nko ke tiisa phatla.	I pass a beerhouse pulling my face with contempt.
Ho tloha moo eaba kea tsamaea.	From there I proceeded.
Ke moo ke fihlang ka B.A. Maseru toropong mona.	It's then I arrived in Maseru town here.
Toropo e tsoeu; fate li ntso.	Town is white; trees are black.
Utloang le, teng melele ea batho,	Listen here, you vagabond men,
Teng ke qeta matsatsi a mahlano;	There I spent five days;
La bosikisi ke be ke tholoa.	On the sixth I was hired.
Ke tholoa sekoting ha Ramonate.	I'm hired for mining at Ramonate's.
Mohla 'tsatsi leo 'ne ke saene lefu,	The time that day I signed for death,
Ka nka bophelo.	[But] I grasped [earned] life.

(Moroba, in Mokitimi 1982, 295–96)

The traditional greeting to any stranger, "Greetings, child of God!" bespeaking unknown, absent parentage and commendation to the Almighty, is a frequently used salutation in *sefela*, where it suggests the migrant has no parent but God. Restless and unrested, the migrant must keep traveling, a "foreign native" (in the old official usage) in South Africa, a stranger to his wife and children in Lesotho. Yet the spirit of the migrant is best summarized by the poet who exhorted his comrades:

Koete, ha habo monna ke hohle;	Gentlemen, a man's home is everywhere;
U nke molamu u k'u itekile.	Take up your stick and ramble.

(Thooboe Ratalane, in Mokitimi 1982, 330)

In *sefela*, as in life, a man meets homeboys and the men of neighboring districts, some who have worked with him on the mines, upon arrival at the labor depots of the western border towns. There they club together, undergoing induction and passport formalities, lamenting the economic crises that have driven them from home, singing *lifela*, awaiting the special trains that will take them to the mines. The train is of particular importance as a kind of master metaphor for the multidimensional, unending life process of labor migration. There is no longer rail service from Maseru for migrants, and most who do not use private taxis to the mines take the special red and yellow buses provided at the border by South African Railways. Depending where they are bound, they may transfer to a train once inside South Africa. While most of these are diesel powered, in *sefela* migrants still thunder over the countryside behind the clouds of black smoke puffing from the nostrils of the *khomo ea 'muso*, "the cow of the government," the hundred-wheeled centipede of the plains. Trains in *sefela* are a set piece, a near-obligatory subject of praises in which nearly every *kheleke* attempts to prove his eloquence by creating fresh and revivifying images. The migrant's train, the "deserters' train" as it is invariably called by its passengers, who have "deserted" Lesotho to stay too often and too long at the mines, is thus painted as a protean hero, praised with its own onomatopoeic names: Makholi Makholonkhotho, "Owner-of-Gunsmoke Hundred-Footed Trudger." The train is also a mythical, devouring water snake called Khanyapa, tutelary diety of diviners and spirit mediums that travels in a cyclone (iconically referenced by the smoke spouting from the engine); it shake-dances like a Xhosa initiate or an entranced diviner; it's an adventurer, a warrior, a madman, a raging prairie fire, a whole menagerie of wild, swift animals, a centipede, a millipede, a swallower and disgorger of the "people of Moshoeshoe" like the fabulous Kholumolumo.[2] In between such fancies, the train covers real territory, with the Free State and Transvaal towns through which it runs lovingly cataloged like the pit stops in the old popular tune "Route 66." The train praises of each *kheleke* have things startling and clever to recommend them. That accepted, we can enjoy the following example, a text as refined as any chiefly *lithoko*, by the outstanding thirty-four-year-old migrant poet Majara Majara (Ngoana Rakhali):

Re kene ho 'masetrata oa reilooa;	We came to the railway magistrate;

Re fihla re 'motsa ea
  rona ea machepa e kae.
	We came and asked him where
	  our deserters' [train] was.

A re e sa eme ka setaleng, phala-fala—	He said it was still in the stable, the favorite cow—
Balisa ba eona ba sentse ba e policha.	Its herders are still polishing it.

Ka 'ma pele-pele, le thoehile
  Bolomo, le khaotse lekanyane.
	Instantly it came down from
	  Bloemfontein, short-cutting hyena.

Oa tseba, ka re, bashanyana ba ntate,	You know, I said, sons of my father,
Le e kene le maphakong mona;	You enter it through the sides here;
Ke pere ea bo-ntate ea khale-khale;	It's the horse of our distant forefathers;

2. The word for centipede in Sesotho is *mosika-phalla*, literally, "thing-parallel-flowing," an exact description of the sickening waving of the two rows of this poisonous insect's legs in motion. Here that motion is compared to the many wheels of the steam engine, connected by the up and down motion of the rods that connect them. The train is also nicknamed millipede, *lefokololi*, because of its ponderous, segmented body supported on rows of tiny, fast-moving wheels. One must have actually seen these animals to appreciate how perfect these entomological metaphors are.

E ne e thapisoe ke Maburu,
mehleng ea khale.
Oa tseba, ke moo bahlankana ba neng
ba tsaba ho palama,
E palangoe, ke,'na Ngoana Rakali.
Terene ha e tloha joale, e ne e entse
mehlolo;
E ne e qala ho etsa makhobonthithi:
Letokisi e tloha; e le o tla morao.

Oa tseba, masaeteng mona e fetile feela,

Che, e ne entse monyenyetsi e patetse. . . .
. . . Ha e tloha mona, e tla khaola—
che, terene.
E ipaka e kalangoe ke molele oa motho.

Ha e tloha joale, eaba ea nyonyoba,
E nyonyoba e ka e tsoa utsoa.

Ea khohlela eaka e tla tsoela;
Ea tsetsela eaka e tla bua.
Terene ea tsetsela se ka Mofu Makhaola.

Oa tseba joale teng ha e kena
Bolomo Sengae,
Ke moo e neng e qala ho kokota.

Batsoari ba tsoereng ka Bolomo

Liponcho ba li bule tsohle.
Terene ho ipaka ekalangoe
ke molele oa motho.
Ho no buoa 'Misisi, mosali oa lekhooa,

"Terene ena e entse joang?"
"Haeka! E matha nomoro sebentine.

Oa tseba, leqaqa le matha,
Le soaile katiba ea kepe.
Tau e matha, e hlanotse 'mala,

It was tamed by the Boers,
in times of old.
You know, there when young men
feared to ride,
I rode it, I, Child of Rakhali.
When that train moved, it performed
miracles;
It began to do amazing feats:
Rail spikes popped, joints
jumped up and down.
You know, at the sidings
it passed in a hurry,
Well, it took notice of no one. . . .
. . . When it leaves here, it will
run fast—yes, the train.
It showed it was ridden
by a wandering man.
When it left, it went wandering,
It went wandering as if it had
stolen [something] away.
It coughed as if it might spit;
It murmured as if it would speak.
The train rattled like the
dying Chief Makhaola.
You know when it entered
Bloemfontein Sengae,
That's when it began
to knock [at the door].
The managers in charge
at Bloemfontein
Opened all the crossings,
The train showed it was ridden
by a true wandering man.
Up spoke the Madam, wife of
the whiteman,
"What's wrong with this train?"
"Haeka! It runs Number 17
[too fast]."[3]
You know, a poor Boer was running,
His cap twisted sideways.
A lion was running, its colors [hide]
turned inside out,

3. When held upside down, a bottle or can of LION, a popular lager in South Africa, appears to read "NO17." In local slang, "No. 17" can refer to anything speeding out of control.

Oa tseba, ha e ne e fihla ka mose,	You know, when it came to the other side,
Tikoe, Sekhooeng,	[To] Tikoe, the European place [mines],
Ke ne ke re maoka a na a tla e hlaba.	I was saying these whitethorn trees would spear it.
Maoka, terene ea phunya maoka bohlasoa.	Whitethorns, the train pierced the spear-sharp whitethorns.
Sethotsela sa moroa se be se tlole kotopong—	A Bushman's ghost jumped from the culvert—
Le ka mahlo re kile ra se bona;	With our own eyes we saw it;
Sethotsela sa moroa ha se ho tsabeha.	The ghost of the Bushman was dreadful.
Banana ba lisang teng ba ne ba e topile;	Girls herding there headed for the train to stop it;
Le ho ema ea seke be ea ema.	It did not even wait.
Ba e roaka, ba re, "Jo moru terene ea Maburu."	They insulted it, saying,"You [ass]hole Boers' train."
Oa tseba o kolokile o ea kae?	Do you know where you are filing to?
Lehlanya le maoto a litsepe,	A madman with iron legs,
Lekanyane, la sekamaqa.	Hyena, it rocked side to side.
Ha leea, mamela bo-ntate,	You listen, my fathers,
Metsoalle ea me, ke utloa le rata ho roka terene.	My friends, I feel I want to praise a train.
Le buoa ka terene le sa e tsebe?	You say a train does not know [appreciate] it?
Le tle ho 'na,Ngoana Rakhali;	You come to me, Rakhali's Child;
Ke tlo le utsoetsa tsa terene. . . .	I may reveal for you things about the train. . . .
. . . E ne e bone e likhoale li ntse li thoena;	. . . It saw Francolins [birds] hopping quickly;
Ea bona linku li ntse li fula;	It saw sheep grazing;
La tsoha lekanyane la lahla seporo.	It took fright at a hyena and lost the rails.
Ke makhooa, o tla bona a e kentse litsepe tse marameng tsena;	Its whitemen, you will see they put these iron [blinkers] on its cheeks;
Ke hore e tloaele ho talima tsela.	It's so that it gets used to looking down the road.
Ho reng ke buoe ka mokhoa ona?	Why should I speak this way?
Bo-ntate, batsoali ba me,	My fathers, my parents,
Pelo ea ka e utloa bohloko.	My heart is in pain.

As Majara suggests, Basotho men have been riding and praising trains since the Afrikaners tamed the iron beast generations ago. Even Molahlehi Makakane, a poet who begins the subject with a the following disclaimer, immediately proceeds to praise the train himself:

Terene molele, terene ea be se e fihla,	Vagabond train, train just arriving,
'Na ha nke be ke roke terene ke se mpara.	I never praise the train like fools do.
Liroki tsa terene, ke tsena li e-tla.	Praisers of the train, it's these that are coming.

The "deserters' train" is a ubiquitous focus of praises because its ultimate identity is the migrant himself, the fearless vagabond, burning up the country, frightening man (always an Afrikaner) and beast on his heedless race to the mines. Trains are at once takers of men and bringers of wealth, totalizing symbols of the heroic productivity (and reproductivity) that comes from a single-minded, go-the-distance pursuit of a living:

Terene ke manka ke mabusetsa. . . .	The train is a taker and a returner. . . .
. . . Ha e fihla Motselekatse,	. . . When it reached Moselekatse,[4]
E fihla e tsoalla Moshoeshoe batho;	It arrived and gave birth to people for Moshoeshoe;
E tsoalla makholo a batho.	It delivered people in hundreds.
	(Makeka Likhojane)

When the migrants finally arrive at the mines, *sefela* songs cover a variety of experiences, including the punishing, often humiliating, rites of liminality imposed on novices by the recruiting agencies and mine management. Aptitude tests and heat acclimatization training are disliked and feared, and the health inspections and communal showering that require older men to appear naked in the presence of teenage recruits violate Sesotho norms of modesty. All that is nothing, however, compared to the fear experienced as the crowded "cage," the mine elevator, rumbles endlessly down into the black belly of the earth.[5] At the destined level, the miner and his comrades are met by a crowd of workers from the previous shift, jostling impatiently to get into the cage and be lifted out of the shaft alive one more time. His ancestors had better help any poor novice who gets in

4. Moselekatse (Mzilikazi) is an important labor disembarcation and processing center on the Witwatersrand.

5. In 1989, Anglo-American Corporation graciously took me on a tour of Free State Geduld No. 2, one of their mines in Welkom. They were at pains to point out the improvements in training facilities, continuing education, and living and working conditions instituted in recent years. I am grateful to mine management and to the underground shift boss, an Afrikaner veteran of twenty-five years' service, for enabling me to have a first-hand look at deep-level gold mining.

the way of the veterans, who mercilessly test the mettle of young newcomers. From the cages, a kind of miniature train takes the miners to the stopes, the ore-faces where "drill boys," wound with cables and hefting heavy rock drills, are drilling holes for the setting of dynamite charges. The working area is about three feet high, the floor covered with loose rock, and severely uneven, so that moving about may require an inverted scramble on hands and feet. The air is thick with noise and dust. In other places, the miners can stand, but up to their knees in water. These days, special ventilation and refrigeration systems keep the temperature down to the maximum allowable, if not exactly bearable, 92 degrees Fahrenheit. Once charges have been set, the stope is cleared and blasting commences. Miners crouch in their waiting areas as the blasts resound through the tunnels. At the all clear, "lashers" (shovel crews) return and shovel the broken rock down through the ore-passes into trapezoidal ore-buckets, wheeled steel carts that are drawn up by the cables and huge winch surmounting the tall headgear at the surface. To make a profit in 1989, a ton of rock had to yield at least six ounces of gold.

South African deep-level mining has always been particularly dangerous. Injury and death from pressure blasts, rock falls, collapsing tunnel supports, gas poisoning and explosion, fire, and fierce machinery that can mangle and amputate with the slightest malfunction or inattention remain terrifyingly common, with annual fatalities still averaging 800. Jean Leger has calculated the total number of mining deaths at 60,000 and injuries at over 1 million since 1900. Despite ever more stringent safety measures, major disasters such as the one at Kinross gold mine in 1986, in which 177 miners were killed and 234 were injured by poison gas, continue to occur (James 1992, 100). Not surprisingly perhaps, life (and death) underground is only rarely sung about in *sefela*, although the changing room where miners clean up after a shift is a favorite place for exhilarated *likheleke* to burst into spontaneous *lifela* at the pleasure of finding themselves once again on the earth and not in it. Life in Lesotho, on the roads and rails, in the city bars, even in remote regions and countries seem preferred topics to the inexpressible terrors of the shaft. Yet the more prolific and talented poets do offer stark images from the emotional wellsprings tapped by experiences underground. Here is a complete passage, marked off by transitional lines, by Ngoana Tooane Motsoafi, who was only twenty-five when Mrs. Mokitimi recorded his *sefela* in 1981:

> I looked toward the mines; I was going to work.
> An ambitious, successful worker,

I was working at "Seiman Jack."
When we are among the shovels there, the ruffians of the mines—
Men, it's those of the shaft—how they tear into it.
They tear into it [with] shovels there.
Khati! Those in-a-file people!
Drill boys defecated in their mine overalls;
Many there were blinded—
I should not be relating this, [I,] a child of God.
The sidekicks[6] died for their veterans,
Some even jumping between [their bosses and danger].
You must see, it was such problems;
Such problems are disastrous evils.
The tough guy injured is a dangerous man.
Injured is Ngoana Tooane, people—
I'm put on a stretcher and brought out,
[Me,] the sidekick, to the main mine hospital;
I was closed in for five days.
When the seventh day came, I was released,
But you know now, they took me to the morgue.
They said, "It's no longer Tooane;
Now he's a dead man, really a goner,
Not even a corpse but an ancestral spirit."
Men, dear old Ngoana Tooane, people—
You know, the people they all cried, "Tooane!"
If it's Tooane, [then] a poor vagabond has died,
Died, an untrustworthy thief of a man.
The reason I do speak in this manner—
Listen, travelers of my home—
When I was shut up in the morgue,
I dreamt badly in my dreams:
I dreamt of death,
Men's corpses forming a line,
Bones of the dead hanging above me.
From there I fled running, people!
I fled while still snoring,
But it appears it was just a dream.
The vagabond, dear old Ngoana Tooane, people—
As night was ending, some of us saw wonders:
We saw beautiful ghosts,
Fires burning for hours [but] warming no one,

6. This is my gloss on the mine term *pekenene* (from English "pickaninny"), specifying a black mineworker of any age who serves as personal assistant to the white shift boss, doing everything from carrying his lunchbucket and other gear to protecting him from any danger. Basotho I spoke to generally liked this job but had little respect for it.

Even those who had lit them having run away—
I should not be relating [these things], travelers.
(Mokitimi 1982, 494–95)

In the midst of their Herculean labors, a rock burst explodes in the faces of the drillers and lashers, and the singer leaps in to protect his shift boss, for whom he is a personal assistant. Ngoana Tooane is injured and brought out of the mine, where he is taken to hospital and after some days given up for dead and left at the mortuary. But he is only unconscious, plagued by dreams of death in the mines so terrifying he rouses himself and runs rather than walks in his sleep to get away. But it seems the explosion, his injury and stay at the hospital and morgue, the walking corpses and flying skeletons underground were all a dream. The passage ends with cobwebs, dawn visions of the uncanny: beautiful ghosts and abandoned campfires in a landscape depopulated by fear.[7] Perhaps the most moving such passage in my own collection comes from Majara Majara (Ngoana Rakhali), a self-proclaimed Mosotho hero:

Ho tsoella, pele ke reng ho lona, bana ba Molimo?	Furthermore, I say what to you, children of God?
Oa tseba Fereginia, V.A. Tikoe Maokeng,	You know Virginia, Tikoe-among-the-Whitethorns,
Thaba-Mashai, ea heleela batho.	Mountain-Mashai, it fell on people [miners].
Ke moo ho shoeleng lekholo la batho.	It's there a hundred men died.
Ho setse 'na, lelimo la motho.	It's me who survived, a cannibal of a man.
Ke setse ke le moneketsana ke le mong.	I alone survived among that tribe [of corpses].
Ke ne ke hula litopo tlasa mafika.	I was pulling corpses from under rocks.
Bana ba batho ba bolile; ba nkha.	People's children have rotted; they smell.
Ba se bile le ba nyeunya litsenyane—	They already swarm with maggots—
Che, litaba tsa mokoti, le mpe le li tlohele.	No, but these mine affairs, you can leave them.

Virginia is a mining center on the Tikoe River in the Free State, called "Tikoe-among-the-Whitethorns" by Basotho, and the site of Harmony

7. The beautiful ghosts here may refer to Basotho witch lore, explained thus by my poet friend Tieho Rakharebe (Hulas Ralipotsotso): "When you are walking the trails at night you may see a beautiful woman coming towards you. Naturally you seize her to make love, only to discover that you are making love to a monkey [*thokolosi*], a deadly monkey that may strangle you."

Mine, which in the mid eighties employed so many Basotho that their remittances accounted for 9 percent of Lesotho's total gross domestic product (Seidman 1993, 2). Here it is made the setting for a mine disaster so terrible it is as if Mount Mashai, a tall peak in Lesotho, has fallen on the miners. The singer, who alone survives, is sent in some days later to help retrieve the rotting corpses of his comrades. No wonder he's ready to change the subject, and no wonder so many poets never even broach it. Elsewhere in the same text, however, Majara returns again to the world underground, this time transcending the description of disaster and death to create an extended trope of praise for his own powers as a poet:

Ke se ke khema lipenta telele:	I am already running long distances:
Ke thapo ea o leche matontsantsima.	I [recite] as long as the cable pulling ore-buckets around the scotch-winch.
Ke hana ha likokopane li teromong,	I refuse [to empty] into the collecting drum,
Le moepeng ke ntse ke li tlatsitse.	Even back down to the diggings still full.
Likomponeng tsena, khale ke li sebetsa. . . .	These mine compounds, I've long worked them. . . .
. . . Ke reng ho lona, likempolara?	. . . What do I say to you, gamblers?
Ke qati ea ntja; ha ke butsoe.	I am a dog's stomach; I don't get cooked.
Ke lekoko le linta; ha ke aparuoe.	I am skin with lice; I am not worn.
Ke serobe sa botsikoane; ha he ke kenoe.	I am a nest of mites; I am not entered.
Ke ka holo e setseng sekoereng—	I'm like a charge that remained in the ore-face [unexploded]—
Bona, e hanne mochini-boi o chaise.	Look, that stopped the drill boy from working.
Mochini-boi, ke o pomme hlooho;	Drill boy, I slashed his head;
Sepannere, ke se pomme letsoho.	Drill guide, I slashed his hand.
Ke moo sepannere se neng se qala ho omana:	It's then the drill guide started to scold:
"Uena, pekenene; uena, thimba-boi,	"You, charge-setter; you, timber boy,
Koala metsi, u koale limoko.	Shut off the water, so you stop the steam.
Thapo tsena li se li re chesitse;	These cables have burned us;
Mali a batho a kopane le majoe."	Men's blood is mixed with the stones."

In the first part, Majara uses cables, ore-buckets, and other mining machinery as a metapoetic metaphor for his own ability to extemporize in *sefela* performance. Then he inserts a burst of characteristic migrant irascibility and toughness, comparing himself to infested clothing and shelter and inedible animals, for a traveling man and a champion poet is not to be used or digested by others. Shifting into high gear, he uses the theme of a frequent workplace oversight, leaving an unexploded charge in a drill hole, as a metaphor for his own explosive poetic powers. But he returns to his first metaphor to do the real damage, slashing and burning the miners with the long (winded) cables of a performance now too hot for other poets to handle. Never has the power of performance been figured in speech more potent.

Fears of death and injury below ground are not the only worries troubling a miner's mind. Unless he is a permanent *lekholoa*, "deserter," a *lechepa* who goes from one contract to another, one mine to another without going home, he will have to steel himself against heartsickness over his family's welfare. It is the central contradiction of migrancy that the male head of household is its least frequent resident, that the migrant must leave his family in order to sustain it. Lack of education not only narrows a Mosotho's job prospects outside mining, it can come to embody and in a way symbolize his frustrations:

Ho se ipalle ke taba e bohloko:	Illiteracy is a sad matter:
Lengolo le baloa ke motho chomeleng.	Your letter is read by someone at the chimney.
Oa tseba? O tšeha pele ho mong a lengolo.	You know what? He laughs in front of the letter owner.
O bolela, "Taba tsa hao, *kea li utloa, morena:*	He remarks, "As for your news, I understand it, sir:
Ba ntse ba bolela tlala,	They report starvation,
Tlhobolo, seboko masimong koana."	Lack of clothing, corn worms in the fields over there."
Banna, phakoe ea selomong sa Maboloka,	Gentlemen, the hawk of Maboloka cliff,
E hana ha litsuonyana li fula;	It prevents the little chicks [children] from foraging;
E ntse e li ubella khafetsa.	It swoops on them continually.

(Serame Thuhloane, in Mokitimi 1982, 276)

Poor Serame has to ask a stranger to read his letter for him. He sits impatiently as the man reads by the light of the hostel coal stove, laughing to himself over his friend's personal affairs. But these are anything but funny: his family famished and naked as parasites destroy the crops. Unprotected in a world of sharp-eyed predators, his children cannot fend for themselves. The ability to read, of course, may only facilitate the arrival of complaints from home:

Lengolo la 'me la be se le fihla—
La 'me, motsoali'a me,
Mosali e mosa 'mae a Mahase,
Mosali ea tsoetseng Mahooana.

E ka ba ho uena Mosotho, Tsokolo:

"Nyoloha, ngoan'a ka mohlanka;
Nyoloha joale u tl'o nyala.
Thaka li nyetse kaofela u setse,

Le bana ba ba nyane ba malom'au;
Le bona ba nyetse sethepu.
Bofutsana, ha bo tsekisoe Molimo;

Hojaneng e be bo ne be tsekoa,
Molimo re ka be re mo tsamaisa linyeoe.

Re lula makhotla a maholo.

"Ha e le bona bo ntsoa ke ho sebetsa feela."

Ke leshano; ba ea re thetsa.
Le hoja ho ea ka ho sebetsa hoa ka,

Le li khomo, nka be ke li rekile,
Le mohoma ke lema ka o lesiba—

Sefofane, ke kalama se sefubelu!

A letter from my mother arrived—
Yes, from my mother, my friend,
The kindhearted mother of Mahase,
A lady who has given birth to
Mahooana clansmen.
Also included is you Mosotho,
Tsokolo:
"Come home, my child;
Come home now and get married.
All your comrades have married
but you,
Even the younger ones of your uncle;
They even have married polygynously.
For your poverty, God cannot be
blamed;
If poverty were contested,
God would be tied up endlessly
in court.
We would sit in High Court
against him. [People say,]
"Poverty is eliminated by hard work
only."
This is a lie; they deceive us.
If this went in accordance with my
working,
Even cattle, I could have bought them,
Even a plough that ploughs like
a feather [strong and light]—
Yes, I would have bought a jet plane!

(Tsokolo Lecheko)

While Tsokolo has been toiling at the mines, his comrades have been paying bridewealth, some for more than one wife, and even his younger cousins have surpassed him. The Sesotho proverb says that poverty is expelled by work, but in Tsokolo's experience, his rewards have not nearly repaid his efforts.

Such deadly seriousness and pathos is more than balanced in *sefela* by the wry humor of comic predicament. There is more to the migrants' world than trains and mines; the whole of Lesotho, the open plains, the way stations, the urban and industrial environment are available through experience as (very) raw material for the creative culture of laughter. Asked why they are so given to comedy in the midst of tragedy, some black South Africans talk about keeping fear and pain at a tolerable distance: laugh now; save your tears for what's coming. Others simply shrug and explain,

"Laughter is cheap entertainment." And a good thing, too, since it is so often at one's own expense. Thus Majara Majara, trying to make his way among the "smart people" of the city:

Ke re'ng ho lona, likempolara?	What do I say to you, gamblers [poets]?
Ke ne ke le mabalane oa potje—	I was the clerk of the toilet—
Motho, ke phakela batho maphepha;	Man, I was serving people [toilet] papers;
Ke ka mehla ke hlolang ke bone *libono tsa batho;*	I was forever viewing the backsides of people;
Ke ne ke bala linkho ho ea letsemeng.	I was counting out beer pots as if at a work party.
Ke re ho lona, likempolara,	I say to you, gamblers,
Ke letsa okono lekeicheneng *lelinyane la moroa le tantše.*	I played the organ at the location for the Coloured girlie to dance.
Ke be ke bone le phethoha se ka *melekorone.*	I even saw her spin like a merry-go- round.
Ke 'na, Ngoana'a Rakhali—ee!	It's I, Rakhali's Child—ee!
Mahure, le tantse, ke semate—le se ke la *nhata.*	Whores, as you dance, I'm smart— don't step on me.
Ke motho ea ratoang ke semate:	I'm a man suited by smart attire:
Ke roala lieta tse ntso, maru matso,	I wear shoes black as storm clouds,
Likausi ranta le halefo korone—moo li *tlohang teng, metsoalle ea me,*	Socks a rand and a half crown—where they come from, my friends,
Ka mose lejuteng, Khobolo. . . .	That side at the Jew's, [at] Khobololo [Vlakfontein]. . . .
. . . Bo-ntate, batsoali ba me, *le tle le utloe,*	. . . Fathers, my parents, you should hear,
Ha ke hlahlela letekatse,	When I break off with a barfly,
Ka lona, ke qala ka lionnoroko;	With her, I start with [take away] the petticoats;
Ke be ke re lerole lesale tse beng lekhona.	I even remove her earrings as she snores.
Ke be ke le rohake, "Kotemete!"	I even curse her: "Goddamit!"
Moleko, oa lehure ke khale o e- *ja mashome a batho—*	Evil whore, long has she eaten men's ten shillings—
Saka le u lekane, mokhothotsi.	A sack will suffice you, thief.

Having made his way to the mines, Majara has like so many Basotho "jumped ship" for easier employment in the African urban townships. Unfortunately this turns out to be the rather humiliating job of a public lavatory attendant, which includes doling out portions of toilet paper to men as they enter the doorless stalls. Other times he pours out cans of sorghum beer at a municipal beer hall, and plays organ for sexy dancers at an illegal bar. This seems to pay a bit better, for he is able to buy smart clothes at the Jewish-owned and therefore stylish shop at the Vlakfontein mines of the Transvaal.[8] He can also afford to keep one of the bar girls as a mistress, but when he leaves he is careful to repossess all the gifts he has lavished on her. The contemptuous manner in which he discards his lover is unfortunately characteristic of migrant attitudes toward the town women who offer them companionship at the price of their money, health, and peace of mind. Indeed, Moodie (1983, 18), rightly in part, describes the relationships contracted between male migrants and female "sexual workers" (an unfortunate term) as mutually exploitative. While such relationships and the associated camaraderie are a major focus of migrant leisure activity, they are also a source of considerable fear: through such dissolution one may end up a broken, diseased, and penniless alcoholic, too ashamed to return to a rural family, who have little to offer in any case.

Ke ratile ngoanana oa Mothepu;	I love a child of the Thembu;
Letebele la nka moea oaka:	A Xhosa has taken my love:
Le fofa ka ona hara litoropo	She flies about with it in towns
Hara litsotsi, hara malaeta.	Among gangsters, among thugs.
Le matha ka thipa;	I run about with a knife;
Ke matha ka thipa libeseng mona,	I run about with a knife in buses,
Ke sena le soka ea ho palama bese:	Not having even sixpence for the fare:
Lampisi o batla batho lipasa;	The inspector wants people's tickets;
Liphomene li batloa ke Matatane—	The cheats are wanted by Matatane—
Oa tseba, le teng ke qhala le joala lekeicheneng.	You know, at that time I splashed beer [drunkenly] at the location.

(Majara Majara)

Partly in response to these dangers, the mine compounds, like prisons in the U.S., provide an environment in which male homosexual relationships between veteran migrants and young novices flourish. As Moodie (1988) has bravely argued—some of our colleagues would rather this aspect of migrant life be left unexamined—homosexuality is a structured expression of relations of dominance and subordination in compound social organization. Boys who are expected to dress and act in a feminine manner for their "husbands" will in time grow their beards and become masculine veterans with boy-wives of their own (ibid., 236). These relationships are strongly regularized, involving verbal contracts between the "husband" and his "wife," who is paid a substantial portion of the older man's income

8. "Jewish labels" is local African slang for expensive, upscale clothes. In the days before designers started printing their logos on the chests and derrières of their products, the wearers of Jewish labels in the townships often contrived to wear them with the labels showing.

in return for his domestic and sexual services. Such contracts were formerly enforced by the *lintona*, the African compound overseers, who use the trade in sex and drugs to extend and reinforce their authority (ibid., 233). The *lintona* could make sure that a favored associate obtained a desired recruit, and could even arrange for the boy to be paid a miner's salary while spending his time around the compound performing light domestic tasks. Miners told me that these "mine marriages," encapsulated within compound and homeboy social networks and governed by *mthetho ka sokisi* (ibid., 236), literally the "rules of the sock" (see van Onselen 1982, 179–89), were far more reliable and safe than transitory liaisons with women in the township and shantytown bars. They also spoke about emotional rewards, referring matter-of-factly to the attachment they had felt for certain long-term partners, but adamantly insisting that all such contacts ceased when they returned to Lesotho and their female wives and lovers became available. Many miners, though, maintain casual relationships with town women alongside a deeper attachment to male "wives of the mine." When a tasty young novice arrives in the compound, veterans vie for him, as much to enhance their reputation as their physical comfort. The *lintona* organized competitive dances called the *seakhi*, held at midnight, where miners danced naked to be awarded the boy, who also danced, dressed in towel, earrings, and other ornaments to arouse the ardor of the competitors. Moodie (1988, 241) quotes a police report from October 1941, in which twelve miners were dismissed by a compound manager for holding *liakhi* dances. The police had to be called owing to the near-violent insistence by an entire working shift that their comrades be reinstated, a clear expression of worker solidarity in support of the "rules of the sock." Truth to tell, I have not witnessed this dance, but I did manage to get a group of migrant enthusiasts to perform the *seakhi*, clothed and in daylight, in a rundown area of Maseru, though they warned me the performance wouldn't be very inspired in the absence of a prize boy. Here is the text of the dance song:

CHORUS:

E ne e le mona, Khanyapa.	It was just here, the Water Snake.
E ne e le mona, Khanyapa.	It was just here, the Water Snake.
E ne e le mona, Khanyapa.	It was just here, the Water Snake.

SOLO:

Hoa buoa ke ngoana separola-thota,	Sings the child of a traveler,
Lijo ke jeleng, litsamaea-naha?	What food have I eaten, travelers?
Ke papatlele, motho oa ha Malebanye;	I am a wanderer, a man of Malebanye's;
'Na ha kea, chona ke tabohetsoe.	I am destitute, dressed in tatters.

Ha e le Maseru, teropong mona,	When in Maseru, right in town,
Ke ntse ke phela, leha ke phela mahlomoleng.	I still live, although I live in misery.
Botsotsi, ba hlola ba nkotlile;	Thugs, they overpower and beat me up;
Ke se bile ke ba fetotse metsoalle.	I've even turned them into friends.

[CHORUS]

SOLO:

Ke tla bona mang, ke mo rome a—ee!	Who shall I see, who shall I send to [for help]—ee!
A joetse ntat'e Lesotho ha ke tle.	Tell my father [back] to Lesotho I'm not coming.
'Na, batho ke ba na ba ntjela pereko.	Here, people are eating up all [the fruits of] my labors.
'Na, ha kea tsoaloa, ke emotsoe;	Me, I wasn't just dropped, I was [in purity] conceived;
Ke theohile ha ha molimo ke tsotse.	I descended naked from heaven.
Lefatla lena ha le ea tla hobane ke fakachile	I didn't get this bald head from wandering
Ho ipaka hore ke se ke le moholo.	To prove that I'm now an elder.
Se 'nang le botsana, ka 'na le sa mpotse—	You shouldn't be asking each other, but not asking me—
Le ntse le botsa, hore na ke haile kae?	You keep on asking, where is my home?
Tajane mona, keha Mohale hantle;	Tejane's here, right at Mohale's;
Sekhutlong mona ke ha Rakhoboso;	Here at Sekhutlong rules Rakhoboso;
Mokhehle ke ka nokeng ka—mona o shebe,	Mokhehle's at the river here—you can see
Ke lihaka li tala ke nkha boqheku.	I've got green wisdom teeth that show my age.

[CHORUS]

SOLO:

Mosali ea mobe ha a bapalisoe, ha u 'mapalisa	An ugly, bad woman is not trifled with, lest as you play
Okare o mo betile, Jonana—oe!	She claims you've raped her, Jonana—oe!

[CHORUS]

SOLO:

Mokola ha ke le makhooeng Koana,'na ha Kea Kholoa;	A stout lad when I was in the mines there, I never returned;
Ke titimetse State Mine No. 4.	I made a run for State Mine No. 4.

[CHORUS]

SOLO:

Li ka ja chelete, litsamaea-naha,	They can eat up [their] money, the travelers,
Li ithetsa, li re li tla boela li sebetsa hape.	Spend on themselves, saying they will just return to work again.
Re be re li jelle le leshome la ho qetela,	We even ate up their last buck.
Athe ke hona ho sa tla lelekoa batho.	Whereas they are still going to lay off people.

CHORUS:

E ne e le mona, Khanyapa.	It was just here, the Water Snake.
E ne e le mona, Khanyapa.	It was just here, the Water Snake.

My circumspect, Christian Basotho friends must forgive me for reproducing and translating this howlingly blasphemous song. The name of the dance itself comes from the verb *ho akha*, which describes the flapping motion of a young boy's penis as he runs carelessly clad about the fields. The movements of the miners' dance do involve the waving of the arms, as if the dancers were attempting to fly about, but as it is performed in the nude there's plenty of flapping on the part of other loose bodily appendages as well. The chorus of the text refers to Khanyapa, the mythical water snake and dread master of magic that lurks in deep pools and travels in a cyclone, embodiment and symbol of heathenism to the Mosotho Christian, and here, obviously, patron of a devilish dance. The opening solo recounts plainly the misery of unemployment as a stranger in Maseru. The second solo begins with a reply that South Africa too is a trap, where money is earned and just as easily used up or lost. Abruptly, though, the singer turns to assert that far from being born in the bush, he's like the Christ child, conceived in purity and sent naked as he is right now from the place of God. His baldness and discolored teeth reveal his long, hard life as a migrant, but he is not a mere vagabond but a man with an ancestry and a home. Yet after an admonitory joke at the expense of mine-shanty (*mekhukhu*) women, the singer admits he's a "deserter," a false friend who helps waste the money of improvident migrants who think they can always take another contract. Under today's changed labor conditions, however, the mines are reducing their work force and even experienced veterans can no longer count on employment.

Does homosexuality appear in *lifela?* Yes indeed, though not very often, to judge from the collections of Mrs. Mokitimi and myself. A good example, though is found in a *sefela* by the redoubtable former "drill boy," good husband and father, and invaluable friend and informant Molefi Motsoahae, "Ngoana Sebili." Motsoahae is prominently featured as a performer in *Songs of the Adventurers*, and when the film was screened at the United States Information Service Library in 1988, I took Motsoahae along and introduced him to the audience. Motsoahae frequently taught younger composers, including one of his sons, and we shared an interest in the techniques of Sesotho composition in *sefela*. He was most forthcoming in explaining the following passage:

Ka mokhoa moo la e ratang bashanyana!	In such a way [how much] I love boys!
Tsoakeletsane maoto li betheng,	Legs entwined in the bed,
Botsikinyane maotoana monate.	The fondling of small thighs is sweet.
Khomo ke tseo leotong la bethe.	Cattle [blankets] are there at the foot of the bed.
Moikutloa pelo ha a tlo li khanna;	A rival can come to drive them off;
Ha a hana, le lona a li tlohelle:	If he's unwilling, he should leave them:
Likobo tsa ka li aparoa bochabela;	My blankets are worn in the east;
Tse ling li aparoa bophirimana.	Others are worn in the west.

The opening lines need no comment, but the reference to cattle actually means the blankets Sebili has paid as bridewealth for his boy in the compound. Anyone brave enough to challenge him can try to take those blankets; others had better leave them where they are. Nor is this his only boy-wife; his "blankets," it seems, are worn all over the map.

Moodie has analyzed the decline of "mine marriage" during recent decades as rural marriage and household institutions have themselves disintegrated under the pressures of rural underdevelopment and proletarianization. More migrants are landless and divorced, while the trend toward mine employment as a "career" encourages mineworkers to maintain families in closer proximity to the workplace. More destitute rural women come to the mining areas or the Lesotho border towns to be closer to their men or to new men or to the female occupations that working men sustain. The system introduced in Free State mines whereby migrants can take a three-day weekend after every eleven consecutive shifts has enabled them to see their wives more often, especially as many families have now moved to the periurban settlements of the border towns. The more flexible, mobile, and accessible long-term relationships with women that proletarianization has made available, Moodie suggests (1988, 254–55), have doomed not only the rigidly separated institutions of "mine marriage" and "village marriage," but the entire system of migrant labor. All of this brings up the issue of the shifting reality and construction the bipolar opposition of Lesotho and *makhooeng*. Passages detailing migrants' amorous adventures and disappointments with women, especially in Lesotho itself, where loving, marriage-worthy girls are supposed to be found, are far more common in *sefela* than those dealing with "wives of the mine." Men's views of women and love are just one of a set of topics that pertain to and derive significance from this duality debate: migrants, travelers of two worlds, or creators of one?

Following Sandra Wallman's pioneering study of family economy in Lesotho, *Taking Out Hunger* (1969), Harold Wolpe (1972) published a seminal article arguing that South African industry was using the homelands and peripheral states as a location and a means toward the cheap reproduction of their African labor force. Since then, social scientists have first developed and then (inevitably I suppose) sharply criticized and limited the model of a dual economy in which rural family agriculture and the social services provided there by women and the elderly were held to supplement the wages of migrant workers. This dualist notion has been taken up in cultural anthropology, notably in Botswana by Alverson (1978), who studied psychocultural adaptation to labor migrancy, and by John and Jean Comaroff (1987), who analyzed the articulation of pre- and postcapitalist ideologies and relations of production. The dualist view has depicted migrants as men of two worlds—women migrants have been largely ignored—people who maintain a symbolic discontinuity between the structure of social relations, patterns of interaction, and cultural norms encountered in South Africa and those governing social participation in the home communities in an effort to resist marginalized incorporation into the regional capitalist economy (Comaroff 1985; Comaroff and Comaroff 1990).

Murray (1981), Spiegel (1980), Simkins (1981) Bardill and Cobbe (1985, 28,42 n), and most recently Ferguson (1990) and James (1992, 57–58) have examined the model of dual economy in rural Lesotho, convincingly demonstrating that the dual economic model of migrants as proletarians in South Africa and peasants in Lesotho is no longer an adequate representation of social reality. In truth, such family-based mixed pastoralism as there is in Lesotho is almost wholly dependent on infusions of capital in the form of migrant wages. Agriculture, which is said to employ 92 percent of Lesotho's resident work force, produces only 6 percent of average disposable household income (Van Der Weil 1977, 88). Only 7 percent of rural households control enough land for cultivation and herding or own enough livestock to make self-sustaining agricultural and pastoral enterprise possible. The Comaroffs emphasize a conceptual opposition in Setswana between *go dira*, "working," referring to autonomous, socially productive activity in the home community, and *go bereka* (derived, significantly, from Afrikaans *werk*), referring to work for whites, the proletarianized, unequal exchange of labor for wages on the farms and mines. At first blush this conscious opposition would seem ideal for differentiating between *Sesotho* and *Sekhooa*, the culture of the whites, or *mthetho*, the culture of the mines. Ideally, perhaps, this is so. Looking at the situation ethnographically, however, the discontinuity between Lesotho and *makhooeng*, the "whiteman's place" (the mines) appears as a putative representation, a fiction useful in the defense of *Sesotho* and its attached situational entitlements.

Lesotho is far more dependent on migrant labor than Botswana, with the customs union with South Africa and most recently the Highlands Water Scheme the only other major domestic sources of capital. The term *ho lira* (for *go dira*) is uncommon in Sesotho and is regarded as a South African synonym for *ho etsa*, "to make, do, create." The verb for working, *ho sebetsa*, can be used for any kind of work, in South Africa or Lesotho. *Ho bereka*, though less common, does have the connotation of "working for whites," but again the term is regarded as a South African loan and is not categorically opposed to *ho sebetsa*. Moodie, who has done the most consistent research on the topic, appears to be of two minds about the "two worlds" concept. On the one hand he identifies two Sesotho words, *tiro* and *mmereko* (*pereko*?) as the functioning cognates of the opposition in Setswana, and asserts that "migrant miners . . . bear the scars of the articulation of two modes of production" (1991, 47). On the other, he admits that miners are permanently marked by their work experience regardless of the strength of their rural orientation and that rural social structures have been transformed by the impact of returning migrants and the migrant labor system (ibid., 48–51).

In Moodie's view, Alverson ignored migrants' self-reformulation on the mines because he depended for data on miners' recollections at home. Rather than maintaining an identity on the mines that is fundamentally continuous with rural identity, the migrant creates a new self-definition consistent with *mthetho* and, then, to the extent that he wishes to and succeeds in doing so, reconstructs continuity upon his return to rural life (Moodie 1983, 5, 29). Migrant experience, of course, is not of one piece and varies along with responses to it, depending on the historical changes in rural social organization and economic conditions, the nature of migrant labor and mine work, and the sort of men, career migrants or target workers, those with continuing rural projects and those without, that one is talking about (Moodie 1991, 41). Most important, in a situation in which a migrant's grandfather may just as easily have been a migrant, there is no reason to assume that working on the mines is as anomic for the Basotho as the Comaroffs say it is for the Batswana. Indeed, the noun form of *ho bereka* in Sesotho is an honorific: *seberekane*, meaning a successful, prosperous migrant worker. A migrant's identity as a *Mosotho oa mankhonthe*, "a true Mosotho," is a unified concept that includes the willingness to do whatever is necessary to support his family. Mining can be part of such an identity, a career in a sense, involving what Moodie calls a "purposive organization of life-worlds" (ibid., 44). The Basotho claim "We opened the mines" is a reference to their established preference for the dangerous but high-paying work of shaft-sinking.

At the recruitment offices, the switching stations, and at the mining centers, the men are subjected to liminal experiences—stripped and run in droves, kicked and pushed to the doctor, cold showers, heat training. They conceive of themselves as soldiers in an economic war, singing *merkorotlo* anthems on the trains, while in *sefela* the very rails answer with a chorus. It is no coincidence that in Sesotho the domain of play, *ho bapala* (which includes games of all kinds from soccer to dance to *sefela*), is not opposed to *ho sebetsa*, "work," but rather to *ntoa*, "war," a domain that includes not only fighting but the disputes, anxieties, disruptions, discontinuities, and conflicts of life in general (Adams 1979b). An integrated, positive, cross-border self-concept has been maintained in the face of systematic displacement, fragmentation, and dehumanization by the development of "migrant cultures which both modified home realities and created mine lives appropriate for maintaining such changed rural identities" (Moodie 1991, 55). Migrants belong at once to Lesotho and to their own occupational culture. That is why even in Lesotho many prefer the company of their fellow migrants and tavern girls to that of their families, clubbing together and indulging in the rude, aggressive industrial manners of the workplace that have earned them the local nickname *likoata*, "uncivilized ruffians." When I asked one migrant why *sefela* contained a great deal more narrative and commentary about Lesotho than about the mine environment, he answered simply, "At the mines we think of Lesotho; in Lesotho we think of the mines."[9] Since this was early in my study, I might be forgiven for missing a deeper reality: much of the narrative imagery of Lesotho used in *sefela* is every bit as much about the mines.

Moodie has emphasized the role of performance in creating and sus-

9. It is fatuous of course, but this statement instantly brought to mind Papa Hemingway's famous reflection on the Moveable Feast: "When I'm in New York, I miss Paris; when I'm in Paris I miss New York."

taining the meanings that unify migrant identity and experience (ibid.). What light, then, does *sefela* shed on the two worlds controversy? Many texts contain evidence that Basotho migrants no longer regard the environments of the mines and the home villages as two separate social fields. *Sesotho*, we might reemphasize, extends beyond the boundaries of Lesotho as a national state, and operates also among Basotho in the Free State, Transvaal, and Transkei. In his *sefela*, Makeka Likhojane (Ngoana Mokhalo) sings about a *thokolosi* (Ashton 1952, 294–96), a witch's demon familiar and poetic/ritual/medical symbol of social evil, sickness, and disruption. A diviner can chase a *thokolosi* out of a village with powerful herbs and magic, and here the traveler poet as healer expels the demon, which physically resembles a monkey, by relentless pursuit over the countryside. At one point, the chase brings Ngoana Mokhalo to his wife's natal village:

Ha Pechela thabeng ke *fihlile teng e le hoseng;*	At Pechela's in the mountains I arrived in the morning;
Ba bohoeng ba ka ba loea.	[There] I discovered my wife's parents bewitching.
Ba le nokaneng mona, ba otla seakhi;	I found them down in the river, beating out *seakhi;*
Moruti a tsotse.	The pastor was naked.
Tšoene ea bona e le thokoana,	Their monkey [*thokolosi*] sat by,
E supa ka koebe e ntse e thotse.	Pointing with a barbed spear in silence.
Ke bonne ba haroloha, baloi.	I saw them file past, the witches.
Ba entse khati ba tšela nokana.	They filed across the river.

The *thokolosi* has taken refuge among the singer's in-laws, who are busy bewitching people, including our hero, while performing the *seakhi* dance. This seems peculiar, since the *seakhi* is performed only by mineworkers in the dead of night in the mine compounds in South Africa. Why should a miner's rural in-laws perform it? Both witchcraft and homosexuality are considered inverted forms of social behavior, and no one admits to practicing them in Lesotho. It is believed that witchcraft, however, can be practiced by and upon anyone, even white people, anywhere. The associated images of demon-familiar and witchcraft here unify the social field, since jealous in-laws are quite capable of sending a *thokolosi* to bewitch, afflict, injure, or kill a mineworker when he is down in the shaft. Further, witches, like *seakhi* performers, dance naked.

Another folk demon, Satane Mautla (Satan the Ravisher), Christian counterpart of the *thokolosi*, is nearly as popular a character in *sefela*. Encountered as easily in Lesotho as in the mines or urban African locations,

Satan can be the maker of evil mischief, bedeviling efforts to bring moral order to Basotho life. The semiotics of the mines as a kind of hell, a land of spiritual as well as physical darkness where the Devil rules in place of God, is well known from the folk religions of miners elsewhere in the Third World. In the tin mines of Bolivia in particular, Nash (1979) documents the existence of an inverted cosmology, a literal underworld where the Devil rules over the life and death of miners and must be propitiated with prayers and ritual sacrifices. Though Satan is an impostor whom the poet, with his divinatory knowledge, magic, and cunning, is committed to driving out, there is as we have seen a certain identity, kinship, or comradeship between devil and migrant:

Ke mohla Mautla a na qala
ho nehoa linotlolo.
O behoa Molimong, ho thoe;
Leholimo lena, o hl'o le buse.
Moshanyana a busa, le bo-ha-ntat'ae.

It's the time Mautla was first
given keys.
He was put in God's place, it's said;
Up there in heaven, he should reign.
The boy ruled,
even in his father's place.

Manyoloi a ka mo hana, a re:
"Ha e le uena, Morena Mautla,
Leholimo u ke ke ua le busa le khale."
Basotho ba leshano ba lefatse:
Ba re, "Leholimong koana, Satane o teng.

The angels can refuse him, saying:
"As for you, Lord Mautla,
Heaven you shall never rule."
Basotho are liars on earth:
They say, "In heaven yonder,
Satan is there.

O re a le teng mehleng ea pele-pele,
pele ho leroele—
A lelekoa; re ne re sebetsa
le eena Khotofolei!

He was there in olden times,
before the mighty storm—
He was expelled; we worked with
him at Grootvlei [mine]!

(Majara Majara)

When I asked Makeka Likhojane whether Satan was a white miner or a black miner, he replied that he must be black, for only black miners "work like the devil." In a passage by Mphafu Mofolo, Satan is identified with the most flamboyant migrant *sekoata*, the sort who wears the ornaments of a country pagan and a felt hat with the brim cut into fringes (*litjobo*) after the style of indigenous beaded headgear. Guarded by such a "policeman of hell," how will the prayers of netherworld miners be heard?

O masale o manaila, Satane,
Lepolesa la liheleng, Mautla.
Katiba o roala e mekali-nkatahoshe.
Banna ba heso, ka bona meleko.

He has earrings and ankle bracelets,
Satan,
A policeman of hell, the Devil.
He puts on a hat with *litjobo*.
Men of my home, I've seen
misfortunes.

Lentsoe ke lena la Molimo	Here comes the voice of God
le fihla le manyeloi;	and the Angels;
Moporofeta oa Molimo, Mphafu,	A prophet of God, Mphafu,
Molimo o koetse monyako marung.	God has closed the doors in the clouds.
O likoetse litora tsa maholimo.	He has closed the towers of the heavens.
Ha o na le leseli;	There's no light;
Ha o na le letho.	There is nothing.
Thapelo tsa bahetene ha li kene.	The heathens' prayers cannot enter.

South Africa and Lesotho thus become a single social world, full of evils and dangers that the migrant performer must uncover and overcome at every turning in his endless road. A man's home is everywhere: take up your song and ramble. The fact is that few migrants can or would even wish to resist the process by which rural relations of production have been thoroughly transformed by incorporation into the South African political economy. What they resist is low pay, poor living and working conditions, and racially structured systems of authority and promotion in a cash-down world. True, in home communities where a man has rights (not in the border towns to which so many migrant dependents and rural poor have moved), chiefs and the better-off are held ostensibly to the values of Sesotho hierarchical reciprocity. Lesotho thus becomes a separate landscape of the moral imagination, a useful fiction providing location for structural values and practices that give content to an autonomous social identity that predated colonial rule and that Basotho are determined must survive both apartheid and its demise. Again Makeka Likhojane:

Ha-Tsekelo, Phutiatsana,	At Tsekelo's, Phutiatsana River,
Lipoli tsa teng li tsoala mafahla,	Goats there give birth to twins,
Mapotsanyane ka bararo ka bone,	Kids in threes and fours,
Ka bohlano joale ka botselela.	In fives now and in sixes.
Theka la poli le lumetse hantle,	The wombs of the goats are up to the task,
Le ka bosupa li ntse li fihla.	Even in sevens they still arrive.

But what of the others found in the two worlds, the women? When marriage is sung about, it is virtually always the Basotho sport of *chobeliso* (elopement) that is recounted. It may be, however, that this sport is a deviation only from an ideological norm. Statistics are hard to come by, but Poulter (1979, 106) estimated in the mid 1970s that over half the marriages in Lesotho began with elopements, in which girls are stolen—sometimes involuntarily—without any bridewealth given to her parents. If caught, the groom can be made to pay a seduction fee of six cattle, but only when a larger share of an adequate bridewealth is paid will the children be counted as his legitimate offspring. Still, *chobeliso* is an effective strategy for getting the parents of one's intended to trim their bridewealth demands:

Ra buoa ka ho nyalana kese;	We talked of marrying each other;
Ke rera hore kea shobelisa—	I now planned to elope with her—
Joale ke utsoa morali oa motho.	Now I am stealing this man's daughter.
Ha kele Borokhong baka Tsoaing,	When I was at Tsoaing Bridge,
Lumela ha-Bele pela Motsekuoa,	Good morning at Bele's place near Motsekuoa,
Ke rekela setšoana kobo;	I bought a blanket for the dark-skinned one;
Mose le lieta hake eso li reke.	I didn't even buy her a dress and a pair of shoes.
Sa nkhula ka kobo, sethojana,	She pulled me by the edge of the blanket, that beauty,
"Ntat'e Kanono Nthako, ha ku hlahe kantle lebaleng mona—	"Father Kanono Nthako, just come outside and see—
U shebe tlasa leralla la ha Nkofi."	Look below Nkofi's hill."
Leroele la qoba hara masimo a batho.	Some dust blew up in the fields of the people.
"Ke malinyane a lintja tseso:	"Those are the young hounds from home:
Kea kholoa ntat'e u ntse a etla.	I am sure my father is still coming.
Ka 'nete u tlilo re bolaea—ee!" feela ngoana enoa a tihisitse.	Truly he is coming to kill us—ee!" this girl was swearing.
Lelimo le fihla moo le halefile;	The cannibal [father] arrived there angry;
Countara u rata le ho li tlola	He wanted to jump over the counters.
Litlelereke, banna, li ea mothiba,	Shopkeepers, men, are stopping him,
Le sechaba se tlileng lebenkeleng:	And the people who had come to buy at the store:
"E seng u bolaee ngoana enoa oa motho.	"You should not kill this child of someone.
Molao u teng; u ilo motšoarisa."	The law is there; you better go have him arrested."
Ka tsoelipana, e seng hobane ke le bohlale;	I managed to escape, not that I am clever;
Ke leka leqheka feela la hore ke mpe ke phele.	I was just trying to save my life.
Ka tsoa ka lifenstere ka matha—	I came out through the window running—

Ha! U ne u ka mpona ka letsatsi leo!	Hey! If you could see me that day!
Lebatha ke le ala ka mokhoa ona,	I was running in my bandy-legged way,
Molula u hanella thlabele.	Grass sticking between my toes.
	(Hlalele Mabekanyane)

Other poets emphasize the troublesome aspects of life with women, warning against the fickle and exploitative attitudes of town girls of other nations or the worry and discord that come with marriage. Makeka Likhojane searches for his beloved all over the district only to be jilted when he meets her, while another poet returns from the mines apparently so changed and forgotten that neither his fiancée's sister nor his sweetheart herself recognize him. Among the most pathetic passages is the following by Sebata Mokokoane, for whom marriage turns out to be poor investment:

Banna, le nyale basali le tle le bone,	Men, you marry women and see,
Banna, meleko e ata joale ke le siko.	Men, evil doings multiply now in my absence.
Ke le siko, Ngoana Molete,	In my absence, Molete's Child,
Ke le siko, Ngoana Mokokoane.	In my absence, Mokokoane's Child.
Banna, ke le siko, Morena Sebata,	Men, in my absence, Chief Sebata,
Joale ke le siko ke le makhooeng koana,	While I was away at the mines yonder,
Lapa la ka le fetohile lithako, Paape.	My homestead turned to ruins, Paape.
Bana ba ka ba fetohe lihase,	My children became motherless orphans,
Kobo tsa ka li jeoe ke lifariki—	My blankets eaten by pigs—
Banna, ke bolela tsa likonyana.	Men, I mean those of lambskin.
Ke fihla ka Tsoane mabalane koana,	I arrived at Tsoane in the lowlands,
Ke fumane ntja, ho se le e 'ngoe.	To find a dog, there was not even one.
Ke qalelle, ntat'a Tholang,	I began anew, father of Tholang.
Banna, le beisini ho se le e'ngoe;	Men, a basin there was not even one;
Banna, le khaba ho se le e'ngoe.	Men, a spoon there was not even one.
	(Mokitimi 1982, 346–47, 474)

Certainly it's a world of uncertainty, where town women can cheat you and rob you, while at home your wife takes your furnishings and leaves you. But Lesotho and South Africa are not the only two worlds ambiguously yoked together. Mirroring the world of male migrants is the world of their women, with difficulties, hardships, and voices to celebrate them as great as those of their men.

Chapter Six

"I'd Rather Die in the Whiteman's Land"

The Traveling Women of Eloquence

Don't play the [accordion] keys of war, boys—I am leaving.
Give me the black-and-white spotted cattle [passports] of my family,
The black-and-white spotted ones, so I know [I can travel].
What day should I ride, girls?
Sunday or Saturday, the day for loafers [off-duty miners].
'Mamosali Alinah Tsekoa

Winter, June 1984, at a small crossroads just behind the main shopping area of Hlotse, capital town of Leribe District in northwestern Lesotho. A great many migrants come from Leribe. It is cold but sunny, and hardly a breeze stirs the bits of paper and plastic bag caught in the barbed wire fencing the rows of mud-brick, two-roomed houses flanking the dusty street. I am standing around in front of Mrs. Motolo's popular *shebeen*, talking with her nephew Samson Motolo, a Johannesburg studio musician and bass guitarist for local singing star Apolo Ntabanyane. When he's home, Samson is the male managerial presence at the tavern, and he has most graciously and for a nominal sum provided his premises for today's order of business. That order is to film the singers, especially the women, who frequent Motolo's *shebeen*. The footage will later appear in Gei Zantzinger's *Songs of the Adventurers*. The principal *chanteuses* concerned, Nthabiseng Nthako, Pontso Moohali, and Thakane "Tholi" Mahlasi, all in their twenties, have gone off with my wife to change into their best: white face powder, fresh, light-colored blouses, modest skirts falling below the knee, black low heels, jaunty berets and caps.

Meanwhile, the crew pulls up in the white Land Cruiser that transports our entire technology. Thomas Ott, cameraman and a professor of film studies at Boston University, examines critically the site for the shoot while Zantzinger and I schmooze with Motolo. My assistant, Seakhi Santho, and I will have the principal task of communicating the director and cameraman's needs to the participants, and keeping the crowd cooperative and calm. The set: a long, rectangular drinking room, with a single narrow door and small, high windows; liquor and band instruments at one end, the floor clear, as always, for dancing. Ott will shoot without lights as always (too intrusive), depending instead on the wan illumination framed in the windows. Youngsters in their caps and ragged pullovers, some in brightly patterned Basotho blankets, hang around outside, waiting for something unusual to happen and hoping there might just, eventually, be drinks. Inside, the more established patrons—adult migrants and retirees in work clothes, sports jackets, and narrow-brimmed fedoras; women in blankets with stockings and black flats—sit drinking pensively, reserving their seats on the benches against the walls. The usual serious drinking has taken on an unusual seriousness. Basotho *shebeen* drinkers, early on, are dour, contemplative, intense rather than gregarious.

Samson is relaxed; he's used to the recording process and he's more or less in charge. Ott insists as forcibly as he can that the door and windows must be kept uncovered and clear of the light-obstructing faces of the curious outside. This proves to be an impossible task. The regular customers are already inside, ranged on the long row of benches, many wrapped in blankets, smoking and talking in low tones or affecting the pose of silent, watchful inscrutability for which Basotho are famous among workers of other origins on the mines. A good-sized crowd of the curious of various ages is milling about outside, ready, at Samson's instructions, to get in for a piece of the action. Nthabiseng, Tholi, and Pontso arrive at last in a flurry, their loud talk and laughter setting a more ebullient tone. The band is all set up by the bar in front, the accordionist perched on the bar itself, the drummer seated facing him. They strike up a slow, strongly Sesotho three-chord melody with heavy downbeats where, were men dancing *ndlamo*, the stamping would be. A young man wrapped in a bright yellow-and-black blanket and waving a *molamu* (fighting stick) warms up the crowd with a *shebeen sefela* in full, vibrant voice. The real attraction, however, are the three women, who begin their performance dancing in unison the gentle, bouncing Basotho women's style of *jaife* (jive). As they slowly break off from each other, wheeling and crouching, Nthabiseng Nthako, aged twenty-one, smiling radiantly, starts her *seoeleoelele:*

> Helelele! Let me whisper to you, you men from the highlands:
> At my home, no horrors exist.
> Helelele!
> Hela! You sweet little Tholi, let me whisper to you:
> I'm clearing out of here;

I cannot stay here any longer—
Yes, here in Hlotse—
For indeed I'm living in hardships.
At my home, they're awaiting my return:
Father, you consider me dead;
Mother, you know I'm alive.
Fighting is terrifying;
I'm off like a shot!
I'm so poor that you could give me your last garment.
Tsotsis, they're always in jail—
How they insulted me. Oh, the devils!
Yonder in heaven, hard are the questions;
With great difficulty must we reply.

Moved by her words, shaking their heads at the sheer juiciness of the performance, the other women move up beside her again, echoing her steps in support. Then abruptly the accordionist sets a new chord sequence and a faster, *jaife* rhythm, challenging Nthabiseng to step and sing ever faster, the movement and word music picking up centrifugal force:

Let me tell you in whispering tones:
Oh, the young prostitutes,
The young prostitutes, girls—
We, the new recruits, live in difficulties.
What kind of people are you russians [gangsters]?
You fight each other each time you meet.
I have left my poor child Thabang;
Yes, I have left my sweetheart behind crying .

Her solo, her "chorus" taken, Nthabiseng closes with a final crouching whirl back to the dance line and a shrill, ululatory melodic whistle. Pontso steps forward, but rather than taking center stage with a show of physicality, her dance is minimal. Her face pinched with concentration, eyes closed, breath short, trancelike, she lets off an intense burst of song:

Hela, my little girlfriend,
I cannot stay here any longer.
I, the young girl from Leribe will go away, telling no one.
I shall leave my old lover without his knowledge,
My feet padding softly away,
Folding up my blankets as I go.

Now the accordionist, playing the singers and the situation in a deft display, once again calms the mood and supplants the hot *jaife* with a slower Sesotho rhythm with a more local feel. The three singers join together in a choral refrain: "We are cleansed with blood/money (*mali*)."[1] Dancing slowly with eyes open, less tense but more serious, Pontso sings over the supporting refrain:

> Hela, my child, my girlfriend,
> Hela, my young fellow of a boy!
> I feel like leaving here at a moment's notice.
> I shall go unnoticed,
> Folding my blankets as I go.
> Yes indeed, I the little girl from Leribe;
> I cannot stay here any longer.
> This Hlotse camp,
> The place of misfortunes,
> Alas! in what great difficulties I live.
> But you, my little girl-child!

In the midst of this solo, our young male warm-up artist, perhaps jealous of the attention the girls are getting, moves up behind Pontso and hangs on her ear, moving his hips suggestively, his face in a lubricious (but harmless) grin. She ignores him so totally that he is compelled to retreat sheepishly. Pontso has her say, and the chorus ceases as the queen of the Hlotse *famo*, Tholi Mahlase, drifts effortlessly to the center and begins, in those high roof tones that produce hot chills in the chests of her listeners, to sing:

> What cruelty awaits you across the border, girls!
> Those purveyors of mischief in the whiteman's country.
> I'm riding an electric train to the Republic,
> To rightfully claim my blankets left because of fighting.
> Helele, you, my young fellow!
> I wish my voice would ring like a bell
> To let the miners know that I live under hardships here in Lesotho.
> I deeply fear the government in power!
> Hae oeleleoelele oelele oelele!
> I recall when the russians in Johannesburg beat me
> Because of the blankets [lovers];
> I have escaped from the hands of thieves
> Who had snatched me away from you
> As ordered by Raliemere [russian gang leader].
> Oele oele oelelele oelelele!
> People always get in my way,
> But we still disappear into mountain hideaways.

1. The word *mali* in Sesotho carries both its original meaning, "blood," and its more recent Sesothoized loan from English, "money."

When you pass through,
I love young boys!
I make them fall for me, leaving their herds of goats.

It is not so much the sense of Tholi's words as the rhythm and timbre of her voice, so completely commanding the performance, disciplining the accordion player, whose chords now strike a more contemplative mood. Tholi ceases and without a visible cue the accordionist, embracing the rhythm with his instrument, begins a lustrous solo break. A male singer quietly interposes a few supportive lines and ceases. The women dance in small circles amid the sweat and smoke and fumes of sorghum beer, heads rocking back and forth to the compelling chords. Tholi's voice floats over the thickening air:

Go away from here, you with porridge between your teeth;
Go away from here, you with your stinking body.
Return to your cattle posts!
I will not die, because I have paid for my life:
One pound I have paid as ransom against God's design on human life—oe!

Each woman moves separately now, head bobbing down, dancing her own thoughts. Some woman shouts, *Nebo Nebo Nebo Nebo Nebo!* Another whistles shrilly in praise. Tholi, smiling almost broadly, hands raised, lets loose a final round:

Here in Hlotse town, in bed I outstretch myself,
But I do pay dearly for the rent.
It is hard to forget about this place once and for all;
I will never forget Fobane location of Leribe.
Hey boy-child, a creature [only] of God,
Helele helele helele!
Attention! Tell [Chief] Matsekha's men to bring back Uelala's child.
All these gunshots make my jumpy!

The accordionist, aware that something definitive has occurred, changes the rhythm once again to a fierce black South African 8/8 jive, the kind of thing that often serves as "traveling music" in these traveler's bars. The patrons, male and female, rise as one to dance, and the younger set pour in as the large, orderly oval of the *motjeko* is formed, the dancers executing solo footwork in place as the ellipse rolls slowly around the floor. The drummer has his day, dominating even the accordion as it blares like the horn on a wedding Buick. Anybody sings, and thoughtful or impetuous solos are taken in turn as each dancer comes before the ultimate orchestration of the camera. Our three stars whistle and wave the men's fighting sticks they have appropriated. There is rhythmic release, and the cathartic self-articulation of bodies, of the solidary social body of Motolo's *shebeen*. The rubber sticks and drumhead of the *moropa* resound thickly like shotguns heard across hills. There is a pleased satisfaction: they have really shown us something, and later "the nations," through film, will see it too.

Tholi says she has learned a lot from listening to *famo* singers on the Free State's Radio Sesotho, and she's had experience singing in a semiprofessional band. Here in Lesotho she doesn't get any money directly for singing, except that she once won 60 rand in a *shebeen* competition. She sings to feel better, and to share experience with her listeners. "We sing a lot about men," she shrugs, "but I don't think about them unless I want money from them, or if they are my friends like Ntate Motolo; I've got three children but I'll never marry." We pack up, pay up, and leave with our treasure. Later, when the *shebeen* regulars are shown the rushes, there is pandemonium among the women when female performers are on camera, polite boredom when it is the men. For their part, the men reciprocate, but in the *shebeen* sequences the women are clear winners, making the most of home field advantage. For our part, we end our film with this day's footage, virtually unedited—or edited for us by the performers in performance. Who is the maker of an ethnographic film?

HALFWAY THROUGH my first lengthy period of research in Lesotho in 1984, I discovered that the relatively brief, strophic songs sung by female brewers and barflies to the accompaniment of piano accordion and drum in the back-street beer bars bore a strong generic relationship to the men's *sefela*. Women, too, it appeared, could be *likheleke*, "eloquent ones." Some women's texts and important performative clues had been available to me since 1978, and I had already speculated about them in my book *In Township Tonight!* (1985, 98–101). What took me so long to follow through? A conspiracy of silence, and witting and unwitting misconceptions about the place of women and their forms of self-expression in Basotho migrant society on the part of my assistants, key informants, and myself had blinded me to the potency of women's arts of words. What tipped me off? I think the decisive event, in retrospect, was the brashness and self-promoting hoopla with which Apolo Ntabanyane, Lesotho's best-known popular vocalist, recording artist, and showman, proclaimed himself "King of *Famo* Music" at a concert at the old Airport Hotel in Maseru in 1984. The queen of Lesotho, 'MaMohato, wife of King Moshoeshoe II, trumpeted the announcement, would be in attendance. King of *famo? Famo* was a term for a kind of dance party that originated in the 1920s in *shebeens* run by Basotho women in Johannesburg, where bar girls danced suggestively before male seekers of sexual entertainment. The word comes from the ideophone *ho re famo*, "to flare the nostrils, to throw up one's garments," and is defined in the dictionary as mine slang for "an indecent dance" (Mabille, Dieterlen, and Paroz 1983, 70). Originally, the key to the dance was *hoa fecha* (from English "fetch"), a more or less exaggerated version of the backward bobbing of the hips (*ho tsoka*) characteristic of rural Basotho female folk dance, fetching enough to begin with. As Mphafu Mofolo sings in a *sefela* passage praising "wild country girls":

> Girls danced and the boys performed ndlamu—
> Dark beauties with glossy buttocks billowing out behind.
> Girls from my home wear floating skirts:
> The dress rises well above the knee.

When intensified to a thrust and performed wearing a short, full skirt, the movement has the effect of flipping up the garment as high as the waist, revealing the ample attractions underneath. *Famo* performers were careful not to wear any underwear. This, Basotho women assured me (I saw no reason to doubt them), was the means by which bar girls or rivals "fetched" their husbands and lovers away.

Now students of the social history of music are well aware of the process by which the dances of the streets and saloons are transformed and domesticated for the ballroom, the gala, and the concert hall. So the *kalinda* of Cuban slaves became first the sensuous rumba, then the demure cha-cha; the fiery *samba* of Brazilian carnival became the bossa nova; and of course, the waltz and other folk and popular dances have long featured in European philharmonic repertoires. In the case of *famo;* this process is very far from complete. I was aware, by the time of Apolo Ntabanyane's self-crowning, that the accordion-band music played on commercial cassettes by migrants on trains and buses, in beer bars, and at get-togethers of all kinds was directly derived from the accordion and drum songs performed at *famo*. But how could a male performer become the king of *famo*, and play before the Queen?

Though I had often dropped in at *shebeens* in search of *sefela* singers in a mood to hold forth, the eloquent ones always refused to perform in them, saying the raucous, noisy atmosphere was not conducive to serious extemporization or listening. Unlike *shebeen* songs, *lifela* are not performed to instrumental accompaniment. Now we were going back to the bars to hear the women instead. Negotiating for the services of a young female research assistant (struggling middle class), I explained to a male visitor that we were "studying women [oral] poets." He gave me a look of concern: there were, he stated categorically, no women poets; women were "singers," a less authoritative and prestigious category of wordsmith. I could have mentioned the well-known praise poet 'MaMpho Chopo and the outstanding published poetry of Mrs. B. M. Khaketla, but I didn't. Back at the *shebeens*, I inquired if women had their own genre; that is, what were *shebeen* songs called? They didn't have a name, just *lipina tsa Basotho* (songs). I suggested terms I associated with them: *famo?* No, that was just the special dance party for gangsters and their molls. *Focho?* (from *fecha?*): that was just the wild dancing, or more nearly, the lethal concoction that made drinkers dance like that. If I wanted to refer directly to the singing itself, I found I had to imitate performance, pronouncing the high-pitched, hortatory vocable *seoeleoelele!* (*se-we-le-we-le-le!*)—no mean feat—singers use to claim the attention of their listeners at the beginning of a song.

I wasn't really surprised. In rural life there are few occasions for a woman to express herself directly to a mixed audience. Before the pervasiveness of male migrancy made this untenable, a Basotho woman (like a child) was not allowed to speak on her own behalf or to give testimony at the chief's court or public assembly—except of course for the chief, who was quite often a woman! If she sought to express explicit disapproval in the presence of authority, she affected a stony, sullen silence that spoke more powerfully (and more safely) than angry words. In conversation a married woman was forbidden to use the personal names or even words whose sound resembled the names of her senior male affines, using instead *hlonepho* (respect), the vocabulary of avoidance. Ironically but unsurprisingly, women used *hlonepho* as a form of verbal competition (Kunene 1958, 162), testing one another's knowledge and cleverness in the elaboration of "restricted synonyms" that could at once avoid an in-law's name and praise or skewer him by veiled metaphor. Another episode in the gender politics of Sesotho, I thought: men withholding authority from women's words by denying women's most formidable genre a name.

But the reality was far more complex and dialogic: I had forgotten that song is the one medium where Basotho women enjoy poetic license, and that seventy years ago Dutton (1923, 75) had observed that Basotho women could gain through performative eloquence a degree of personal authority otherwise denied them. Even in *hlonepho*, the designated substitute for *ho bina*, "to sing," is *ho kelekenya*, "to speak out with eloquence" (Adams 1974, 131). Study of *shebeen* performance revealed that the personal compositions of women were as intentionally artful, as reflective and critical, and as persuasive and cathartic as the *lifela* of their men. It is precisely for this reason that *shebeen* songs have no generic name. Socialized to avoid direct public criticism of men, Basotho women have no interest in identifying and thus singling out for condemnation a genre in which their most serious complaints are publicly, evocatively, and viscerally expressed: "These are just songs, Ntate David." On a close listening, I was more than tempted to simply call them women's *lifela*, but I could get no Mosotho to call them that unless I reverted to that fieldwork favorite, "leading the ethnographic witness." Just songs they may be, but that did not stop male customers from jumping up to sing angry ripostes when stung by women's lyrical barbs (if the shoe fits), nor did it stop the women from pushing a man back down when they were in no mood to be interrupted. The *shebeen* is a public domain where, as the *maele* says, *mosali ke morena*, "woman is chief," providing a rare public forum for women's discourse on problems that are unacknowledged in other contexts. To understand how this came to be requires the location of *shebeen* songs both in the wide domain of Sesotho auriture, and along the highroads and crossroads of Basotho migratory experience.

Whether they comment on the general disabilities of Basotho women or narrate a personal plight with which female auditors easily identify, women's genres both old and recent are freighted with the catharsis of affliction. Oldest among them is the *koli-ea-malla*, an archaic lament sung only by women on the death of a husband or close male kinsman. Apparently no longer performed, there is no more beautiful and touching example among the surviving collected texts than the one published by Guma in which solo and chorus echo one another in the darkening atmosphere of desolation:[2]

SOLO:

Ke mohibi, mosala-suping.	I am a wailing fool who remains among ruins.
Ke mohibi, mosala-palapaleng.	I am a wailing fool who remains in a bare, open field.
Ana ke setse hokae, *Ka rare, ke setse le mang?*	Where do I remain, By my father, with whom do I remain?

CHORUS:

Ha eshwa batho; ra sala le mang? *Ha fela batho; ho sale diesola.*	Men died; with whom do we remain? Men departed; only the worthless remain.

2. Researchers' pronouncements of the death of genres are notoriously questionable. Upon the publication of this book, I shall not be surprised to hear from a Mosotho colleague that somewhere in Lesotho he or she has heard *koli-ea-malla*. Let us at least hope so.

Ha fela banna; ra sala le mang?	Real men departed; with whom do we remain?
SOLO:	
Ke mohihi, mosala-suping.	I am a wailing fool who remains among ruins.
Ha le feletse makobotelo,	When the sun has sunk low,
Halfing ke a ya,	To the door I go,
Ka tsetsekwane ke a nanya,	On tip-toe advancing slowly,
Ke hloma a itlela,	Supposing him coming alone,
Ke hloma a itswela tsholong.	Supposing him returning from the hunt.
CHORUS:	
Ha eshwa batho; ra sala le mang?	Men died; with whom do we remain?
Ha eshwa batho; ra sala suping.	Men died; we remained in ruins.
Ha eshwa batho; ra sala palapaleng.	Men died; we remained in a bare, open field.[3]

(Guma 1967, 109–10)

In the *mokhibo*, "kneeling dance" (*ho khiba*, "to kneel"), Lesotho's most popular and widely performed female folk genre, dancers sing a chorus of a single line or couplet, which by itself can attain widespread popularity if it indexes some telling social reality. Supporting singers alternate with responses, and a senior woman leader (*sephoko*) plays the *moropa* (drum) and sings the solo. Hugh Tracey recorded a solo in 1959 (AMA. TR 104 B-1 N2G11) that expressed in a tone not unlike that of the *koli ea malla* the sense of abandonment and resentment felt by women left in Lesotho or forced into migration themselves by absent and unsupportive husbands:

> Taung, Moletsane's place, my home!
> If I speak, I shall cause sorrow: some would remember things,
> And I would be bringing back the dead.
> Women on the Rand are vagrants; they wear shoes without stockings.
> You can see our mountains in Basutoland.
> The hawk which dwells on the cliff at Ramalile
> Catches the chickens when they go out to feed.

Another of Tracey's recordings (AMA. TR 103 B3), which he describes as a women's "feast or party song," has even more the tone of affliction and rebellious complaint characteristic of *shebeen* songs:

3. My transcription here retains the South African orthography of Guma's original, but I have made some revisions of my own in the English translation. Sesotho speakers will note the occurrence of several archaic words in this text.

Aunt, stretch out the blanket;
There are two of us.
Stretch out the blanket;
I'll be coming. I'm going out to smoke [make love].
When I leave here, going away,
Montsala remain here and look after my children.
Look after Mamotolo and Malerato and Toma.
Toma, look after these children of mine,
Particularly Mamotolo and Malerato.
It looks as if I'll be going away.
I feel I'm going.
I really feel I'll be crossing the [Caledon] River
[to South Africa]

This potential migrant is perhaps luckier than many of her counterparts, for it appears she may be going to South Africa with her man, rather than in search of him or even to get away from him. The truth is that though they may not face the immediate threats of injury and death in the mines or the violence of the mine compounds, women's lot under the migratory labor system is on a continuing basis more fraught with insecurity, dependence, and hardship than that of their men. What, then, are the afflictions, the thousand unnatural shocks that Basotho women's flesh is heir to?

There is a small but superb literature of the life of "peasantarian" women in Lesotho, including accounts by van Drunen (1977), Spiegel (1980), Gay (1980a, 1980b, 1980c), Gordon (1981), Murray (1981), Wilkinson (1985), Bonner (1988), and Heap (1989). I would rather commend interested readers to these scholars than repeat their findings here, but because three of the five full-length monographs cited are unpublished doctoral dissertations and a fourth is available only at the Centre for African Studies at the University of Cape Town, I may perhaps be doing both my colleagues and my readers a service by summarizing some of their most salient points. Certainly these authors' conclusions are reflected in *shebeen* songs. It is especially regrettable that Judith Gay's thesis was not published and now, as she told me, it may be too late since a major update would be required. Indeed, with the changes afoot throughout South Africa and Lesotho almost all sociological data seem to require constant updating, so I will attempt a few contemporary observations as well.

When a young girl comes of age, her heart will want to marry, for only her own house and children can bring her the respect, security, and identity due to a "mother," as all adult women are properly addressed. Yet she may not: given imbalanced gender ratios and the absence of so many men in their twenties and thirties, a husband can be hard to find. Further, except among the small Westernized elite (and sometimes within it), so hard will be her lot as a young wife that a husband, if found, may not be wanted. Still, the alternatives to marriage are certainly no bargain.

Basotho marriage within the migrant labor system (and for the people we are talking about there is hardly any concept of marriage apart from labor migrancy) is both a crucial and precarious partnership. A man marries "with cattle," a prestation that demonstrates his identification with and investment in his rural community, validating, symbolically at least, the expression heard so often in village conversation: *Khomo ke bophelo ba Mosotho*, "The cow is the life of the Mosotho" (Gay 1980c, 190). Of course, he doesn't yet have these cattle. So he heads for the mines, where whatever else he does, he is supposed to remit a large portion of his wages to support his homestead and its inhabitants, and if possible to buy livestock for bridewealth, plowing, and capital. In exchange, his wife manages the homestead and its resources in his absence, cares for children and aged relatives, and preserves his social and material investment against the day of his permanent homecoming. But this paradoxical bargain, in which the homestead is augmented through the subtraction of its owner and managed in the absence of his authority, is subject to nearly unbearable structural and psychological pressures.

Upon marriage, a woman passes from the jural control of her father to that of her husband and his agnates. A man's identity derives from the chief who controls the land where he homesteads, but as Chief Jobo said in 1873, "A women has no chief but her husband" (Duncan 1960, 5). But like her father, this husband is hardly ever around. Who is around? A mother-in-law (a father-in-law if he's not at the mines or dead) whom she must obey and work for and live with if her husband has not yet built her a house of her own. Above them is a chief whose interest is in making sure that the women of his absent followers "behave" and stay put. If she has her own house, she is almost totally dependent on her husband's earnings and on rights to land and property established by marriage; yet she must still contend with his parents both for these earnings and for household authority (Showers 1980, 55–56). While her husband is away, she must be an independent and resourceful household manager with neither the jural rights nor the economic autonomy to fulfill the responsibilities she must bear (Gay 1980c, 132).

As much trouble as that is, it is often when her husband comes home that the real trouble starts. Subordinate to mine regimen and discriminatory authority in the "whitemen's country," he may be overly eager to reestablish his command over his own homestead, compensating for his own powerlessness and stress at the expense of his wife. Why has she not spent his money as he has instructed in his letters, and why was so much spent on food and clothes and household utensils? Who (which other man) has paid for all these new dresses and blankets? Why did she allow others to steal livestock, plant on parts of his fields, feed their animals on her crops, cheat her out of her share of the communal yield? Who is she to question why he needs a horse to canter from beer joint to beer joint on Saturday, drinking with his migrant friends? What are her friends saying about him behind his back? Used to self-reliance, the wife must endure the countermanding of her experienced management by a sometime visitor working to master his own feelings of alienation. As Gay puts it, "The wife who has been sleeping in the bed, eating at the table and entertaining her friends in the best room or building relinquishes the bed to her husband except when he calls her, serves him and his male friends at the table, eats her own food on the floor with the children, and entertains in the cooking hut or kitchen" (ibid., 177–78).

Because rural Basotho boys spend years herding, a wife may well have more formal schooling than her husband, but direct protest or self-assertion is unlikely to be tolerated. Relatives burdened by their own problems may not offer much assistance or relief for her loneliness, stress, and fragile self-esteem. Sex and money are interrelated causes of marital conflict, with both husband and wife worried about the loss of earnings and conjugal rights through adultery. Yet it is only through marriage that a rural woman can hope to improve her life. Judith Gay once asked a village girl who was about to marry what she expected to find in marriage. "Babies and troubles and beatings every day," she said, "and a house and furnishings and dishes and all the nice things I want." She will be lucky if she receives her share of this bargain. Many husbands send too little money, entertain too great expectations, visit too seldom, take too little interest, have too little understanding. Elizabeth Gordon's research (1981, 61–67) revealed the self-perception of many migrants' wives as one of loneliness, helplessness, and poverty.

People, even the wives of migrants, are of course not always as powerless as they might wish others to think. A "good husband" in the terms of the system may suffer from his dependence on his wife's management of household resources in his absence. As one such husband, a mineworker, testified:

> When I think about the last sixteen years, then I should stop working here. For years I've been sending money home, but don't think I'm exaggerating

> when I say after ten years my wife hasn't even managed to save R50 [in 1992 about $20]. Imagine now I lose my job and I'm forced to leave this place of gold. What then have I been doing in the mines for all those years?[4]

Just keeping yourself, your family, and your marriage alive is the answer, for as one of his co-workers argued, only money can keep a migrant's marriage together. While a man may feel more affection for an urban girlfriend than a rural wife, a wife too may come to feel greater attachment to a present lover than to an absent husband. Among a migrant's most nagging fears is that expressed by another mineworker:

> I go home for a weekend on leave. Before leaving to come back here, I give my wife R600 [1992 value $240]. She goes with me to the bustop, to make sure that I've gone back to the mines. Then she grabs her boyfriend going to the nearest joint for a drink, "Look at all this wild money the gold digger left. Come on, darling, let's go and tame it; the gold digger is gone."[5]

Many wives bemoan the unavailability of active fathering and the burdensome decision-making and familial conflicts that make their periods of independence less than enjoyable, yet they would not want to live with their husbands in South Africa even if that were allowed. Both husband and wife have too much invested in their rural base and social identity as Basotho to abandon them for a "government of the Boers" (post-Boers for that matter). Nor do I wish to imply that Basotho marriages are incapable of withstanding the pressures of migrancy, or that there is something inevitable about the conflicts I have rudely typified. Mphafu Mofolo (Ngoan'abo Mokhoati), a renowned *sefela* composer, worked nearly forty years on the mines. Though he was given no pension, he retired to his village of Ha-Shale in Maama's District, where he eked out a living until his death in 1987 with the help of his wife's earnings as a part-time domestic and contributions from a son living in the Free State. I cannot think of a couple more devoted to each other than Mphafu, the grizzled career miner, and his wife. All right, every ethnologist must mind the Yiddish proverb, "'For example' is no proof," but marriages that survive long droughts of separation only to flower emotionally in the partnership of maturity are both aspired to and often achieved in Lesotho. Interestingly, Mphafu's *lifela* are replete with hilarious and often self-deprecating amorous adventures, a veteran miner's stock-in-trade:

4. On camera testimony of a mineworker in Don Edkins and Mike Schlömer's excellent film, *The Colour of Gold* (Medienwerkstatt Freiburg 1992).
5. Ibid.

Mphafu, ha ke atamela litšoana,	Mphafu, when I approach the black complexioned ones,
La ntebaetsa letsoalo.	I became faint-hearted.
Mocha, ka utloa mangoele ho khoehla.	A youngster, I felt my knees go weak.
Le banana ba bile ba ncheba;	Girls even looked at me;
Ka bona ba ncheba ba sheba koana.	I saw them looking at me and looking away.
Qetellong eaba ba ea li opa;	At last they clapped hands;
Joale ba li opa liatlanyana.	Now they clapped the small hands.
Ba le tšeha ba le re qhoa, "A khae je."	They laughed and laughed, "*A khae je.*"
Papatlele, e tsoa kae, basali	A vagabond, where does he come from, ladies?
Tseke-tseke o sena le mehopolo	A dull man without thuoghts,
Latha-latha o sena le pelo ea lerato,	A fool without a heart for love,
Ekaba ea ratang ntho ena ke mang?	Who could love this thing?
Moitšepi ea joalo oa motho,	A proud person like that,
Lijo tsa malapeng, oa li hana.	Food from other families, he refuses them.
Le ha a tla ja, o batla a sikoe.	If he should eat, he wants to be held in your arms.
A sikoe joalo ka ngoana oa lesea—	He's held in the arms like a baby—
Ntle ho, tseo tse joalo o tla o hlala!	Besides that he will divorce you!

Mphafu: in life a steady migrant worker, soldier (World War II), hardscrabble farmer, husband, and father; in auriture a rake, a boozer, a marijuana smoker, a singer, a Christian sinner. We are reminded again of the complexity of the relationship between experience and art: when analyzing products of the imagination, as W. H. Auden admonished, "Thou shalt not commit a social science."

The point is really that migrant husbands and their wives are vitally dependent upon one another. A man can neither take his family to South Africa nor remain there himself if he is injured, ill, or too old to work, and so he must build up his rural security while he can. The entire migratory labor system and thus the South African economy itself depends as much upon rural women as it does upon migrant men (Gay 1980c, 126). As long as the system persists, the preservation of marriage and the reciprocal obligations defined by the Basotho family system are essential for everyone's economic security; but it also creates conditions that undermine the patrilineal structure and make it difficult to develop close conjugal bonds (ibid., 310). In the crucial matter of child care, the sibling relationship is often as important as the marital one, as sisters and brothers care for each other's children through cyclical reciprocity and fosterage. Sesotho is therefore still a source of values needed to cement ties on which everyone depends, not despite, but because of migrancy (ibid., 89–92). Basotho institutions like bridewealth do not simply persist but have taken on new functions in the maintenance of family networks (see Spiegel 1980).

At any one time, roughly half of all married women in Lesotho are wives of absent migrants, and their experience is the backdrop against which women *shebeen* singers are silhouetted. But they are not in general the singers themselves. The *basali ba bokheleke*, the women of eloquence, are those who, married or not, have taken up options other than or in addition to dependence on a husband's remittance. What are these options? Despite its drawbacks, most women need to be married and to avoid spinsterhood, separation, and divorce if they can. It is only through legal marriage that a girl can break from childhood dependence, be respected as a woman, and obtain lifelong rights to a homestead and a house of her own, to the labor and cash support of a man, to fields and livestock, and be assured the legitimate right to the labor and earning power of her children (Gay 1980c, 45–46). Even within marriage, a personal cash income, however small, can add enormously to a woman's autonomy, self-confidence, and leverage within the household. Perhaps for this reason, many men formerly resisted wage labor or self-employment for their wives, though today the financial relief it provides is a powerful counterweight to fears of female independence.

In the rural areas, however, jobs are very few, and only the informal sector provides much opportunity for women to earn a cash income. Self-employed women in both rural and urban areas can knit and sew, sell cooked food, trade in pottery and other homemade goods, run small shops, or "cafes" as they are called, sell old clothes or even illicit diamonds; but most often they brew. Farming, once women's work, is impossible without the capital investment of migrant wages, and plowing is male labor that women must somehow engage and supervise. Decades ago migrants came home for plowing, sheepshearing, and other essential labors of the agricultural cycle. Today, career miners fortunate enough to have jobs must hurry back from short-term leaves lest their reengagement certificates expire and they find themselves replaced by one of the thousands of job-hungry unemployed. Many continuing migrants are gentlemen farmers, spending what little time they have at home sitting about with friends or strolling the fields gazing proprietarily at their scrawny stock and the uneven, stunted rows of corn and sorghum clinging to thin-skinned hillsides or huddled between the huge erosion gullies. The fact is that in this broken, weatherbeaten land, women without their men cannot add substantially to household production through cultivation. Even so, agriculture remains a central activity of rural women as a source not only of food and psychological security but of cash from the sale of beer.

Beer has always played a central role in the spiritual and social life of Basotho communities, and it remains crucial to contemporary social relations. Routine hospitality at the chief's residence, feasts for the ancestors, rituals of the life cycle, the naming of a newborn, Christian celebrations, and numerous other occasions all require the much appreciated and remarked upon contribution of beer brewed by women. Gay notes (ibid., 239) that beer is also essential to meetings of the special women's court, *lekhotla la basali*, called under the leadership of a senior wife or mother of a chief, at which all women who have borne children gather in a secluded spot to listen to cases exclusively involving women. The consumption of quantities of beer is also a prominent feature of occasions celebrating "the company of women," ritual dance feasts known as *litolobonya*. Mutual support among Basotho women centers in multigenerational, matrilineal female networks that have developed among women in response to male migrancy. Both within marriage and without, female networks involving both kin and kith are a major source of social support. *Sesotho* designates reproduction as an exclusively female domain, and customs that emphasize this responsibility are intensified by the absence of men. The support that mothers give to those newly joining their numbers, for example, as well as the social power that accumulates from female solidarity under labor migrancy, is expressed and exemplified by the growing popularity of the rural village dance feasts formerly known as *pitiki*. Gay believed in the mid 1970s that *pitiki* performances were declining, but my experience in the late 1980s, as well as participants' own observations, testified to its increasing visibility in rural Lesotho. This is partly because the occasion has developed from a ceremonial feast marking the end of a new mother's period of confinement (about two months after the birth) to a form of dance competition among teams of mothers from various district villages.

Pitiki (*ho pitika*, "to roll in a circular motion") centered on the "outdooring" of the new mother and infant and feasted all the mothers who had attended at the birth of the child. A man entered the *motsoetseng*, the room of confinement from which all males had formerly been barred, and came outdoors with the infant, where he was greeted by women performing *mokhibo*. Then the women went back inside and performed the special *pitiki* dance, which was strictly off-limits to men. The costumes consisted of very short feather or fringe skirts, open in front, and specifically constructed to show off the expertise of the dancers in the suggestive *hoa fecha* movement on which the dance was centered. The sequence of movements mimed the procreative process from conception through pregnancy, labor, and delivery, and the idea was to celebrate womanliness among women. More recently, more or less regular teams of dancers have sprung up in urban neighborhoods as well as rural villages, and they may travel to compete against one another at feasts at which no newborn need be involved, though membership is still limited to those who have borne a child. These occasions are now called *litolobonya*, a delicious but untranslatable term whose root words refer to "a rolling or protruding flirtation." The real meaning is that inexpressible delight that both men and women feel when women bob their derrières seductively when dancing before men. But at *litolobonya* there are no men. The men gather outside the house, drinking the women's beer and conversing dyspeptically as the women's songs and lusty cheers filter out from behind the tightly shuttered windows. What, then, is being communicated, what feelings expressed?

I was myself allowed to witness two performances of *litolobonya* and even to record the occasions on film and tape, authorized by the idea that since I was not a Mosotho I was not really a man. I have no evidence that having a non-man as a non-normative male spectator added anything to the women's fun. The women wore underwear, top and bottom, along with berets and fringe skirts, but a few asserted that at some performances, particularly those held after dark, only the little open fringes were worn. The texts are short and repetitive, and not uncommonly include the church hymns that have entered the corpus of Basotho folk music. Others celebrated the dancing itself, boasting of the team's prowess and scorning that of their rivals, especially in *hoa fecha*. After all, if a woman can't *fecha* enticingly, she invites those who can to entice away their husbands. Some songs employ lyrics suggestive of a certain freedom as well as sexuality:

Nyatsi ea ka bapala, bapala, bapala—oe!
Aee! Ha o bapala, o etsise monna oa ka—oe!
Ha o bapala, bapala—oe!

My lover, move it, move it, move it—oe!
Aee! When you move it, really do it like my husband—oe!
When you move it, move it—oe!

Still others are openly critical of men who condemn this celebration of motherhood while avoiding their own manly responsibilities:

Banna ba sejoalejoale,
Le hana ka pitiki; le hana ka lenyalo.
Lea hana, lea hana.

These very contemporary men,
They refuse *pitiki;* they refuse marriage.
They refuse, they refuse.

Yet another condemns women who betray the secrets of the dance to curious men:

Ke mongala.	It is deserting [our sorority].
Le sa tla ngaloha—	Some of you shall flee from there—
Lona bo-me le joetsa banna lintho tsa pitiki.	You women who are telling the men our secrets of *pitiki.*
Le sa tla ngaloha; ke mongala.	You will flee from it; it's desertion.

One woman suggested a parallel between these songs and men's *mangae* songs, since *litolobonya* like male initiation is secret to its participants, but there is no connection between female initiation rites and *litolobonya.* Rather, she explained, *litolobonya* is the female counterpart to *mohobelo*, the dance that displays both individual manliness and male comradeship and social coordination. Queen 'MaMohato (now Queen Mother), ever an enthusiast of *Sesotho* folk performance, held *litolobonya* regularly in the royal palace in Maseru during the mid 1980s. But what *litolobonya* appears to be celebrating is the growing emergence of "a more self-sufficient female world" (Showers 1980, 57) among women, married or not. This growing independence of women can be seen as part of a worldwide trend, which may be irreversible and profound in its effects because it challenges both the conjugal relation and the patriarchal family structure (Gay 1980c, 308–9). The self-assertive, independent attitude ever more prevalent among Basotho women is rooted in their growing reliance on networks composed of other women rather than or in addition to dependence on the advocacy and money of men.

Gunner's (1979) discussion of Zulu women's praises describes a performance context akin to Basotho *litolobonya* but a content similar to *seoeleoelele.* Zulu women perform their personal praises essentially for one another at feasts where female group identity and solidarity are emphasized. There, stretching out in the security of their own subculture of laughter, the whole nine yards of poetic license is taken. As in a Basotho *shebeen,* vigorous solo dancing and intense audience-performer interaction dramatize recitations elaborating and assessing the performer's personal identity within a shared experience. The praises grow in length over the years, combining the themes of affliction with sexual braggadocio (ibid., 242–45), serving as both weapons and celebrations of the singer. These are the unzipped nineties of course, even in Lesotho. Since *litolobonya* has become so secular and popular, its performance detached from the context of parturition, girls without children and even men have begun to infiltrate. No longer a kind of *koma*, a secret, *litolobonya* is now witnessed by men and performed in a casual manner by girls in the village streets, and even by male dancers, dressed in the usual female garb, on "Ezodumo," SATV's weekly television program of "traditional music." Of course, I would like to blame the latter spectacle on the propensity of South African state TV to serve up artificial studio refuse as African tradition, but I cannot. We anthropologists are doomed, it seems, to lament the contravention of convention (or our structural analyses of it) while our subjects unapologetically get on with their culture. Men doing *litolobonya?* What is *Sesotho* (or my beautiful model of it) coming to?

Seen today in every village is the white or yellow *phephesela*, a rag or plastic bag flapping on a tall stick to advertise the sale for cash of one or another variety of home brew, a material symbol of the hard struggle for both survival and personal autonomy among women. The houses where it flies have become informal centers of sociability, where migrants on leave, the unemployed, and retirees can spend their time agreeably together, but also where women run the show and in the context of market exchange socialize on a more equal, characteristically proletarian basis with men. Canned European-style beer and brandy may also be sold, at a profit of around 35 percent. Even so, there's not much money to be made in a village. Those who brew for cash are not much respected, and it is considered suitable employment only for the otherwise destitute, those who have lost their men. Women who brew and sell beer are believed to exercise a dangerous power over men who drink. Judith Gay offers the following story as typical of those that circulate regarding the unscrupulous power some women who brew are believed to exert:

> A young migrant had stayed in South Africa for many years. Finally he returned home unannounced and decided to stop at a beer house before going home. The proprietor and her daughter plied him with beer until late into the night when they robbed him of what little money remained, took all his clothes, and pushed him into a reservoir to drown. Only the next day when the police arrived did the women discover that it was their own husband and long-lost son whom they had destroyed. (1980c, 257)

Certainly married women who have become successful in selling beer (or have gained income from any other source) are in a stronger position when their husbands return. In addition to the daily round of brewing, special rotating credit associations or temporary brewing and cooking partnerships called *setokofele* (from South African *stokfel;* see Coplan 1985, 102–5) may be formed to hold weekend-long fetes to fund a major capital expenditure. A woman with enough capital resources and enough clientele may turn her place into a regular village *shebeen*, complete with accordion and drum band and soloists to sing. The *shebeen* was imported during the 1920s by women who themselves migrated to South Africa specifically to enter the liquor trade. Returning along with their migrant menfolk, they established the *bara* (from English "bar") or *sepoto* as a fixture of both town and country life in Lesotho itself.

This brings us to the option most popular with women who have decided to take their chances outside the hardships and disappointments of marriage, or who have suffered the loss of their husbands through desertion, separation, divorce, or death: migration. Of course a woman who leaves or loses her husband can return to her natal home, but she is unlikely to get much support or respect from her parents, brothers, or their wives, to whom she and her children are an unexpected, illegitimate burden. With neither agnatic, conjugal, nor affinal rights or social position, it is better to strike out on your own.

Despite the extreme difficulty of obtaining a legal divorce in Lesotho and attestations to the stability of traditional Basotho marriage, de facto divorce has been part of Basotho life since the mid nineteenth century (Phoofolo 1980, 11–14). These were cases of desertion and sometimes remarriage by women whose frequent intention was to follow the trails well-traveled by men. The distorted social system that no longer provided social security for women in return for their continuing subordination made migration to South Africa an attractive, sometimes necessary alternative. Local authorities attempted to deal with this problem by collaborating with South African attempts to prevent women from crossing the Caledon River and to repatriate them when they did, but with little effect except to keep female migrants on the move, wherever they were. Such women became known as *matekatse*, a term universally translated in Lesotho as "prostitutes." It is derived, however, from *ho teka*, "to roam about," and *ho tekatsa*, "to abandon one's husband," and so signifies an independent woman, free of the control but bereft of the support of father, older brother, or husband. The wives themselves, however, protest that they go to *itsebeletsa*, "to work for myself," or to *phelisa bana ba ka*, "to support my children" (Gay 1980c, 275). As one of the most renowned *shebeen* singers, 'Malitaba, complained:

'Malitaba oa Mphoso—oe! *Ba mpitsa molele,* *Ha ke molele; ke phetha mabaka.*	I, 'Malitaba of Mphoso—oe! They call me a vagabond, But I am not a vagabond; I am taking care of business.

Helele! Ke tsoteletseng ha ncheba lenyemo-nyemo?	Helele! Should I mind when they wink at me?
Ba seba ka moea, hoba ba tsaba ho buoa.	They spread evil of me in secret whispers, yet they fear to speak out.

If a woman has lost her husband, or even if she hasn't, she may decide it is better to go away where she can live independently, support herself, and establish new liaisons. As early as 1906, British officials in the Mohale's Hoek district reported complaints about women "absconding from their husbands and taking refuge in the colony [South Africa]" (Gay 1980c, 275). The numbers involved were significant, causing concern among South African authorities about "undesirable Basotho women" plying their trades in mining areas and urban townships (Bonner 1988). The presence of such women helped create a stabilized urban African population and threatened the rural base of the migratory labor system in the so-called homelands, both consequences that the strategists of segregation and white supremacy, not to mention Basutoland colonial administrators and Basotho chiefs, were at pains to prevent. For any woman in difficulty, South Africa offered a refuge from marital problems, an alternative means to support herself and her children, and an attractive if risky road to freedom from rural poverty and subordination. In her epochal study *Reaction to Conquest*, Monica Hunter wrote of urban South Africa in the 1930s: "The deserted and deserting wives form the nucleus of a very large class . . . which is swelled by numbers of unwed mothers and widows . . . driven by poverty to come to town to earn money to support their children and themselves (Hunter 1936, 484). While their songs may not be termed *lifela*, women *shebeen* singers are *litsamaea-naha*, worldly travelers as intrepid as their men.

Up until 1962, 27 percent of known Basotho migrants were women (Gay 1980b, 40), but then South African law made female migration from Basutoland illegal, and those who could not fix their papers or disappear somehow into the urban woodwork were sent back. Since then the official numbers have steadily declined, and since the enaction of even tougher new "influx control" legislation in 1979, the total is now about 7 percent (Gay 1980a, 24). Today younger women resent the restrictions and envy their mothers who had the opportunity for legal migration. To Basotho men, migration meant wage bondage, even if they accepted its necessity and used it to their advantage. But to a woman, paradoxically, South Africa represented something like freedom, however much they might fear and resent the brutal triple oppression they suffered there as Africans, as women, and as illegal migrants. Town is the only place where a woman's chief might be herself, rather than her husband. A strong recent trend among younger women is internal migration to Lesotho's border towns, where in certain quarters females between the ages of twenty and thirty-four outnumber their male counterparts by four to one (see Wilkinson 1985, 136–61). Many of these women have moved along with rather than without husbands. Rather than relegating them to a remote and unproductive rural homestead, many migrants these days prefer to have their families in an urban center where they can reach them more frequently and easily from their South African workplace and where their wives may get some work in the informal sector. Marion Heap (1989, 75) observes that women who do manage to secure their own steady source of income often refuse to marry, protecting themselves against male control, appropriation, and dissipation of their earnings. For most of the women who drift to the border towns without husbands, however, there is little decent work (Gay 1980b, 50), and brewing is a popular occupation. So Thakane "Tholi" Mahlasi, prevented from migrating and harassed by chiefs, local officials and former prime minister Leabua Jonathan's Lebotho la Khotso (literally and ironically: "Peace Corps," the high-handed and violently repressive civil guards) calls out to her male comrades in South Africa:

Heee! lentsoe la ka e ka b'e le tloloko,	Yea, If my voice could be like a clocktower chime,
Nka be ke memetsa.	I could call out loud.
Ke bitsa banna ba Khauteng ke ba joetse,	I'd call the men at Johannesburg and tell them,
Kea sotleha, Lesotho mona;	It's oppressing me, Lesotho here;
Kea hampe, Lesotho mona.	It's awful, Lesotho here.
Ha ke loana, ke isoa moreneng;	When I fight, I am brought before the chief;
Ha ke loana, ke bitsoa khotla.	When I fight, I'm brought to court.
Ke re ke otla kamehla,	I say I am always beaten up,
Ke se ke bile ke otile—	To where I've become thin—
Oelele! oelele! oelele!	Oelele! oelele! oelele!
Ke tsabile 'muso oa mathata;	I've fled from a government of miseries;
Ke tsabile Lebotho la Khotso	I've fled from the "Peace Corps."
Heela, uena ngoan'a moshanyana!	Heeyyy, you man-child!
Ho betere ke shoele lefatseng la makhooeng—bo!	It's better I die in the whitemen's land—bo!
Nkeke be ka koenehela likano;	But I can never betray my oaths;
Nka mpa ka shoela borasheeng koana.	I'd rather die among russians (gangsters) yonder.

Hele helele, Ngoan'a Mathopela!	Hele helele, Mathopela's Child!
'Me' le ntate—oeeeee!	Oh mother and father—oeeeee!
Ua ithaba u na le 'mao,	You are happy you have your mother,
'Mao le ntat'ao,	Your mother and your father,
E tle e re ha u shoele, ba u llele:	So that when you are dead, they will bewail you:
"Hele helele, Ngoan'a Tsele,	Hele helele, Tsele's Child [her lover],
Ke mofu a ithobaletse;	She is dead and gone to sleep;
Ke e motle Mofokeng."	She was a beautiful Mofokeng."

Brewing and entertaining in a *shebeen* is one of the best available ways for independent women to extract some money out of the migrant labor system, not only illegally in South Africa but in Lesotho's urban lowlands as well (Gay 1980a, 26–27). There money can be demanded from regular migrant boyfriends without foregoing the rewards of moonlighting among the local leftovers or, better, with *ma-weekend*, migrants living it up on a three-day pass. One of the Maseru neighborhoods formerly most notorious for *shebeens* was named after this social scene: Thibella (Prevent), refers to the ways bar girls catch hold of returning migrants as soon as they recross the border, preventing them from ever reaching their rural homes and families. Conversely, as I talked to migrants heading back to South Africa at the Maseru borderpost one Boxing Day (December 26), I noticed a number of wives who had come to say goodbye. "Do you always come to see your husband off?" I asked one. "Oh yes," she replied, "to make sure he really goes, and doesn't slip back to the *shebeens* for a few days instead." Once she is sure he is gone, of course, she may not fear to spend her migrant husband's money with a boyfriend at a *shebeen* herself.

Tholi, meanwhile, was trapped as a barfly among scruffy bumpkins in a *sepoto* in Hlotse, capital of Leribe District. Rather than put up with this kind of clientele and with her current boyfriend, Tsele, a lovable man but born under a bad sign, she'd take her chances as an illegal migrant and gang moll in South Africa:

> Go away from here,
> You with porridge between your teeth.
> Go away from here,
> You with stinking body.
> Return to your cattle posts. . . .
> . . . Here is Hlotse town in bed I outstretched myself,
> But I do pay dearly for the rent. . . . [6]

6. The first part of the passage comes from the film *Songs of the Adventurers;* the second follows it, but this is a separate redition of the same song sung on another occasion.

. . . Woe, my child [lover] Tsele,
Yes, don't cloud me with misfortune.
When I run, I stumble into a stone;
I sink into thick grass taller than me.
I wish I could live and increase.

Not long after she sang these lines, Tholi Mahlasi—age twenty-nine, shoot-out veteran, never-married mother of three, semiprofessional band vocalist and brilliant *seoeleoelele* composer—her beauty but not her spirit a little the worse for wear, disappeared once again into South Africa.

Since the mass retrenchments of Basotho mineworkers that began with more than 5,000 sent home during the massive strike of 1987 and swelled to an additional 25,000 in the nineties, increasing numbers of women have followed her. In Lesotho today we are confronted with a new social pattern: the male-headed single-parent rural household. Unemployment in Lesotho itself is nearing 40 percent. Men, without jobs or the legal right to seek work for more than two weeks across the border, are forced to extract what subsistence they can from the land. Women, however, can often find jobs—however poorly paid—in domestic service, the informal sector, or light industries in Maseru and other border towns. More important, they find it far more easy to simply disappear into South Africa's swelling periurban slums now that internal influx control has been abandoned. All a woman really requires is to find a man, or series of men, usually migrants from within South Africa, or perhaps Mozambique, to provide accommodation, protection, and a little working capital. Hence many a wife who has told her retrenched and despondent husband that she is going off to look for work to support him and their children has not been heard from again. Others just go away, with no word of farewell. At an informal gathering (*pitso*) of retrenched migrants I held in Roma District at New Year's, 1994, a question about deserting wives produced a great angry chorus of confirmations and complaints.

If a woman's life in Lesotho is a rock, though, then for a woman migrant South Africa has always been a hard place. Some women are driven by broken relationships into migration, and others choose it as their main chance, but they all leave homes where they are someone and travel long distances alone to seek work. There they live independently but in narrow circumstances in bleak hostels, rented rooms, mine shanties (*mekhukhu*), or servants' quarters. Domestic service is the most popular employment among Basotho women migrants, but many prefer a dangerous mobility to the "degrading subservience required in working for a white 'madam'" (Gay 1980c, 285). A risky but more diverting and profitable alternative is domestic and other service for male migrants, not usually Basotho, who provide them with a feeling of conjugality, however fleeting, along with the diversions of the industrial workplace. These women are much more on their own than contract male migrants, and their patterns of self-reliance are much more extreme than those of women who remained as wives of migrant workers living near affines and agnates in the rural areas. Male migrants visit home more often, spending more weeks at home and fewer uninterrupted months at work every year than do women migrants (ibid., 290–93). Women, unlike male migrants, hardly ever get to see their children, because they cannot risk trips home. They enjoy far more autonomy in their relationships than do actively married women, but their "romances" are often simply mutually exploitative, and many are confirmed in a view of men as by nature unreliable, as "a resource which could be used to meet their immediate needs, but not as dependable partners with whom they could hope to build close conjugal relations and stable homes" (ibid., 294).

Under such conditions female networks, based as much on friendship as kinship, become as important as they are to rural women. Networks on the South African side help a woman with advice, housing, food, employment, men, and entertainment, while rural ones look after interests and property at home and provide the all-important service of child care in a mother's absence. The reality of female migration alongside that of men has abolished the residential linkages among kindreds and lineages. Families and young women crowded into the Lesotho lowlands will commonly have some members giving migrant-subsidized mixed pastoralism a try, along with others who are effectively permanent emigrants to South Africa. Just as *Sesotho* transcends Lesotho, the Basotho are a borderland and cross-border society. This reality gives a new social history and cultural meaning to Moshoeshoe I's ironic reference to the Sesotho name for the Caledon River (*Mohokare*, "Amidst") after the Afrikaners and British made it the border of Lesotho in 1869: "How can they make a border amidst our land?" With bureaucrats on both sides of the current political border dedicated to stopping the flow of Basotho work-seekers forth and back across it, the answer from *Sesotho* is that you cannot. Like the witchcraft and misfortune metaphorized as a fatal disease in the following passage from a *sefela* by Majara Majara, the experience of migrants, women as well as men, knows no boundaries:

Ha le sa tseba le lefu le leholo	You don't even know the serious disease

La ho khetha baimana,	That chooses pregnant women,
Lefu le qhoma Russia libotlolong koana.	A disease that bursts from Russia in bottles yonder.[7]
Le qhomme likepeng, ha Sefee.	It has burst from the ships, but it's not papaya-drink.
Ke moo le neng le qala ho thobela Manyesemane,	That's where it first escaped from Englishmen,
Makhoahla, bashemane ba boko bo thata.	Whites, boys with strong brains.
Mokoting joale le theohile ka likeche;	It has entered the mines now by the cages [elevators];
Litraighting le lihile mafolo;	Into the straights [tunnels] it has toppled loaded ore-buckets;
Masaeteng la isa mofufutso.	At the ore-faces it caused sweating.
Lireiseng, le hloele ka lilata;	The risings [vertical tunnels], it climbed by ladders;
Litonorong, le entse limeche.	In the new galleries, it has caused explosions.
Mali a batho a matha liphororo—	Men's blood runs in streams—
Ba ba khutsoanyane e ba tlola holimo	Short men stood covered [in blood];
Ba batelele a ba ema tlasa,	Tall men stood submerged to their chests,
Lifuba ba ananang Senatla, Morena Mosiea.	Including Senatla, Chief Mosiea.
Motho ke buoang ka eena,likempolara,	This person I'm talking about, gamblers [competing poets],
O mo telele ekang ba lifate:	He is as tall as the trees:
Ha a le lekhoa, o bona Lesotho.	When he's at the Vaal, he sees Lesotho.
Che, teng nkekebe ka tlohela ho cho.	No, there I can't stop talking.
Ha ke tloha joale, eaba leea sesela;	When I left, the sickness moved slowly.
E nkile tselana e tlang ka Lesotho.	It took a little road to Lesotho.
Banna, le kene teropong ena ea Bolomo.	Gents, it entered that town of Bloemfontein.
Le nke matekatse a moo kaofela,	It took all the prostitutes there,
Basali ba lahlileng banna.	Women that have lost [thrown away] husbands.
La ba pomaka menoana ea maoto le ea matsoho.	It diced their toes and fingers.
Ha ba tloha joalo, eaba le ea tšela	When it left, it took the road

7. In describing this animated and deadly disease, which behaves suspiciously like witchcraft, the poet sought to add a touch of exoticism to its origins by suggesting that it had exploded from some bottles shipped in from Russia. (Could it be Communism, the whiteman's bugaboo?)

Le kene Maseru Mejametalana.
Le nkile 'maseterata oa Maseru;
Letsohoana la jesi, le feta ka eona;
Esita le joale, re ntse re le batla.
La potela ka Boleka Manyareleng:
Ke moo le neng le fihla le re nka
bana ba likolo,
Bashanyana ba e-shoa ba ngannge lifuba;
Banana ba e-shoa ba ngannge matsoele.
Oa tseba, la potela ka
Boleka Manyareleng:
Ke moo le fihla le hanella lekhoareng.

Oa tseba, le nkile tonki;
Le ne le romelletsoe ka tsintsi e tala,
Sebenfolae.
Ke reng ho lona, likempolara?
Bo-ntate, bastoali ba me,
Hanyane ke mpe ke le utsoetse.
Ke 'na, ke etsoa ka mokhoa ona:
Le 'nokile maqeba ka letsoai.

Banna, e se 'nore ha a opa,
Le be le ntlohela
Ke be ke sale ke teka-teka sebakeng,
E ke ke khutsana.

And entered Maseru Mejametalana.[8]
It took the magistrate of Maseru;
The arm of a sweater, it passed with it;
Even now, we still search for it.
It went round Boleka Manyareleng:
There when it came to take
schoolchildren,
Boys died with chests exposed;
Girls died with breasts exposed.
You know, it went round
Boleka Manyareleng:
That's when it climbed into
the reed windbreak.

You know, it had a donkey with it;
It was accompanied by the greenfly,
Sebenfolae.[9]
What am I saying to you, gamblers?
Fathers, my parents,
A little I may steal for you.
Me, I'm treated in this way:
You have poured salt on my
wounds [teased me to sing].

Gents, when these wounds are sore,
Don't leave me alone
To be roaming about aimlessly,
As if I were an orphan.[10]

8. Majametelana is a dam in Maseru, so the capital is frequently referred to in story and song as Maseru Majametelana.

9. *Sebenfolae*, "greenfly," is a *sefela* term for a particular green insect. More recently, "greenfly" has become a slang term for the bothersome and dangerous green-uniformed Bophuthatswana homeland police.

10. The poet has been goaded into performing, and those who have done so must now stay to hear him out, as the feelings aroused by poetic inspiration can only be assuaged by an attentive and appreciative audience.

Chapter Seven

"My Heart Fights with My Understanding"

Bar Women's Auriture and Basotho Popular Culture

They ask where I was born—"T. Y."
[Teyateyaneng] at the trees yonder, at my father's, at Marentintsi.
Helele Mathoalenyama! It is better I go, a mere girl.
I can't stay here; I can stay among white people at Johannesburg, anywhere.
You russian gangsters, what sort of people are you?
When you meet, you fight;
When you greet each other, you fight.
They ask why I am so lean—
I am lean because of my bad temper.
A wife of the russians, girls, she is never fat—
I should have a plump backside.
Nthabiseng, from my mother, girls,
Heee! the cruelty [to] my mother!
Nathabiseng Nthako

Barflies and canteen-keepers, single, deserted, deserting, or married—these were the "undesirable women" who developed the *seoeleoelele* genre amid the sexual bravado of the *famo* dance. The *shebeens* not only provided women with an independent albeit hard-won means of livelihood, they created a female-controlled arena for extended individual textual composition. True, Guma (1967, 104) cites women's corn-grinding songs sung by female orphans or *lingoetsi* (newly married wives) with long soliloquies lamenting hardships and sufferings under a stepparent or mother-in-law. Among the rural 'Tlokoa, Ashton (1967, 97) observed women's singing contests, and also noted that women's initiation dances were accompanied by long thematic poems sung as women rotated around the night fire, but these are not the generic antecedents of *seoeleoelele*. The latter are also "songs of affliction," enveloping grief in a celebration of the sisterhood of the unsubordinated oppressed, but the most direct influence on their development was the *sefela* of male customers and friends. There is precedent for female performance of male genres in Sesotho; for example, the songs of female intitiation rites called *metsetselo* are in fact female versions of the *mangae* of male initiates (Sindile Moitse, cited in Wells 1994). Research both for *In Township Tonight!* and for this account revealed that male folk genres such as *mohobelo* and *mangae* were popular in *shebeens* in Basotho-speaking urban neighborhoods around Johannesburg starting at the turn of the century. There is every reason to believe that *lifela*, then as now, were also performed within the hearing of *shebeen* women. In form, the only significant differences between *sefela* and *seoeleoelele* are due to the rhythmic influence of the instrumental accompaniment and the shorter, more repetitive and strophic structure imposed by the "dance and song" context of *shebeen* performance. Men, too, as I have noted, are *shebeen* singers, performing in exactly the same style as the women, though interestingly they prefer the opening salutation *Helele helele!* used by women also, to the uniquely female call of *Seoeleoelele!* Their right to sing out was ensured by the intoxicating (in every sense) freedom of the "immoral," illicit, but for that very reason indispensable, *shebeen*. In this context, the contradiction of women appropriating the forms and usurping the expressive privileges of men is resolved not only by the ambiguous, independent social position of *shebeen* women, but also by the Sesotho metonymical principle whereby individuals performing unaccustomed roles can be reclassified with the category of persons who ordinarily perform them. So a woman can be referred to as a man if she is performing a role socially identified with males. Soloing to beat the band, a woman can be hailed as *Ntate!* (literally, "My father," but also the equivalent of "Mister" or "Sir") by her entranced supporters. Openly urging a prospective lover to come and "play the husband," Nthabiseng Nthako belted out:

> What do you say, you men of Lesotho?
> When I leave, I clear out;
> I am the donkey stallion, girl
> The donkey stallion, neck-bridle breaker:
> When I leave I travel.[1]

In greeting a stranger among Basotho, "Where do you come from?" (Who is your chief?) is asked of a man, while the parallel question asked of a woman is "Whose child are you?" (Gay 1980c, 6). The *shebeen* songs of the *matekatse*, though, start with an obligatory declamation of the town or vil-

1. There is a song about this donkey so obscene that only children are allowed to sing it, and then only if no adults are within earshot. Since this is not a children's book and virtually all my readers are surely adults, I am not going to repeat it here either.

lage the chanteuse hails from. Pursuing the male metaphor from sung rhetoric into dance, it is only in *shebeens* that I have seen women, singing and moving to the music of accordion and drum, snatch up and wave (quite aggressively) the massive and beautifully decorated *melamu* fighting sticks of the men.

The mirrors of imagery that men and women migrants' texts hold up to one another, and the images of self each projects in return, are significantly different. Men's *lifela* are most often egocentric, reflecting the male migrant's existential self-concept as a contemporary hero in the established Sesotho mold (Kunene 1971, 41), an ordinary man confronting extraordinary dangers in an alien place, exiled from the home, family, and community he is (often thanklessly) fighting to preserve. Like American bluesmen, they sing of affairs and faithlessness, not marriage; doubt and danger, not certainty; wage labor, not agriculture; trains and trails, not home and family. Here is former hayseed Majara Majara: dressed to kill, tickling the ivories, astonishing the foreign city girls in the shantytown *shebeens.* What does it matter if his shanty is built of chicken feathers!

Ke moo ke neng ke qala ho etsa mehlolo:	It's there I began to perform miracles:
Ke re ho lona, likempolara	I say to you, gamblers [poets],
Ke luthara ea malofa.	I am a Luther [founder of the church] of the Loafers.
Makhooeng koana, motho, ke ne ke lula,	At the mines yonder, man, I was staying nicely at my home,
Lekeicheneng la heso, la Bilone hantle.	The location that is my home, that of Benoni[2] truly.
Motho, joale ke letsa okono lekeicheneng leo:	Man, now I was playing an organ at the location:
Lelinyane la moroa le be le tantse;	A Coloured's offspring [young girl] even danced;
Ke bone le phethoha seka 'melekorone.	I saw her go round like a merry-go-round.
Ke checha sa khofu kapa maofane.	I crept backwards like a snail.
Ke be ke khalengoele ke ngoanana Motsoana.	I was even scolded by a Tswana girl:
"Ntate Rakhali, se 'na o letsa ka mokhoa ona—	"Father Rakhali, don't play this way—
Ke tloha ke tantse tsa mohlanyeng;	I will soon dance like a lunatic;
Ke be ke poma mese ena ea monna oa ka.	I shall shorten these dresses of my husband.

2. Benoni, a town on the East Rand near Johannesburg, was famed for its Basotho location infested with gangsters and rough *shebeens;* it was one of the birthplaces of the *famo* dance.

Motho, e tlabe e se ke etsa khoba;
Ke tlabe ke etsa seo 'Me'
a shoeleng a se etsa."
Oa tseba, ho khalengoa
ke, 'na Ngoana Rakhali
"Mahure le tantse ka se mate;
le seke la nkhata":
Ke motho ea ratoang ke semate;
Ke roala lieta, tse ntso maru matso,
Likausi, ranta le halefo korone—
moo li tlohang teng, ntho tsena,
Ka mose, lijoteng Khobololo.

Ke haile ntlo ka holima terata;
Ke haile ka masiba likhoho.
Letolo ha leluma, e ea sekama.

Man, I shall make miracles;
I shall be doing what my mother
was doing before she died."[3]
You know, I was scolding,
me, Child of Rakhali:
"Prostitutes dance gently;
don't step on me":
I am a person suited to smart attire;
I wear shoes, black as storm clouds,
Socks, one rand half-crown—
where they come from, these things,
That side, at the Jews' place
at Khobololo [a mining town].
I have built a house beyond the fence;
I have built it with chicken feathers.
When lightning and thunder strike, it
shakes.

Women's songs do in fact proclaim a resolute, individualistic, and adventurous spirit imitative of male itinerant heroism, deliberately contrary to the stationary domestic commitment expected of adult women in Lesotho. Today many girls do not even wait for a marriage to fail but avoid early marriage and the danger of forced elopement, preferring to take their chances in the informal sector in Maseru and other border towns in a pattern of female internal migration described by Wilkinson (1985). Both the forced repatriation of the 1960s and internal migration since have brought many superbly talented female *shebeen* singers to the border towns, though many of the most renowned are among those who have eluded the immigration dragnet. Their flight from the normative is an enforced one, however, and the accompanying sense of displacement profound. Theirs is an explicitly shared affliction, "in mourning for their lives," as Chekov put it, grieving the loss of kinship and marital security; friendship found, sundered, and betrayed; the embattled reality starkly outlined against the conjugal and communal ideal:

Heee! Sehloho sa 'me motsoali,
Sa 'me, 'mosali oa batho, o lla mehla—oe!
Ka mehla pelo ha e tele.

Heee! The cruelty [to] my mother,
To my mother, an unfortunate woman,
she cries daily—oe!
Always my heart never forgets.

3. The implication is that his playing will cause her to make short, sexy skirts out of the modest dresses bought for her by her husband, giving in to temptation like her mother, who, it seems, died an untimely and unnatural death.

Chabane, kea tsamaea.
Ke motho ea phelang ka bothata:
Ke phela ka ho khothotsa basebetsi.
Ha ke sebetse; ke mahlalela,

'Na, ngoananyana oa Lesotho.
Mpheng tekete, banna,
tekete le molamu oa ka.
Ha ke tloha, kea tsekela;
Ke ikela haeso, haeso Lesotho koana.
Ha ke tloha, kea kolla. . . .
. . . Hele helele, ngoan'eso Anna,
Bo-malimabe bo ntsoereng!
Hobaneng kea tsamaea?
Ke 'Mamanyaloa. . . .

. . . Basali, ba na ba nrerile;

Ba buoa ka 'na, ngoanana, ka
'na likhutlong tsa matlo.
Ke ba sheba; ba sheba, koana.
Hee oena, ngoan'aka ngoanana,
Ntate kapa Nthako,
Ke siea bana beso;
Ke ba na kampong ea Hlotse, banana—

Ke ba siea ke ba tsepisang mang?
Ke tsepile Ramaseli—ee!

Ke tlohele, nthapelle,
Che, hobane ke letekatse.
Ba botsa hore, na ke busoa kae?

Ke tseba moo ke phelang, banana:
Kampong ea Hlotse.
Helele, helelele, helehelele,
Ntate kapa Molefi, helele!
Nka siea ngoan'eso, Tholinyana.

Pelo eaka e loana le maikutlo,

'Na, ngoananyana oa ha-Masupha.

Chabane, I am going away.
I am a person living indifficulties:
I live by cheating [migrant]workers.
I'm not working; I'm a wandering
divorcer [philanderer],
I, a little girl of Lesotho.
Give me a ticket, gentlemen,
a ticket and my stick.
When I leave, I wander about;
I am going home, home to Lesotho.
When I leave, I move fast. . . .
. . . Hele helele, my sister Anna,
The misfortunes that have seized me!
Why am I going?
I am the mother of marriages
[I have many men]. . . .
. . . These women, they speak about
me;
They speak about me, girl, about
me at the house corners.
I look at them; they look away, yonder.
Hee you, my girl-child,
Father or Nthako,
I abandon my sisters [fellow barmaids];
Here they are at Hlotse camp [town],
girls—
In whose trust do I leave them?
I have entrusted them [having no
husbands] to God—ee!
I have left, pray for me,
Yes, because I am a prostitute.
They ask of me, where am I
ruled [staying]?
I know where I live, girls:
At Hlotse, the camp [town].
Helele, helelele, helehelele,
Father or Molefi, helele!
I can leave my sister [friend],
Tholinyana.
My heart fights with my
understanding,
Me, a little girl of Masupha's.

Nthabiseng Nthako, the composer/performer of this passage, was twenty-two years old, an unmarried barmaid afraid that the miner who paid the rent on her tiny ramshackle bedroom might forsake her, but confident of attracting a replacement when he did so. The male dimension of her stance is exemplified by the rhetorical request: "Give me a ticket, gentlemen, a ticket and my stick," referring to the train ticket and heavy wooden fighting stick (*molamu*) that symbolize the intrepidity of the male migrant. Her friend and fellow singer Thakane Mahlasi (called Tholinyana in the passage above) performed the following admonition to "little boys" (reluctant migrants), reminding them of their responsibilities, and that women's struggles are equivalent to their own:

He ee oele oelele oele!
Dying at one's home, little boy,
Yes, one dying in his home
Is no meat for his relatives:
A man's home is everywhere.
Hello, Child of Mathopela—
A man is never overwhelmed by troubles:
Even women do overcome them,
Oh, little girl of [the] Kholokoe [clan].

This genre that dare not speak its name achieves its purposes by traveling incognito—pointed commentary, emotional community, aural art, and low comedy—licensed by conspiratorial nonrecognition somewhere on the borderlands of what passes as categorically *Sesotho.* The provision of the *shebeen* as a space for women's defiantly deviant behavior, self-expression, and gender crossing helps to reduce the stress caused by the need to maintain the more general operation of social norms (*molao*, "the law") as useful fictions. This principle of the useful fiction allows the reproduction of social ideology as both a moral and historical template for cultural identity and integrative behavior, while reducing the disruptive consequences of what people actually wish or have to do. The well-known proverb, *Leshano le pholosang le molemo*, "The lie that rescues is good," is widely cited to sanction the white lies and inadmissions that smooth the surface of social interaction or prevent public injury to the feelings or pride of people "caught out." It is also much quoted by non-Basotho as proof that unapologetic prevarication is a normative strategy of Basotho social interaction. The deeper meaning of this proverb, however, is that neither competing personal interests and loyalties, nor intractable social and material realities, nor even plain human frailty ought to be allowed to fracture the general acceptance of and attempts to approximate stabilizing structural ideals. Cynicism, an attitude bespeaking a lack of faith in social values in both motivation and conduct, is therefore an inappropriate alternative to social naïveté. A negative effect of this principle, however, is that appearances are often necessarily deceptive. As the *maele* warns: *Motse o motle kantle*, "The village looks pretty from outside."

Victor Turner was among the first ethnologists of symbolic process to justify explicitly the attribution of meanings in conflict with those held by informants and obtained through their exegesis. In so doing he was defending his own method and by extension that of Max Gluckman, who regarded exegesis as a red herring, and of Evans-Pritchard, who went so far as to suggest that ritual symbolism would lose its efficacy if its practitioners understood its meanings reflexively. Turner's predecessors based their practice on the unexamined contention that ritual practitioners simply cannot see the Forest of Symbols for the trees, and that the wider system of meanings is revealed only in the synthetic, higher-order structural analyses of anthropologists. In response, Monica Wilson and S. F. Nadel argued that *only* exegetical meanings and locally "comprehended" symbols had value in social analysis and anything else was "bespattered" with ethnographic guesswork (cited in Turner 1967, 26). In the next generation, Thomas Beidelman, a self-identified opponent of Gluckman and Turner (though not of Evans-Pritchard), gave renewed analytical substance to Wilson's position (Beidelman 1966, 1986).

Turner's further "structural" analysis of the problem of interpretation, however, is not easily dismissed. Although the participant, the one using the symbols, is not blind or contextually myopic, "his vision is circumscribed by his occupancy of a particular position, or even a set of situationally conflicting positions. . . . Moreover, the participant is likely to be governed in his actions by a number of interests, purposes, and sentiments, dependent upon his specific position, which impair his understanding of the total situation" (Turner 1967, 27). Even more serious, conscious and therefore ideological explications of totalizing symbols, implicitly expressing what Geertz called "importunate claims to humanity . . . cast in the accents of group pride" (1973, 22), demand adherence to habituated, "axiomatic" values (Turner 1967, 27): "One of the main characteristics of ideological interpretations is that they tend to stress the harmonious and cohesive aspect of social relationships. The exegetic idiom feigns that persons and groups always act in accordance with the ideal norms" (ibid., 33). The distance between generalized values as useful fictions and the less conscious concept of cultural hegemony is bridged by the recognition that in every community and social category, no matter how "dominated," there are those whose self-perceived interests, whether material or psychosocial, rational or valuational, lead them in varying degrees to collaborate in the operation and reproduction of the dominant discourse.

Their social practice clearly reveals that Basotho are aware of and exploit the transformational potential embedded in structural contradictions. Looking at a Turnerian problem, for example, the ideology of "cousin marriage" in this partilineal society gives preference to unions with the mother's brother's daughter, based on values of cooperation and equality among affines. In practice, however, the preference is for marriage with a father's brother's daughter, which infuses these affinal behavioral norms and expectations into the hierarchical and competitive relations that inevitably undermine the solidarity expected among agnates. As Kuper explains: "This is not stressed in the ideology, and it does not appear in the ideal order of close-kin marriages, since a preference for this sort of marriage [father's brother's daughter] implies that relationships with close agnates are fraught with difficulty and need to be translated into something else. The Sotho prefer to see their endemic fraternal conflicts as occasional and lamentable deviations from the ideal amity" (1975, 74).

Indeed, the concept of *molao* is actively employed to bring normative and actual patterns of behavior into greater harmony or agreement (*tumelano*). Among the most striking examples is *bonyatsi*, a non-normative but virtually institutionalized form of adultery in which married men or women contract extended extramarital relationships in the frequent and lengthy absence of a spouse (Spiegel 1991). *Bonyatsi* for a man is condoned on the basis of the once-normative institution of polygyny, forbidden by the Christian denominations to which the vast majority of Basotho nominally belong. *Bonyatsi* among women is probably no less common, but may be overlooked rather than condoned since Basotho seek to prevent human weakness, however understandable or prevalent, from threatening the overall maintenance of social harmony and customary law. Women point to accepted notions of the universal human need for emotional and sexual satisfaction, and to beliefs about the harmful physiological and mental effects ("stagnant blood") of celibacy in justifying *bonyatsi* for themselves. There are, however, clear socioeconomic motivations for female *bonyatsi*, since the cattle paid as bridewealth for a woman by her husband go to her father and other consanguineal relatives, while the secret but mandatory gifts from a *nyatsi* (lover) are hers alone, free even from the restrictions that a husband may place on the disposition of other family income (ibid., 150–51). On the other hand, a wife's lover can be a significant drain on an absent husband's income, since her emotional attachment makes her generous, and as one woman said frankly, "You have to give the man something if he's doing the work." As early as 1897, the missionary Jacottet transcribed the following comic song performed by two choruses of *bale* initiation girls:

> First group:
> Listen, thus! The adulterer, it's the woman.
> Second group responds:
> Listen thus! The adulterer, it's the man.
> First group responds:
> And the woman also.
> (Jacottet 1896–97:128; my translation)

Among the *likoma* (secret lore) taught to girls during the *bale* rites are instructions in how to conceal adultery from their future husbands and, in the event her transgressions are discovered but tolerated by an understanding or equally guilty spouse, how to keep her affairs from causing him intolerable public embarrassment. It is for such reasons, and not only because of their deep historical and cultural embeddedness and authority, that the Basotho say *koma ke nnete*, "a *koma* is truth" (Guma 1967, 117). Marriage is a social and economic partnership, preserving the male migrant's investment and entitlements in his home community and providing identity and security for women and children. Hence *bonyatsi* is virtually never discussed in public (why spoil things?), and the lie that rescues social structure is a higher truth than the truth that fosters stress and discord.

The parties, music, and dancing that accompany *shebeen* singing go beyond *bonyatsi* into *botekatse* (prostitution), a publicly recognized (and rather less concealable) arena for "deviance" in which the very harshness and social fragmentation of migrant life becomes a basis for commiseration, commensality, and collective self-expression. In the Basotho areas of South African towns, the original instrument for *famo* dancing was the pedal organ (*okono*), which might even be loaded into a horsecart or taxi and moved when occasion demanded. In the smaller depots and country junctions, the portable German concertina (*korosetina*), adopted from Afrikaner farmers, was the ubiquitous accompaniment.

Famo apparently originated among the gangs of Basotho thugs who began making a name for themselves around Johannesburg early in this century. City gangs, whether composed of urbanized criminal predators called *tsotsis* (from English "zoot suit", see Coplan 1985, 162–64) or ethnically oriented arrivals from the homelands, identified themselves with fearsome and racy names drawn from popular culture and the current scene. During the Second World War, many gangs took names referring to the combatants, for example, the *tsotsi* "Berliners." The Basotho originally ganged together as vigilantes determined to protect themselves and their women from attacks by other black ethnic groups and by criminal *tsotsis*, but it wasn't long before they moved into protection, extortion, gambling, bootlegging and marijuana selling (teaming up with the *bo-mamosali*, the "queens" of the *shebeens*), and other rackets themselves. They called themselves *majapane*, "japanese." In early 1947 a dispute broke out between gang members from northern and southern Lesotho over the alleged failure of the northerners to come to the aid of southerners when they got embroiled in a battle with police while returning by bus from Kroonstad (south of Johannesburg) after having recaptured their leader's abducted mistress. From that time, the Basotho gangs divided into two factions, the Ha-Molapo (allied with the Masupha) from the north and the Matsieng from the south. As a whole, they became known by the name of one of their internal subgroupings, calling themselves *marashea*, "russians." This name was inspired by the paranoia the white government and media expressed over the new, postwar threat from Stalin, and provided a suitable antonym for one of their most feared enemies, the *tsotsi* "Americans" gang of Johannesburg.

Borashea, "russianism," was far more than a distorted and violent byproduct of African proletarianization and urban social dislocation, having roots deep in Sesotho and rural male Basotho experience and its ethos. The pitched battles fought between the local branches of russian factions were to begin with a recrudescense of the fierce stick-fighting that erupts when the herdboys of one village try to prevent the cattle of an adjacent one from grazing near them, or deliberately graze their stock in the *maboella* (reserved, fallow pastures) of their neighbors. Like herdboys, faction branches had their pastures, city turf they were determined to extend and protect. The factions of Matsieng and Ha-Molapo/Masupha reproduced and reignited the historical antagonism between the royalists of south Lesotho, followers of Moshoeshoe's heir, Letsie I, with his capital at Matsieng, and the restive collateral nobility of north Lesotho led by Moshoeshoe's second and third sons, Molapo and Masupha, whom he installed at Peka and Thaba Bosiu, and who consistently defied or rebelled against the paramountcy. Both factions wore wide black trousers and two-tone black and white (Ha-Molapo) or red and white (Matsieng) shoes. The Ha-Molapo wore red Victoria blankets with black designs and four white vertical stripes, while the Matsieng uniform was a black blanket with a large white emblem in the middle, called *thapo ea Seeiso*, "mourning badge of Seeiso," the paramount chief of Lesotho who died in 1940 (Litabe 1986, 10). The Matsieng also shaved their heads, a Sesotho sign of mourning.

Violence between factions could occur upon chance meeting or by ambush, after the practice of *khoaletsi*, when herdboys assault country wayfarers without warning. Most battles were prearranged for Saturday afternoons or Sunday mornings, however, as a sort of blood sport that left the rest of the week for normal pursuits or for fighting non-Basotho antagonists (Thabane and Guy 1983). The night before a battle, faction members would gather for a *famo* at their favorite *shebeen*, where their women would brew, cook, sing, and dance for them in encouragement. Molefi Malefane, a Masupha member known among russians as "Ntsasa" (Greased), described the competitive ribaldry of these occasions:

> A *famo* is like a [church] "tea-meeting" with an accordion [laughter]. The women are there. And the men are naked under the blankets, and we are in a circle, and there is a command: *Likepi!*[4] Then we lay out our pricks on the table. And the women are not wearing any panties under their skirts. It's a *stokvel*, for money. When the *famo* dance is done, there shouldn't be any laughter; it's quite serious. They display themselves to the men. They even shave their vulvas, and put some lipstick, called "stoplight," around them. The man who is the good dancer and a good stick fighter is the one who the women want, and he gets whatever woman he wants.

Let it be noted that among South African peoples in precolonial times, it was customary for women to disrobe flamboyantly before the troops, flinging off their blankets to inspire, excite, or shame their men as circumstances dictated. As Alinah Tsekoa, "'Malitsepe," a veteran observer of many russian battles, sang in her Maseru *shebeen:*

Ha e loana, e ea tsabeha:	When it's fought, it is fearsome:
nka e hlobolela likobo.	I can fling off my blankets.

The *famo* dance was both a lusty good time and a preparation for battle, at which women did and said everything possible to fire up their men. Some russians emphasize that the admiration of women was a major reason for their participation. Not only did women lavish their favors upon them as protectors and heroes, but a russian could live quite comfortably as an adjunct to a woman's economic activity based in the *shebeens* or in the legal informal sector, a preferred alternative to migrant laboring.

At dawn the men would take up their formation outside the bar and

4. A *kepi* is a steel pick or chisel used by herbal healers to dig medicinal plants and roots out of the ground. Here it is a euphemism for a man's sexual "magic wand."

begin their dance. Rather than the *mokorotlo*, the dance songs of war emphasizing individual prowess, the russians chose *mohobelo*, the highly stylized and synchronized dance of male fellowship, unity of purpose, and team display—a dance of social agreement—as preparation for the fray. While *mokorotlo* symbolized national unity, *mohobelo* is performed in Lesotho as well as in South Africa in two distinct southern (Mohale) and northern (Leribe) regional styles that originated in the civil conflict between Lerotholi I (son of Letsie I) and his uncle Masupha in 1898, further expressing the opposition between Matsieng and Ha-Molapo/Masupha russians (Adams 1974, 170). Among the Matsieng faction in Johannesburg, the men's dance was supported by women singing the following chorus:

Moshanyana, oa ka ha ke tloha mona,	My boy [lover], when I get out of here, [I will depart,]
Ke ea tsamea, tloho ke u pepe.	Leave, carrying you on my back [like a baby].
Moshanyana, ha ke tloha mona, ke ea tsamaea,	Boy, when I get out of here, I will depart,
Ke u tšabisa masholu a banna.	Fearful for you of the thief-men [*tsotsis*].

As the enemy approached, a whistle was blown, and a brutal clash would commence, resulting on occasion in numerous deaths. Other favorite venues included township railway stations, where both ambushes and prearranged showdowns took place. Classic russianism reached its height around Johannesburg during the later 1950s, when general war broke out between Matsieng and Ha-Molapo, ultimately involving opponents from the Hlubi ethnic group, the *tsotsi* gangs, and urban black vigilante groups called "civil guards," armed by the police. The fighting sticks and axes concealed beneath blankets were replaced by pistols, greatly increasing casualties.

During this period, russianism as a concept demonizing rural-based Africans entered popular consciousness in urban South Africa, as law-abiding city folk, black and white, as well as *tsotsis*, shivered with fear at the shadowy groups of blanketed men stalking the night streets and mass transit stations. As my colleague, the renowned historian Stanley Trapido once told me, "When I was a boy in Johannesburg, my mother always threatened that if I misbehaved, 'the Basuto' would get me." Harsh enforcement of apartheid and influx control regulations in the mid 1960s reduced formal russianism, but the russians' organization, their battles, and most important, their legend persisted. Today the term "russian" is used to label everything from petty thugs to armed robbers, strikebreakers, police goons, and hired assassins, perpetuating and inflaming the antagonism between rural and urban Africans. The older Matsieng and Ha-Molapo/Masupha veterans to whom I talked repudiate all these activities, claiming that russianism was a *koma*, a male secret society, honorable in love and war, and that their criminality was confined to small-time vice rackets and the skin trade. The continuity and loyalty of the russian membership is demonstrated in the welfare functions they provided, pensioning off their leaders and burying their members with ceremony and at great expense, and paying out a death benefit to the families of fallen comrades.

Philip Bonner (1990) has studied the russians as a means of understanding the complex and often contradictory relationships between social experience, social forms, and organized political action on the Reef. These Basotho do not fit Philip Mayer's (1961) classic dualistic model of townsmen and tribesmen, urbanites and migrant workers in the social structure of the black townships. At first go, the russians appear to embody one of the fundamental social consequences of "grand apartheid": a perpetually unsettled African population from which neither a self-sufficient rural peasantry nor a permanent urban working class is permitted to emerge. In their own logic of social action, however, the russians attempted to resolve or at least domesticate this contradiction by extending *Sesotho* to the heterogeneous and, in their view, uncivilized and cultureless urban environment to which perforce they had emigrated. An obvious sign of this attempt was the predatory violence and contempt they directed toward urban black youth, whether or not the latter were in fact social predators themselves. Hence the military allegiance to regionalism that Moshoeshoe had tried to control was revived in the russian factional battles on the Reef, complete with factional uniforms, traditional doctoring, and a moral *code de guerre*.

The russians may have lost their physical links with the land and drifted into permanent immigration in the urban areas, but they still regarded themselves as *Basotho a 'mankhonthe*, true Basotho of Moshoeshoe. They were among the first to act upon the reality that they were not "men, or women, of two worlds" but actors in a single social arena that included both South Africa and Basutoland. Russians uniformly insisted that russianism was something enjoyable or necessary only in South Africa. Factional, intercommunal, or interpersonal violence is considered uncultured and antisocial in Lesotho, and russianism is disparaged as imported South African *bokoata*, "uncivilized ruffianism." Yet interpersonal violence is common in Lesotho, and it's easy enough to pick out the russians (on vacation) in any border town, labor depot *shebeen*. More significant, the russians' recognition that their social reality was "a rat race, where only a rat can survive," as the Temptations sang in "Cloud Nine," has since come to permeate social relationships among migrant Basotho in general, even among kin.

In sum, the russians, both male and female, were "encapsulating" themselves, not in homeboy networks or urban residential or occupational relationships, but in an ethnically based, culturally grounded subculture of their own, competing strategically and violently with each other but wrapping their blankets and shaking their fighting sticks at settled urbanites, other ethnic groups, and landed Basutoland Basotho alike. Gender relations in *borashea* were and are an expression of this intent to create autonomy in the cracks of a world ill-fashioned for them by enemies both foreign and domestic. Bonner (1990) notes that control of independent women, *matekatse*, was an important competitive russian agenda, and the immediate cause of many a murderous encounter. This control, however, was predicated upon the reestablishment and defense of normative neomarital bonds, notwithstanding the common-law nature of the majority of russian domestic relationships. Russians and their women were mutually supportive and independent counterparts. Like female *shebeen* singers, male russians often began their anthems with the salutation *Ngoana moshanyana!* "Man-child!" When a woman grabs a man's fighting stick and rises to do lyrical battle with her circumstances, betrayers, and detractors, men cheer her on with shouts of *Famola bo, ngoanana! . . . Iketle thope, ngoananyana! . . . U tsamaile; u lahlehile!* "Do the famo, young girl! . . . Take it easy, little girl! . . . You have traveled; you are lost! [You're on your own; why hold back?]" (Coplan 1985, 100).

Conversely, identification with the russians and the marginal position to which they are both socially consigned leads female singers to express admiration for these stouthearted men and to appropriate images of male battles to express their own existential struggles:

Hae oele oele! You, Child of 'MaKhalemang [a male russian,
friend and fellow bar singer],
Blow the whistle so the russians may fight—oe!
When it's fought, it is fearsome;
When it's fought, it is fearsome:
I can fling off my blankets [in anguish, aggression, sympathy, excitement, desire].
He! I, the Child 'Ma'tsepe—oe!
The loafers' [russians'] whistle-blower, Khalemang,
Whistler of loafers, Khalemang, you, man of Mokotane's,

Makotane's at Mantsonyane,
Lead them into the way [of battle]; they know it [well].
Hee! [So] I seize the black [heavy] fighting stick;
I'm fighting.
I cannot be stopped; I am fighting.
(Alinah Tsekoa, "Malitsepe")

Nevertheless, women singers are almost universally critical of russian *likoata* (uncultured ruffians), and of the domineering, rude, egotistical, and violent behavior that they see as the anti-*Sesotho* side of *borashea.* A verse appearing in many *shebeen* songs runs:

What kind of people are you russians?
Each time you meet one another, you fight.
After greeting one another, you fight.

Other songs, such as 'Malitaba's below, identify russians with cannibals, while still others invoke the folk character of Satane Mautla, as in this 1950 recording, *Famo Ngoanana* by Mamapetle Makara koa Famong (Gallotone GB2012):

Aoelele, ngoana moshanyana!
Leholimo le ka be le na le 'tulo:
Mor'a Molimo e moholo ke mang?
Hela! Oa mantlha oa matsibolo Satane.

Mohla a qalang ha ntsoa motsana;
Hela! Na ntsoa sekoti sa lihele.

Hela! Ke eo ba mo, tsoere ka toropong;
A le thipa a le selepe sa hae.
Hela! A le kobong tsa lefu a feletse.
Hela! Khomo li besua ka mollo, Satane;

Ha li le tala li ka u
hlatsisa (Mamapetla Makara)

Aoelele, man-child!
Heaven should have a place [for you]:
Who is the eldest son of God?
Hey! The very first of the firstborn is
Satan.
At first he was allotted a small village;
Hey! Then he was given the pit
of hell.
Hey! There he is, caught up in town;
On him are a knife and an axe.
Hey! He is in full funeral attire.
Hey! The cattle are burned with fire,
Satan;
If they are raw, they'll make you vomit.

Mamapetla's song plays on the biblical legend of Satan as God's original favorite among the angels, who, like a firstborn son of a chief, is given his own village to rule over. Rejecting his father and his patrimony, the song's migrant Lucifer ends up in the social hell of the townships. Now a proletarian gangster, the absconder is warned that "the cattle"—a metaphor both for stolen goods and dangerous, diseased town women—will bring him only misfortune and sickness.

Local recording companies had been on the lookout for material for the growing African market since the 1920s. The Basotho concertina tradition was already highly developed, and in the 1940s a number of recordings of solo male singer/players appeared that featured astonishing virtuoso performances on that small instrument (T. Makala, *Tshetla* and *Kroonstad*, Gallotone GB1604.Y591). Complex melodic runs that imitated the vocal qualities of sung poetry were not suitable for dancing, however, and thus lacked an important selling point. The rhythmic three-chord instrumental accompaniment made women's *shebeen* singing a good sales prospect, and by the 1950s migrants could buy *seoeleoelele* recordings spiced up with tell-it-like-it-is female vocals, like Mamapetle Makara's song, transcribed above. Perhaps the most renowned of all the singers is 'Malitaba, now retired in Lesotho, who for decades ran a *shebeen* in Moletsane location, Soweto, Johannesburg, and attended her husband Sanaha, a Matsieng faction leader, at numerous battles in the Johannesburg area during the 1950s and 1960s. Asked what role women played during the actual fighting, she replied, "Why, to carry on singing, to give them courage to win the fight!" When hiding from the police, russians often gave their guns to their women, who also brought them food when they were arrested and jailed. In 1960, the great 'Malitaba was "discovered" singing in her Soweto *shebeen* by a talent scout and made several recordings that brought her fame throughout Lesotho and Sesotho-speaking South Africa. 'Malitaba's long and faithful marriage continues despite her husband's continued absence in South Africa, and her songs express a tenderness and respect for her mate (as well as a few of her other favorite men) in the midst of accounts of harrowing russian battles, pleading her desire to return with Sanaha to Lesotho:

Hau oelele! oelele! oelele!	Hau oelele! oelele! oelele!
Helele! Ke hopotse koete Makhaba.	Helele! I remember handsome Makhaba [Maize Fields].
Lekhaba le mona leso, banna—oe!	That green maize field of our home, men—oe!
Ea lulang ha Sekekete koana—	He stays at Sekekete yonder—
Jo! Motho oa ha Nkoebe,	Jo! A man of Chief Nkoebe's,
Nkoebe Sebapala, Matsela-ha-Beli,	Nkoebe's [at] Sebapala, Matsela-ha-Beli
Qomo-Qomong ha Lesala, ha habo koete Patsi.	Qomo-Qomong at Lesala's, at the home of handsome Patsi.
Bashanyana ba heso, 'Molo,	Boys of my home, 'Molo,
Baheso ba ntse ba lla.	Those of my home are still crying [missing her].

Ba botsana, ba sa ntsebe,
'Malitaba oa Mphoso;
Ba botsa ke lula kae—oe!
Ke tsoaletsoe Thabana Morena—
jo! Motho oa ha Konote.
Mohale's Hoek ha Malebanye,
Kampong ea Mafeteng, ha habo 'na,

Ke lula ha Ntsane, Nyakosoba,
Ha-Chele, pela ha Monyohe,
ha habo Sanaha, monna—oe!
Tloho re tsamaea, Ntate Sanaha—
jo! Mong'a lerato, lumela!
Re ikele Lesotho koana;
Nke ke be ka shoela mona Khauteng.
Molumong moo setopo se
tseloang ka meokho,
Betlile, ngoana moshanyana
oa ka lumela—oe!
Helele! Hele! 'Mankokosane, pula ea tla.

Ha ke bapale le bashanyana,
hoa ipaka ke se ke le moholo.
Ke ba joetsa ka mehla,
ha kea tsoaloa ke feteletse.

Jo! Ngoana'ka Lenka,
Ha a le teng, 'Malitaba oa Mphoso,
u ke ke be oa bona bothata;
Bo hlaha ke manolo feela.
Ba ka nketsang ha kena,
senatla se tletse bohlale.
'Thipa, li ka nkobesa;
Melamu e ka ntlola holimo,
Ntsekalle, Madoda—
jo! melamu ea banna.

Tse mpe, li botsoe mang?

They ask each other, not knowing me,
'Malitaba of Mphoso;
They ask where I stay—oe!
I was born at Thabana Morena—
jo! A person of Konote's.
Mohale's Hoek at Malebanye's,
The camp [town] of Mafeteng,
at my place,
I stay at Ntsane's, Nyakosoba,
At Chele's, next to Monyohe,
home of Sanaha, the man—oe!
Come let's depart, Ntate Sanaha—
jo! Master of love, hello!
Let's take ourselves quickly to Lesotho;
I should not die here in Johannesburg.
Amidst noise there at a
funeral flowing with tears,[5]
Greetings, Betlile my son—oe!

Helele! Hele! 'Mankokosane, the rain
is coming.[6]
I don't play with boys,
for I am now a grown woman.
I always tell them I am not born [a
shebeen singer],
but compound my mistakes.
Jo! My child Lenka [the accordionist],
When she's there, 'Malitaba of
Mphoso, you won't see hardships;
Things just go smoothly.
I'm not afraid of a muscleman,
even one full of cunning.
Knives, they can miss me;
Sticks swing over my head,
Cracking [together] over my head,
Madoda—
jo! the fighting sticks of men.
Of bad news [her death], who can be
asked?

5. In Johannesburg, people weep loudly at funerals, both because there is inordinate suffering and because the funeral has become a noisy, spontaneous vehicle for political mobilization in the South African townships since 1976.

6. *'Mankokosane*, "Mother of Water," is a song in praise of rain after a drought.

Li ka botsoa Sanaha, monna—
jo! Mong'a lerato.
Ke ba joetsa ka mehla—cho!
Motho oa Chele hantle oe!
Nke ke be ka lula Naledi—
Jo! Motho oa ha Shale hantle—
oe! Haeno!
Nke ke be ka lula Naledi, Tlali,
le Moletsane, ngoana'ka;
Ke re, malimong koana,
Mapetla le Senaoana,
Ha e loana Qomatsi

E felile; kea tsamaea.
Ke chaile; kea tsamaea.
Ke chaile; kea tsamaea—
Tafeeta, u lula kae?
Roma, tuma lichabeng!

They can be asked of Sanaha, the
man—jo! Master of love.
I always tell them—cho!
The person truly from Chele's!
I won't stay in Naledi [Soweto]—
Jo! A person truly of Shale's—
oe! To your home!
I won't stay in Naledi, Tlali,
or Moletsane,[7] my child;
I say, among cannibals [russians]
yonder, in Mapetla and Senaoana,
When the State of Emergency[8] was
fought.
It's finished; I'm leaving.
Time up; I am going.
Time up; I am going—
David [Coplan], where do you stay?
[At] Roma, renowned among the
nations![9]

It was also during the early sixties that the piano accordion (*koriana*) appeared in South African music stores and was adopted by Basotho instrumentalists in the mining compounds and *shebeens* in preference to the pedal organ. Combining the portability of the concertina with the musical range and full-textured volume of the organ, the piano accordion enabled its most serious exponents to make live performance something like a full-time profession. *Shebeen* owners could afford to buy accordions and supply them to musicians playing in various locations. A musician could sling the instrument over his back and tour by bus and foot from the black townships of urban South Africa to the remotest village *shebeens* in Lesotho. Others made long-term agreements modeled on mineworking contracts with *shebeen* queens in the border towns to stay and play daily for the patrons. Ensembles were completed by the addition of a drum (*moropa*) con-

7. These are all separate African townships within the large residential complex of Soweto (an abbreviation for South West Townships). Moletsane was the location of 'Malitaba's own *shebeen*.

8. 'Malitaba compares the faction fights of the russian gangsters to the fighting that took place when Prime Minister Leabua Jonathan declared the State of Emergency in Lesotho in 1970 and violently suppressed the singer's party, the Basutoland Congress Party.

9. 'Malitaba praises herself by concluding with the observation that she is not singing in the village *sepoto* but giving a "command performance" for Professor Coplan at the National University of Lesotho.

structed of a twenty-liter can topped with a piece of inner tube, above which was fastened a row of bottle caps or metal jangles (*manyenenyene*) to provide a jingling beat to alternate with the thump on stretched rubber of drumsticks made from slices of tire. Trendsetters included Forere Motloheloa (Pau Manyetse), who made enough money with his band on the mines to give up mine work altogether. Adding singer/composer Apolo Ntabanyane in 1980, the band went professional as the recording ensemble Tau ea Matskeha ("Lion of Matsekha," the performers' home district in northern Lesotho). Apolo had been a *kheleke* of *sefela* on the mines, and that genre greatly influenced his popular compositions for accordion band. The band name became virtually synonymous among migrants with the musical form (which had no real name, remember), and despite Apolo's departure in 1983, the group remains one of the most popular exponents of the male-dominated, studio *seoeleoelele* style. On 45 rpm records and, later, cassette tapes, the music rode on buses, trains, and taxis and could be heard over the radio in any Basotho home. Live, *famo* and *seoeleoelele* were now everywhere that working-class Basotho gathered for drink and entertainment, with most of the singing provided by the brewers and customers themselves.

Dominating the live performance domain of the *shebeen*, good female singers are much respected and sought after, and *shebeen* owners in the towns stage paid competitions between the top singers among the *matekatse*. Of the women, the long-time and current champion is indisputably Puseletso Seema, who in forty-some years has suffered all the slings and arrows of outrageous fortune that comprise Basotho female proletarian life. Puseletso was born in Seteketekeng (Place of [drunken] Staggering), a raucous section in Johannesburg's old Western Areas. In the early 1960s she was removed with her mother to the Soweto township of Orlando East, where they both presently reside. At twelve she was sent to stay with her grandmother in rural northern Lesotho and, there being no boy available, put to a boy's tough task of herding cattle. The village proved no safer for the maturing girl than the city, and within a year she was kidnapped into marriage (*chobeliso*) and gave birth to her first child. Escape from her abusive in-laws did not prevent her "husband" from tracking her down and impregnating her once again, and at fifteen she was back in Soweto with two infants to care for. Working in her mother's *shebeen*, she developed her performing talents and soon set off on her own itinerant career, brewing and singing in shantytowns throughout the Free State and Transvaal. The object of rivalry among russian commanders, she contracted lengthy liaisons with three of them, and attended numerous russian faction fights around Johannesburg. After the death of her last man in 1976, she began her professional recording career. In the mid-1980s, she mysteriously suffered a loss of voice for an extended period. The diviner diagnosed "spirit sickness" and prescribed initiation as a traditional diviner and healer. During her training her voice returned, and she is now a medical as well as musical practitioner.

So has she achieved a *summa* of proletarian Basotho cultural knowledge, combining the three professions of migrant *shebeen* queen, "eloquent one," and herbalist/diviner. Her shield has been that powerful voice that sends *seoeleoelele!* chills down her listeners' spines, and led russian commanders to kidnap her just to sing for their side in *famo* competitions. The success of her recordings, backed by the superb accordionist Maele Phuthiang and studio singers, guitarists, and drummers, has enabled her to retire to stable single motherhood in Soweto. During 1991, Puseletso and her group appeared regularly on South African Television's "Ezodumo." The studio process has affected her performances, forcing her to shorten solos to fit arrangements for popular singles. Perhaps as a result, each of her songs on record focuses on a different aspect of her experience, rather than building experiences into a resonant concatenation as is usually the case with extended *shebeen* performances. The following text is from an album she made in 1981 with male vocalist and composer David Motaung and Tau ea Linare, *He O Oe Oe!* (Globe Style ORB003):

He! Ke le mose hara makhooa mona,	Hey! When I'm across among the whites yonder,
Le hoja ke ne ke le monna—oe!	If I was a man—oe!
Nkabe ke lula seporong	I would sit at the railway
Ke hapa likobo tsa batho.	And seize people's blankets.
Taba li ka botsoa buti Manocha,	Matters can be asked of brother Manocha,
Sethlare, sea ngoana Moriana ho!	Medicine, of the child of medicine.
Hee! Bashanyana, kea tla,	Hee! Boys, I am coming,
Hee! Ke saletseng marena ha boloaoa—oe!	Hee! Why am I left behind when chiefs are killed—oe!
Hee! Lefu la motho e mong, bana beso,	Hee! The death of another, children of my home,
La motho e mong ha le rekoe.	That of another isn't bought.
Hee! Nkabe ke ntsitse chelete, banana,	Hee! [Or] I would have taken out money, girls,
Ka reka lefu le Ngoana Santho—oe!	And bought the death of Santho's Child—oe!
Motsoalle, mong'a marato,	Friend, master of love affairs,
Ntat'e, buti Tselinyana 'nake, ngoana'ka ngoanana.	Father, brother Tselinyana dear, my girl-child.

Ke mofu hobane, a robetse, oaka oa litjepa.	He is dead, for he sleeps, mine who married me by oxen.
Hee! Oaka oa lilemo, mose khateane,	Hee! Mine for years, everywhere over there,
Mose hara makhooa mona.	The other side among whites there.
Hae! Oelele! Oelele! Banana, motsoalle ngoana moshanyana.	Hae! Oelele! Oelele! Girls, [my] friend the man-child.
Hala! Uena! Jooe!	Hey! You! Jooe!
Hae! Oelele oelele! Khauta oe!	Hae! Oelele oelele! Khauta oe!
Ntat'e, buti Khauta, namane e tsehla—	Father, brother Khauta, the yellow calf[10]
Hee! Ke le mose hara makhooa mona.	Hee! The other side among whites there.
'Na, 'Me' Khubelu, ke sa khantsetsa baeti.	I, mother of Khubelu, I used to enlighten visitors.
Ke hopotse mehleng ea khale,	I recall in times past,
Khale-khale hosa phela marena,	In times long past when chiefs still lived,
Paolosi, nogana oa Makoetje.	Paul, the child of Makoetje.

The passage begins with a humorous reference to the petty criminality of some of Puseletso's russian associates, who lurked by the railway lines to steal blankets off the backs of unsuspecting travelers. Next she asks not to be left behind in South Africa at a time when russian commanders—whom she calls "chiefs," of course—are being killed. Among these is a husband named Santho or Tselinyana, whose death she would gladly have given everything to prevent, if only life could be bought. Finally, she recalls better times, when she "enlightened" customers with the brilliance of her songs, a time when the redoubtable russian chieftains she knew and loved ruled the townships. Puseletso's success has evoked some jealousy and gentle satire among Lesotho's *shebeen* singers, including Hlotse's Thakane Mahlasi:

> We met at the crossroads;
> We didn't recognize one another—jo, my darling girl!
> Puseletso, little girl of Seema.
> Her short stature is hers by nature;
> Her light complexion is self-made [with skin-lighteners]—
> Oh girl!

Interestingly, male *shebeen* singers and *sefela* performers rarely give *borashea* more than a mention, and almost never sing about russian battles.

10. This expression "yellow calf" means "lion cub," referring to the lion clan, Bataung, to which Khauta, meaning "Gold" (yellow), belongs.

Former Matsieng commander Molefi Thabane, who, remarkably, had a flair for praise poetry as well, was the only *sefela* performer I met who was also a russian. The women, who ordinarily fight only with one another over the men, sing about the men's battles in detail, praising the valorous and handsome, mourning the fallen, projecting themselves into the fray. Clearly these fellow migrants, male and female denizens of the social wil-d(er)ness, identify with one another. Just as the term *matekatse* for barmaids derives from the verb "to wander about," male migrant performers commonly refer to themselves as *lipapatlele*, "vagabonds"; *likhutsana*, "orphans"; *likeleme* (from Afrikaans *skelm*), "rogues"; *melotsana*, "deceivers"; *likempolara*, "gamblers"; *makholoa*, "absconders"; and most categorically, *litsamaea-naha le liparola-thota*, "inveterate travelers of the wilderness." Their fellow travelers, the women of eloquence, sustain themselves and their companions in affliction with songs of innocence and experience (Gunner 1979) in which their misfortunes are lamented but their care for true friends and lovers never dies:

Ntate Kapa 'Muso, monna oa ka,
o ntse a itlela.
Ba pepesaka ke letekatse.
Ha ke 'tekatse;
Ke phetha mabaka:

Lelapeng la 'me', banana,
La 'me' ho jooa ka thata;
Che! Ke letekatse.
Ntate o ne a shebile sakeng;
'Me' o ne a shebile mots'eo.

Che hobaneng? Ke letekatse.
Ke sa nahana ke tla tekatsa;
Bothata bo hloele, manolo holimo. . . .
. . . Nka siea monn'a ka lla,
Ntate, kapa Sello.
Ke Sello le Fosa;
Ba botsa ke nyetsoe kae.
Ke Matsitsi Letebele—
Helele, ngoan'a ka ngoana!
Le nthlotse kea tekela;
Le nthlotse kea tekela.
Helele, ngoananyana Lioling!

Mr. Kapa 'Muso, my husband,
he comes on his own account.
They slander me as a prostitute.
I am not a prostitute;
I narrate the causes [of my
circumstances]:
At my home, girls,
At home eating is difficult;
Yes! I am a prostitute.
My father looked away to the kraal;
My mother looked away deep
inside the hut.
But why? [because] I am a prostitute.
I still think I shall go wandering;
Hardship piles up, quietly higher. . . .
. . . I can leave my man and cry,
Sir, or Sello.
It is Sello and Fosa;
They ask where I am married.
It's Matsitsi the Letebele—
Helele, my girl-child!
You have left me wandering about;
You have left me wandering about.
Helele, little girl of Lioling
[Teyateyaneng, a border town]!

O ke ke be oa bona ke nyetsoe;	You will not see me married;
Ke nyaloa ka mehla.	[Yet] I get married [fall in love] daily.
Ka mehla pelo ha e tele;	Daily my heart is long [hopeful];
O ke ke be oa bona ke koatile.	You will never see me surly.
	(Nthabiseng Nthako)

The question might be raised as to whether and in what sense women's *lifela* can be construed as "heroic." Certainly their performance does bring forth women's grievances in a public context. Male *shebeen* patrons, stung by the critical barbs of female performers, routinely rise to sing spontaneous retorts. On occasion, they are shouted down or even pushed aside by *matekatse* determined to hold the floor. More significant, singers like Thakane Mahlasi embody, in their lives as in their songs, the refusal to conform to the normative, dependent role of the married female Basotho peasantarian. Risking arrest and bodily harm to remain a *setsamaea-naha*, a traveler, Thakani exposes yet another, painfully ironic gender contradiction of the migratory labor system. For men, South Africa is the land of wage slavery; for women, it represents relative choice, opportunity, and independence. For both, "traveling" provides resources for domestic social power. The *shebeen* operator and the *letekatse* live in willfull defiance of the identity that both Basotho society and the migratory labor system as a whole prescribe for them. The trenchant mix of pathos, protest, and bravado in their *lifela* reveal a consciousness of the overall injustices of the South African political economy as well as of their disabilities within it.

Chapter Eight

"Eloquence Is Not Stuck on Like a Feather"

Sesotho Aural Composition and Aesthetics

> [Here] enters a man of eloquence,
> A poet who goes mad telling stories.
> The little owls are dark in plumage [their noise disturbs]—
> The poor reciters spoil the music of the learned;
> The bad singers interfere with my [expert] performance.
> I no longer know the old owl.
> I am not an owlet but the great horned owl.
> I am the owl that lives in the forest.
> *Mphafu Mofolo, "Ngoan'abo Mokhoathi"*

To this point I fear I may have erred in not saying something about how Basotho travelers put their self-defining songs together. The issue reminds me of the masterful seminars in ethnopoetics led by the great folklorist Richard Bauman, during which he admonished us first to inquire "How is it made?" before considering the social embeddedness of a genre or performance.[1] Bauman makes the analysis of craft a priority, not only because this is the folklorist's stock-in-trade, but because he understands how complex and unobvious, how culturally particular rather than commonsensical, is the relationship between experience and its performative, transformative representation. The nature of this relationship was elucidated by the late lamented John Blacking (1973), whose insights continue to inspire students not only of the music of southern Africa and of African music more widely, but of ethnomusicological theory at its most general. No one understood or explained more clearly than Blacking how great a "pleasure principle" exists within cultural performance for creating models of psy-

1. The National Endowment for the Humanities Summer Seminar in Ethnopoetics, held at the University of Texas at Austin, 1985. I wish to express my gratitude to Professor Bauman, now director of the Folklore Institute at Indiana University, Bloomington, and to the NEH for the seminar's lasting intellectual benefits.

chosocial coherence that answer a questionable moral reality with an artful moral imagination. In its condensed and virtual landscape, art orders the world as we would do if we could. The perceptions of empowerment created in migrants' auriture, evidenced by its persistence and elaboration from nonliterate through illiterate to postliterate cultural contexts, requires an exploration of both Basotho ethnoaesthetics and of the craft of aural composition itself.

The single outstanding student of Basotho performance aesthetics to date is Charles Adams, and much of the following account derives from his pioneering work (Adams 1974, 1979a, 1979b).[2] Adams's researches of Sesotho genres did not include *sefela* or *shebeen* songs, but they provide a conceptual framework within which these song types can logically be placed, a schema of ethnoaesthetic categories in the performative domain. As with any cultural philosophy, these categories must first be presented as ideal-typical, with the understanding that they are differentially shared, understood, and defined by individuals in practice. *Sefela*, along with sporting contests, various kinds of public spectacles, displays of beauty and skill, and performances of all kinds, belong to the overall domain of *lipapali*, "games," derived from the verb *ho bapala*, "to play, playing." So the concept of disciplined, performative recreation that underlies the connection between such American phrases as "Play ball!" and "Play the blues!" is explicit in Sesotho. Both sport and performing arts are associated further with the notion of *ho bapa*, "to be parallel or commensurate," from which *ho bapala* is derived. The enactment of this concept is glossed by the intensified form of *ho bapa*, *ho bapisa*, "to make parallel," or freely, "to make metaphor," from which the noun *papiso*, "metaphor" is derived. Not surprisingly, some *sefela* performers use sporting metaphors metapoetically, as a vehicle of self-praise in competitive performance. Here Mphafu Mofolo depicts his victory over his local rivals, including one Kotsiea, on a visit to the capital:

Monongoaha Kotsiea o raha bolo.	This year Kotsiea plays football.
Baheso ra tena limolo.	Men of my home have put on soccer trunks.
Re leba Maseru teropong;	We go to Maseru town;
Ha re fihla ka hare ho teropo—	When we came right into town—
Banna, likhomo, ngoanabo Makhoathi!	Gentlemen, cattlel, brother of Makhoathi!

2. The following discussion of Basotho ethnoaesthetics is in part a revised version of that published in Coplan 1988, 350–66.

Morao ba li opa liatlanyana:	Behind they clapped little hands [applauded]:
Mphafu o le tabotse letanta.	Mphafu has torn the goal net.

Basotho "games" are thus enactments that at once produce and reproduce cultural knowledge. Following this logic, activities that do not both follow from and represent socially derived understandings cannot be "played" (Adams 1974, 240).

The ability to make metaphor is an essential aspect of talent and expertise for musicians as well for the composers of verbal texts. On the *lesiba*, for example, expert players can sound the quill and produce a vocal, syllabic hum at the same time, creating the sense of "part performance" so fundamental to indigenous southern African music. *Lesiba* performers compose short, breath-rhythmic tone passages variously called *linonyana* (birds), *linong* (vultures), and *linonyana khajoane* (jackal buzzards). Such melodic passages are intended as sonic representations of specific events that at once reveal, express, and explain them (*ho hlolosa*). A competent *lesiba* player is said to have "knowledge" or "understanding" (*ho utloaisisa*, from *ho utloa*, "to hear, comprehend, feel, sense"). This concept of understanding has an explicit sensory dimension: *linong* are musical metaphors that conjure images in the mind's eye; like ritual symbols, they have both emotional and ideational content (Turner 1967, 27–32). These sensory understandings are unavailable to those without "deep Sesotho," and exemplify those opaque, nondiscursive expressions that differentiate one culture from another. Beyond that, "a *lesiba*'s components are symbolic of the 'vibrations' of the social, as well as the physical, environment of the individual performer. . . . A *lesiba* is the means by which these become manifest in sound and thereby make sense. . . . Hence the musical continuity and cohesion of stick-string-quill . . . and voice express an interpenetration and unification of self and circumstance, of player and instrument. *Lesiba* performers contend that it is by means of this esthetic 'communion' that communication and community are possible" (Adams 1986, 4,6). Similarly, *lifela* are sung in praise of horses by their riders at the popular country race meetings, using sounds as well as words to address the horse and to provoke a winning performance:

Motleli, Motlola-tsethe,	The jumper, the skip-jumper,
Motlola-tsela li ea ka makhooeng,	The jumper of roads going to the mines,
Seberekane, se setso maroboko . . .	The industrious migrant, the black spotted . . .

(Mokitimi 1982, 189)

Mekorotlo anthems are often sung on horseback, as riding songs and, reinforcing their association with heroic travel, in praise of trains by their migrant passengers. In one *sefela* the train itself sings the anthem, cheered on by the veld over which it rumbles:

Oa tseba utloang, makareche *a o lumela mokorotlo;*	You know listen, the carriages sound the *mokorotlo*;
Matsiri a na a bina, "ielele-ielele."	The grass then sings [responds], "ielele-ielele."

(Mabote Nkoebele, in Mokitimi 1982, 317, 442)

The creation of insightful, affecting metaphors, whether verbal, aural, kinesic, or visual, is a distinctive characteristic of Basotho games. Directly associated with this attribute is the contention that games help construct society, giving connective, harmonious, and mutually supportive relationships a degree of self-consciousness (*boikutlo*, from *ho utloa*) and emotional reinforcement. In this sense they are semantically contrasted, not with work (*sebetsa*), but with war (*ntoa*), a domain that subsumes all kinds of social anxiety and conflict, including the social disruptions of the migratory labor system itself. The competitive dimension of *sefela* performance expresses the social tension inherent in the notion of games as a friendly fight, a conflict that unites people in a common excitation over the display of individual prowess in social accomplishment. Indeed, competition is regarded by many performers as the central dynamic, the point of performance. Some singers, encountered by chance, declined to perform without a partner and rival, someone to resound for and against, while others consented to imagine an interlocutor[3] for the occasion, as long as some prize money was provided as a stimulation. Still others I met at home in rural Lesotho explained that, while they enjoyed performing for a local audience, they seldom did so since their village lacked suitable competitors. *Sefela* is for travels. The widespread practice of praising oneself as a performer in performance is often a direct challenge to others to compete, and such challenges are especially common during travel to and from the mines (Mokitimi 1982, 72). Citing the standard closing formula, "Amen, I have finished," Rabonne Mariti uses such a challenge to conclude his *sefela:*

Nkabe ke re, "Amen, ke phethile";	I should be saying, "Amen, I have finished";

3. Yes, my use of "interlocutor" is a pun on the stock minstrel show character "Mister Interlocutor."

Nke ke siele 'mate a buoe:	I should give my friend a chance to perform:
Terene e ratang ho haka, e hake.	The train that wants to hook, it can hook on [couple].
Sebuoe se ratang ho buoa, se buoe.	The speaker that wants to speak, let him speak.
Banna! Joale se buoe ka lentsoe le monate:	Men! Now let him recite in a voice that's sweet:
Nkang pina ea lona!	Take your song!

My lecture audiences, students, and fellow academics often ask me how *sefela* contests are decided, and who the judges are. Among performers these questions were always greeted with the same mild surprise. The judges are the most senior, renowned performers, *lingaka tsa sefela* (doctors/teachers of *sefela*)—if there are any about, they explained—but everyone present can hear who is the winner. Often a loser is the first to acknowledge the result by shaking the winner's hand. Can a relative amateur defeat a "professional"? Not usually, though genuine feeling and a particularly persuasive or original evocation can on occasion overthrow more practiced, but studied eloquence. But it takes courage and *savior faire* for an amateur (*ngakana*, "apprentice doctor") even to attempt such a feat: there is money at stake, and the veterans are cunning linguists and much feared. Broadly, the superior player bests his rivals in a comradely contest over the most convincing aural representation of shared experience. For listeners who are not migrants, the winner is the performer who enables them to participate most vividly in his itinerant exploits, to travel his imaginative and emotional landscape.

Games, in short, model reality and suggest evaluative and constructive modes of feeling about it. In this they combine the three forms of cultural knowledge recognized in Sesotho: normative wisdom (*bohlale*); empirical, operational competence (*tsebo*); and sensory, perceptual awareness (*kutlo*) (Adams 1974, 22). Specific games are classified "by the channels through which they are performed and the perceptible qualities inherent in those modes of production" (Adams 1979a, 305). So there are games that are realized through "doing" (*ho etsa*) and others through "sounding" (*ho luma*). *Ho luma* implies composition (*boqapi*) in contrast to mere noisemaking (*lerata*), with connotations of social agreement and connectedness: "harmony" (*tumellano*, from *ho luma*) in both its musical and social senses. Hence the universal greeting in Sesotho, *Lumela!*, "Believe!" ("to believe, accept, agree"; literally, "to sound/resound for"). Song promotes social agreement in part because it creates shared pleasure: it's aesthetically agreeable. Sound, rather than sight, is the primary communicative channel through which Basotho apprehend, appreciate, interpret, and reorder experience as social reality and relationships. For them, the mutuality of sounding/hearing has greater validity and force than showing/seeing. Understanding in Basotho culture is more attuned to the African-American phrase, "I hear ya" than to the Euro-Americanism "Seeing is believing." Basotho ethnoaesthetics are a literal realization of Blacking's famous dictum: "The forces in nature and culture would be expressed in humanly organized sound, because the chief function of music in society is to promote soundly organized humanity by enhancing human consciousness" (1973, 101).

The constant input of energy and feeling involved in the act of sounding is the source of the social continuity and shared comprehension that results from it. The temporal dimension of performance, found in its most admired form in dance, which artfully combines feeling, energy (movement), showing, and sounding in time, is fundamental to its socially constitutive capacities. As Wainwright (1979, 130) found among Xhosa miner praise poets, *lifela* singers frequently create poetic turns through simultaneous semantic and auditory plays on words. The most important quality of a good song is agreement between rhythm and words, and as Basotho say, *Nako ke litumellano lipakeng tsa batho*, "Time is the agreements between people" (Adams 1979a, 317). As word music created through performance in time, *sefela* involves the agreeable transformation of both self and social relations. This notion of agreement, achieved through the performative, rhythmic, and therefore temporal representation of feeling in sounded metaphors, applies equally to the agreements one must reach with oneself. In the following passage, Makeka Likhojane (Ngoana Mokhalo) recalls such an agreement over his departure for the mines. For added dramatic effect, he uses the device, popular among Sesotho poets, of switching from the past to the present tense, placing both himself and his listeners within the immediate time frame of the event and its emotional context.

Ke lesole la habo 'Mamokhesuoe.	I am the soldier of 'Mamokhesuoe's village.
Ha ke ne ke tloha ke eea makhooeng,	When I was leaving to go to the place of the whites [mines],
Ka bua le pelo ra ba ra qeta,	I spoke to my heart and we finished,
Le moea ra ba, ra utloana.	And my soul, we understood each other.
Mahlo a ka a lla ke sa fahluoa;	My eyes cry though nothing has got into them;

Pelo e nyeka ke sa ja letho.	I felt like vomiting [though/because] I've eaten nothing.[4]

In asserting their right to sing and be heard, *sefela* poets often make metaphoric reference early in their texts either to the sounding/hearing complex or to the aural qualities of their voice:

Tholang lerata e be tsiee, lala;	Stop your noise and cease buzzing, locusts;
Fatang litsebe, Basotho, le utloe.	Prick up your ears, Basotho, so you hear.
	(Sporti Mothibeli)

This formula echoes the standard call to attention, *Tsie, lala!* (Quiet, locusts!) used by chiefs to open their court proceedings, and is similar to the opening formulas *Thea tsebe u mamele* (Open your ears so you hear) and *Thola u mamele* (Quiet so you hear) found in both praise poetry and *lifela* (Damane 1963–64, 46). Singer Phoofolo Pitso is explicit about the connection between sonority, timbre, and other musical aspects of vocalization and the qualities of self-expression in *sefela:*

I shall speak into the distance,
And then keep quiet;
Otherwise my ribs might get tired
Because of endless shouting.
How does my voice sound, Basotho?
It sounds badly;
It sounds hoarsely;
Always it sounds like a *setolotolo* [mouth-resonated bow];
It sounds like *lithomo* [gourd-resonated bows],
[Like] things [instruments] of the girls. . . .[5]
. . . I speak through my soul;
I am afraid to speak up:
Would that my voice rang like a bell.
I would ring it,
[And] make it sound at Thenefa [a place in Johannesburg].

4. The final line makes use of ambiguities in Sesotho that are unavailable in English. *Pelo e nyeka* is an idiom for nausea that literally means "sickhearted," and the last phrase may mean he was nauseus either because or although his stomach was empty.

5. The *thomo,* a gourd-resonated one-string bow, is traditionally an instrument played by girls. Perhaps because of it's vibrating, steep-fronted sound, the name *thomo* is also given to European organs and harmoniums. For a description of the *thomo* and the *setolotolo,* see Kirby [1934] 1965, 202–3, 233–34.

Not coincidentally the *setolotolo*, a braced mouth bow, is said to combat fatigue on long journeys by foot (A. G. Mokhali, cited in Adams 1974, 109). By the late nineteenth century, it had been supplanted as a mode of transportation among migrants by the concertina (*korosetina*), which could be played under a man's blanket, the pumping of his arms and fingers heating his body as the words and music beguiled his intellect and warmed his heart.

In games, the domain of sounding (*ho luma*) matches and overlaps the domain of acting or doing (*ho etsa*), which includes dance. Within the domain of sounding, games are divided into categories, based on their modes or qualities of sound production. These categories are generally ranked (not always consistently) in terms of their prestige and putative capacity to reconstitute social relations. The highest category consists of dance-songs, based upon the agreement (*tumellano*, from *ho luma*) of sounding and doing, of text, tune, physical movement, and rhythm. This category includes men's *mohobelo* and women's *mokhibo* (kneeling) dances, and the *mokorotlo* dance songs. Next is *ho bua*, "speaking," which has special application to contexts of social change and power relations, followed by *ho bina*, "singing," implicated in education and changes in social identity and status (ibid., 257), an association that strengthens the conceptual linkage between initiates' praise songs and *sefela*.

In abstraction, men's *sefela* is always referred to as *ho bina*, "singing," and thus ranked below praise poetry, which is *ho bua*, "speaking," yet in mode of performance *sefela* clearly falls ambiguously between song and aesthetic speech. As we have seen, *lifela* are identified, along with *likoma* and *mangae* initiation songs, as *lipina tse binoang ho nngoe*, "songs which are sung standing [still]," in contrast to dance-songs, which are *lipina tse binoang ka maoto*, "songs sung with the feet." Both performer and audience remain relatively motionless during *lifela*, in order to focus attention on the sounds and the texts of songs (ibid., 134). In *lifela* texts, moreover, performers frequently refer to their performances as "speaking," as in the typically alliterative/assonontal closing formula, inviting other performers to follow: *'Bui tse ratang, ho bua li bue*, "Speakers who want to speak, they should speak" (Mokitimi 1982, 27).

As song, *sefela* employs stabilized pitches, but in a declamatory style in which the tune is made to serve textual rhythm and emotional impact. Indeed, performers consistently referred to rhythmic organization (*morethetho*) rather than to melody as the defining quality of *'mino*, "music, song" (from *ho bina*). Rhythm is also an important performative criteria of praise poetry, though relatively less regular or strict than in *sefela*. But in both genres rhythm is "neither rigid nor uniform. It is thought-rhythm rather than vowel rhyme, and it is accompanied by thought arrangement rather than word arrangement, with a parallelism of ideas, whose poetic melody is ensured by rhythm" (Guma 1967, 180).

In *sefela*, the overall style of delivery is based upon the principle of rising attack followed by falling release that is so often found in solo song parts and sung poetry throughout subsaharan Africa. Spoken Sesotho, like most other black African languages, uses a system of inherent syllabic tones to make semantic distinctions. Sesotho has two tonemes, high and low, but these values are relative to the tonal environment of each syllable, rather than absolute. A toneme is high or low only in relation to the pitch of its neighbor(s) (Guma 1971, 26). Over the course of a sentence, there is a tendency for lower tones to pull down high tones that follow them, producing an overall downward drift of intonation. This pattern is exaggerated in *sefela*. The major unit of vocalization is the "breath group," which may extend from a single line of poetic phrasing to four or more. The Sesotho idea of breath includes not only physical respiration but something of the European notion of "breath of life." The word *moea* can thus be translated as "wind," "breath," or "soul." The vitalizing role of breath and rhythm in *sefela* performance is illustrated in the following passage, in which the poet Majara Majara praises his own style of intonation:

Ke reng ho lona, likempolara tseso?	What do I say to you, gamblers [poets] of my home?
Ho buoa kata-kata ea motse oa Mahaese,	Speaking rollingly of Mahaese's village,
Kata-kata ea motse oa Ramanki.	Rollingly of Ramanki's village.
Ke buoa feela, ke sa tsotelle letho.	I speak freely, not minding anything.
Ke nka ka moea; ke lahlela koana.	I sieze [it] with the breath (soul); I cast [it] forth yonder.

Rising attack becomes an immediate swoop upward of perhaps a minor third, and the rise is maintained until the final third of the poetic line or even longer, at which point phrase downdrift is introduced until the line ends. If the performer's breath is not exhausted and there is semantic linkage between this line and the next, he may start the next phrase or line somewhere in the middle of the downdrift pattern, maintain this level for several syllables, and then continue downward to the end of the breath group/semantic unit. When the declamatory mode is employed, in Sesotho speech as well as in poetry and song, heightened dramatic and emotional intent is expressed by deemphasizing the internal rise and fall of intervening syllables, and by exaggerating the normally extended length of the penultimate syllable in the final word of each line or breath group. Frequent use of phrase-initial and phrase-final ideophones and interjectives increases this effect (ibid., 28).[6] The following transcription of the opening lines of a *sefela* by Rabonne Mariti (ex. 1) illustrates this performance style. Here, breath groups are enclosed within brackets. Capital letters indicate the beginning of poetic lines, corresponding to the written transcription and translation that follow.

[Khoali ee!]	[The black and brown spotted ox ee!]
[Khoali ahlama, ba o bone manong;	[Mottled one open your mouth, so they see inside;
Ba bone moo o jelang.]	They should see you where you eat.]
[O jelang lijabatho tsena?	[Why do you consume these cannibals?
Letsa la thaba,]	A mountain Springbok,]
[Letsa la thaba ka mahlong le letšo,	[A mountain springbok is black-faced,
Letso joalo ke ho koma lithlare.	It is black from chewing medicines.
Le tle le mamele;]	You should listen;]
[Le tle le mamele, banna ba thota:	[You should listen, men of the veld:
Papatlele ea naha,	A vagabond of the country,
Esale ke theosa le mafatše.]	I have been going down along the lands.]

Interestingly, the strength of this pattern and especially the structural force of the breath group will sometimes overrun a semantic unit, so that the first word or so of a line may be intoned at the end of a downdrift. The performer then takes a breath and begins in the middle of the line with a rising attack. This asymmetry may continue for another line or two, but a performer will soon correct it and return to the normal pattern where intonational pattern, breath group, and semantic unit are matched. Here, for example, is another passage from the same *sefela* by Rabonne Mariti:

[Le se ke mpe la ikhoela, Basotho,	[Please do not harm yourselves, Basotho,
Kapa la tsoha le joinela bosoleng.]	Or jump up to join the soldiering.]
[Ntoa etlaba teng, banna, le tsebe:	[A war will break out, men, you should know:

6. "Ideophones" are ideas, concepts, actions, or images expressed by lexemes or compound lexemes representing sounds. Extremely common in ordinary as well as aesthetic Sesotho, they represent the most naturalized form of sonic metaphors in the language (see Kunene 1965). As Burbridge put it, "The ideophone is the key to native [Basotho] descriptive oratory. I can't imagine a native speaking in public with intense feeling without using it" (quoted in Finnegan 1970, 66).

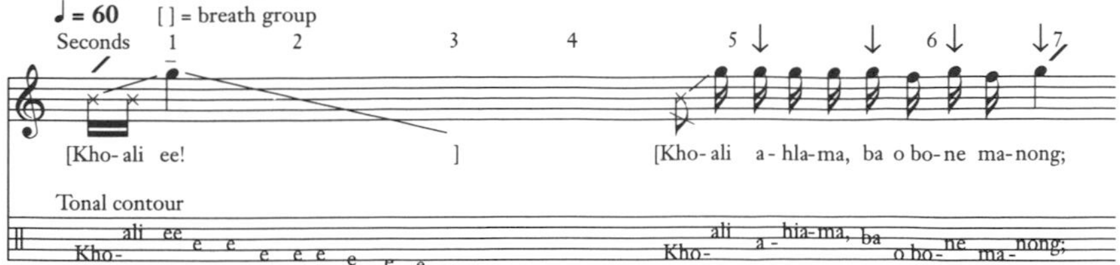

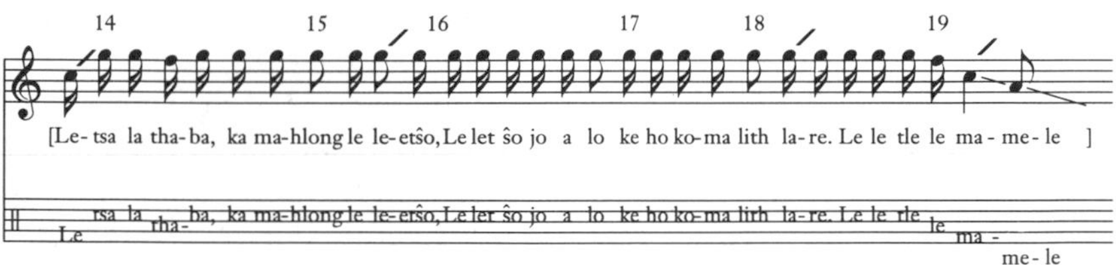

/ = accent

↓ = tone flattened due to tonal progression of syllables.

* Thanks to Alan Berg, James Perla.

Hitlilara] [o qabane le Monyesemane. ↓	Hitler] [is quarreling with the English. ↓
Mohlomong] [le tla bitsoa, Basotho bo! ↓	Probably] [you will be called, you Basotho! ↓
Ka ha le ntse le le batho ba likorone.]	Since you are still people of a colony.]

Here the word *Hitlilara* ends up isolated at the end of a breath group, as indicated by the end bracket. The next tone begins with a rising attack on *o qabane*, and ends with *Mohlomong*. The mid-downdrift pauses, indicated in the transcription by a down arrow that marks the end of semantic units at *Monyesemane* and *Basotho bo!* show the performer already correcting the asymmetry, and the normal conjunct pattern is back in place by *likorone*. What this slight, accidental variation implies is that the repeated performance of passages originally composed in performance or in rehearsal prior to performance gives them something of a fixed status as textual units, whose content the force of rhythmic organization and breath may occasionally override.

In the next transcription, part of a women's *shebeen* song entitled "Peka" (a town in northern Lesotho), Thakane Mahlasi holds strongly to the rhythm of the accompanying accordion and drum (ex. 2). Women's bar songs, unlike men's *lifela*, are said to have names, but these refer to the short choral refrain for which the solo serves as leader. As in traditional southern Bantu song, the soloist follows the principle of "staggered entry," overlapping her breath groups with the phrase cycle of the chorus, which in this instance is both played on the accordion and sung by the male accordionist. Similarly, her melody accords with the polyphonic "root progressions" employed by the accordionist (Rycroft 1967, 96), although the intensity of her declamation leads to only microtonal variation within the body of a given breath group, and her tones are often pushed beyond stabilized pitch to forced palatal head-tones, virtual shouts or vibratory cries.[7] Unlike male *sefela* performances, *shebeen* songs are organized both rhythmically and tonally by their instrumental accompaniment, and female performers universally declined to sing without it.

[Hae hae haeeeee!	[Hae hae haeeeee!
Khahleli-a-Nkhahle,]	Khahleli of Nkhahle,]
[Che ea, Nkhahle, batho:	[Oh yes, of Nkhahle, you people:

7. In *In Township Tonight!* I referred to root progressions as "the short sequence of bass roots and the melody or melodies moving in relation to the tone center in multipart structures of African music. Rycroft used the concept of root progression as a substitute for 'chord sequence' because African polyphony does not have real chords or a fixed harmonic scheme" (Coplan 1985, 258).

Women's *Sebeen* song, "Peka"

3
3
Hae Hae Haee kha hla li a Nkhahleeee
Che ea Nkha hle be tho Ra kha bla na Re

kha hla ne tea nong Re sa tse bane jo 'nake ngoa na na

Pu se le tso ngoan an ean 'a See ma

Bo khut soan ea na bo na ke se bo pe ho Bo se hla na ba

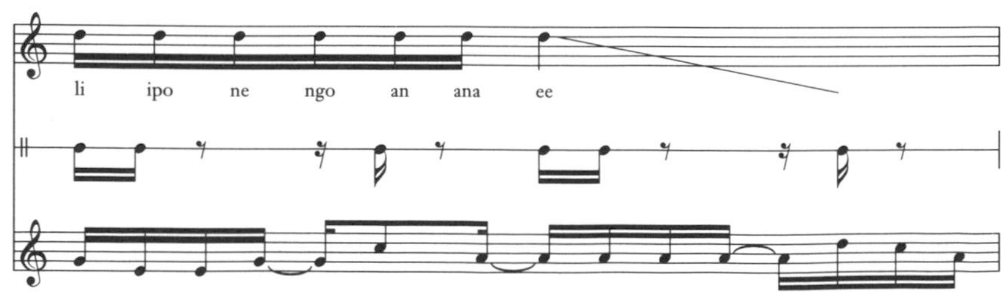
li ipo ne ngo an ana ee

Ra khahlana,	We met,
Re khahlane teanong;	We met at the crossroads;
Re sa tsebane—	We didn't recognize one another—
jo 'nake ngoanana!]	jo, my darling girl!]
[Puseletso, ngoananyan'a Seema:]	Puseletso, little girl of Seema:]
[Bokhutsoanyane bona ke sebopeho;	[Her short stature is hers by nature;
Bosehlana ba liipone—	Her light complexion is self-made—
Ngoanana!]	Oh girl!]

In past times, the songs of the *shebeens* ranked even lower than *sefela* because of where they are performed and because of the kind of dancing and musical instruments that serve as their accompaniment. European instruments such as the guitar, concertina, accordion, and drum are "played/resounded with the hands" (*letsa ka matsoho*) and thus had less prestige than the *lesiba* and *setolotolo,* which are "played/resounded with the mouth" (*letsa ka molomo*), with the "breath" of life. The verb *ho letsa* is derived from *ho lela, ho lla,* "to cry," and "refers primarily to sounds which sign and signal affective conditions" (Adams 1974, 100). Women's *seoeleoelele* are sung amid dancing but are classified under "instruments" (*liletsa*) rather than as songs "sung with the feet." This played agreement of sound and movement, however, does not shift attention away from sound and sense, but rather reinforces them with the rhetoric of the female body in emphatic motion, commanding the emulation of women and the attention of men.

Emotional communication through sounding leads informants' to refer to *sefela* as "mouth played," in the same category as a *lesiba.* It is this marriage of music and speech that shapes the narrative progression of texts, providing an aesthetic structure for both the display and the creation of cultural knowledge and feeling. The intense emotionality of games like *sefela,* combined with their capacity to reconcile disparate and even antagonistic domains, provides expressive mediation of the complex contradictions of Basotho migrant life (Adams 1979b). In Basotho performative theory, the elaboration of metaphors through the musically structured sounding of the soul, the emotional rhythm of the breath of life, recreates continuity among opposing social worlds, divided relationships, fragmented selves (see Comaroff 1985, 111). As Harold Scheub has commented, "The purpose of metaphor . . . is to harness the emotions of the members of the audience, trapped as they are in images of past and present, thereby divining paradoxes and resolving conflicts, and to move that audience into a new perception of reality" (1985, 6).

It is not my desire to inject the "semiotic mediation" of Sesotho metaphor into the continuing debate over culture and practical reason (Sahlins

1976). There is no doubt some validity in Paul Ricour's claim that metaphor is not merely illuminating but predicative and world-creating (Ulin 1984, 108). "Power exists not in control over a problem situation itself," argues Abrahams, "but in the ability to objectify the situation in symbols—words, pictures, enactments—and in the presentation of the problem in a context that not only gives the situation a name or an image but also provides for its resolution" (1972, 19). Modes of signification, however, are part of practical action and historical process, and they both structure and are structured by inequalities in interaction and the concrete institutional limits on human action (Ulin 1984, 121). The metaphoric process, in revealing and creating unlooked-for continuities and identities, articulates social contradictions and holds them in balance within a single cognitive and experiential frame. Poetic narrative shifts freely among first-, second-, and third-person voices as the performer becomes his own interlocutor and his *dramatis persona* moves from identity to address to detachment. Here is a remarkable example from one of *sefela*'s great entertainers, Molefi Motsoahae (Ngoana Sebili) of Thabana Morena:

Banana ba heso, mabitso ke ana:	The girls of my home, their names are these:
'Mapepang o pepile Pepang;	'Mapepang is carrying Pepang;
'Matenane o pepile Tenane;	'Matenane is carrying Tenane;
'Malesala o pepile Lesala;	'Malesala is carrying Lesala;
'Marantso o pepile Rantso;	'Marantso is carrying Rantso;
'Mamonyane o pepile Monyane;	'Mamonyane is carrying Monyane;
'Mabereng a pepa Bereng—	'Mabereng carried Bereng—
Banna! 'Masebili o pepile Sebili!!	Men! Masebili is carrying Sebili!!
'Makonote o pepile Konote.	'Makonote is carrying Konote.
Joale, ha re fihla ka lebenkeleng,	Now, when we reach the shop,
Ho 'na, separola sa motho, ke reketsoe lipompong!	For me, the traveling man, sweets are bought!

In this passage, the singer takes an original approach to displaying his acquaintance with the girls of his village, a popular topic in *sefela*. He imagines each girl carrying her baby on her back and creates an intense parallel series by using the Basotho custom of female teknonymy, *'Ma*, "Mother of," plus the name of her child as a polite form of identification. In line eight, the singer varies the pattern with the direct interjection "Men!" to call attention to one particular mother, 'Masebili, who is imagined carrying Sebili, the singer himself, as a child on her back. There is a colloquial notion in Sesotho that a man's lover is like a mother to him, cradling him tenderly in her arms, no surprise to amorous Americans among whom

"Baby" as a term of endearment is widely overused. These are the darlings of Sebili's village, remember, so perhaps 'Masebili is really that special girl, cradling her "traveling man" as she goes for those "sweets" her "baby" likes so much.

In *sefela* as in chiefs' praises, people are transformed into metaphors that may be mixed or switched or so sustained they create a new, virtual level of existence for the text (Kunene 1979, 60). Taking on a life of their own, such "total identification" metaphors creatively link one domain to another through chains of imagistic association and synonymy, prescribing choices in narrative voice or point of view. In this way the techniques of shifting person and "impersonification" are complementary and mutually illuminating (ibid., 74–76). Migrants become and behave like the train they ride, and the comparisons (without "like" or "as"!) of this composite traveler with the creatures and features of the landscapes it travels creates cognitive continuity between home and mine compound (Mokitimi 1982, 211). Foreign words are Sothoized and used in preference to Sesotho alternatives as a means of domesticating and incorporating the dominant relations of production (ibid., 237–39). So *mteto*, the Xhosa word for the informal rules governing mine life becomes *mthetho;* "miner" becomes *maenara* and by extension *maeneng*, "at the mine"; while many terms assume the singular and plural prefixes of the Sesotho noun classification system: "squatter/squad/*kwaad*" becoming *sekoata, likoata.* In Sesotho, the verb "to be" is often understood rather than stated; in other cases, the invariant particle *ke* establishes identity between subject and object. The language is by construction intensely metaphorical, and easily establishes identities and equivalences that make parallelism of form and meaning automatic. Indeed, a complete, elegant balance of ideas and form—parallelism of position, syntax, idea, part of speech, stress pattern, sound, syllable, and intonation—is an aesthetic value in Sesotho (see Lestrade 1937, 307), most refined and intensified in the genre of *maele:*

Ha se motho; ke seka motho.	He is not a person; he only resembles a person.[8]
Motho ke motho ka batho ba bang.	A person is a person through other people.
Morena ke morena ka batho.	A chief is a chief by the people.

Basotho poets give new meaning to Edgar Allen Poe's self-exemplary dictum for successful poetic effect: "The sound must seem the echo of the

8. Although he may possess the appearance of a human being, this individual's conduct is unbecoming to a socialized person.

sense." Grammatical and phonetic rules may be bent to accommodate the demands of rhythm and melody, and words are often chosen to give sonic emphasis to a visual image, as in the praise lines:

Kanono tsa tla li kutuma tueta e luma.	Canons came roaring, the field resounding.
Lisabole tsa tla li ketema kahohle.	Swords came jangling on all sides.

(Mofokeng 1945, 119–20)

The syntactic structure of Sesotho possesses an inherent wealth of alliterative and assonantal sound patterns and parallelistic rhythms, of which *sefela* performers make full use. Sesotho nouns, for example, are attached to verbs and modifiers by a set of pronominal concords based on the identifying prefixes of the singular and plural noun classes. This creates natural sequences of repeated consonant and vowel sounds, frequently reinforced by syntactic and semantic parallelism. In performance this tendency is heightened for aesthetic effect, as in the classic opening line of the *tsomo* (folktale) *Moleso oa Likhomo: Boholo-holo-holo ho bo le basali ba babeli*, "Once there were two women." *Sefela* is no exception, as this passage by Tsokolo Lecheko, for which I have inserted an interlinear word-by-word translation:

Ke tila fatse ka lento lena la ka; *[I hit earth with foot this of me]*	I hit the earth hard with this foot of mine;
Ke tila fatse hoa nyoloha methokho. *[I hit earth so to arise medicines]*	I hit the earth to bring up medicines [my song].

In Sesotho, a language that makes semantic discriminations by contrasting patterns of syllabic tone, there is the additional possibility of "tone parallelism," but my research is so far inconclusive on this point. A. C. Modan notes in addition the richness of verb forms in southern Bantu languages: "Any verb stem . . . can be made the base of some twenty or thirty others, all reflecting the root idea in various lights . . . each bearing the whole luxuriant super-growth of voices, moods, tenses, and person forms, to the utmost limits of its powers of logical extention" (cited in Finnegan 1970, 61). In sum, performance involves an interpenetration of sound and meaning in which music is inseparable from verbal interest (Finnegan 1977, 118–19).

All of these texts and the many forms of parallelism—repetitions with a difference—raise the question of oral "formulas" and their uses in *sefela*. One cannot, I suppose, even mention the subject of oral composition without addressing Milman Parry and Albert Lord's concepts of the formula and "composition in performance" (Lord 1960) and more recently the theories of Father Ong on orality (1982). Finnegan (1976, 1977) and more recently Vail and White (1991, 21–30) have incisively criticized Lord along with Marshall McLuhan, Walter Ong, and Jack Goody, relieving me of the duty to comment on the "orality and literacy" debate or its literature. So I would like to confine my observations to formulas and oral composition in *sefela*—if only I could. There is the immediate problem, however, that the notions of "formula" and "oral composition" (if it exists as a discrete process) are so ill-defined and unconstrained that they lose all meaning through retrodictive inclusiveness. Thus "formula" devolves into any form of repetition, assumed (rather than proven) an aid to "oral composition." Milman Parry's definition of the formula as "Any group of words 'regularly employed under the same metrical conditions to represent a given essential idea" (Lord 1960, 71) certainly fails to fit *sefela*, which employs rhythm but not meter, but we can extend the concept usefully if we take formula to indicate any set of structured formal devices that aid in composition and performance through repetitive patterning. Formulas in *sefela* are used to open and close performances, mark transitions or periods between thematic units, give rhythmic structure to the flow of a text, or just to keep the song idling while the performer searches instinctively for his next trope. But however they are employed, there is virtually always an intention of heightened aesthetic and emotional effect, creating a state of feeling or remembrance. So Makeka Likhojane:

Ke re'eng, litsamaea-naha?	What do I say, inveterate travelers?
Likepechele, batho ba makhooeng,	Knobkerrie-poets, men of the mines,
Lirurubele, ba kile ba nkotla,	The Butterflies, they once swarmed on me,
Ha e tla ba ke nepile.	If it should be I am right.
Ke tloha Mpohlo, banna;	I left Mpohlo, men;
Ke rongoelloa bosoleng,	I've been sent into the army,
Ha e tla ba ke nepile.	If it should be I am right.
Ha kea tata; ha kea potlaka.	I'm not in a hurry; I'm not in a rush.
Ha kea khena; ha kea hlabeha.	I'm not impatient; I'm not offended.
Bo-ntate, banna ba makhooeng,	Fathers, men of the mines,
Ke sebelitse lae malimo a batho;	I have worked with cannibal men;
Malimo, liphakoe bo-Motlalentoa	Cannibals, hawks of Motlalentoa,
Bo-Keresemese, litjaka bo, Tokelo lehlanya . . .	The Christmas boys, proud swells, crazy Tokelo . . .

Having sung of misfortunes and wonders, the singer recalls the rough and ready "knobkerrie poets" (are they poets carrying knobkerries or poets in the use of knobkerries?), the "butterflies," "cannibal-men," and "proud (but dangerous) swells" of the mines, invoking the cooling, worldly-wise patience of one of his favorite, oft-repeated formulas:

Ha kea tata, ha kea potlaka	I'm not in a hurry; I'm not in a rush.
Ha kea khena; ha kea hlabeha.	I'm not impatient; I'm not offended.

I asked Makeka what the line about "butterflies" meant, and he said these were russian gangsters who sometimes forced him to perform, and used *sefela* mostly as an excuse to club together. "Why call them 'butterflies?'" I asked. "'Butterflies' refers to their colorful blankets," he replied, "and anyway, I wouldn't have dared call them russians."

Ironically, *lifela* generally feature far fewer formulaic usages than do praise poems, which have a more fixed idea of text and employ more conscious memorization. Lord himself doesn't believe in memorization and has argued that by definition "oral mentality"—we must forgive this terminology in so venerable a scholar: we all stand on the shoulders of giants—means having no idea of a fixed text, so that each performance is a new composition, created by remembering rather than by memorization (cited in Opland 1983, 154). Then again, while Lord regards repetition as the "hallmark of oral poetry," *sefela* performers lose competitions (and money) if they repeat themselves without obvious aesthetic purpose. *Sefela* performers do not favor the "formulaic metaphors" common in chiefs' praises (Swanepoel 1983, 8), but do appear to manipulate an established "thematic repertoire," as Lord's prescription for oral poetry provides (1960, 63), blended with entirely original ideas and subjects. But as Mokitimi has pointed out (1982, 56), formulas are not "thematic" in function and tend to be hortatory, phatic, or for maintaining rhetorical and rhythmic flow while marking time or making a transition.

As to the reified notion of "oral composition," Ruth Finnegan (1976, 135; 1977, 20) doesn't believe it has any identifiable empirical basis, not even in that folklorists's favorite, "oral transmission." Praise poetry, she observes (1970, 105–6), is modified, "reforged" in performance by performers who are not in fact regarded as the composers. Style in auriture may be fundamentally social, but this does not prevent the *sefela* composer from putting his individual name and stamp upon his work. Goody's (1977) helpful replacement of the false notion of "collective composition" with the more accurate "concatenated recomposition" is even more applicable to *sefela* than to chiefs' praises. Lord's definitive criteria for oral literature is that it must be "composed in performance," but Vail and White (1991, 30) point out that much oral poetry isn't. In *sefela*, apprentices tend to compose their texts in advance with the help of their teachers, while the real *likheleke* maintain their reputation by virtuoso extemporization to suit the occasion and the context of competition with formidable rivals. The status of *sefela* poets is somewhere between professional and amateur, so recruitment and training are semiformalized to informal. A poet's central personal text develops over time, incrementally, through a combination of rehearsal and improvisation (Mokitimi 1982, 70). Lord's Macedonian poets can (and do) consult published versions of their epics, and these days the *lithoko* of Basotho royals are often learned from Mangoela's ([1921] 1984) written collection (taught in primary schools). *Lifela* are not so much handed down as looted (with or without citation) or broken into fragments and handed around, but their creators, like the famous *liroki* of Basotho kings, are not anonymous.

Finnegan cites many illustrations of the interpenetration of literate and nonliterate contexts and the co-occurrence of expressive devices in written and oral forms. In *sefela*, illiterate (not nonliterate) singers often satirize the control that documents and written contexts exercise over their destiny, even extending to the existential plane of the ancestors:

Hoja leholimong ho oa ngolla,	If it were possible to write to heaven,
Ke ne ke tla romela maqheku teng,	I would send the old folks there,
A tle a fumane Jorodane e tletse,	So that they find Jordan flooded,
E tseloang ka libuka	Which is crossed by books,
Banna, le ka mangolo, Basotho.	Men, and by certificates, Basotho

(Mabote Nkoebele, in Mokitimi 1982, 235)

Unlike Finnegan's (1976, 130) Limba storytellers (or Lord's Slavic epic singers), who asserted they were telling the same story exactly despite recorded variations, Basotho singers regard each performance as "another *sefela*" no matter how similar or different. "Orality," Finnegan argues convincingly (1976, 137–41), is relative and "oral composition" unqualifiable: performance is the crucial criteria.

In *sefela*, singers blend aural and metaphoric resources to create aesthetic worlds of feeling from shared experience and knowledge. For the Basotho, these "cries of the heart" constitute a cultural articulation of sound and sentiment (Feld 1982) that both ravels up the tattered sleeve of care and knits together the rent fabric of social relations for people living divided and dependent lives. In this sense a *sefela* is both a personal and collective autobiography, an aesthetic reflection on experiences at once deeply individual and widely shared. Here there is no opposition between orality and individuality, and the listener understands what his or her levels of personal experience, empathy, and cultural knowledge permit. A *sefela* has an immediate level of meaning apparent to any casual listener, including women and older children. Second, there is a level apprehended by other Basotho men who have shared with the performer such experiences as mine labor and ritual initiation. Third, there is the level communicated to other expert poets, who share a heightened appreciation of aesthetic techniques and qualities of *lifela* performance. Finally, there is the meaning caught only by the performer's closest associates, who are intimately acquainted with both his personal history and his *lifela.* This complex, socially constitutive relationship between individuality and commonality is reflected in the constitution of cultural knowledge in the domain of games, which is at once broadly possessed and creatively and interpretively individuated. It is variously expressed in the competitive efforts to bring fresh images and new life to near-obligatory motifs such as the moving mine train, in personal narrations that relate a familiar story, and not least in the tendency of poets to steal from one another (see Mokitimi 1982, 51, 56): next to prize money the highest collegial accolade. *Lifela* are formed out of an entire life experience in the creative crucible of extemporaneous competition. Every performance is a reordering of materials used in previous recitations combined with original passages composed on the spot. In a sense, poets have just one *sefela:* a poetic life-narrative made up of materials variously composed and acquired, and continually recomposed, lengthened, and recombined throughout their performing lives. Most poets begin their careers reciting a great deal of what they've learned from their seniors, gradually replacing it with material of their own. Ambitious youngsters may willingly lose their share of a prize kitty for the opportunity to study and appropriate the choice phrases, narrative episodes, performance techniques, even the singing names (much to the consternation) of renowned opponents. Long *lifela* most often contain images and passages donated by teachers or stolen from other poets one has heard or competed against. Freely mixed in with personal material are textual resources drawn from a loose corpus widely employed and freely exchanged among experienced poets and their pupils.

On another note, experience itself may be empathetically borrowed. The ethos of sisterhood that underlies female networks among bar women, for example, are aptly expressed in a passage from one of Thakane Mahlasi's songs, "Bakhototsi" (Thieves):

Hele helele ngoana moshanyana!	Hey there man-child!
Ke lahlehetsoe ke motho tsamaeong;	I've been abandoned by [my] man amid [my] wanderings;
Jo, 'Malebenyaeeeeeee!	Jo, 'Malebenyaeeeeeee!
Hae oele oelele le le oele!	Hae oele oelele le le oele!
Menejara komponeng koana, bo!	The manager of yonder compound, bo!
Ke re, 'menejara komponeng koana,	I say, the manager of yonder compound,
U romme manekapotene komponeng.	You sent the compound captains [on your business].
Heela uena, ngoana moshanyana!	Hey, man-child!
'Maene kapotene, Satane,	Mine captain, Satan,
Jo! O moleko oa ho qetela.	Jo! You are misfortune itself.
Hele helele, ngoana moshanyana!	Hey there, man-child!
U nkile themba la ka;	You have taken my [one] hope;
O le behile merafong koana.	You have kept him at the mines yonder.
Hela uenaeeeee!	Hey you heyyyy!
Ke eane, u chofa likolofane,	There he is, pushing ore-buckets,
Mose hara makhooa koana.	There among the whitemen yonder.

The events recounted in the first person here actually concern a friend of the singer's who was living with her man near a mine compound in South Africa. When the man was suddenly transferred to another mine, she was unable to follow and had to return to Lesotho. Asked about this passage, Thakane replied that her friend had little talent or self-confidence as a performer, so she composed and sang these lines for her—and for all the women who suffer the pain of forced separation from their men.

The aesthetic of social harmonization is also characteristically expressed in metapoetics, what Adams refers to as the principle of "intrinsic evaluation" (1974, 248), in which imagery of aesthetic value provides evaluative commentary within the process of performance itself. Further, because games both embody and communicate cultural ideas, their enactment obviates external commentary. Games exist only in performance, so their reality is their truth, their identity their evaluation. In Sesotho auriture, the better the performance, the more true the form (ibid., 160, 195). The one genre that can with confidence be evaluated "systemically," that is, with reference to preexisting cultural concepts of it, is (not surprisingly) chiefs' praises, whose "truth" exists apart from its performance. Appropriateness in this Sesotho form of "selective tradition" depends to an extent upon the status of the praiser and his aristocratic subject and upon the context of performance. New verses may be admired, but there is an idea of a fixed text that the praiser must "get right" even though the text is never fixed in fact (ibid., 193–95).

Sefela though, applies a generic language "specifically energized by its processual and eventual nature, rather than by some set of qualities or formal conditions imposed according to an aesthetic" (George Quasha, cited in Tedlock 1977, 514). Majara Majara sustains a metapoetic reflection upon his process of composition, breaking the trope with his favorite formula:

Ha hona le letho, 'mino ona:	It contains nothing, this singing:
Ke re thapo ena ke e loha,	I say I know how to make this rope,
Ebile ke tseba le ho e phetha.	And I know how to finish it.
Ke re ho lona, likempolara?	What do I say to you, gamblers [poets]?

The very notions of genre and ethnoaesthetic systems of classification, of course, raise certain culturally embedded expectations about performance. Images that both invoke and demonstrate performance values—such as extemporaneous long-windedness (with repetition allowed only for poetic effect), originality, precise observation, ethical reflection, brilliant evocation, narrative interest, thought-provoking sequencing and linking of themes, unpredictability, display of knowledge of "deep Sesotho" and of a wide range of cultural domains, humor, a captivating vocal tone and an intuitive feel for verbal rhythm and melody—are common elements of superior *lifela* (Mokitimi 1982, 58). As Bauman observes (1977, 29), metapoetics—the capacity of semiotic structures to comment imaginatively upon themselves—represents a process of personal cultural self-definition by their performers. Sesotho games actualize personal and group experiential understandings, so that their meaning is entailed in their doing in a particular way, uniting concept, process, and performance product: *Ba li etsa ka molomo ho li hlalosa ho binoa ka nako e le 'ngoe,* "People make songs with the mouth to explain them [express their meaning] while singing at the same time" (Adams 1974, 160). Performance is therefore at once a vehicle and a frame of display, setting the communicative act itself apart for contemplation. An admirable performance is a sufficient claim to knowledge about a genre, so that "talking about performance and what is performed tends to be superfluous if not presumptuous without the ability of demonstration" (ibid., 140). Performers do have an ordinary speech vocabulary of aesthetic commentary, and when asked "What makes a good *sefela?*" replied with the following:

"The voice should be high" (intense, clear).

"The singer should know Sesotho" (display extraordinary linguistic competence and thus cultural knowledge).

"The singer should have substance in his song; he should have seen places and be able to make the people see them" (be a person of experience and able to share them with others).

"He should be able to go on for a long time with out stopping, and without repeating himself" (be capable of flowing, extemporaneous, original composition in performance).

In general, however, performers showed little interest in extrinsic discourse about formal values, and referred to the "music" or the "substance" (images) of the songs themselves. As the poet Holomo Tsauli sang, *'Kheleke ha bo hlomeloe lesiba*, "Eloquence is not stuck on like a feather" (Mokitimi 1982, 263).[9] In *sefela*, performers demonstrate their mastery of poetic composition in the rhythmically driven roll of spontaneously concatenated episodes and images, and in original metaphors or fresh reworkings of established ways of commenting both on *bokheleke*, "eloquence," and on the *kheleke*, the "man of eloquence" himself. During a competition at Ha-Mafefoane, Roma District, Mphafu Mofolo and his rival, Phoofolo Pitso, employed the familiar imagery of water fauna in their efforts at once to claim and prove that each was the better poet. First Phoofolo Pitso sang:

> I plunge [into performance], *Phaka!* [Go to it!]
> Like a kingfisher into the water.
> As it sits like a duck-bird,
> The child of the waters dives deep into the song;
> I was swimming, swimming up the deep pools [of poetic meaning].

Later, when his turn came, Mphafu Mofolo:

> As I arrived there,
> To me Chieftainess Matsepo and others paid respect.
> They said to me, "Brother of Makhoathi,
> You should just sing for us, father of Thabang."
> Don't you see, even at Maama's here, I am treated as a person.
> You should know, I am given the recognition [due to] eloquence:
> They say to me, "Just go on singing."
> He! I can never just sing;

9. Although I have no way of finding this out, it may even be that Holomo's line referred directly to the renowned singer and teacher Hlalele Mabekanyane of Mafeteng, who was known at the mines in Welkom, Orange Free State, by the singing name "Lesiba" (Feather), after the feather he sported in his Sesotho straw hat when he performed *sefela*.

I don't just plunge in, [I] the father of Thebang.
Don't you see I am received at the chief's place?
I am a certificated man of eloquence:
Sons of my home, my eloquence rises from the outset—
He! Men! Cattle! [I salute you.] [I] brother to Makhoathi!

One dimension of *sefela* performance for which there are seemingly no rules and perhaps no established patterns is narrative time, space, function, or sequence in the Proppian "syntagmatic" sense. As with all "trickster" genres, the central character (here the singer) and the theme of traveling are the only unifying elements (Babcock-Abrahams 1975, 166–67). Singers usually start with formulas or statements calling for attention, identifying themselves and boasting of or deprecating their performing prowess, and end with calls to their comrades and rivals to follow their act if they can. In between almost anything can happen. Emotional dynamics and their musical expression govern the spontaneous progression of linked, polysemantic images in a *sefela* performance. Since complete texts often run to between 500 and 900 lines, illustration and analysis here has been confined to illustrative passages, but comparison of *lifela* texts by different poets or of several texts by the same poet reveal no overall patterns or rules of thematic arrangement or sequence. While themes are varied and numerous, the selection is not infinite. The order in which relatively stable thematic passages occur, and even the length of such passages, varies unpredictably from poet to poet, master to apprentice, performance to performance. The important thing is to keep the recitation going, and transition depends upon the musical and emotional continuity of the performer's verbal inspiration.

Perhaps *lifela*, like praises, are not narrative in the formal sense, but more a series of pictures whose ordering is layered and intensifying like the superimposed scenes and figures of a cave painting. Forged in a language much given to figuration and "picture-talks" (Franz 1930, 145), the images of *sefela* are bound by metaphor rather than by chronology, event sequence, or interior narrative. More generally the patterning of images, rather than of time or story, may be as Scheub says "the single most important characteristic of African oral performances" (1985, 10). The structuring of images as a progression is enabled by the nature of metaphoric implication, which "moves thought not by identities, but by equivalences that are unities of identity and difference [moving] ceaslessly through a genealogy of concepts . . . sometimes even coming back to what might seem a point of origin" (Tyler 1987, 173–74 n). Like the trickster tales for which African folklore is famous, form follows character in *sefela*, and traveling is the only thread that sews narrative episodes together. In *sefela sa litsamaea-naha*, songs of the country travelers, the poet transcends boundaries in space, time, and narrative structure as the migrant transcends the political borders of Lesotho and the structural boundaries of Basotho society.

Among the most pervasive and commanding metaphors in *sefela* apart from the many modes of travel is that of traditional medicine and the afflictions and uncertainties to which it ministers. As Heap explains, disease is a metaphor used to describe the unifying role of conflict in society. Disease both literally and figuratively indicates a rift in social relations, so sickness and curing become part of a wider Turnerian "social drama" of breach, response, and restoration (Heap 1989, 102–7). Ashton, who worked among the mountain Batlokoa clan in the 1940s, described the *ngaka* (pl.: *lingaka*) as a professional man of superior knowledge and experience, called on for any problem people cannot deal with themselves. His knowledge is obtained through purchase, cunning, inheritance, apprenticeship, and of course can be created through intuition and experimentation. Many *lingaka*, like the legendary Mohlomi, are great travelers in search of experience, new knowledge, more business, prestige, or simply from wanderlust (Ashton 1967, 282–87). As the *maele* has it, *Ngaka e shoa e etile*, "A doctor dies abroad" (Guma 1967, 82). Ashton suggests that for Basotho, knowledge and ritual action are identical as forms of power: "The use of medicines does not stop at the curing of sickness but extends far beyond, to almost every situation where a man requires help to control nature and social phenomena, or is faced with difficulty, danger, and uncertainty" (Ashton 1967, 303). As the missionary Casalis observed of *lingaka*, "there is in fact, no manner of question which they do not undertake to answer" ([1861] 1965, 288). Despite a widespread fear of *boloi*, witchcraft and sorcery, Basotho regard divination as essentially supplementary to plant pharmacopia and theraputic technique. Though physical, social, and spiritual relationships belong to a single moral universe, the *ngaka* is less a technician of the occult than of herbalism and healing (Kunene 1972, 340–41). Indeed, despite the legends of fearsome diviners who draw down lightning bolts to strike at one another, the popular mediumistic tradition is not strictly *bongaka* but *bothuela*. This form of divinatory performance is said to have been imported from the Nguni-speaking people of the Cape and is also referred to as *bokoma*, from *ngoma*, the Nguni word for dancing and drumming. Many of the invocations and prayers of *bothuela* are of

Nguni origin, including the famous southern Bantu healers' equivalent of "Amen," *Siyavuma!* "We agree!"

Operating metaphorically, the title *ngaka* is extended as a recognition of expertise in any domain of cultural knowledge. Hence Casalis noted that a blacksmith was called *ngaka ea tsepe*, "doctor of iron," his specialty, like *bongaka*, requiring ritual purification and a long apprenticeship (Casalis [1861] 1965, 131). The mutuality between the living and dead members of kindreds and totemic clans (*liboko*) that comprises the essence of Sesotho non-Christian religion sanctions the moral ideology of social harmonization through the offices of the *ngaka*, who ritually mediates relations between ancestors and their descendants and among living members of communities and kinship groups. In contrast to Nguni-speaking peoples, Basotho see most important problems as arising from relations with other people, not from relations with nature. All such relations must be kept in harmony and balance, or sickness, evil, and misfortune follows (Hammond-Tooke 1974, 323–35). Casalis ([1861] 1965, 302–3) noted that morality among the Basotho depended on social order, and that political disorganization led to collective moral collapse and individual crime. Moral evil itself was represented as ugly, damaged, afflicted, faulty, or incapable. Mediation though *bongaka* can of course, foster the disruption as well as the reordering of social relations. Master *lingaka* work in partnership with spirit mediums and are often diviners themselves, as much feared for their ability to confront and reveal witchcraft as they are needed to restore physical and moral composure to the sick and conflicted. Though traditional healers are still very widely employed in both the medical and ritual exigencies of everyday life, they have largely lost their historical position as seers and councilors to the powerful. Though the famous *ngaka* Chapi was a close confidante of Moshoeshoe I, the worldly-wise king publicly lamented the rapid increase in the numbers and kinds of diviners during his reign, and excoriated them for their quackery and greed (Lagden 1909, 1: 301–2). Today *bongaka* is a form of institutionalized liminality discredited by educated resident elites, sharing in the categorical marginality of migrancy, though in Lesotho migrancy is a marginality that has overgrown the center. As Murray points out, though, "Apart from the chieftainship, the profession of medicine is the only sphere of traditional male prestige which remains viable today, and is certainly the most lucrative activity in rural Lesotho" (1975, 67), and thus one of the few alternatives to labor migrancy open to landless, unschooled rural Basotho.

A renowned singer of *sefela* who is in demand among his juniors as a teacher of composition is known as a *ngaka ea lifela.* In bringing the causes of social disaffection to public attention through heightened modes of aesthetic discourse, the *kheleke* shares in the ritual functions and authority of the *ngaka*, creating the opportunity for cognitive and social reassessment and reintegration through "illocutionary acts" both in and of performance. Both *likheleke* and *lingaka* retain a certain prestige as what Gramsci termed "organic intellectuals," purveying the knowledge underlying the historical continuity of Sesotho in aesthetic or ritual performance and discourse. I asked my good friend and mentor Nthebe Bulara, a well-known *ngaka* of Mafeteng and a Sesotho organic intellectual *par excellance*, about the roles of word music, speech, and song in *bongaka.* Breaking through into performance, he prefaced his reply with a divination song. "It is light," he continued,

> we ask for light (*leseli*). To see the light; be observant (*qamako*) regarding the patient, clairvoyant. In songs the words are to ask the ancestors, so they in turn can ask God,[10] so you can disclose the illness, it's cause and cure. . . . The need of music, dancing, is for observation, relaxation. After you have sung and danced, you are going to feel relaxed, and it brings up your *bongaka*, your power to cure. After you have sung and danced at length, it makes clear your visions in the night. Otherwise we sing church hymns, because they bless.

Among diviners, the standard greeting is not *Lumela*, but *Khanya*, "Bright"; the reply is *Leseli.*

Like singers, traditional healers are classified not by their varied divinatory techniques but by personal reputation. Both *bokheleke*, "eloquence," and *bongaka*, "healing," are repositories of *Sesotho*, and the singer as traditional diviner/herbalist is one of the most popular tropes through which composers dramatize the authority of "eloquent knowledge" (Coplan 1987b). In some *lifela*, singers represent themselves narratively as doctors:

Ke pelo ka utloa bohloko,	My heart felt such pain,
Ka nka kepi ka nyolosa thaba.	I took a digging rod and ascended the mountain.
Ke ne ke ilo cheka lithlare tse thata feela:	I was going to dig the strong medicines only:
Ke cheka maime;	I dug *maime;*
Ke cheke mabophe;	I dug *mabophe;*
Ke nka feko le lirahalibone.	I took *feko* and *lirahalibone.*[11]

10. As the ancient Sesotho diviners' prayer puts it, *Molimo o mocha, rapela oa khale*, "New god, pray to the old."

11. Each of these medicines, composed of a single plant or a mixture of plants, has a specific purpose, usually signaled by its name. So *maime*, from *ho imela*, "to lie heavily upon, be too difficult for," is used to make a chief lenient in his judgment when one is brought

Tse metseng ka lithakong, le tsona ke li etsa motsoako.	Herbs from village ruins, of those I made [them].
Feela ke ne ke re 'mampharoane a seke a li tlola;	But I said the zonure lizard should not leap over them;
Etle ere ha a ka a li tlola, a qale ka ho khaoha noka.	The time he leaps over them, he will first lose a leg.
Joale ha ke tloha, ke etsa mohlolo.	When I leave, I'm first going to make miracles.

(Tieho Rakharebe, "Hulas Ralipotsotso")

Tieho's knowledge of herbalism was not entirely casual or metaphoric: he had served for some months as a *lehlaahana*, an apprentice who carries the *khetsi* (medicine bag) of a *ngaka* on expeditions to dig herbs in the countryside. It is therefore not accidental that the medicines he names are the major ones used by doctors in preparing and strengthening the *seriti* (shadow, dignity, personal authority) of a migrant prior to his departure for the mines. The application of these medicines in a ritual context will ensure the safety and success of the migrant, and protect his *seriti* from attacks by witches at home in Lesotho. Once underground, many miners use magical/herbal protections, and *lingaka* do a thriving mail-order business in *meriana* (medicines), used to establish certainty and control over one's situation (Gordon 1977, 210), or to bring luck, promotion, money, lovers, victory in court cases, sporting matches, and yes, *sefela* competitions. In *lifela*, doctoring is often a metaphor of metapoetics, a means to both assert and demonstrate expressive prowess:

Ngaka tse ngata, li tloha mona ke ho tsaba.	Many doctors, they leave here for fear of me.
Le tse setseng ha li ntsebe;	Those who remain do not know me;
Li se bile li nahana.	They are still figuring it out.
Ho falla Ralilochane, oa ngaka, matsetsele.	Even Raliochane, the specialist [in eloquence], intends going.
Bana ba kula: keng u cheka?	The children are sick: what herbs are *you* digging?
'Na, ha ke sale ngakana; ke ngaka.	Me, I am not an apprentice; I am a doctor.
Ha ke 'nke kepi ho cheka lithlare:	I don't take a pick to dig medicines:
Ke qale pele ka ho opa liatla;	I start first by clapping hands;
Ke tila fatse ka lento lena la ka;	I hit the earth hard with this foot of mine;

before him for a serious infraction; *mabophe*, "binding," is used to delay the pursuit of enemies so as to provide time to flee to safety; *feko* allows one to pursue a course of action unobserved, while *lira-ha-libone*, "enemies do not see," makes one invisible to one's pursuers.

Ke tila fatse hoa nyoloha methokho.	I hit the earth hard to bring out my song.
Ho nyolohile litlhare tse thata feela, khelebetla le lehabeea.	I bring forth strong medicines only [for your appreciation], *khelebetla* and *lehabeea*

(Tsokolo Lecheko)

Eloquent ones, like diviners, have the capacity to articulate the social realities and contradictions that lie beneath the surface of institutional and community life, and so to help reestablish the moral basis of productive and satisfying social relations. As Adams memorably put it: "The connection of verbal expressiveness and social process is fundamental in Basotho society" (1974, 128). This connection is emphasized in Makeka Likhojane's endless pursuit of the *thokolosi*, the demon witch familiar, a trope used to illustrate the unity of the migrant's geographical and social environments. In another performance (let me not say "another *sefela*"), Makeka's efforts to drive out evil in the form of the *thokolosi* demonstrate the universality of conflict, venality, and misunderstanding, ameliorated by the *kheleke/ngaka*'s eloquent articulation:

Litsohatsana bo 'ma ea Motolo,	The old women of Mother Motolo's,
Ba roetse mokopu ba tsoa masimong.	They balance pumpkins as they come from the fields.
Joale ba joetsa Ngoana Komane,	Now they tell Komane's Child,
Ngaka e teng masimong koana;	A doctor is over there in the fields;
Motho eo ke Ngoana Mokhalo.	That man is Mokhalo's Child.
Ha ke fihla, ba 'mpitsitse;	When I arrived, they called me;
Ke fihla ho Ngoana Komane.	I came to the [chief] Child of Komane.
Ke li qhala—lifalafala,	I scattered them [bones]—*lifalafala!*
'Taola tsaka tsa bohlokoa, bana ting,	My precious [divining] bones, you children,
Ke li qhala ke li qamaka.	I scattered them and examined them.
Ke moo ke joetsang, Ngoana Komane,	It's then I told him, Child of Komane,
Mokuli tsoha o ba latele;	The sick must get up and follow them;
Ba ja khomo o qele.	Those eating a cow you ask [for meat].
Masapo a khomo, kunutoll'a batho,	Cattle bones, the revealers of people,
Ka seea letlalo la ntja e khunong;	I skinned a brown dog;
Ka nka le bohloa bo, botona,	I took a male ant, men,
Haholo banna le le tsehali,	Especially the females,
Mafura a tsoene le boko ba 'mutla,	Monkey fat and rabbit brain,
Tsikitlane ke etse mothamo:	A mouthful of marigold:
Thokolosi ea baleha ka hara masimo;	A *thokolosi* ran away from the fields;
Ea hla ea leba sakaneng koana.	It even went to the kraal yonder.

Bashanyana ba ntjoetsa, Moleko
o teng sakeng koana.
Ea baleha ea leba sakeng la pere;
Ea baleha ea leba masimong;
Ea fihla ea leleka batsosi.
Ha ke fihla ka masimong,
Batsosi ba baleha ka masimong.

Ba re, ha ba fihla ka hara motse,
Moleko o teng masimong koana:
E choatla mokopu, e siea 'tjoto;

Poone tsena e lipoma chakatsa;
E li fetolela bolepo;
Litapole e li fothotse metloang.
Ha ke fihla ka masimong,
Ea kena tlasa lefika.
Moo ke ntseng ke e bona;
e rola lieta tsa litopo
Le likausi tsa boea ba lipoli—
Li ne li tsoehla, haholo li lakalisa, batho,
nama.
Ke re ho eona—banna, le 'mamele—
Ke moo ke ntseng ke e bona.
Ea rola katiba tooane;
Ea e beha tlasa lefika.
Ka tsoela mathe letsohong mona,
Ha ke ntse ke pikitla ho tsoela pele.
Linotsi li fofa—
Joale tsa semana, li ea e hlola:
Tsa entsa ka tlasa lefika.

Ea baleha ea leba lebenkeleng,
Ha Fako ha Masupha.
Ea reka bohobe le kofi;
Ke tle ke e setse morao.
Ha ke fihla ka lebenkeleng,
Ea baleha, e so thole chenche;
Ea leba Matsieng.
Ha-Ramokoatsi teraeshareng,
E ripota ho molula-setulo.
Samane e tsoile teraeshareng,
E mpatlang—banna, le ntsebe mabitso.

Ha ke fihla ka teraeshareng,

Boys told me, there's an evil spirit
in the kraal.
It ran to the stable;
It ran to the fields;
It chased away the bird-chasers.
When I came to the fields,
The bird-chasers ran away from
the fields
They said, when they came home,
There is an evil in the fields:
It breaks pumpkins, leaving
wild watermelons;
It cuts maize in flower;
It pulls out the corn silk;
It pulled out potatoes by the roots.
When I came to the lands,
It went under a rock.
There I saw it;
it pulled off its gumboots
And the stockings of mohair—
They were so oily, they'd make one
long, people, for meat.
I said to it—men, listen to me—
It's there while I still saw it.
It took off a grass hat;
It put it under the rock.
I spat in my hand,
Then rubbed it continuously.
Bees came flying out of my hand—
Now bees, it's afraid of:
They chased it out from under the
rock.
It ran away to the shop,
At Fako's at Masupha's place.
It bought bread and coffee;
I came following it.
When I came to the shop,
It ran away, leaving the change;
It ran away to Matsieng.
At Ramokoatsi's court,
It reports to the chairman.
The summons was issued,
Calling me then—men, you should
know my names.
When I came to court,

Ea leba ha Mojela,	It ran away to Mojela's,
Mapotu ha Mojela,	To Mapotu at Mojela's place,
Ha 'Mikiea pela ha Rabuka.	To Mekiea's near Rabuka's place.
Joale e ea ha bo mosali—	Now it goes to my wife's place—
Ke thotse ba bohoeng baka ba loea,	I was silent as my in-laws cast spells,
Ba le pineng ea bosiu ba khiba.	Singing at night and dancing the girls' knee dance.
Ka ba feta ka nokaneng;	I passed them at the river;
Ka botsa 'maea mosali,	I asked my mother-in-law,
"Chaile ea lona e tlaba neng?"	"When are you dispersing?"
A re, "Oena monna oa ngoanaka,	She said, "My daughter's husband,
Foho ha e otla, re tla qhalana.	At the stroke of 4 [A.M.], we will disperse.
E ea lapeng o itulele; re sa le papaling mona."	Go and stay home; we are still playing here."
Ka bona ha ba fihla ba ntikile;	I saw them come and surround me;
Ba pota-pota motseng.	They surrounded the village.
Ba le melamu ba le likoa-koa;	They had fighting sticks and war-axes;
Ba batla le ho mpolaea.	They wanted to kill me.
Empa ha ba chaisa baloi ka foho ea bosiu,	But when the witches dispersed at 4 o'clock in the night,
Ho fihlile 'maea mosali.	There came my wife's mother.
A re, "O kae monna oa ngoanaka?"	She said, "Where is my daughter's husband?"
Ha ke fihla oa ntjoetsa,	When I came she told me,
"Re ne re ile papaling koana."	"We had gone for games yonder."

Here the poet portrays himself as a well-known *selaoli*, a "bone thrower," a *ngaka* who divines through the use of four major and a variable number of additional "bones" (*litaola*) (actually pieces cut from the front of the hoofs of cattle). Incised with specific patterns, each bone has a name and represents a significant actor in the oracular drama, including the patient, close kin and associates, witches, lovers, and so on. The diviner himself or herself (*lingaka* and especially *mathuela* are often women today) is a performer, throwing the bones on the ground and interpreting their *leoa*, "fall, scattering," while singing curing songs and chanting *lithoko tsa maoa*, "praises of the falls" (Leydevant 1933). These praises employ compositional devices characteristic of Sesotho auriture, including numerous ideophones and citations of other genres such as riddles (*lilomo*) and proverbs (*maele*):

Fiela-fiela, Nkoko a tswale;	Sweep a little, that Nkoko may bring forth his child;
A se nne a tswalla matlakaleng.	He should not do so in bits of straw.

The first line of this couplet is a riddle, the answer to which is *litaola*, "divining bones." In the next praise, the last line is a proverb entrenched in Sesotho legal usage, preventing the brothers of a deceased man from consuming the patrimony of his sons:

Phae o ja mangana;	The uncle eats cattle;
O jele kgomo tsa kgutsana kgudu ya Maphaong.	He has eaten the cattle of an orphan at Maphaong.
Mohla e hlolang kgutsana	The day the orphan grows up
Kgomo e tla di tseka	It [He] will demand them
Hobane tsabo moshemane ha di jewe.	Because "those [cattle] of a boy's family are not eaten."
	(Guma 1967, 150)

Having discovered the presence of the *thokolosi* through the bones, "the revealers of [the wicked designs of] people," Ngoana Mokhalo undertakes a powerful exorcism. Driven from it's hiding place, the demon abandons its characteristic grass hat and miner's rubber boots and flees to the local shops, where it is again forced to flee the hot pursuit of the poet. From there it runs to Matsieng, capital of the kings of Lesotho since its establishment by Moshoeshoe I's son Letsie I (hence *Matsieng*, "Among those of Letsie"), showing that misrepresentation, intrigue, and social immorality are practiced even in the highest places. Fortunately for the nation, Ngoana Mokhalo harries it on, so that the demon proceeds to the local court to lay a case against our avenging hero. Unsuccessful at court, the *thokolosi* takes refuge with the poet's in-laws: not surprising, since most witches are women, cannibals who kill their own kin for provision at witches' ritual feasts. Indeed, *boloi* is believed to occur most frequently among close kin, and the most frequently accused are a man's wife and mother-in-law (Hammond-Tooke 1974, 357–58). Here is the testimony of Nthebe Bulara:

> As it is known by miners nowadays, sometimes their women want to kill them while they are still at the mines, so as to get the death compensation money. So the miners go to see their *lingaka*, who prepare them the *lenaka le meleko*, the "horn of evils," before they go to the mines. . . . But nowadays we are preparing the *lenaka le sireletsa*, the "horn of protections," because your mother-in-law, anybody can just try to kill you or bewitch you over there, so stronger protection is needed. And your wife can bewitch you by taking your *seriti*, your shadow. . . . She takes your shadow while you are still at home. And at some time they will decide to kill you through your *seriti* over there. They can make a *tebello*, normally a wake-keeping the night before a corpse is buried, singing songs and drinking and eating; they make

> that while you are still alive in the mines, and they say, "I wish you can get killed in a mine accident."

Sure enough, the poet finds his mother-in-law and her coven having a high old time. Retreating to the village, the witches surround him, threatening to kill him: is he not a great diviner, exposer of witchcraft, exorcist, eloquent truth-teller? His mother-in-law intercedes for him, however, explaining that her friends were "just going for games yonder." The task of the poet as *ngaka*, explained Ngoana Mokhalo after the performance, was to use eloquence to drive out disharmony, wrongdoing, ignorance, and poor self-expression wherever they are found.

Another favorite figure in *sefela* is Khanyapa, the mythical water snake or python and patron diety of diviners, a monster who lurks in deep river pools, luring cattle and people to their deaths with its hypnotic gaze. The image of a predatory "deep-pool monster" plumbs the deepest wellsprings of southern Bantu narrative symbolism. Readers familiar with Thomas Mofolo's early Sesotho novel *Chaka* ([1925] 1981) will recognize Khanyapa in the figure of the water monster who anoints the young Chaka (Shaka Zulu) with the magic of kingship as he bathes in a brooding river grotto. In praise poetry the pervasive metaphor of the crocodile (*koena*), totem and eponymous symbol of the ruling Bakoena clan, is sometimes subsumed with that of the water snake. The following passage commemorates the victories of Moshoeshoe's grandson Lerotholi (1836–1905) over Cape colonial forces in the Gun War of 1880–81:

> Deep in the pool the Crocodile opened his eyes.
> He stared with eyes that were red,
> And the sons of the whiteman fell in.
> The boys have fallen in the mouth of the snake!
> Black snake, deep pool monster of the king;
> He belched forth lightning. . . .
> . . . This year he draws them in, deep-pool monster;
> Deep-pool monster, Python of the house of Seeiso,
> He swallowed a Boer, contained him in his stomach.
> Vainly his comrades searched for him,
> Up and down among the hosts, they failed to find him.
> (see Damane and Sanders 1974, 143, 150)

Khanyapa often appears to diviners in dreams, giving insight and instruction on medicines, beads (essential to *bothuela* regalia and curing paraphernalia), and the afflictions and treatment of both current patients and those yet to appear. Such knowledge is believed to come ultimately from the ancestors, who govern social relationships. Xhosa speakers regard water snakes as river spirits representing evil aspects or manifestations of the ancestors (Hammond-Tooke 1974, 322). Some healers claimed to have spent months at a time under water, studying herbalism and divination with Khanyapa. A diviner with divinely given powers of second sight is known as *senohe*, "seer," from *noha*, "snake." When drought forces Khanyapa to move to another river or pool, it travels in the form of a tornado, making it a formidable destructive force:

Tlatlametsi ea Makhaleng	Water Coluber, snake of Makhaleng River,
Khanyapa, lelinyane la eona e le siele malibohong koana.	Khanyapa, it has left its young at the river crossing.
E leshano: e sa tlabe khutle e ilo lelata.	It is lying: it will return and fetch it.
Mohlang e khutlang, ea Makhaleng,	The day it returned, thing of Makhaleng,
Khanyapa, ea tsosa meea ea mefuta.	Water Snake, it caused a mighty storm.
Joang bona e bo poma litsoala;	It mowed the grass;
Metso ea lifate e shebisitse holimo.	Tree roots were made to look at heaven [upside down].
Lipoone e li poma lichakatsa;	It cut the ripe maize flowers;
Mabele e ea pooma likopo.	It cut the cobs of sorghum.

(Majara Majara)

Indeed, *khanyapa* means "cyclone" or "thunder storm," and when Sebata Mokokoane tells his rivals "You will see Khanyapa" in his *sefela*, he means "I will destroy you" (Mokitimi 1982, 479). The cyclone is also the iconic link, along with the sinuous length of the serpent, by which the steam train, with its thick spiral of black smoke, becomes Khanyapa in *sefela*, carrying along its bundle of associations and its belly-full of migrants. Murray (1980b, 68) has also noted the importance of the water snake in Basotho ritual symbolism. Khanyapa controls rain in *bongaka*, and its riverine haunts are associated with fertility. During the *bale* rites for girls, it emerges from moist erosion ditches (*dongas*) to instruct the initiates, where it is called *motanyane* or *ngoan'a madiba*.[12] In this landscape of the imagination, everything is potentially a symbol of everything else. So Nthebe Bulara elaborated: "*Khanyapa* is not a living creature. It can stand very high temperatures, like under the earth with the volcano. While I was still a security official in the mines, there were some whites who wanted to take

12. Readers interested in the associations between rivers, the water snake, sexuality, and female initiation in Sesotho should consult the beautiful folktale "Monyohe" in Jaccottet 1908, 126–40.

a picture of the *khanyapa* in the mines, because it is also there, but it's a mine fire."

Ghosts, *lithotsela* (from *ho thola*, "to remain silent") are another form of supernatural being associated with the human capacity for creating evil. They are conceived not as the unquiet souls of the dead but rather more like zombies, people whose *liriti* (shadows, essences) have been magically captured and who now walk the earth as living dead, played with and manipulated by their captors. A reciter known as "Separola" (Wanderer) from Mafeteng District, whose physical constitution could not stand up to the rigors of mine work, attributed his poverty and failure to the *boloi* of his relatives. As Heap (1989, 94–95) discovered, Basotho witchcraft is not an explanation for ordinary sickness but a resource for explaining misfortune in extraordinary conditions, for making sense of uncanny evil, a disease of social context and circumstance. Separola's *lifela* are so redolent with the folklore of witchcraft that my annotations are longer than his texts. Here is his promiscuous young aunt, made into a ghost by her own grandmothers, but perhaps not much worse off than Separola, whom others pay a pittance for odd-jobbing on their lands:

> Their dogs are Sporty and Spider;
> They have eaten a person's child.
> They have eaten the young one, the firstborn slut [his aunt].
> Since then, they [the old women] have left;
> I saw them marching [her] at a run over the veld.
> You know, there is one very bad thing in Lesotho:
> It is to rise very early in the morning;
> It is to rise to carry the harness [as a beast of burden].
> You know, ever since I arrived in the fields, I'm standing idle.
> I'm standing, motionless in futility;
> I am seized by the medicine-charms of my relations.
> Hurry soon doctors, and come cure me;
> You should cure me because I am not respected.
> The back of my neck is [smeared] black
> [with the medicines rubbed into the cuts made in ritual scarification];
> On my shoulders here I've got halters.

My mention of ghosts is triggered by Nthebe Bulara's comment that the watery Khanyapa can be, in its destructive, mobile phase, a mine fire. Basotho make no clear distinction between Sesotho and Western medical systems (Heap 1989, 92); neither do they place any boundaries around the environments or contexts where *boloi* is held effective. The Indian community in Lesotho and Europeans at the mines are held to practice witchcraft and be affected by it just like Basotho. Nthebe Bulara put it clearly:

> The *lithotsela* are known by you whites. Once we were three working in the mines, and a man that had killed a miner by crushing him with the sidecar created his victim into a ghost that only the murderer could see. Ghosts are those of miners killed underground, whether by accident or otherwise. And some of them are whites who have been killed also at times. The whites know how to expel the ghosts from the mines, so the work won't be interrupted. . . . When you see the ghost of the white miner in the mines, it is going to write a large sum of money on you; you are going to look like a check, and when that amount is seen on you, you are going to be paid that amount and then fired, because that is the secret of how the whites get their wealth.

For the country travelers, there is only one moral world, in which the migrant himself or his rival in *sefela* competition can be a ghost, the water snake, or (you guessed it) a cannibal:

Hoa kena Mareka oa Mothibeli,	There entered Mareka of Mothibeli,
Phathakalle e maoto a sehole;	Varana lizard with its crippled feet;
Khanyapa, lelimo le mona la Khojane,	Water Snake, cannibal of Khojane's,
Monna enoa eaba oa nthlola:	This man defeated me:
Ho tloha moo eaba, kea tsamaea.	At that I left, and traveled.
	(Sporti Mothibeli)

Finally, we must be aware that *sefela* performers are first of all entertainers, and like them, we must not take all this too seriously. Satan, the *thokolosi*, Khanyapa, ghosts, diviners—these are also comedic characters, overblown like their creators with melodramatic prowess. There are no *lifela* more rich in humor than those of the loquacious Mphafu Mofolo:

Lithabaneng moo Ha-Keiso	In the mountains there at Keiso's,
Ho omana litšoana teng,	Shouting the black-skinned women there,
Mosali a roaka monna oa hae:	A woman insulting her husband:
"Forotomo, lumela Seforonyaki, o tšuba le ho ea tokho."	"Greetings, you fool Seforonyaki; you smoke [fuck] even when you go to work."
Re sale re senya ngoana enoa oa hae. . . .	We remained and got his daughter pregnant. . . .
. . . Ke fihla ke phunya kakana; sehlahleng	. . . I arrived and made an earth-pipe; we smoke:
Mphafu, ke itsubela matekoane;	Mphafu, I smoked marijuana;
A ntaile matekoane.	I got stoned.
Ke tšeha feela ke sa buoe le motho;	I was just laughing without speaking to anybody;

A ntsoantsa le libaesekopo.	I imagined I was a cinema.
O khena feela, ntata Moliehi;	He becomes angry for nothing, father of Moliehi [Mphafu];
Ho khaleoa ke, sekeleme sena.	He [I] was overcome by sleep, that rascal.

Among the most clever and ironic of *sefela* poets is my great friend Molefi Motsoahae of Thabana Morena, who helped immeasurably in my research and starred in *Songs of the Adventurers.* In that memorable cinematic "command performance," Motsoahae introduced a verse dramatizing the flight of rival performers in the face of his eloquence:

Batho ba tloha ho 'na, litšiba li lla!	Men fled from me, their underwear crying [chafing as they ran]!
Lihempe li nqamathela 'mele;	Shirts stuck to their bodies;
Joale ba baleha ba e ea lifemeng.	They ran away to the factories.

Vivid, but not remarkable. Some lines later, however, he returned to the theme, but with a surprise twist:

Ha Raliemere pela Mafeteng,	At Raliemere's near Mafeteng,
Joale kampong ea Mafeteng,	Now the town of Mafeteng,
Seithleko ha a leleka matekatse,	When Seithleko expelled prostitutes,
A re: "Tlohang mona, le libono li kholo."	He said: "Away with you, you fat derrières."
Ba kene Maseru letatsi le rapame:	They arrived in Maseru in the afternoon:
Le Maseru, e ntse le loana,	Even in Maseru, you are still fighting,
Le ngoana Pasa le Shebile Boleka.	[You,] daughter of Pasa and Shebile Boleka.
Lits'oana bo Ngoana Mareka,	The pretty black ones, daughters of Mareka's Child,
Le bona, ba tloha mona,	You see, they left here,
Batho, ba tloha ho 'na, litšiba li lla!	People, they left me, their underwear crying!
Ba baleha ba ea li femeng.	Away they ran to the factories.

Here, a chief called Seithleko has chased away prostitutes who were fighting near Mafeteng. They flee to Maseru, where they continue fighting. What's the ruckus? Turns out these "pretty black ones" were fighting over our poet, who were forced to leave him in Mafeteng, and that's why their underpants are crying! The double claim of performance prowess (or is it his money the girls are missing?) turns on the word *litšiba*, "undergarments," which like the English equivalent does not specify male or female, top or bottom. Did this ironic little boast *need* explaining? In any language, it's funny. Richard Abrahams has said, in grandly intellectual terms, that "for a piece of folklore to control by suggestion and then guide future action, it must first provide the release afforded by pleasure, a release accomplished by projecting, objectifying and impersonalizing the troublesome situation, thus linking individual experience to public concerns" (1972, 19). As a Basotho proverb succinctly puts it: *Lefu-leholo ke litseho*, "Laughter is greater than death."

Chapter Nine

"Laughter Is Greater than Death":

Migrants' Songs and the Meaning of Sesotho

It contains nothing, this singing:
I say I know how to make this rope,
And I know how to finish it.
I say to you, long-time poets,
The days are two you [Coplan] visited me;
This is the last day:
You will respect me, the honorable one, truly.
I am not an apprentice but a doctor—
I am the horned one;
I'm no longer an owlet but a great horned owl.
What am I saying to you, my parents?
I'm the horned one who stays in the trees.
Majara Majara

In the great tradition of Basotho name-dropping (Dan Kunene's "eulogues of associative reference"), these lines by Majara of Ha-Abia Matsotso, Maseru, praise the poet by evoking the research encounter. If Majara isn't a renowned poet, why has his fellow *ngaka* (Ph.D.!) from the American university come to him? This is a good question, but not for that reason. The passage at once asserts, analyzes, and demonstrates his eloquence, confirming the magical elevation of his talent—a secret and a thing apart, the horned one who stays in the trees.[1] Perhaps I am hopeful that repeating Majara's lines as an epigraph will inspire in me an equally eloquent answer to his rhetorical poser: Why *have* I come? Why did I leave my beloved Manhattan for the rigors of the Mountain Kingdom, a stingy, stony fastness into which the Basotho were driven by the rapacity of empire, attrac-

1. Majara is very likely punning here on the concept of the poet as *ngaka*, the herbalist who keeps his most powerful preparations in a hollowed animal horn. So he is a "great horned owl," a bird closely associated with the spiritual dimensions of healing; and "the horned one," a doctor possessed of powerful medicine horns.

tive only to the Basotho themselves and to those travelers who sojourn long enough to fall under its elevated spell. English fails and I retreat, like a Mosotho, to Sesotho: *Ke hopotse Lesotho*, "I recall/reflect upon/long for [all at once] Lesotho."

Why all this travel for some travelers' songs? Of what real moment or significance are they to us, or even to blanket-wearing Basotho? Beyond the opportunity to boast of being "renowned among the nations," as 'Malitaba sang it, the presence of the Western auditor means little to the *likheleke*. Only their own colleagues, companions, and comrades can comprehend what they are doing or saying, and those are the audiences who put down, year in and year out, the real money for their art. One reason I was treated to so many superb, unselfconscious performances, I suspect, was because the performers could enjoy the cachet of my attendance (documentation technology and all), safe in the assumption that I understood virtually nothing of what they were singing. But to their sometimes pleased, sometimes discomfited surprise, I did at length come to understand some things. It is my pleasure to pass them on to you: I speak freely, not minding anything.

In brief, as material conditions and social forces distort and transform their "whole life process," Basotho migrants recompose (and sometimes perform) their personal and collective narratives because the unauthored life is not worth living. Imagination is a mode of thought in which performers consider how their experience and action in society as they find it—"under conditions not of their own choosing"—have made them what they are (Beidelman 1986, 9). As Johannes Fabian comments:

> the kind of performances we find in popular culture have become for the people involved more than ever ways to preserve some self-respect in the face of constant humiliation, and to set the wealth of artistic creativity against an environment of utter poverty. All this is not to be dismissed offhand as escape from reality; it is realistic praxis under the concrete political and economic conditions that reign. (1990, 19).

And, I might add, in expressing in forms such as *sefela* the existential ground of social being, a coherent purpose, and a sense of life as journey, it is this praxis that makes perfect amid the most imperfect concrete conditions. *Hlapi, folofela leraha, metsi a pshele o a bona*, "The fish, seeing the water has dried up, struggles mightily in the mud" (see Guma 1967, 91).

Migrant performers participate in a larger sense in the social "dialectics of culture and power, ideology and consciousness" (Comaroff and Comaroff 1991, 6) through a dialogic of metaphor. Through *ho bapisa*, "to make parallel, to bring near," social practices and rationalizations are measured against authoritative cultural values, dominant discourse against social reality, selective tradition against emergent culture, *Sesotho* against Sesotho. As to Giddens's (1979) by now perennial problem of the relation of "structure and agency," migrants' *sefela* are of course simultaneously systemic and contingent, reproductive and productive of Sesotho. More specifically, they are directed toward transforming structure in ways continuous with a historical ideology and moral economy more honored in the breach by powers that be, and so at once conservative and subversive of the discourse of authority in Lesotho. Most important, however, what the foregoing account demonstrates is the effectiveness of the study of popular performance as a means to address the problem of "how to represent the embedding of richly described local cultural worlds in larger impersonal systems of political economy" (Marcus and Fischer 1986, 77). In the end, it is sufficient if this account reveals to my comrades in history and the social sciences the treasure trove of perception and motivation contained in auriture—however much it may become "another thing" (like a ritual mask hung in a museum) when mediated by abstraction, transcription, translation, fragmentation, interpretation, and integration into an alien ethnographic narrative. The notion of a useful fiction, extended to its dia-logical conclusion, becomes a metaphor for ethnography itself:

> It is fiction—fiction, not falsehood—that lies at the very heart of successful anthropological field research; and, because it is never completely convincing for any of the participants, it renders such research, considered as a form of conduct, continuously ironic. (Geertz 1968, 154; cited in Clifford 1988, 80).

Not only the conduct but the inscription of culture becomes inescapably ironic, and one wonders if we will not soon weary of reading accounts (like this one) in which analysis is written almost wholly in invisible quotation marks.

Cultural anthropologists have spent, or should have spent, the last decade admitting to the doubtful epistemology and overdetermined quality of "realist" ethnographic discourse. This trend was given impetus by similar developments in history, literary criticism, and language philosophy, which have undermined modernism as the foundation of Western intellectual life. Pretensions to objectivity and positivistic methods in cultural description have been rejected as both inherently colonizing and patently discontinuous with the actual conduct of the ethnographic project (see

Clifford and Marcus 1986; Clifford 1988). Unreflective of the field encounter, the synthesized, omniscient, temporally distanced voice of classical ethnography has lost its status as an empirical representation of the perspective of the subject others who in anthropology have replaced the objectified Other. No longer, it seems, can one write or speak of "the Zulu" or "Zulu custom," for instance, without suffering the retort, "Oh yes, which few dozen so-called Zulus do you mean?" Hence the call for a postmodern ethnography of social fragmentation and cultural diversity, one suited to a field "where we encounter neither social order nor equilibrium, nor a homogeneous shared culture embodying undisputed values and norms" (Fabian 1990, 13). Cultural analysis must be decentered, and multiple, equivalent voices heard. In interpretive anthropology such as that practiced here, social reality as well as its meanings must be revealed as situationally contested. The legacy of Victor Turner and Clifford Geertz in the analysis of totalizing symbols must be reexamined so as to account for the ways the negotiated quality of relationships and the improvised nature of social action influence the pragmatics of "master tropes."

In a parallel effort, the guilt-ridden inheritors of intellectual imperialism are attempting to decolonize the study of other times and other customs by granting subjects' own representations epistemological equality with their own. Yet "antiessentialist," postmodern characterizations of culture as mobile, unbounded, hybrid, and decentered do not advance this project as much as the characterizers would wish. As David Scott has pointedly observed:

> for whom is "culture" unbounded—the anthropologist or the native? Is it in other words, for (western) theory or for the (local) discourse with which theory is endeavoring to engage, to inquire upon? . . . To say a priori that "cultures" are not "bounded" therefore is misleading since local discourses do, in fact, establish authoritative traditions, discrete temporal and spatial parameters in which it is made singularly clear to cultural subjects and their others what is (and who are) to belong within these parameters, and what (and who) not. . . . the important issue here is . . . the political one of how and in what kinds of material circumstances, through what kinds of discursive and non-discursive relations, claims about the presence or absence of boundaries are made, fought out, yielded, negotiated. (1992, 375–76)

Perhaps it is at once ironic and eminently sensible that positivist notions of truth and authoritative narrative should have lost their validity just when their inheritors have agreed to listen to Other voices.

If we are genuinely willing to recast anthropological subjects as autonomous social actors, then proper weight must be given to the implicit, fundamental identification people have with reified notions of group culture, history, and belonging. Given the upsurge in segmentary cultural nationalisms and community identifications, "imagined" or otherwise, not only in South Africa but seemingly everywhere else, it appears that the world and therefore anthropology is not ready for poststructuralist demystification. No, people would prefer to live—and die—as Zulu or Croat and not as simply the Wretched of the Earth, thank you very much.

So we need to approach expressions of ethnic identification as internalized, inextractible constituents of the self and social reality as well as resources for conscious mobilization. Conversely, one of the problems facing scholars who seek in a real sense to historicize southern African societies is the degree to which ethnicities conceived and disseminated in the context of colonial displacement have inevitably been accepted and internalized by Africans themselves. So "oral tradition" is not simply a matter of an African reality struggling to emerge from a European myth. When entitlement and power are involved, what is useful becomes what is true and "the lie that rescues is good." Africans, like postcolonized people everywhere, have become not only objects but participants in the process of ethnogenesis, terms in the discourse of primordial cultural oppositions. Indeed, the ongoing process of "othering," in which both colonizer and colonized equally contest and participate, is one of the central concerns of contemporary cultural anthropology.

In such an intellectual environment, where informants' and anthropologists' modes of ethnographic representation contest one another while serving as the subjects of much reflexive analysis, Johannes Fabian's recent call for a "move from informative to performative ethnography" may provide one means to harmonize internal and external accounts (1990, 5). Following the logic of his methodological metaphor, Fabian practices performance ethnography by making cultural enactments explicitly recognized as performances his focus of study. Studying popular culture in Shaba Province, Zaire, Fabian observed that "'performance' seemed to be a more adequate description both of the ways people realize their culture and of the method by which an ethnographer produces knowledge about that culture." Performance ethnography is thus "appropriate to both the nature of cultural knowledge and the nature of knowledge of cultural knowledge" (ibid., 19). Recognizing that ethnographic research itself is a dialogic enactment, Fabian tries to get away from ethnography as answers to questions, since even the answers to "our ethnographic questions can be interpreted as so many cultural performances. Cultural knowledge is always mediated by 'acting'" (ibid., 6–7). The study of performances reveals both explicit, reflexively formulated cultural categories, values, and meanings, but also implicit, nondiscursive aspects of the cultural knowledge from which identities are constituted. This is one of the benefits that I have suggested (Coplan 1987b) anthropology and history can derive from examining forms that "privilege actors' interpretations of their own conduct" (Rosaldo 1986, 97), in particular those, like performance, created by people themselves to reflect upon experience. Broadly, performative ethnography attempts to discover how people constitute identity in realizing their culture, and of finding a method of producing our own empirical knowledge and defensible interpretations of that culture. Fabian readily admits that pursuing a communicative and dialogic ethnography is no guarantee of "power-free" interaction on equal terms. "It's not just a matter of protesting our goodwill," he insists; "knowledge depends on what actually happens in communication and dialogue" (1990, 5).

As I argued in chapter 1, the power relations in which performance is embedded and out of which it emerges are crucial to its analysis. In the Basotho case, the relationship of power and performance centers around Basotho nationalism and the meaning and reference of *Sesotho*.[2] The question of the interests that underlie contesting definitions of Basotho identity is of the greatest importance for this relationship, as the intensifying conflict over the meaning, possession, entitlements, and authority of *Sesotho* vividly illustrates. The current polyvocal discourse of Basotho nationalism is rooted in class differentiation and conflict (Frank 1992, 29), with all the parties engaged in the struggle over social change seeking to mobilize the concept of *Sesotho* and the practices and institutions it glosses. The patent contradictions and problematic status of these practices and institutions does not inhibit their exploitation as social resources. As the ruling elites, colonial and postcolonial, over the past century have each in turn refused to support in practice any autonomous, locally comprehensible political vision or broad-based economic advancement, the appeal of *Sesotho* as self-identifying "tradition" has revived and strengthened among the powerful and privileged and the dominated and exploited alike. Members of the emergent classes in Basotho society have, each in their own strategic ways, retreated to the protection of Sesotho as a last existential redoubt. Like a cultural correlative of the impassible but sheltering ranges of the Drakens-

2. I have recently addressed this issue in a lengthy occasional paper entitled "The Meaning of Sesotho" (Coplan 1992).

burg up against which the Europeans drove them, the "secrets" of *Sesotho* have taken on the character of a defensible symbolic landscape, ringed by an implicit supposition of authoritative knowledge and a reified identity: *Ho checha ha pheleu, hase ho baleha,* "When a ram retreats, it is not running away" (Guma 1967, 89).

Ultimately, the internal debate turns on the question of whether Lesotho should maintain its existence as an independent nation-state. The Basotho achieved the rare distinction of defeating or at least holding at bay both settler colonialism and imperial militarism (in part by playing these two forces against one another). They were hard pressed to save much from the jaws of Afrikaner and British collaboration, however, and so their prize was a mountainous rectangle of rocks and ditches completely surrounded by the most predatory neighbor within which an African nation could have the misfortune to survive: that cannibal of cannibals, white South Africa. For this very reason the Basotho, whose recalcitrance is legendary, are most stubborn of all in their attachment to the autonomous concept of Lesotho, to the institutions like the chieftaincy (however problematic) that have embodied and defended this concept, and to *Sesotho*, the language and culture in which it is expressed.

With so much original Basotho territory incorporated into the Orange Free State, and so many Basotho residing in South Africa, cultural symbols and practices have become the most significant markers of national identity. Such representations are constructed on the basis of geographical origins and political allegiances within what remains of Moshoeshoe I's monarchical/military state. In this sense, Lesotho anchors a historical patrimony that extends well beyond its present physical borders. Indeed, Basotho nationalism as an explicit agenda still centers on the demand for the return of the "Conquered Territories," no matter how unlikely its fulfillment. As South Africa undergoes dramatic political change, Lesotho's independent existence, already so precarious and artificial in an economic sense, may cease to be worth defending except to the interlocking military, professional/bureaucratic, and aristocratic elites who have a vested interest in structures of government and patronage, land allocation, the political economy of migrant labor and the "donor mode of production."[3] Other Basotho may have actually found a way to repossess the Conquered Territories. Like the Mexican immigrants presently reoccupying the American Southwest, they may simply move there, provided the joint effort of the

3. I am grateful to Judith Gay for this ironic but accurate characterization of "development" in Lesotho.

current Lesotho and South African regimes to prevent this is abandoned or can be circumvented.

From the point of view of the migrant workers, the independence of Lesotho represents a profound social and economic dilemma. In the mines, the disadvantages of foreign status are rapidly coming to outweigh the advantages, as those Basotho who were dismissed and deported to Lesotho during the 1987 National Union of Mineworkers' (NUM) strike will readily attest. The political integration of Lesotho, bringing with it the rights of citizenship and formal recognition of union membership, is the most reliable road to employment security and labor mobility in a future South Africa. Otherwise Basotho will suffer continued discrimination in the workplace and exclusion from the benefits of programs of land reform and reallocation. As Roger Southall puts it, South African politics determines life in Lesotho and on the mines (1991, 225); it's time for the Basotho to be players in that process, not bystanders in the struggle for their own economic future. Indeed, a visit to Lesotho by a high-level delegation of the NUM in May 1991 confirmed their support for an official union resolution passed the month before suggesting political integration as the "only realistic answer which is in the best interest of the people of both countries" (Weisfelder 1992, 26). A year earlier, Mafa Sejanamane of the National University of Lesotho's Academic Staff Association received a letter whose author claimed to speak for a majority of Lesotho mineworkers in voicing opposition to the further issuing or carrying of Lesotho travel documents called "local passports."

On the other hand, there are powerful reasons why Basotho migrants cling to Lesotho's national sovereignty, no matter how impoverished. The proud history of Lesotho with its distinctive institutions, social structure, and resistance to incorporation is a hard thing to abandon. Just as important, *Lefatse le la sechaba*, "The land belongs to the nation": a married man is theoretically entitled to pasture and fields for cultivation as "free goods," and in genuine practice to some ground on which to build his house regardless of the privatizing impetus (so far unenforced) of the 1979 land legislation. The attempt by the former military government to limit unproductive overgrazing and generate revenue by a head tax on cattle has now been abandoned by the civilian administration in the face of widespread resentment, often voiced as anger over the trampling (yet again) of *Sesotho*.

Lesotho is a member of the United Nations Organization, with a distinctive political history, monarchy, chiefship, land tenure, and legal system. Both during and after its separate British colonial history, it defined itself in opposition to being part of South Africa (Southall 1991, 217–18). The platform of the unanimously victorious Basotholand Congress Party (BCP) in the March 1993 elections emphasized Basotho nationalism rather than incorporation, which the party does not favor. So great has been the upsurge in nationalist feeling in the face of the political turmoil taking place across the border, that both the African National Congress and the NUM have been taken by surprise. At present, no one materially involved in the debate would use the term "incorporation"; the less total and more equivocal word "integration" is now preferred.

In addition, the rights to residential stands, fields for cultivation, and pasturage that attach to social identity as a member of a Basotho family, clan, and chieftaincy, as well as that identity in and of itself, represent precious entitlements to a great many migrants, the more so as they have to spend so many hard years away from them. Current and, perhaps more significantly, retrenched migrants with whom I have recently spoken state they would gladly throw away their Lesotho passports if a government that was "good for blacks" came to power in South Africa. They are skeptical, however, that the elections scheduled for April 27, 1994, will install such a government or bring peace and prosperity to their neighbors. Further, those who would prefer to carry South African identity documents still resist the idea of "incorporating" Lesotho into its hegemonic neighbor, just as they prefer not to relocate their families to the workplace, even if there proves to be a future administration that is certifiably "good for blacks": "That would mean the end of *Sesotho*," they protest. By *Sesotho* they mean far more than their "language and culture," narrowly conceived. It means a social identity and its entitlements, reciprocities and their resources, investments of the self and substance, a personal as well as communal, genealogical, and national history, and a secure, self-comprehending way of life. In the Times of Cannibals, Basotho have always had Lesotho; without it, can there be *Sesotho?*

That aside, all the retrenched Lesotho mineworkers interviewed by Seidman (1993) stated they would relocate across the border if they could, as there is no hope of work in Lesotho. Whether a future South African government will let them come, however, is doubtful. For some time the Chamber of Mines has been under pressure from the South African government to "internalize" its labor force. The result is that currently approximately half of all mineworkers are from South Africa and its homelands, and that foreign workers find it very difficult indeed to get a job on the mines if they have not worked there already (Cobbe 1985, 8). Still, the skills, experience, and work "traditions" of foreign migrants have enabled them to carry on their mining careers, so that Lesotho, for example, which provides more than half of all foreign labor in South Africa, still accounts for over a quarter of all labor in the mining industry (TEBA 1992, 19). In the past, when the Chamber of Mines sought to maintain a diversity of labor sources, there were trade-offs, advantages as well as disadvantages in Lesotho migrants' foreign status. Currently and for the future, however, any advantages have completely disappeared (Southall 1991, 223), and their only hope of survival in the industry is as full-fledged union members (largely a fact) possessing the same rights as South African workers (a fond hope).

Jean Comaroff (1985, 197–98) has argued that both reinterpretations and continuities in cultural practice can be explained essentially as forms of resistance to incorporation in a capitalist political economy. Rugege (1991, 158), however, has shown how the rulers of postindependence Lesotho have continuously sought to entrench their authority by propagating the ideology of tradition, a strategy that is something of a tradition in itself, going back to the British colonial codification of the *Laws of Lerotholi* under chiefly supervision in 1903. In this, Rugege observes, Lesotho is just one of many places in Africa where an ideology of hierarchical reciprocity and communalism is used to mask real power relations in the political economy. This tallies with Waterman's (1990, 9) conclusion in a recent discussion of Yoruba ethnicity in Nigeria that both continuity and transformation in cultural usage can as easily mask empirical structural relations through the upholding of the "selective tradition" of hegemonic social understandings as they can serve the interests of the oppressed. Yet Rugege points out that it is precisely when African postcolonial states fail to deliver that people revert to support for chiefs and other focal points of traditionalism. The chieftaincy is seen as a political recourse in fending off the predatory interventions of the centralized, externally dependent military and state bureaucracy. Its use as a resource, however, is greatly affected by the complex overlapping of Lesotho's aristocratic, military, civil service, and commercial elites.

The latest attempt by the central government to exploit traditionalism came just after the 1986 coup, when the military regime recruited King Moshoeshoe II to serve as head of state, and, ironically enough, revived the notion of "Moshoeshoeism" first formulated by the ousted Leabua Jonathan, a great-grandson of Moshoeshoe I himself. "This linked the father figure of Moshoeshoe I with the new regime and a series of progressive social values it proclaimed. It emphasized reconciliation, development, and human rights, all associated with Moshoeshoe I" (Frank 1992, 17). In reality, however, the new military rulers wanted anything but increased political participation on the part of the aristocracy (or anyone but themselves). The repression practiced by the military made a mockery of Moshoeshoeism as enlightened despotism and undermined the king as well. Conflict over the king's strong anti–South African sentiments (the military preferred close collaboration with the South African "securocrats" who had helped them come to power by blockading Lesotho in advance of the coup) and the challenge to Major General Justin Lekhanya's authority as head of the Military Council by aristocratic senior officers (Lekhanya is a commoner) led to the removal, exile, and abdication of the king in 1990. As the king should have understood, the real Moshoeshoeism (going back to the 1820s), like *Sesotho* itself, is not a political ideology but a politics of survival (ibid., 23): The lie that rescues is good.

Meantime the migrant workers show signs of developing into Lesotho's "labor aristocracy." Massive retrenchments of 20 percent industrywide over the past decade (Coplan 1993, 1), due to capital investment in new technology, response to political and industrial action, and the unprofitability of many mines brought on by the continuing uncertainty of gold and coal prices have reduced the number of Basotho mineworkers during the 1990s and made it very difficult for novices or men who did not quickly renew their contracts to get employment. While the reliability and accumulated skills of experienced Basotho miners in the new structure of the industry should have given them an advantage, many veterans have nevertheless been retrenched and their accumulated service benefits appropriated by the "cannibals" of the mining bureaucracy—the African clerks (*mabalane*) and other low-level administrative personnel: retrenchment as an industry. The mines benefit from longer contracts, shorter leaves, very high return rates, and low novice intake. Seidman's worker informants at Harmony Mine, Virginia, Orange Free State, complained that despite all the talk about "career miners" and the efforts by management to define and expand this category, the mines continued in practice to treat all migrants as if they were occasional, temporary contract workers whose real homes were in the rural areas (Seidman 1993, 16). There, career mining, or more properly, "inflexible migrancy" (Crush 1992), has increased stratification, heightened social tensions, reduced productivity, and (like retrenchment) accelerated the disintegration of family life. Career miners are more proletarianized, more prone to alcoholism, sexually transmitted and respiratory diseases, and suffer more keenly the hardships of compound life (Crush, Jeeves, and Yudelman 1991, 151–52), but in the current situation they must be grateful to have a "career" at all. Indeed, the latest trend is not to offer retrenched mineworkers their old jobs when they are rehired, but to employ them as "casual" workers on contracts without security or service benefits and at vastly reduced wages.

In *sefela* performance, the division between active migrants and unemployed is sadly evident. *Sefela* competition is as popular as ever among those who have jobs, and the performance of this boastful genre is itself a boast that one has a contract and therefore a reason to lift one's singular voice in song. Among the retrenched, skills in *sefela* also abound, but are little exercised by those who feel trapped, destitute, and dispirited in Lesotho's periurban labor reserve. On the other hand, a number of senior, renowned performers I know who no longer go to the mines proudly maintain their skills at home and pick up a nice bit of change teaching younger upstarts a thing or two in competitions at the local *'joaleng* (Sesotho sorghum beer houses). Radio Lesotho, say the veterans, no longer calls them to record *lifela* for broadcasting, while Radio Sesotho, in the Free State, still does. Perhaps, but listeners to Radio Lesotho's traditional music program at midday on Mondays are regularly treated to beautiful *lifela*.

Official unemployment in Lesotho grew from 23 percent in 1986 to 35 percent in 1991 (Frank 1992, 24), and the actual figure is probably much higher. One result was the "race riot" of May 1991, in which Maseru's urban underclass, expressing a sentiment of "Lesotho for the Basotho," attacked the Korean and Taiwanese shopkeepers who have recently become so visible in Lesotho's consumer economy, as well as members of the Indian merchant community who have lived in Lesotho for generations, carry Lesotho passports, and might properly be regarded as Basotho. The Asians were targeted despite the origins of the disturbance in the beating death of a Mosotho woman accused of shoplifting by local security guards at a white South African-owned franchise outlet. However little, or perhaps because there is so little that the national state does for them, Lesotho's new underclass expressed revolt in nationalist terms: for them the only viable moral economy or even claims on the entitlements of humanity subsist in *Sesotho*.

It seems very unlikely that Lesotho will soon give up its formal sovereignty, even if, with the coming abolition of the ethnically designated, variably autonomous African homelands, Lesotho remains the last de facto enclave in South Africa. In a final irony, it may be that if the Basotho were at last prepared to drop their objections to reincorporation, a future South African government might well decline to have them (Southall 1990, 225–26). The two-billion dollar Lesotho Highlands Water Scheme, the largest development construction project ever undertaken in the region, essentially guarantees that the government of Lesotho will continue to exist in order to collect the revenues from the supply of water to South Africa. It is those very revenues that will finance this continued existence. Virtual sovereignty over extensive portions of the highlands have been ceded to the South African-dominated Joint Permanent Technical Commission in overall charge of the project. The people who have had their lands and homes expropriated and their lives disrupted by the project have been treated dismissively by the local Lesotho Highlands Development Authority and by the private South African companies who have brought in their personnel (labor migration in reverse!) to do the job. The imposition of the Highlands Water Scheme has revivified Basotho nationalism in the areas affected (Thoahlane 1991, 343), but how futile is the appeal to the moral economy of *Sesotho* when the chips are down. Not that the project is a bad idea. South African agriculture needs the water, Lesotho has it, and there is no reason for the government not to profit by it. It is just that, as Thoahlane observes, "the state responds more to the needs and interests of international financial and social institutions than to local concerns because of the growing control over the domestic and social economy held by these institutions. Rather than representing its own people, the state can easily become a manager for these international concerns" (ibid., 331). In reality there will be more people, facilities, services, goods, and money in the mountains (if little direct employment) as a result of the water project, and one cannot expect the needs and cultural sensibilities of rural villagers to get much attention: they are hamburger people in a world of big stakes.

In March 1993, Lesotho elected its first real parliamentary government since 1970. The Lesotho government since independence has been the main beneficiary (along with South Africa itself) of the migrant labor system, just as it is of the Highlands Water Scheme. Its fear that Basotho will vote increasingly with their feet instead of their ballots and leave their rulers with a territory but no productive citizenry from whom to extract revenue is evident in a 1991 regulation laid down by the former Ramaema military government that forbids any Lesotho citizen from working in South Africa without first getting permission from their own Department of Manpower. Workers already employed in South Africa must return to Maseru and obtain permission before work permits are renewed. Under this regulation, all Basotho seeking to work in South Africa are treated like migrants. The South African Ministry of Home Affairs, happy to see their counterparts in Maseru riding on the backs of their citizens more heavily than ever, has been only too ready to enforce this regulation on the Lesotho government's behalf. The BCP government is not likely to change this regulation because, like their military predecessors, they are concerned about the continuing brain-drain of qualified Basotho into South Africa. The current policy, however, is entirely counterproductive from that standpoint. Highly skilled and qualified Basotho (such as my numerous Basotho colleagues at South African universities) can easily get their prospective employers to ensure that legal obstacles to emigration are waived, while an artisan or domestic worker is consigned (at least officially) to desperation and unemployment in Maseru. One can only hope that more enlightened and humane officials in future on both sides of the bureaucratic fiction of the Lesotho border can be persuaded to delete it, at least in practice.

Not surprisingly, it is members of the elites who most pointedly represent cultural and political identity as coterminous, bottling up *Sesotho* in Lesotho. As a prominent Mosotho professor complained to me, "These things you are studying from the migrants and bars and prostitutes, they were never in Lesotho, they have been brought in from South Africa." The self-appointed "Sesotho Academy" of elite Basotho intellectuals locates the performance domain of *Sesotho* in the *lithoko* of deceased aristocrats, rural dance/song genres (Matsela 1987), and written Sesotho literature (which quite a few Basotho write, but only a very few ever read). Yet it is the nature of culture to be suffocated by a too self-conscious and solicitous (hegemonic) embrace. The continuing development of Sesotho (no italics) as a living culture guiding autonomous social action has passed in large degree from aristocratic retainers and praise singers to the *litsamaea-naha.* As other Basotho educators have come to realize (Mokitimi 1982; Moletsane 1982, 1983), it is the performing artists and genres among migrants, both male and female, that have expanded and kept open the boundaries of Sesotho, while still reproducing its collective understandings and historical representations for the affective encoding of social experience. Migrant working men and women have created new performance genres that enlarge Basotho cultural boundaries and increase their permeability, challenging idealized, authoritative, and "selective" notions of what constitutes *Sesotho.*

The migrants' self-preserving image as rural yeomen and keepers of the true cultural knowledge of Sesotho is tempered by their ambiguous investment in the present boundaries and existence of Lesotho as a political state. Among Basotho migrant singers and their listeners, there is no confidence whatever that the Basotho economic or political elite have any commitment to practicing or upholding precolonial values of hierarchical reciprocity or communal social exchange. Hence the assonontal parallelism *'khooana tsoana* (little black whitemen) as a working-class term for the Basotho bourgeoisie is contemptuous rather than critical, suggesting a self-defeating abandonment of *Sesotho* while still falling short of European status. The army, during their rule, fared even worse. Although the rank and file and many of the officers come from humble backgrounds, their exercise of power was more repressive than that of the most autocratic colonial chief. "When you ask the soldiers the reason for something," despaired an elderly wisehead, "they show you a gun." Some individual chiefs and the chieftaincy in general have been contingent exceptions to these negative views about resident elites. An important reason why there is little sentiment for abolishing the chieftaincy among working-class Basotho commoners is the conviction that as the institutional representatives of *Sesotho*, chiefs can be weighed in the scales of the hierarchically reciprocal social values their hereditary offices embody. This accountability is demanded despite (or because of) the involvement of the aristocracy in the operation of the bureaucratic state. Leabua Jonathan himself was an important northern chief (descended from Moshoeshoe I's second house) and, ironically, a one-time migrant mineworker. During his rule, local administration was severely harmed by the forced assimilation of village chiefs and development committees into his Basotho National Party (BNP) structure. On the other hand, resistance to "development" and other forms of political and economic high-handedness centered on certain courageous (or just plain stubborn) chiefs not involved in government.

David Ambrose, working on a new, detailed map of Lesotho and its communities, has discovered that the government lists of officially gazetted chiefs do not often reflect the situation on the ground. The de facto chiefs in many subdistricts are not those gazetted but those with *litempe* (stamps), rubber stamps for official documents that are obtained from their immediate chiefly superiors, ultimately reaching up to the twenty-two principal ward chiefs. Only gazetted chiefs get the small salary attached, a policy going back to the official gazetting of chiefs by the British administration in 1938, but de facto chiefs continue to perform the duties of local administration and land allocation without it because of the fees and tributes these functions command. At local level in many cases, the chieftaincy is in the hands of the *liboko* who originally settled the area, such as the Taung, Tlokoa, Fokeng, Phuthi, or Hoja, and not of the aristocratic Bakoena at all, let alone of Moshoeshoe I's Bakoena ba Mokoteli section, despite the efforts of successive monarchs to place descendants of Moshoeshoe in every local chieftaincy. So there appears to be a reemergence of not only pre-1938 patterns of local authority, but patterns existing in the nineteenth century and even before. The identification of the chieftaincy with Leabua's discredited BNP, however, continues to hamper local administration.

Chief M. K. Lerotholi argues that there is no substitute for chieftaincy in the rural areas, that they anchor society, that many people are attached to the institution and its abolition would be too radical (Rugege 1991, 164). So the chiefship, like custom itself, is really a social resource, appealed to and mobilized by any and all Basotho when and where it appears useful, and shunted aside, often rudely, where it does not. The chieftaincy is still obliged to acknowledge and carry along all its adherents, the unconditionally and the conditionally loyal, the useful and the useless, the reliable and the perfidious alike: *Morena ke khetsi ea masepa*, "The chief is a shoulderbag of shit." For aural composers, the chieftaincy comprises a political geography and a source of identity, though as individuals chiefs are either disparaged or hailed in *sefela* to the extent that they are seen to violate or uphold the social morality of *Sesotho*. With print and broadcast journalism largely closed to the migrants, urban workers, and resident "peasantariat,"[4] communal and popular song becomes a vital and significant medium for creatively reflecting on their experience and inserting it into public political discourse (Waterman 1990, 10,88)—especially when the cassettes of *seoeleoelele* bands are played endlessly over the radio!

Forms like *shebeen* songs have long been extending Basotho culture into new domains of experience and across the borders of Lesotho. But never have the boundaries of what is regarded as *Sesotho 'nete 'nete*, true Basotho culture, been more strongly defended than they are today, when Lesotho has little economic or political autonomy. In such circumstances *Sesotho* becomes a reservoir of identity, self-expression, and social entitlement that appears crucial to any meaningful form of national survival. Moshoeshoe I understood this when he sent his sons to be initiated with the sons of his allies and vassals, and it is no accident that institutions such as *lebollo* are increasing in attendance. Migrant workers and their women, without whom there really is no Lesotho, are producing aural genres that do not simply preserve but enlarge and revitalize Sesotho in direct confrontation with the social forces that threaten it. Migrant performers do not cast aside historical Basotho culture but root themselves deeply within it. The reso-

4. An exception is Transformation Centre, a Christian progressive social welfare organization in Maseru that focuses on the concerns of ordinary Basotho workers and their families in its publications, *Work for Justice* and *Litaba tsa Lesotho*.

nant images and shared understandings of Sesotho are used to comprehend, assess, decry, and even celebrate the quality of Basotho participation in a world they cannot control, but that must not be allowed, at any cost, to control their collective and individual sense of self, their continuing reformulation of a national culture.

Recorded in Johannesburg, *seoeleoelele* is the nearest thing to a contemporary Basotho national music. It was the female barflies and canteen-keepers who first developed the dance and song genre on which the studio form is based. Although male performers now largely dominate the broadcasting and cassette market, the indestructible Puseletso Seema can often be seen on SATV's "Ezodumo." Today *seoeleoelele* music is popular to some extent with virtually all segments of Lesotho's resident and nonresident population. The urban youth and middle class have little interest in it, but, the Sesotho Academy excepted, they readily acknowledge it as *Sesotho*. For the exclusively Sesotho speaking, this is their favorite music; but even the highly educated enjoy it, no longer look down upon it, and appreciate its sagacity, pointed humor, and Sesotho aesthetic and cultural qualities. *Sesotho*, as an invented and guiding metatradition of useful fictions, would become not a saving but a patent falsehood without the infusions of performance from and through the border, the songs of its migrant *lintho tsa Molimo*, "things of God."

The indigenous concept of *Sesotho*, like any other reified and consciously mobilized notion of tradition, is composed of continuities, reinterpretations, syncretisms, and inventions that are situationally contested. The Mosotho migrant *kheleke* may recognize that his people are today divided by social class, but in a deeper sense they all do share *Sesotho*, just as they share the larger disabilities historically enforced by the leviathan next door and its economic partners abroad. Men's *lifela* establish a multiple dialogue between the poet and mines, and between identity as a Mosotho and as a migrant. *Sefela* performance helps to domesticate the intractable contradictions between the symbolically reconstituted past and the uncertain constitution of the present, between life at home and at the mines, between family solidarity and long-term separation, between autonomous self-image and identity as a labor unit, between idcal relationships and the reality of migrant and village life, between the migrants' thirst to determine their own destiny and the dry well of their alternatives.

In brief, we have a situation in which performance as a social process actively constitutes social reality as it imaginatively encodes it. There arises, then, the question of the relation of day-to-day events to the construction of experience in *sefela*. How, for example, might the structure and severity of unemployment, unionization, or the recent interethnic and political violence on the mines affect the context and content of *sefela* performance? Asked about this, a group of eloquent ones in Maseru said that while they certainly could sing about such things, it would have to be in terms of things that had actually been experienced by themselves or people they were close to. Further, working these quotidian events into the aesthetic medium of *sefela* requires lengthy effort and reflection: "We analyze to see how we can compose it into song, and that takes time. We work on how to put things into words for a long time after it happens." While poets deal explicitly with external forces and events as they are personally affected by them, their fundamental concern is with the central contradictions of structure and meaning in Basotho historical and social experience. Social facts, such as increasing landlessness or female independence, are assimilated into the central metaphors from which social reality and moral attitudes are constructed. As Ellen Basso has written:

> Since the reality of performed cultural events is not literal representation of the day-to-day life of narrator and listeners, these events have a universal quality of truthfulness because they are unbounded by relativistic necessity. . . . Because many elements of a performance do not match everyday life, the listener can interpret them only through reference to "normal" or, more accurately, common and expected experiences. (1985, 3–4)

Unlike the praise poet and his chiefly subject, the *sefela* poet is at once culture hero and marginal man. *Sefela* singers, Victor Turner (1969) might have argued, establish *communitas* with their audiences, an emotionally immediate categorical identification in which performance provides a collective evaluation of social structure and suggests more "liberated" alternatives. Beidelman suggests we view performance as a universal means to construct images not only of the world in which people live, and of how that world may change, but also of the "ways that a society's members may stand back to scrutinize, contemplate, and judge their world. In this sense, imaginative exercise constitutes a means for criticism, for distortion, even subversion, of the social order" (Beidelman 1986, 2). The art in question is poetry, not in its textual but in its aural form, "which, by means of its performative break with everyday speech, evoked memories of the *ethos* of the community and thereby provoked hearers to act ethically" (Tyler 1987, 202). As works of moral imagination, *lifela* are a fertile source of metaphors that span "a range of seemingly otherwise unbridgeable realms" (Beidelman 1986, 3). Performance itself is an attempt to use the dialectical structure of metaphors to articulate inherent contradictions and bridge the discontinuities of Basotho migrant experience. The practical success these performances achieve in unifying migrants' identity need not prevent workers from seeing themselves as rightful petitioners for social and economic justice in South Africa itself. On the contrary, Basotho make up a large proportion of NUM membership and leadership, and Basotho migrants insouciantly wear the badges of both the African National Congress (with which the NUM is allied), and the Basutoland Congress Party (allied to the Pan-Africanist Congress and a long-time antagonist of the ANC). *Sefela* demonstrates how people struggling to deal with exploitative and disintegrative social conditions may create for themselves a sense of personal autonomy from within which they may truly act. For Basotho migrants, this autonomy is built upon the positive redefinition, through performance, of their human value, in opposition to their identity as mere labor units in the political economy of South Africa. For the migrants' women, their own form of *sefela* provides a medium of collective self-expression and emotional reflection on the quality of their lives, their hopes, and their inalienable human dignity. The study of such forms as *sefela sa litsamaea-naha* may illuminate migrant workers' consciousness and the cognitive sources of the African struggle for self-determination in Southern Africa.

In *The Predicament of Culture* (1988), James Clifford has criticized performance ethnography, especially the past sins of performance ethnographers, deriving most often from too narrow a focus on the microdynamics of performance situations. Among these deficiencies are distorted or nonexistent context, the limited number and possibly unrepresentative nature of the local voices we hear, and the essentially static, dehistoricized portrayal of the performers and their communities. It is my hope that the work of scholars like Fabian and myself has begun to remedy these shortcomings in the "performance paradigm." As to the problems of translation raised by Clifford, they have been and will remain a creative intellectual challenge to anthropologists engaged in the work of cultural interpretation. The accounts of performers and performances never arrive unmediated; they cannot "speak for themselves." We must acknowledge that we inescapably speak for them, and show our respect for what they do by doing it well, in a manner not idiosyncratic but ethnographically committed, contextualized, and defensible. As Evans-Pritchard asked (1937, 4–5), what after all is anthropology but translation, and bad translation at that? But the point of the whole enterprise is to improve our translations through cultural knowledge. Performance ethnography is simply one means by which the inheritors and creators of the cultures we seek to translate can assist us through greater participation in the translation.

> Jo! Eloquence is not stuck on like a feather [in a cap]:
> The year before last I should have been respected,
> For showing I know how to speak.
> The Lion is here, at the ridge on the plain;
> Its eye shines with anger:
> Heroes lost their minds
> When they saw the Lion roaring. . . .
> . . . These little creatures of God, men,
> People who speak by shells [behind cupped hands],
> They whisper breathily.
> They fear to speak; they are noiseless, soundless—
> Jo! evil words or innuendo.
> Let unity be written, peace increase;
> Cases should cease to take up appeals.
> Let the guilty be forgiven at the courts here,
> Men guilty of great crimes. . . .
> . . . However well you may sing,
> I, Sporty, can never be beaten.
> The way I speak, travelers,
> This eloquence runs in my family:
> My father Mareka was born eloquent;
> My mother Mary was born eloquent;
> My sisters and brothers were born with this eloquence.
> Father surpasses in [singing] the *likoma* of the veld [initiation lodge];
> My mother surpasses in ululation;
> My sisters and brothers surpass in dancing—
> The beautiful initiation girls, whose women are they?
>
> (Sporty Mothibeli)

Appendix One

Thakane Mahlasi

Originally from the remote mountain areas, Thakane Mahlasi spent much of her youth in Johannesburg. She learned singing from the Sesotho language radio service, and by the time we met her in 1984, "Tholi" as everyone called her, had been a gangster's moll in South Africa and performed with a semiprofessional African jive band around Johannesburg. Only twenty-nine at the time, Tholi was one of the most accomplished women's *sefela* or *seoeleoelele* performers we encountered. She was a friend of professional bass guitarist Samson Motolo, and sang regularly at his aunt's *shebeen* in Hlotse, capital of the northern Lesotho district of Leribe, where the song below was recorded on January 28, 1984, accompanied by Samson Motolo on accordion and Bushy Thobokela on *moropa* drum. Tholi has three children but no permanent men in her life, and she is thoroughly skeptical of marriage as an institution. In contrast to her close friend, singer Nthabiseng Nthako, she doesn't bother to retain the hope of finding a man who will keep the bargain of a normative migrant Basotho marriage. She recounted "the hell my aunts experienced in marriage" and argued that she was better off with the savings and annuity her casual relationships and personal enterprise had earned her. When we returned to Hlotse in 1988, Tholi had disappeared without a forwarding address.

MAMALUNJANE

Hae elelele, haelele, lelele, banana!	Hae elelele, haeelele, lelele girls!
He tholang lerata, ke le joetse.	You be quiet, I tell you.
Le nke mahlokoa, le a robelane;	Take twigs of grass, break them among yourselves;
Le qhoae litsebe, banana.	[Dig] the wax out of [your] ears, girls.
Helele-lelele! Ntema, ngoana Makhaola.	Hele-helele! Ntema, child of Makhaola.

Letsolo le lumme khutlong;	Lightning[1] has thundered in the gorge;
le ka nka ngoan'aka ke enoa—	it can take this child of mine,[2]—
Hee! ke seile ngoan'aka Koete.	Hee! I have left my child Koete.[3]
Mose har'a makhooa, le lumme letolo—	The other side among whites, lightning has thundered—
He-e! Sefofane se teng, banana.	He-e! An airplane is there, girls.
Se teng har'a makhooa koana;	It is there among whites there;
Se ka nka banana ba sekhoo.	It can take girls of the whiteman's ways.
He-e! Sechaba se baluoe letamong koana.	He-e! A nation has been counted at the dam there.[4]
Jo! Ngoan'aka ngoanana,	Jo! My girl-child,
Mohanuoa, ngoananyana Kanono,	Mahanuoa, a little girl of Kanono,
Fosiea, ngoan'eso Tsosane.	Fosia, a little girl of Tsosane.
He-e! Litaba ha li hlaha,	He-e! When the news comes out,
li ka botsoa mang, banana?	who should be asked, girls?
Li ka botsoa ngoananyana Kholokoe.	They can be asked from a little girl of the Kholokoe clan.
Helele, 'na, ngoananyana ngoanana,	Helele, I, little girl of a girl,
Nka siea, ngoananyana Baholo,	I can leave, little girl of Baholo,
Saleng 'Makopo Baholo.	[Of] Saleng 'Makopo Baholo.
Helele-hele! Ke re Paulosi,	Helele-hele! I say Paul,
ngoana Makoetje;	child of Makoetje;
Ke re Masakoane, ngoana Rametse.	I say Sakoane, child of Rametse.
O kae ngoanayan'aka Tello?	Where is my little girl Tello?
Ntate, buti Lebohang—jo!	Father, brother Lebohang—jo!
Ngoana batho, Lesole,	The people's child, Lesole,
Ke ngoana 'Matsaba.	He is the child of 'Matsaba.
Helelelelele, lentsoe la ka le entse joang, banana?	Helelelelele, what has happened to my voice, girls?
He! Ke lena le lla Mathlere-Thlere—ee!	He! It cries Mathlere-Thlere—ee!
He nkalimeng sebuilahole	Borrow me a loudspeaker [so]
Ke roke marena a ka Lesotho;	I praise chiefs of Lesotho;
Ke re Jemeseli kapa Motsoene.	I say Jemeseli or Motsoene.
Hela, oena ngoananyana Sebepila,	Hello, you little girl of Sebepila,

1. Lightning has powerful cosmological significance in Sesotho, and master diviners are said to do battle by sending lightning bolts against one another. Here, lightning appears to stand for the (moral) "wrath of the ancestors," to use the late Professor A. C. Jordan's memorable phrase.

2. Sesotho aural composition makes frequent use of onomatopoeic and ideophonic (ideas or images in sound) terms and phrases. *Letletletle* is one such term, representing the sound of metal weapons striking against one another.

3. She means her lover.

4. There are countless people living at a shanty near a dam outside a mining area.

Ke busoa ke morena oa monna;	I am ruled [only] by a [real] chief of a man;
Ke re, moshemane a ke kebe a mpusa.	I say, a boy cannot rule me.
He-e! Maqai le mathisa—ee!	He-e! The uncircumcised boys and girls—ee![5]
Tlohang mona—ee! Le nkha letsuka—ee!	Get away from here—ee! You smell of a kraal ee!
He oele, oelelele ee!	He oele, oelelele ee!
Lethisa le nkha, sa fariki ea motsoetsoe—ee!	Uncircumcised girl, she smells like a pig with a litter—ee![6]
Ke re ke ratana le bashanyana;	I was in love with boys;
Ke ba theola Metebong koana.	I brought them from the cattle post.
Ke re, ke ba seisa mehlape ea lipoli;	I say, I made them leave flocks of goats;
Ke joetstoe, ke motho nka tlohela.	I was told by somebody, I left them.[7]
He 'na, ngoana oa ngoanana,	He-e me, child of a girl,
Jo! Ngoan'aka ngoanana	Jo! My girl-child.
He, ke hopole har'a makhooa koana,	He-e, I remember among the whites yonder,
Lanse har'a makula;	A lance among [Asian] Indians;
Ke re, 'tlele, le kene har'a metebo.	I say, an assegai, it thrusts in among the cattle posts.
Koana ka robe ke eatla;	Yonder breaking sticks I'll come;
Ke tlo, roba likotelo	I'll come breaking [them], the sticks, to drive away calves—[8]
He! Pholo li baleha ka lijoko.	He! Oxen runaway with yokes.
Batho ba no ba kile ba nkotla;	Those people once beat me;
Ba nkotla ba ntsenya tsobotsi.	They beat me to spoil my face.
Ba nkotla ba nkukela mose har'a, makhooa koana.	They beat me and took my dress away, among the whites yonder.
Helehelele! Ngoana Mathopela,	Helehelele! Child of Mathopela,

5. The singer compares inadequate lovers to uncircumcised, that is, uninitiated boys and girls.

6. It is Christians, *Majakane*, who do not have their youth circumcised, and this line directly echoes the possibly anti-Christian and explicitly traditionalist sentiments expressed in the initiates' praises published by Jankie: *Thisa le nkga sa kolobe ya motswetse*, "An uncircumcised girl smells like a pig with a litter" (quoted in Guma 1967, 140).

7. As a beautiful young girl, Tholi found that she could lure herdboys of her acquaintance away from their cattle posts. She was warned of the severe consequences of this and ceased such dalliances.

8. A *kotelo* is a short stick used to drive away a nursing calf when its mother is being milked. In this passage, Tholi sees herself as causing disruption at the cattle posts, where the herd boys, fierce stick-fighters in any case, quarrel over her sexual attractions. This metaphor is extended to the urban areas as well, for she can also recall causing havoc "among the whites yonder / A lance among Indians."

Seperintsi har'a toropo,
Khotofelei, manyaleng koana
Se ka ntsiea, bonna ba ha Jakobo;

Springs right in town,
Grootvlei, in dirty places yonder[9]
They can leave me, men of
Jacobs' place;

Ke ba siea, ke ba siea ka
mahlomola ka lerato.
Ntate 'Miki a se le ka—ho lelala!

I leave them, leave them in
distress with love.[10]
Father 'Miki can face upwards—ho
lelala!

O ba joetse kea sotleha—jo! Lesotho mona;

You tell them I am bothered—
jo! Lesotho here;[11]

Ke re motho oa Makhuleng Tebeleng
Ha ntate Hemi koana,
Ha ke tantse le bana—ee!
He, le bana; ke se kele moholo.

I say a man from Makhuleng Tebeleng
At Father Hemi's place there,
I don't dance with children—ee!
Heh, you are children [small boys];
I am a grown-up.

Ke thakali ea mekoti e meholo;
Ke selomo sa methati, banana.
Hela, oena ngoana moshanyana!
Thontholi, o ka itholla—
Jo! Ngoan'aka ngoanana,
Ke thola ka lerato; ke lena!
Ntate, buti Tholang, o ba joetse o ba sebele.

I am an anteater of big holes;
I am a cliff of steps, girls.[12]
Hello, you boy-child!
Police pick-up van, you can pick up—
Jo! My girl-child,
I pick up by love; here it is![13]
Father, brother Tholang, you talk
and whisper to them.

Jo! Ngoan'eso, ngoanana,
Se ka ntsiea, 'Malitaba, mosali.
Hee! Ke mo siea, ke mo siea le mang?

Jo! My sister, girl,
Don't leave me, 'Malitaba, woman.[14]
Hee! [If] I leave her, with whom
do I leave her?

Ke Hlotse mona bo:
Bo-telele bona e entse sebopeho;
Bo-sehlana bona se entse thomeche.

This is Hlotse here:
Tallness you have made an appearance;
A light complexion you have made
[one] to match.[15]

9. A well-known mine formerly employing many Basotho migrants. The shanty areas around it are apparently exceptionally squalid.

10. She leaves a trail of broken hearts behind her.

11. Her men in South Africa should know life is bothersome in Lesotho.

12. Tholi said this meant that she has many enemies who plague her and block her way, but that she is not easily denied or overcome.

13. *Thontholi*, "pick-up van," and *thola*, "pick-up" are puns on Thakane's nickname "Tholi" (from English "tall"). Like a police van, she cruises for men, but she "arrests" them through desire, rather than laws, handcuffs, and pistols.

14. 'Malitaba is a once-famous pioneer of *seoeleoelele* singing and in a sense the mother of all *shebeen* singers.

15. The singer praises her own impressive height, matched by her light brown coloration. There is an element of self-satire here, however, as the idea that she has "made" her complexion "to match" implies the use of face powders and skin lighteners.

Hela, oena, ngoan'aka Mphokong,	Hello, you, my child Mphokong,
A beka Elizabeta ha 'Me MaMotolo mona.	She treated Elizabeth at Mother Motolo's here.
Hele helele! Mathopela, nkaikela *Setakaneng—jo!*	Hele helele! 'Mathopela, I can go to a rough drinking place—jo!
Ngoan'eso, ngoanana,	My sister, girl,
Ke re Golgotha motseng oa baitsepi;	I say Golgotha, the village of *baitsepi*;[16]
Ke re Jerusalem, motseng oa balumeli—	I say Jerusalem, the city of believers—
'Nka mpa ka shoela Kanana	I had better die at Kanana [Caanan].
He-e! Lichaba li apara likobo,	He-e! The multitudes wear blankets,
He-e! likobo tse se nang mabitso.	He-e! blankets that have no names.[17]
Batho ke ba na ba apere, lishepa.	Here are people who are [properly] dressed, shepherds.[18]
Ha ke lebale, ke molotsana;	I don't forget; I am a deceiver;
Batho ke ba na ba tlilo mpolaea.	Here people have come to kill me.
He! Nkang melamu, banna;	He-e! You take sticks, men;
Melamu e tiee ka matsohong—bo!	Let the sticks be firm in your hands— bo!
Ke re ke ha li shebisana melomo, *mechinikane;*	I say they face each other, machine guns;
Ke re ha le le banna le lekholo ke mang,	I say when you are a hundred men,
Ea kileng a loana a bona lithunya,	Who has fought and seen guns,
Ha li farela, mose har'a makhooa koana?	When they jammed, among the whites yonder?
Raliemere, monna oa ka Mafeteng.	Raliemere, man of Mafeteng.[19]
Ntate, buti Lekhanya, motho *oa Talimo motseng.*	Father, brother Lekhanya, man of Talimo's in the village.
Helelelele helele! Banana he *ke talenta ea bohlokoa,*	Helelelele helele! Girls are precious talent,[20]

16. *Baitsepi* means the self-confident or proud ones, those who believe in themselves, and so introduces the idea that finishes with "believers" in the next line.

17. A comment on the sort of cultural devolution that the singer finds in urban areas where people of many nations mix. In a proper Sesotho environment, all blankets have factory labels, "names" such as "Victoria" or "Seana-Marena" that distinguish them as to quality, status, and type.

18. They may be only poor, ragged shepherds, but they know how to wear blankets properly; that is, they know their culture.

19. The singer recalls her involvement in battles among Basotho russians in Johannesburg, including Raliemere, a Matsieng captain who was very prominent in the battles between urban vigilante "civil guards," the police, and the Basotho in areas around Newclare in west Johannesburg during the mid 1950s. He is invoked here, not as a personal acquaintance of young Tholi's, but as a historical figure who symbolizes the fierceness of russian warfare—guns and all.

20. The young bar girls ought to be respected and treasured for their singing and sweet attractions and not treated as expendible objects in a "throw-away" society.

Ea bohlokoa, ngoananyana Kholokoe

A precious one, a little girl
of the Kholokoe.

Jo! 'Me', tholang, Kholokoe.
Ha ke lehure; ke letekatsana:

Jo! Mother, keep quiet, Kholokoe.
I am not a whore; I am just a little
newcomer:

Ke ne ke sa tsebe ke tla tekatsa.
Me' le ntate, banana—hele helele!
Kheisara, seporo sa terene,
Kheisara, seporo sa Matlatsane.
Ntja, le liema Khauteng, Kopanong;

I did not know I would be a prostitute.
Mother and father, girls—hele helele!
Kaizer, railway of a train,
Kaizer, railway to Matlatsane.[21]
Dogs, you run in packs in
Johannesburg, South Africa;

Ke ha ke tloha Nyokanada—
Jo! Ngoan'aka ngoanana
He! Ke palama terene ea ho etela;
Ke ha ke lata likobo
mose har'a makhooa koana.
Lieta ke roala, malapi, ke tsoanetse ho
matha lebelo;
Ha ke qeta, ke baleha pekapa—lieta, he!

It was when I left New Canada[22]—
Jo! My girl child,
He! I rode on the last train;
It was when I fetched blankets
that side among whites yonder.[23]
Shoes I had put on, clothes, so I
should run a race;
When I finish, I flee the [police] pick-
up—shoes, hey!

Bona, ka o hata.
He ke tsoere; ke mala a kulang.

Look, I tread on you.
I am suffering from stomachache; I am
sick.

Oele oele oelele oelele!
He! Ha ka motho; ke Satane
Kea beta, ebile kea utsoa—ee!
Nka utsoa mosali oa motsoetsoe
Ke ee le eena makhooeng koana.

Oele oele oelele oelele!
He! I am not a person; I am a devil.
I rape, and I steal also—ee!
I can steal a nursing-mother
And go with her to the
whites' place yonder.

Ke re nka inama tsa fala
Nke ke be ka joetsa le motho;
Ha ke tloha, kea thoba.
'Mathabo thela likhopo;
ke nyemola moprofeta

I say I can lower my face and
I cannot tell anyone;
When I leave, I will steal away.
'Mathabo pays homage at the railings;
I look bashfully at the prophet.[24]

21. There was apparently a Kaizer Aluminium Company installation near the terminus of this train, which runs to the Vaal Reefs mines in the West Rand, called Matlatsane by Basotho.

22. The "dogs" referred to here are gangs of unruly workers, apparently first encountered by the singer at New Canada Station outside Johannesburg, the main switching station between the townships of Soweto and the central city.

23. "Fetched blankets" here is a euphemism for catching up with one's lovers in the urban areas.

24. The singer repents her sins and feels unable to hold up her head in public. Her friend 'Mathabo, evidently a Roman Catholic, confesses and takes communion; Tholi appeals contritely to her "prophet," a minister of an independent African church.

Nka feta ka thota ka ikotsa—	I can pass through the veld asking myself—
E ka nka pheta ka eketsa.	I wish I could recite by adding.[25]
Hela, oena, ngoan'aka Lineo,	Hey, you, my child Lineo,
He! Ntsa le motho a mpitsetse, ngoan'aka.	He! Tell the person who has called me, my child.
Ngoanana, a ntsiea, banna ba kampong;	Girl, he is leaving me, men of the town;
Ea ntsiea, banna ba ha Motapane.	He is leaving me, men of Motapane.
Ke a e, matso Matebele.	It is he, the one of the black Matebele.[26]
Ntate, buti Maphonia,	Father, brother Maphonia,
Jo! Ngoan'aka Polane,	Jo! My child Polane,
Helehelele! Abuti Tseliso.	Helehelele! Brother Tseliso.
O ba joetse, banna o ba Sebele;	You should tell them, men of Sebele's;
Ntate, buti Libono ke enoa.	Father, that's brother Libono.
Molisenyane, o makiri-kiri,	Molisenyane, he is troublesome,
Lefu, la ka monna a ka teropong—bo!	My death, my man in town—bo!
E sale 'Mathato Motebang	It is still 'Mathato Motebang,
Ntate, buti Liphapang,	Father, brother Liphapang,
Jo! Ngoan'aka, ngoanana.	Jo! My child, girl.
He! Ntate kapa Leschecho,	He! Father or Lechecho,
Motsoalle, ngoana moshanyana—ee!	[My] friend, the boy-child—ee!
Ke hlotse ho pheisanoa-khang,	I conquered through a [singing] competition,
Mose hara makhooa koana—ee!	That side among whites yonder—ee!
Hela oena, ngoana moshanyana:	Hey you, boy-child:
Letekatse la mosali le ea tsoaneloa;	A prostitute of a woman is well-suited;
Le monna le ea roneha—bo!	That of a man is unbecoming—bo![27]

25. I wish I could express more of what I have to say in song.

26. Her lover is a Mosotho of Zulu or Swazi descent, who are believed to be characteristically darker skinned than other Basotho.

27. The life of a prostitute is well-suited to composing and performing these types of songs; men's songs are not so well-suited.

Appendix Two

Tsokolo Lecheko

This performance was a favorite of my late friend and assistant Seakhi Santho's, who after eighteen months of research ranked as something of a connoisseur of *sefela.* Oddly, this was the first I ever recorded, only a few days after I arrived in Maseru just before New Years 1984. At the old Labour Recruitment Bureau, behind Fraser's (Mafafa) Supermarket, Joachim Ntebele (another invaluable comrade) and I were inquiring after singers when Tsokolo Lecheko, a short man in his late twenties, presented himself. I hardly had time to get my tape recorder going before he launched into song. Unprepared, my batteries were flat by the time the tape ran out, and we begged him to hang around until we could return with fresh supplies. No such luck. When we got back, other men told us his name had been called and he had taken his documents and boarded a bus for the border. We know nothing about him except what his text proclaims, that he is a Mofokeng clansman from "the village of [Chief] 'Muso Lihloaeleng" in the mountain districts of Mantsonyane in central Lesotho. We have neither a life history nor a textual exegesis nor any personal commentary from Tsokolo. But his is a beautiful *sefela:* make of it what you will.

Nkalimeng okono,	Lend me your organ,
Nkalimeng okono metsoalle ea me,	Lend me your organ, my friends,
Nkalimeng okono nke ke letse.	Lend me your organ so I play.[1]
Hoba khale; 'na ke thotse	For at length you talked; I was quiet.
Le se bile le mphetotse sehole.	You have already turned me into a fool.
Utloang, e ngoe temana ke ena:	Listen, here is yet another verse:
Ke morapeli oa mehla;	I am a daily worshiper;
Ke etsa thapelo.	I make my prayer.

1. *Sefela* performers often compare the sound of their voices to musical instruments, emphasizing sound as the embodiment of sense.

Bongata bo botsana, bo sa mpotse; *Bo botsa lebitso ke mang—* *Motho, tooe oa litouoa, Tsokolo,* *O tloha hae o louoe ke mang?*	Many ask each other, not me; They ask what my name is— You, man of witchcraft, Tsokolo, On leaving your home who bewitched you?
E sita le bo'ma lona ba ntse ba loea.	Your mothers as well are still bewitching.
Le pereisaka boloi; *Ke ngoanana ea chakang ka phirima.*	You boastfully condemn witchcraft; It [witch] is a girl who walks about by night.
Eke lintja li ka tla li molomme? *Li mo taboletse mose holima lengoele?*	Will the dogs make a bite on her? Will they tear her dress above the knee?[2]
Morena o'a fana khotsong ea me:	The chief is dispensing harmony [resources] at my village:
O fana likhomo; o fana lipere;	He gives out cattle; he gives out horses;
Monongoaha, o fana le masimo. *Feela ha a eja, oa nkhetha.*	This year, he even gives out fields. But when he distributes, he discriminates [against] me.
Ke bone ha a khetha macholo-cholo, *Batho ba jakang ka lipere,*	I saw when he favored the swindlers, People who settle by [giving] their horses,
Batho ba jakang ka basali	People who settle by [giving] their wives.
Naha ha e sena tjako u tlohe;	A place where you cannot dwell you should leave;
U eo jaka ho a mang makhosana.	You should settle among those who are [real] chiefs.[3]
Bongata bo botsana, bo sa mpotse; *Bo botsa ke haile kae* *Ke haile nokeng koana Mantsonyane,*	Many ask each other, not asking me; They ask where I live: I have a home in the area of Mantsonyane River,
Feela ha 'Muso Lihloaeleng;	Just in the village of [Chief] 'Muso Lihloaeleng;

2. Among the most dangerous of demon familiars in Sesotho lore is "the monkey that drags a chain," a *thokolosi* and succubus who walks the roads at night in the form of a beautiful girl. Any Mosotho man who comes across such a vision is quite likely to seize her and pull her down for intercourse, only to discover himself locked in the arms of the deadly monkey. Specially trained dogs are supposed to warn their owners of and hunt down such demons, but witches have means of killing such dogs as well.

3. This is a brave challenge to himself, since the shortage of farmland in Lesotho makes it unlikely that a chief will allocate any to a stranger.

Moo ho busang Morena Molia.	Here reigns Chief Molia.
Feela ha ke sheba, ke tla falla;	But on scrutiny, I shall leave the place;
Ho betere ke theohele lebenkeleng,	It is better I move down near the shop,
Moo ho busang Mosotho Lipuo	Where reigns Mosotho Lipuo.
Lipuo, u se khethe batho: u morena	Lipuo, don't discriminate [among] people: you are a chief.
Batho ba khethoa litopong ba shoele.	People are discriminated in the mortuary [when they are] dead.
Chaba ke sena se tlil'o 'mpona;	Here comes the multitude to see me;
Se tlile ka banna le ka bashanyana.	These are men and boys.[4]
Koalang mamati, metsoalle ea me,	Close the doors, my friends,
Koalang mamati kereke e kene.	Close the doors for church to begin.
Seteraeke sechaba sa Noka-ntšo,	The Noka-ntso crowd went on strike,
Seteraeke se hana ho sebetsa.	On strike and refused to work.
Ntsa likhomo u nyale mosali,	You [must] pay cattle to marry a wife,
U tlo u bone ha meleko e ata.	[Then] you shall see how problems multiply.
Likhomo li kenya meleko lapeng;	Cattle herd in problems among a family;
Eang le e nyale metsuku-tsuku—	Go and marry aquiline faces—
E tle, re e tsofala, e le makatse.	Once married [to them], when they grow old, don't be surprised.
Sello sa ngoanana ea mokhunoana,	The cry of a girl with a fair [pretty] complexion,
Ha a tsoa koana bohali ba hae,	When she returns from the husband's home,
Ha a fihla ha habo moholo'a hae,	When she arrives [back] at her maternal home,
O re 'mae a ntate, 'mae a ntate.	She tells her mother to fetch me, her mother to fetch me.
"Ho uena, motsoali oa me,	"To you, my friend,
U ke u thole joale ke u qoqele	May you be quiet now I chat to you
Taba tse koana bohali ba ka:	About the affairs of my husband's home:
Ba re ha ke sila, kea haila,	They [my in-laws] say when I do my work, I am incapable,
Ha ke khile metsi, ke khile bolele,	When I fetch water, I fetch algae,
Ke fepa le bana, ha kea hatlela,	I even feed children [when] I have not washed my hands,
Ha ke ea patsing, ke ea selaetsong	When I go afield to gather wood, [that] I go for love affairs.

4. Because he is a famous performer, men of all ages rush to see him when they hear he is in their area.

U joetse ntate, u joetse malome,	Tell my father, tell my uncle,
Khomo tseo tsa batho, ba li je;	[That] those cattle of [my husband's] people, they may eat;
Ba li siea.	They may eat but leave some.
Khomo ha li sile motho; kea sila."	Cattle are not meant to outwork a person; I do my work."[5]
Utloang, e ngoe temana ke ena:	Listen, here is yet another verse:
Sello sa ngoanana e mokhunoana,	The cry of a girl with a romantic [desirable] face,
Ke katikisimane ea lona, likheleke	She is a catechism [an examplar] to you, the eloquent ones
Ke 'mampoli oa lona, litsamaea-naha,	I'm the chief herdboy [leader], country travelers,
Moporofeta oa Molimo, Mahase.	The prophet of God, Mahase.
'Na, ha kea tsoaloa ke otaruoe:	Me, I'm not born but issued:[6]
Ke theohile ha Molimo Labone;	I descended from God on a Thursday;
Labohlano la nthola tseleng;	Friday found me on the way;
Lefatšeng ka fihla moqebelo.	On earth I arrived on a Saturday.
Ha ke fihla oa heso oa ha 'Muso,	When I arrived in my village of 'Muso,
Litsohatsana li teng har'a motse oo;	There are the aged women in that village;
Bo Nkhono 'Mamokoto,	These include Grandmother 'Mamokoto,
Le mosali e mosa 'mae a Koloi.	And the good-hearted woman 'Makoloi.
Ka utloa ka bona molilietsane:	I heard and saw ululations [of joy]:
"Ka sheko lena re pholohile!—	"By this warrior we are saved!—
Ho tsoetsoe, kheleke, ea motse oa ha 'Muso.	He is born, the eloquent one, in the village of 'Muso.
Kata-kata ea Bafokeng ka lla."	The fluent one of the Bafokeng [clan] cries."[7]
Ka hlola ke nyantsoa heso lapeng:	This revealed itself during early stages of my infancy:
Ke nyanya le 'me ke ntse ke lla;	[I can recall] my mother giving me the breast whilst I cried;
O nqaea motoho ke ntse ke lla.	She forced me to drink soft porridge whilst I cried.

5. If you marry a pretty girl, your family is likely to suspect that she is trading on her looks, and is disobedient and lazy. Here, such a girl asks the singer to plead with her agnates not to eat up all the marriage cattle, because they may have to return some if she decides to run away from her in-laws' harsh treatment.

6. A common South African way of insulting one's subordinates, whether on the mines or the police force, or in other working-class contexts, is to say they were "not born but issued."

7. The implication is that even his first cries or sounds were eloquent and melodious.

Ke hona, ke sa tla, ota mpela:	Time tells, it's yet to be, that I become leaner and leaner:
Ke motho oa moea, metsolle ea me,	I am a spirited person, my friends,
Feela oa moea; ke lakatsa hlophe.	Simply of the spirit; I desire the divination dance.[8]
Ke motho ea binang ka sekupu;	I am a person who sings secretly;
Ke bina ha likupu li lla,	I sing whenever drums sound,
Mechonoko e nyoloha lefehlong.	Like the novice diviners coming up from [their] initiation.
Majakane ha le batho, le baloi;	You the worshipers are not people, but witches;
Le pelo li mekha-mekha, baloi.	You are of devious mind, you witches.
Le hana le ngoan'a Molimo a kula;	You refuse [to relent] even when a poor child of God is sick;[9]
Le mofasitse ka khoejana thekeng.	You have tied him with a string [thinly] around his waist.
Le 'meile tseleng ea selibeng,	You have placed him in the road to the well,
E tl'ere ha le feta le mo komele	So that you may address him in contempt as you pass by,
Le re ho eena ngoana, "Ntja tooe!"	And say to him, "You dog!"
Aowa, nya, nka tsa hau	Oh no, [girl,] take your belongings
U khutlele monneng u ka lehlanya:	And go to your husband like a handicap:
Khomo tsa batho re li jele boholo;	We have eaten most of the people's cattle;[10]
Koalang mamati, metsoalle ea me.	Close the doors, my dear friends.
Utloang e ngoe temana ke ena:	Here again is yet another verse:
Ho se ipalle ke taba e bohloko.	To be unable to write for oneself [illiteracy] is painful.
Tsatsing leleng, metsoalle ea me,	One day, my friends,
Ha ke le makhooeng koana,	When I was in the mines,
Ke re thaka ha li ngolle hae.	I was saying my colleagues were not writing home.
E ilare re sa lutse rea ngola,	It happened that we were seated writing [letters],
Lengolo la 'me la be se le fihla.	A letter from my mother arrived.
La 'me, motsoali'a me,	Yes, from my mother, my friend,

8. The *hlope* dance, which is done as part of the initiation into spirit mediumship, is the cure for the hysterical condition known as *motheketheke*.

9. Migrants are known by the greeting traditionally addressed to strangers: "child of God."

10. Having had his fill of a woman, and so "eaten the people's cattle" (bridewealth), he sends her back to burden her husband.

Mosali e mosa 'mae a Mahase,	A kindhearted mother of Mahase,
Mosali ea tsoetseng Mahooana;	A lady who has given a birth to [children of the] Mahooana clan;
E ka ba ho uena Mosotho, Tsokolo:	Also included is you Mosotho, Tsokolo:
Nyoloha, ngoan'a ka mohlanka;	Come home, my child;
Nyoloha joale u tl'o nyala.	Come home now and get married.
Thaka li nyetse kaofela u setse,	All your comrades have married but you,
Le bana ba ba nyane ba malom'au;	Even the younger ones of your uncle;
Le bona ba nyetse sethepu.	They even have married polygynously.
Bofutsana, ha bo tsekisoe Molimo;	For your poverty, God cannot be blamed;
Hojaneng e be bo ne bo tsekoa,	If poverty were contested,
Molimo re ka be re mo tsamaisa linyeoe.	God would be tied up endlessly in court.
Re lule makhotla a maholo.	We would sit in High Court against him. [People say,]
"Ha e le bona bo ntsoa ke ho sebetsa feela."	"Poverty is eliminated by hard work only."
Ke leshano; ba ea re thetsa.	This is lie; they deceive us.
Le hoja ho ea ka ho sebetsa hoa ka,	If this went in accordance with [the value of] my working,
Le li khomo, nka be ke li rekile;	Even cattle, I could have bought them;
Le mohoma ke lema ka o lesiba—	Even a plough that ploughs like a feather—
Sefofane, ke kalama se sefubelu!	Yes, I would have bought a jet plane!
Tsehlana, itlhatsoe, ke ea lichabeng,	My darling, get clean, I am going among the peoples,[11]
E tl'e re ha ke fihla ka lekhotleng,	So that when I arrive in court,
Ba sheba 'momo ho feta litaba.	They may look more at my calves than at the case.[12]
Ngoan'a khotso ha a lebale tsa khotso.	A peaceful man never forgets a peacemaker.
Khutla, u khutlele khotsong ea hau—	Go, go back to your motherland—
Le ka nketšang, litsamaea-naha?	What harm can you cause to me, you the travelers [migrants]?
Le ka nketšang, ke hlotse boloetsa?	What harm can you cause me, I [who] have triumphed over witchcraft?
Ke qochile likheleke, ka tebela lingaka.	I am superior to the eloquent ones.

11. He is going to the court in the city where there are people of many kinds and nations.

12. They should be so prepossessed by his appearance they don't think to examine the strength of his case too closely!

Ngaka tse ngata, li tloha mona ke ho ntsaba.	Many doctors, they leave here for fear of me.
Le tse setseng ha li ntsebe;	Those who remain do not know me;
Li se bile li nahana.	They are still figuring it out.
Ho falla Ralilochoane, oa ngaka, matsetsela.	Even Ralilochane, the specialist [in eloquence], intends going.[13]
Bana ba kula: keng u cheka?	The children are sick: what herbs are *you* digging?
'Na, ha ke sa le ngakana; ke ngaka.	Me, I am not an apprentice [amateur poet]; I am a doctor.
Ha ke 'nke kepi ho cheka litlhare:	I don't take a pick to dig medicines [herbs]:
Ke qale pele ka ho opa liatla;	I start first by clapping hands;
Ke tila fatse ka lento lena la ka;	I hit the earth hard with this foot of mine;
Ke tila fatse ho nyoloha methokho.	I hit the earth hard to bring out my song.
Ho nyolohile litlhare tse thata feela, khelebetla le lehabea.	I bring forth strong medicines only [for your appreciation], *khelebetla* and *lehabea.*[14]
Utloang e nhgoe temana ke ena:	Here is yet another verse:[15]
Ke ne ke bue joalo, ke sa le moshana Keemela koana Mantsonyane,	I was saying so, when I was a boy herding yonder at Mantsonyane,
Ke lisa likhomo tsa morui—oe e e;	I was looking after the cattle of a rich man—oe e e;
Tsa ntate tsa Lecheko Montsi.	Those were the cattle of father Lecheko Montsi.
Jo, o li ntse li mo tseba—oe e e!	Ah, his flock used to know him—oe e e!
Banna, utloang e ngoe temana ke ena:	Men, here is yet another verse:
'Na, ha kea futsa, ke feteletse,	Me, I don't just resemble, I am the spitting image [of my fathers],
Ka futsa ka mali le ka sebopeho.	By resemblance of blood and by [my] nature.
Ngoan'a mali o latella seboko	The child of the blood is the one that follows the clan

13. The word *matsetsela* here has a double meaning, playing on *ho tsetsela*, "to whine, to be dissatisfied," and *matsetsele*, "perfect doctor, leader, trusted person" (see Mabille, Dieterlen, and Paroz 1983, 425).

14. A love charm used to make a girl love a man.

15. Lecheko begins a narrative episode here, then takes a detour for four lines, only to pick it up again for the final sequence of his text (as recorded). Other singers, including the renowned Makeka Likhojane, "Ngoana Mokhalo," also favor ending their performances with a herdboy adventure.

Letsatsing le leng, metsoalle ea ka.

Ke emele Mphe Lebeko matsatseng;
Likhomo tsa tlola sakeng ke li koaletse.

Ke qetile matsatsi a mabeli holim'a sehlaba

Ke li batla, ke sa li fumane.
Utloang, e ngoe temana ke ena:
Ke liketse kotjana tsena kaofela,
Ke ha ke theosa Mantšonyane
Ha ke fihla motseng,
motsaneng mona, Mokotane
Ke fumane banna ba motse oo—
"Bo-ntate, lumelang mona!
Ke motho oa meraka ke ntse ke batla;

Ntholleng joale, kea batla."
Ba re ho 'na, separola-thota,
"Likhomo tseo u, li batlang;
Tseo likhomo, le ka mahlo ha rea li bona.

Bosiu bo seleng bona, re utloile
namane ea khomo e lla
E tsela nokeng tlaase ha Mokone."

Haufinyane le bana ba Nchela,

Ke e theosa Mantšonyane
Ke fihla motsaneng mona ha Leronti.

Bathepung mona,
Ke kopane le Mokoampe oa Maqhotsa
Ho ho ho, ngoana Mothepu.
Ntholle joale, kea batla;
Ke lahlehetsoe ke khomo tsa morui.
Hoa bua ngoan'a Mothepu,
"Sekeleme, ngoan'a Mahase,
Likhomo tseo u li batlang tseo,

From the very day [he is born],
my friends.[16]

I was in the Mphe-Lebeko grasslands;
Cattle left the kraal at night
despite my precautions.

I spent two days on mountaintops
and in the valleys,

Searching for the cattle, but in vain.
Yet again, here is another verse:
I went over all the hills and valleys,
Then down the Mantsonyane River
Until I came to a village,
the little village here, Makotane.
I met the men of the village—
"Fathers, greetings here!
I am from the mountain area and
am in search;

Help me out now, I'm in search."
They said to me, the veld-tracker,
"The cattle you are looking for,
Those cattle, our eyes have not
seen them.

Last night, we heard a sound of a calf

As it crossed the river further down by
[the village of] Mokone."

But somewhere near the village of
Nchela,

I went further down the Mantsonyane
Until I arrived at the village of
Leronti.

Among AmaThembu-Basotho there,
I met Mokoampe of that Xhosa clan
Making gibberish,[17] the Xhosa child.
Help me out now, I am searching;
I have lost a rich man's cattle.
Then Mothepu replied,
"You, unreliable son of Mahase,
The cattle you are looking for,

16. It's a wise child who knows his own father, but resembling the old man in character as well as appearance helps.

17. Tsokolo rather chauvinistically makes fun of the Xhosa language as "gibberish." It's just a joke.

Khomo li liketse sepetlele;
Likhomo li liketse sekolong."
Ha ke le sekolong ke botsa,
Ho bana ba sekolo.
Hoa bua ngoan'a lesea,
"Sekeleme, ngoan'a Mahase,
Khomo tseo u li batlang tseo
Li sekoting koana 'Malihase."
Ha ke fihla 'Malihase, ke fumane ha ho khomo, ha ho namane.
Ka be ke e theosa Mantš onyane
Ke fihla ha Jeitse, lebenkeleng
Moo ho busang Basotho feela.
Ke botsitse tlelereke ea Mosotho,
"Oho ngoan'a Mothepu,
Ho uena, setsamaea-naha, ntholle joale, kea batla;
Ke lahlehetsoe ke tsa morui."
Hoa bua tlelereke ea Mosotho,
"Ho uena, ngoan'a Mahase
Khomo tseo u li batlang tseo
Li liketse Mantš onyane."
Ha ke le sepetlele, ke fumane nese ea ngoanana:
"Oho ngoananyana, Limakatso!
Ntholle joale, kea batla;
Ke lahlehetsoe ke khomo tsa morui."
"Khomo tseo u li batlang tseo,
Le ka mahlo ha kea li bona."
Ke ha ke theosa Mantšonyane;
Ke fihlile motseng o bitsoang Ntširele.
Ke botsitse mosali a le moholo,
"Oho 'mae a mosali,
Ntholle joale, kea batla;

Those cattle have wandered toward the hospital;
Those cattle have wandered toward the school."
When I came to the school,
I asked the schoolchildren.
The youngest schoolchild said,
"You, unreliable son of Mahase,
The cattle you are looking for
Are in a deep valley at 'Malihase."
When I arrived at 'Malihase, I found no cattle, no calf.
I went still further down the Mantsonyane
Until I came to the village of Jeitse, at the shop
Where only Basotho live.
I asked a Mosotho clerk,
"Oh you of the Mothepu clan,[18]
To you, [I] the traveler, help me out now, I am in search;
I have lost a rich man's cattle."
The Mosotho clerk replied,
"To you, son of Mahase,
The cattle you are looking for
Have gone down the Mantsonyane."
When I arrived at the hospital, I met a nursing sister:
"Oh you little girl, Limakatso!
Come to my aid now, I am in search;
I have lost the cattle of a rich man."
"The cattle you are looking for,
With my own eyes
I've not seen them."
Then down and further down the Mantsonyane I went;
I came to a village named Ntsirele.
I did ask an elderly lady,
Oh you mother-in-law,[19]
Come to my aid now, I am in search;

18. Tsokolo seems somewhat of two minds as to whether the Basotho of Amathembu Xhosa descent, who still speak Sixhosa as well as Sesotho, are Basotho or not. Every Mosotho I have asked has given the same reply: they are Basotho from a AmaXhosa clan.

19. "Mother of my mother" is an ingratiating greeting to an older woman.

Ke lahlehetsoe ke khomo tsa morui."
"E ka ba ho uena Mosotho, Tsokolo,
Khomo tseo u li batlang tseo,
Khomo li kenetse koana ha Mahlong."

Ha ke fihla koana Mahlong,
Ke be ke phallela moreneng:
"Maama, nthollejoale, kea batla;

Ke lahlehetsoe ke khomo tsa morui."
Hoa bua thope, thope ea ngoanana,

Le le tsoana Letebele!
"Sekeleme, ngoan'a Mahase,
Khomo tseo u li batlang tseo
Li theositse Mantšonyane."
Mehlolo!
Ha ke tsela Tenane,
Ke fumane seporo sa manamane;
Ha ke le Matateng, ke fumane
balisa ba manemane.
Ke re ho bona,
"Bashanyana beso, ho lona, lumelang
mona;
Ke utloa ke le lumelisa, sechaba.
Ke motho oa meraka, ke ntse ke batla."

Hoa bua ngoan'a lesea:

"Ho uena, separola-thota,
Khomo tseo u li batlang tseo
Likhomo li tsoeroe Macheseng."
Ha ke le Macheseng, ke fumane
banna khotla ho lutsoe:
"Bo-ntate, lumelang mona,
Khotsong! Kea le lumelisa, sechaba.
Ke motho oa meraka, ke ntse ke batla"
Ba re, "Ho uena, ngoan'a Mahase,
Khomo tseo u li batlang tseo
Khomo li sentse masimong a batho;

I have lost a rich man's cattle."
"Oh poor you Mosotho, Tsokolo,
The cattle you are looking for,
Their last whereabouts are yonder
at Mahlong [village]."
When I arrived yonder at Mahlong,
I reported at the chief's place:
"[Chief] Maama, come to my aid, I am
in search;
I have lost the cattle of a rich man."
Then there replied a young beautiful
girl,
Yes, a dark beauty of a Matebele![20]
"You, unreliable son of Mahase,
The cattle you are looking for
Have gone down the Mantsonyane."
Oh, miracles!
On crossing Tenane [River],
I found a trail of the calves;
When I arrived at Matateng, I found
boys looking after calves.
I said to them,
"Boys of my age, to you, greetings
here;
I hear and greet you, people.
I am from the mountains, and I am in
search."
Then there spoke the youngest of
them all:
"To you, veld-tracker,
The cattle you are looking for
Have been impounded at Macheseng."
Arriving at Macheseng, I found
men seated by the kraal:
"Fathers, I greet you,
Peace! I greet you, people.
I'm a mountaineer, and still in search."
They said, "To you, son of Mahase,
The cattle you are looking for
Have caused great damage to the
people's fields [crops];

20. Basotho of remnant AmaSwazi or AmaZulu clan origin are called "Matebele" in Lesotho.

Feela ke tsane letsoapong thabeng."	It's just those there on the mountainside."
Ba mpatla ponto;	They demanded from me one pound;
Sepacheng sa me, ha ke na ponto.	In my purse, I have not a pound.[21]

21. This is an abrupt—the tape ran out—but narratively consistent and conclusive ending. Perhaps he would somehow have redeemed his cattle, but the point of the story is a larger commentary on migrancy in the allegorical metaphor of herding. Having squandered his patrimony—losing the cattle of his "rich" senior agnate—the migrant is forced to search for it over long distances, seemingly in vain. When he finally finds it, he has not the resources to redeem it or, by implication, himself. How better to summarize the fundamental tragedy of Basotho labor migrancy, and as it happens, to end this book?

References

Abrahams, Roger. 1972. The Training of the Man of Words in Talking Sweet. *Language in Society* 1972: 15–29.

———. 1983. *The Man of Words in the West Indies.* Baltimore: Johns Hopkins University Press.

Adams, Charles. 1974. Ethnography of Basotho Evaluative Expression in the Cognitive Domain *Lipapali* (Games). Ph.D. diss. Indiana University, Bloomington.

———. 1979a. Aurality and Consciousness: Basotho Production of Significance. In *Essays in Humanistic Anthropology: A Festschrift in Honor of David Bidney,* ed. Bruce Grindal and Dennis Warren, 303–25. Washington, D.C.: University Press of America.

———. 1979b. Distinctive Features of Play and Games: A Folk Model from Southern Africa. In *Play and Culture,* ed. Helen Schwartzman, 150–61. West Point: Leisure Press.

———. 1986. Wind, Breath, and Strings Round and Flat. *Experimental Musical Instruments* 1, no. 5 (February).

Alverson, Hoyt. 1978. *Mind in the Heart of Darkness.* New Haven: Yale University Press.

Ambrose, David. 1973. The Basotho Settlement at Griquatown. *Lesotho Notes and Records* 4: 60–64.

Arbousset, Thomas. [1840] 1991. Missionary Excursions. Edited and translated by David Ambrose and Albert Brutsch. Morija, Lesotho: Morija Archive.

Ashton, Hugh. 1967. *The Basuto.* Reprint, London: Oxford University Press. Original edition, 1952.

Auge, Marc. 1979. *The Anthropological Circle.* Cambridge: Cambridge University Press.

Austen, Ralph. 1991. An Opaque Epic: Preliminary Reflections on the Narrative of Jeki La Njambe in the Culture of the Cameroon Coast. Paper presented to the graduate seminar of the Department of Social Anthropology, University of Cape Town, April 19.

Babcock-Abrahams, Barbara. 1975. A Tolerated Margin of Mess: The Trickster and His Tales Reconsidered. *Journal of the Folklore Institute* 11, no. 3: 147–86.

Barber, Karin. 1991. *I Could Speak until Tomorrow.* Edinburgh: Edinburgh University Press for the International African Institute.

Bardill, John E., and James H. Cobbe. 1985. *Lesotho: Dilemmas of Dependence in Southern Africa.* Boulder, Col.: Westview Press; London: Gower.

Basso, Ellen B. 1985. *A Musical View of the Universe.* Philadelphia: University of Pennsylvania Press.

Bauman, Richard. 1977. *Verbal Art as Performance.* Rowley, Mass.: Newbury House.

Beidelman, T. O. 1966. Swazi Royal Ritual. *Africa* 36, no. 4: 373–405.

———. 1980. The Moral Imagination of the Kaguru: Some Thoughts on Tricksters, Translations, and Comparative Analysis. *American Ethnologist* 7, no. 1: 27–41.

———. 1986. *Moral Imagination in Kaguru Modes of Thought.* Bloomington: Indiana University Press.

Biesele, Megan. 1986. How Hunter Gatherers' Stories "Make Sense": Semantics and Adaptation. *Cultural Anthropology* 1, no. 2 (May): 157–70.

Bird, Charles, and Martha Kendall. 1981. The Mande Hero. In *Explorations in African Systems of Thought,* ed. Charles Bird and Ivan Karp. Bloomington: Indiana University Press.

Blacking, John. 1973. *How Musical Is Man?* Seattle: University of Washington Press.

Bonner, Philip. 1988. Desirable or Undesirable Women? Liquor, Prostitution, and the Migration of Basotho Women to the Rand, 1920–1945. Manuscript.

———. 1990. The Russians on the Reef, 1947–1957: Urbanization, Gang Warfare, and Ethnic Mobilization. Paper presented to the SARP Fall Workshop, Yale University, New Haven, October 27.

Bosko, Dan. 1983. Social Organizational Aspects of Religious Change among Basotho. Ph.D. diss., New York University.

Bourdieu, Pierre. 1977. *Outline of a Theory of Practice.* Cambridge: Cambridge University Press.

Burchell, Thomas. 1822. *Travels in the Interior of Southern Africa.* London: Longmans.

Burke, Kenneth. 1945. *A Grammar of Motives.* Berkeley: University of California Press.

Casalis, Eugene. 1841. *Études sur la langue sechmana.* Paris: Imprimerie Royale.

———. [1861] 1965. *The Basuto, or Twenty-three Years in South Africa.* Cape Town: C. Struik.

Clifford, James. 1988. *The Predicament of Culture.* Cambridge: Harvard University Press.

Clifford, James, and George Marcus, eds. 1986. *Writing Culture.* Berkeley: University of California Press.

Cobbe, James. 1985. Lesotho and South Africa: Implications of an Evolving Relationship. Paper presented at the annual meeting of the African Studies Association, New Orleans, November 21.

———. 1986. The Changing Nature of Dependence: Economic Problems in Lesotho. *Journal of Modern African Studies* 21, no. 2: 293–310.

Cobbing, Julian. 1988. The *Mfecane* as Alibi: Thoughts on Dithakong and Mbolompo. *Journal of African History* 21, no. 2: 487–519.

Cohen, David, and E. Odhiambo. 1989. *Siaya.* London: James Curry.
Comaroff, Jean. 1985. *Body of Power, Spirit of Resistance.* Chicago: University of Chicago Press.
Comaroff, John. 1982. Dialectical Systems, History, and Anthropology: Units of Study and Questions of Theory. *Journal of Southern African Studies* 8, no. 2: 143–72.
Comaroff, John L., and Jean Comaroff. 1987. The Madman and the Migrant. *American Ethnologist* 14, no. 2 (February): 198–211.
———. 1990. Goodly Beasts, Beastly Goods: Cattle and Commodities in a South African Context. *American Ethnologist* 17, no. 2 (May): 195–216.
———. 1991. *Of Revelation and Revolution: Christianity, Colonialism, and Consciousness in South Africa.* Chicago: University of Chicago Press.
Cope, Trevor. 1968. *Izibongo: Zulu Praise Poetry.* Oxford: Clarendon Press.
Coplan, David B. 1980. The Urbanization of African Performing Arts in South Africa. Ph.D. diss., Indiana University, Bloomington.
———. 1985. *In Township Tonight! South Africa's Black City Music and Theatre.* New York: Longman.
———. 1986. Ideology and Tradition in South African Black Popular Theatre. *Journal of American Folklore* 99: 392.
———. 1987a. The Power of Oral Poetry: Narrative Songs of the Basotho Migrants. *Research in African Literatures* 18, no. 1: 1–35.
———. 1987b. Eloquent Knowledge: Lesotho Migrants' Songs and the Anthropology of Experience. *American Ethnologist* 14, no. 3 (August): 413–33.
———. 1988. Musical Understanding: The Ethnoaesthetics of Migrant Workers' Poetic Song in Lesotho. *Ethnomusicology* 32, no. 3: 337–68.
———. 1991. Fictions That Save: Migrants' Performance and Basotho National Culture. *Cultural Anthropology* 6, no. 2: 164–91. Reprinted in Marcus 1993.
———. 1992. The Meaning of Sesotho. *Journal of Research* (Lesotho) 3, no. 4: 1–56.
———. 1993. Damned If We Know: Public Policy, Labour Law, and the Future of the Migrant Labour System. Paper presented to the Department of Social Anthropology, University of Cape Town, August 17.
Crais, Clifton C. 1992. *The Making of the Colonial Order.* Johannesburg: Witwatersrand University Press.
Crush, Jonathon. 1992. Inflexible Migrancy: New Forms of Migrant Labour on the South African Gold Mines. In Crush, James, and Jeeves 1992.
Crush, Jonathan, Alan Jeeves, and David Yudelman. 1991. *South Africa's Labour Empire.* Cape Town: David Philip.
Crush, Jonathan, Wilmot James, and Alan Jeeves, eds. 1992. *Transformations on the South African Gold Mines* [in English and French]. Special issue of *Labour, Capital, and Society / Travail, Capital, et Société* 25, no. 1 (April). Montreal: Centre for Developing-Area Studies, McGill University.
Damane, Mosebi. 1963–64. The Structure and Philosophy of Sotho Indigenous Poetry. *Basutoland Notes and Records* 4: 41–49.

Damane, Mosebi, and Peter Sanders, eds. 1974. *Sotho Praise Poems*. London: Oxford University Press.
Davidson, Hilda. 1978. *Patterns of Folklore*. Ipswitch, Mass.: Brewer, Rowman, and Littlefield.
De Heusch, Luc. 1982. *The Drunken King of the Origin of the State*. Bloomington: Indiana University Press. Original French edition, 1972.
Dobb, Alan J. 1984. The Organization of Range Use in Lesotho, Southern Africa: A Review of Attempted Modification and Case Study. Part I. M.S. thesis, Washington State University.
Dornan, S. S. 1908. The Basuto: Their Traditional History and Folklore. *Proceedings of the Rhodesia Science Association* 8, part 1: 65–94.
Dorst, John. 1983. Neck-Riddle as a Dialogue of Genres: Applying Bakhtin's Genre Theory. *Journal of American Folklore* 96: 413–33.
Duncan, Patrick. 1960. *Sotho Laws and Customs*. Cape Town: Oxford University Press.
Dutton, E. A. T. 1923. *The Basuto of Basutoland*. London: Cape.
Edgar, Robert. 1986. *Prophets with Honour*. Johannesburg: Ravan.
Eldredge, E. 1986. An Economic History of Lesotho in the Nineteenth Century. Ph.D. diss., University of Wisconsin, Madison.
Ellenberger, F. D., and J. MacGregor. 1912. *History of the Basotho, Ancient and Modern*. London: Caxton.
Evans-Pritchard, E. E. 1937. *Witchcraft, Oracles, and Magic among the Azande*. London: Oxford University Press.
Fabian, Johannes. 1978. Popular Culture in Africa. *Africa* 48, no. 4: 315–34.
———. 1990. *Power and Performance*. Madison: University of Wisconsin Press.
Feld, Steven. 1982. *Sound and Sentiment*. Philadelphia: University of Pennsylvania Press.
Ferguson, James. 1990. *The Anti-Politics Machine*. Cambridge: Cambridge University Press.
Fernandez, James W. 1989. Coment on Keesings's "Exotic Readings of Cultural Texts." *Current Anthropology* 30, no. 4: 470–71.
Finnegan, Ruth. 1970. *Oral Literature in Africa*. Oxford: Clarendon.
———. 1976. What Is Oral Literature Anyway? In *Oral Literature and the Formula*, ed. B. A. Stoltz and R. S. Shannon. Ann Arbor: University of Michigan Press.
———. 1977. *Oral Poetry*. Cambridge: Cambridge University Press.
Foucault, Michel. 1976. *The Archaeology of Knowledge*. New York: Harper.
Frank, Lawrence. 1992. The End of Ideology in Lesotho. Paper presented at the annual meeting of the African Studies Association, Seattle, November 21.
Franz, G. H. 1930. The Literature of Lesotho. *Bantu Studies* 4, no. 3: 145–80.
Gay, Judith S. 1980a. Basotho Women Migrants: A Case Study. *Institute for Development Studies Bulletin* (Sussex) 11, no. 3: 19–28.
———. 1980b. Wage Employment of Rural Basotho Women: A Case Study. *South African Labour Bulletin* 6, no. 4: 40–53.
———. 1980c. Basotho Women's Options: A Study of Marital Careers in Rural Lesotho. Ph.D. diss., Cambridge University.

Geertz, Clifford. 1968. Thinking as a Moral Act: Ethical Dimensions of Anthropological Fieldwork in the New States. *Antioch Review* 28: 139–58.

———. 1973. *The Interpretation of Cultures.* New York: Basic Books.

———. 1983. *Local Knowledge.* New York: Basic Books.

Germond, P. 1967. *Chronicles of Basutoland.* Morija, Lesotho: Sesuto Book Depot.

Giddens, Anthony. 1976. *The New Rules of Sociological Method.* New York: Basic Books.

———. 1979. *Central Problems in Social Theory.* London: Macmillan.

———. 1981. *The Class Structure of the Advanced Societies.* London: Hutchinson.

———. 1984. *The Constitution of Society.* Cambridge: Polity Press.

———. 1991. *Modernity and Self-Identity: Self and Society in the Late Modern Age.* Cambridge: Polity Press.

Goody, Jack. 1977. *The Domestication of the Savage Mind.* Cambridge: Cambridge University Press.

Gordon, Elizabeth. 1981. An Analysis of the Impact of Labour Migration on the Lives of Women in Lesotho. *Journal of Development Studies* 17, no. 3: 59–76.

Gordon, Robert. 1977. *Mines, Masters, and Migrants.* Johannesburg: Ravan Press.

Guma, Mthobeli. 1985. "Sotho" Male Initiation Rites in an Urban Setting. B. Soc. Sci. Hon. thesis, University of Cape Town.

———. 1993. History and Meaning: Names and the Construction of Personhood among the Southern Sotho. Manuscript.

Guma, S. M. 1965. Aspects of Circumcision in Basutoland. *African Studies* 24, no. 4: 241–51.

———. 1966. *Likoma.* Pietermaritzburg: Shuter and Shooter.

———. 1967. *The Form, Content, and Technique of Traditional Literature in Southern Sotho.* Pretoria: J. L. van Schaik.

———. 1971. *An Outline Structure of Southern Sotho.* Pietermaritzburg: Shuter and Shooter.

Gunner, Elizabeth. 1979. Songs of Innocence and Experience: Women as Composers and Performers of Izibongo, Zulu Praise Poetry. *Research in African Literatures* 10, no. 2 (1979): 239–67.

———. 1986. 'A Dying Tradition'? African Oral Literature in a Contemporary Context. *Social Dynamics* 12, no. 2: 31–38.

Gusfield, Joseph. 1989. *Symbols and Society: The Work of Kenneth Burke.* Berkeley and Los Angeles: University of California Press.

Guy, Jeff, and Motlatsi Thabane. 1984. The Ma-Rashea: A Participant's Perspective. Paper for the History Workshop, University of the Witwatersrand, February.

———. 1988. Technology, Ethnicity, and Ideology: Basotho Miners and Shaft-Sinking on the South African Gold Mines. *Journal of Southern African Studies* 14, no. 2 (January): 257–78.

———. 1992. Basotho Miners, Oral History, and Worker's Strategies. In *Cultural Struggle and Development in Southern Africa,* ed. Preben Kaarsholm, 239–57. Portsmouth, N.H.: Heinemann.

Hammond-Tooke, W. D. 1974. World View I and II. In *The Bantu-Speaking Peoples of Southern Africa*, ed. W. D. Hammond-Tooke, 318–63. London: Routledge and Kegan Paul.

Hamnet, Ian. 1965. Koena Chieftainship Seniority in Basutoland. *Africa* 35, no. 5: 241–51.

Harms, Robert. 1980. Bobangi Oral Traditions: Indicators of Changing Perceptions. In Miller 1980, 178–200.

———. 1983. The Wars of August: Diagonal Narrative in African History. *American Historical Review*, October, 809–34.

Heap, Marion. 1989. *Health and Disease in South-Eastern Lesotho: A Social Anthropological Perspective of Two Villages.* Centre for African Studies, Communications No. 16. Cape Town.

Hobsbawm, Eric, and Terence Ranger, eds. 1984. *The Invention of Tradition.* Cambridge: Cambridge University Press.

Holquist, Michael, ed. 1981. *The Dialogic Imagination: Four Essays by M. M. Bakhtin.* Austin: University of Texas Press.

Hunter, Monica. 1936. *Reaction to Conquest.* Oxford: Oxford University Press.

Hymes, Dell. 1981. Discovering Oral Performance and Measured Verse in American Indian Narrative In *"In Vain I Tried to Tell You": Essays in Native American Ethnopoetics.* Philadelphia: University of Pennsylvania Press.

Jacottet, E. 1908. Treasury of Basuto Lore. Morija, Lesotho: Sesuto Book Depot.

———. 1896–97. Moeurs, Coutumes, et Superstitions des Ba-Souto. *Bull. Soc. Neuchateloise de Geographie* 9: 107–51.

Jakobson, Roman. 1966. Closing Statement: Linguistics and Poetics. In *Style in Language*, ed. Thomas Sebeok, 350–75. Reprint, Cambridge: M.I.T. Press. Original edition, 1960.

James, Wilmot. 1992. *Our Precious Metal: African Labour in South Arica's Gold Industry, 1970–1990.* Cape Town: David Philip.

Johnson, R., et al., eds. 1979. *Working Class Culture*, New York: St. Martins.

Jones, G. I. 1951. *Basutoland Medicine Murder.* London: His Majesty's Stationery Office.

Joyner, Charles. 1975. A Model for the Analysis of Folklore Performance in Historical Context. *Journal of American Folklore* 88, no. 349: 254–65.

Keesing, R. 1989. Exotic Readings of Cultural Texts. *Current Anthropology* 30, no. 4: 459–79.

Kimble, Judy. 1982. Labour Migration in Basutoland, c. 1870–1885. In *Industrialisation and Social Change in South Africa*, ed. Shula Marks and Richard Rathbone, 119–41. London: Longman.

Kirby, P. R. [1934] 1965. *The Musical Instruments of the Native Races of South Africa.* Johannesburg: University of the Witwatersrand Press.

Kottler, A. 1988. South Africa: Psychology's Dilemma of Multiple Discourses. Mimeograph, Department of Psychology, University of Cape Town.

Kunene, Daniel. 1958. Notes on *Hlonepha* among the Southern Sotho. *African Studies* 17, no. 3: 159–82.

———. 1965. The Ideophone in Southern Sotho. *Journal of African Languages* (UK) 4, part 1: 19–39.

———. 1967. A War Song of the Basotho. *Journal of the New African Literature and the Arts* 3: 10–20.

———. 1971. *Heroic Poetry of the Basotho.* Oxford: Clarendon.

———. 1972. Metaphor and Symbolism in the Heroic Poetry of Southern Africa. In *African Folklore*, ed. Richard Dorson. New York: Anchor/Doubleday.

———. 1979. Levels of Communication in the Heroic Poetry of Southern Africa. In *Artist and Audience: African Literature as a Shared Experience*, ed. R. O. Priebe and T. Hale. Washington, D.C.: Three Continents Press.

Kuper, Adam. 1987. *South Africa and the Anthropologist.* London: Routledge and Kegan Paul.

Lagden, Geoffrey. 1909. *The Basutos.* 2 vols. London: Hutchinson.

Lestrade, G. P. 1934. European Influences upon Bantu Languages and Literature. In *Western Civilization and the Natives of South Africa: Studies in Culture Contact*, ed. I. Schapera, 105–27. London: Routledge and Kegan Paul.

———. 1937. Traditional Literature. In *The Bantu-Speaking Tribes of South Africa*, ed. I. Schapera, 297–99. London: Routledge and Kegan Paul.

Leydevant, F. 1932. Religious or Sacred Plants of Basutoland. *Bantu Studies* 6, no. 1 (March): 65–69.

———. 1933. The Praises of the Divining Bones among the BaSutos. *Bantu Studies* 7: 341–73.

———. 1978. *The Rites of Initiation in Lesotho.* Translated by G. Chadwick. Roma, Lesotho: O.M.I. Social Centre. Original Sesotho edition, 1951.

Litabe, James. 1986. Marashea: A Participant's Experience as a Leader of Molapo-Masupha Faction versus the Matsieng Faction, Zulu, Tsotsis, and Police. B.A. Ed. thesis, Department of History, National University of Lesotho.

Lord, Albert. 1960. *The Singer of Tales.* Cambridge: Harvard University Press.

Mabille, A., H. Dieterlen, and R. A. Paroz. 1983. *Southern Sotho-English Dictionary.* Morija, Lesotho: Sesuto Book Depot.

Machobane, L. B. B. J. 1990. *Government and Change in Lesotho, 1800–1966.* Maseru: Macmillan Lesotho.

Makhoali, M. 1985. *Circumcision Poetry.* In *Handbook on the Teaching of Southern Sesotho*, ed. R. I. M. Moletsane and Sr. C. M. Matsoso, 171–79. Maseru: FEP International.

Mangoela, Z. D. [1921] 1984. *Lithoko tsa Marena a Basotho.* Morija, Lesotho: Sesuto Book Depot.

Mapele, Seeiso. 1976. Lifela. B.A. Hons. thesis, National University of Lesotho.

Mapetla, Joase. 1969. *Liphoofolo, Linonyana, Litaola: Le Lithoko tsa Tsona.* Morija, Lesotho: Sesuto Book Depot.

Marcus, George, ed. *Rereading Cultural Anthropology.* Durham, N.C.: Duke University Press.

Marcus, George, and Michael Fischer. 1986. *Anthropology as Cultural Critique.* Chicago: University of Chicago Press.

Matsela, F. Z. A. 1979. The Indigenous Education of the Basotho and Its Implications for Educational Development in Lesotho. Ed.D. diss., University of Massachusetts.

———. 1987. *Dipapadi tsa Sesotho.* Mazenod, Lesotho: Mazenod Printers.

Matsobane, Dan, and Toine Eggenhuizen, eds. 1976. *Another Blanket.* Johannesburg: Agency for Industrial Mission.

Mayer, Philip. 1961. *Townsmen or Tribesmen.* London: Oxford University Press.

———, ed. 1980. *Black Villagers in an Industrial Society.* Cape Town: Oxford University Press.

Miller, Joseph C., ed. 1980. *The African Past Speaks.* Folkestone, England: Dawson.

Mofokeng, S. M. 1945. Notes and Annotations of the Praise-Poems of Certain Chiefs and the Structure of the Praise-Peoms in Southern Sotho. B.A. Hons. thesis, University of the Witwatersrand.

Mofolo, Thomas. [1925] 1981. *Chaka.* Translated by Daniel Kunene. London: Heinemann.

Mohapeloa, M. D. 1950. *Letlole la Lithoko tsa Sesotho.* Johannesburg: Afrikaanse Pers-Boekhandel.

Mohome, Paulus. 1972. Naming in Sesotho: Its Socio-Cultural and Linguistic Basis. *Names* 20: 3.

Mokitimi, Makali I. P. 1982. A Literary Analysis of *Lifela tsa Litsamaea-naha* Poetry. M.A. thesis, University of Nairobi.

Moletsane, R. I. M. 1982. A Literary Appreciation and Analysis of Collected and Documented Basotho Miners' Poetry. M.A. thesis, University of the Orange Free State.

———. 1983. *Lefela tsa Litsamaea-naha le Liparola-thota.* Maseru, Lesotho: Longman.

Moodie, T. Dunbar. 1983. Mine Culture and Miners' Identity on a South African Goldmine. In *Town and Countryside in the Transvaal,* ed. Belinda Bozzoli, 176–96. Johannesburg: Ravan.

———. 1988. Migrancy and Male Sexuality on the South African Gold Mines. *Journal of Southern African Studies* 14, no. 2 (January): 228–56.

———. 1991. Social Existence and the Practice of Personal Integrity: Narratives of Resistance on the South African Gold Mines. In *Tradition and Transition in Southern Africa,* ed. Pat MacAllister and Andrew Spiegel. *African Studies* 49, no. 92, special issue in honor of Philip and Iona Mayer, 39–64.

Mothibe, Tefetso. 1988. Chieftaincy and Legitimation in Pre-Colonial Lesotho. Paper presented to the Southern Africa Joint History Seminar, National University of Lesotho, August 1–3.

———. 1991. Lesotho: Historical Legacies of Nationalism and Nationhood. In *Southern Africa after Apartheid,* ed. Sehoai Santho and Mafa Sejanamane. Harare: SAPES Trust.

Motlamelle, M. G. 1938. *Ngaka ea Mosotho.* Morija, Lesotho: Sesuto Book Depot.

Motsamai, E. [1912] 1977. *Mehla ya Madimo.* Morija, Lesotho: Sesuto Book Depot.

Murray, Colin. 1975. Sex, Smoking, and the Shades. In *Religion and Social Change in Southern Africa,* ed. M. Whisson and M. West. London: Rex Collings.

———. 1980a. From Granary to Labour Reserve: An Economic History of Lesotho. *South African Labour Bulletin* 6, no. 4: 3–20.

———. 1980b. Sotho Fertility Symbolism. *African Studies* 39, no. 1: 65–77.

———. 1981. *Families Divided: The Impact of Migrant Labour in Lesotho.* Cambridge: Cambridge University Press.

Nash, June. 1979. *We Eat the Mines; The Mines Eat Us.* New York: Columbia University Press.

Ong, Walter. 1982. *Orality and Literacy: The Technologizing of the Word.* London: Methuen.

Opland, Jeffrey. 1983. *Xhosa Oral Poetry.* Cambridge: Cambridge University Press.

Ortner, Sherry. 1984. Theory in Anthropology since the Sixties. *Comparative Studies in Society and History* 26, no. 1: 126–66.

Peek, Philip. 1981. The Power of Words in African Verbal Arts. *Journal of American Folklore* 94: 19–43.

Peires, Jeffrey. 1989. *The Dead Will Arise: Nongqawuse and the Great Xhosa Cattle-Killing Movement of 1856–1857.* Johannesburg: Ravan.

Phoofolo, Pule. 1980. *Kea Nyala! Kea Nyala!* Husbands and Wives in Nineteenth-Century Lesotho. Mohlomi Seminar Paper No. 3. Roma: History Department, National University of Lesotho.

Poulter, Sebastian. 1979. *Legal Dualism in Lesotho.* Morija, Lesotho: Sesuto Book Depot.

Rosaldo, Renato. 1986. Ilongot Hunting as Story and Experience. In *The Anthropology of Experience,* ed. Victor Turner and Jerome Bruner, 97–138. Urbana: University of Illinois Press.

Rugege, S. 1981. *Class Formation in Contemporary Lesotho.* Roma, Lesotho: ISAS.

———. 1991. The Future of "Traditional" Hereditary Chieftaincy in a Democratic Southern Africa: The Case of Lesotho. In *Southern Africa after Apartheid,* ed. Sehoai Santho and Mafa Sejanamane, 148–85. Harare: SAPES Trust.

Rycroft, David. 1967. Nguni Vocal Polyphony. *Journal of the International Folk Music Council* 19: 88–103.

Rycroft, David, and A. B. Ngcobo, eds. 1988. *The Praises of Dingana.* Pietermaritzburg: University of Natal Press.

———. 1965. *The Praise Poems of Tswana Chiefs.* Oxford: Clarendon.

Sahlins, Marshall. 1976. Other Times, Other Customs. In *Culture and Practical Reason.* Chicago: University of Chicago Press.

Sansom, Basil. 1974. Traditional Rulers and their Realms. In *The Bantu-Speaking Peoples of Southern Africa,* ed. W. D. Hammond-Tooke. London: Routledge and Kegan Paul.

Scheub, Harold. 1985. A Review of African Oral Traditions and Literature. *African Studies Review* 28, nos. 2 and 3: 1–72.

Scott, David. 1992. Criticism and Culture: Theory and Post-Colonial Claims on Anthropological Disciplinarity. *Critique of Anthropology* 12, no. 4 (December): 371–94.

Scott, James C. 1976. *The Moral Economy of the Peasant: Rebellion and Subsistence in Southeast Asia.* New Haven: Yale University Press.

Sechaba Consultants (John Gay, Debby Gill, Thuso Green, David Hall, Mike Mhlanga, and 'Manthatisi Mohapi). 1991. *Poverty in Lesotho: A Mapping Exercise.* Maseru.

Seidman, Gay. 1993. If Harmony Closes, Will the Last One to Leave Turn Out the Lights? Down-Scaling in the Free State Goldfields. Manuscript.

Sherzer, Joel. 1977. Kuna Ikala: Literature in San Blas. In *Verbal Art as Performance*, ed. Richard Bauman. Rowley, Mass.: Newbury House.

Showers, Kate. 1980. A Note on Women, Conflict, and Migrant Labour. *South African Labour Bulletin* 6, no. 4: 54–57.

Simkins, Charles. 1981. Agricultural Production in the African Reserves of South Africa. *Journal of Southern African Studies* 7, no. 2: 256–83.

Southall, Roger. 1991. Lesotho and the Re-integration of South Africa. In *Southern Africa after Apartheid*, ed. Sehoai Santho and Mafa Sejanamane, 209–28. Harare: SAPES Trust.

Spiegel, Andrew. 1979. Migrant Labour Remittances: Rural Differentiation and the Development Cycle in a Lesotho Community. M.A. thesis, University of Cape Town.

———. 1980. Rural Differentiation and the Diffusion of Migrant Labour Remittances in Lesotho. In *Black Villagers in an Industrial Society*, ed. Philip Mayer, 109–68. Cape Town: Oxford University Press.

———. 1981. Changing Patterns of Migrant Labour and Rural Differentiation in Lesotho. *Social Dynamics* 6, no. 2: 1–13.

———. 1990. Changing Continuities: Experiencing and Interpreting History, Population Movement, and Material Differentiation in Matatiele, Transkei. Ph.D. diss., University of Cape Town.

———. 1991. Polygyny as Myth: Towards Understanding Extra-Marital Relations in Lesotho. In *Tradition and Transition*, ed. Pat MacAllister and Andrew Spiegel, 145–66. Johannesburg: Witwatersrand University Press.

Swanepoel, C. F. 1983. *Dithoko tsa Marena:* Perspectives on Composition and Genre. UNISA Inaugural Lecture, Pretoria, March.

Taussig, Michael. 1980. *The Devil and Commodity Fetishism in South America.* Chapel Hill: University of North Carolina Press.

TEBA. 1992. *The Employment Bureau of Africa Annual Report.* Johannesburg.

Tedlock, Dennis. 1983. The Spoken Word and the Work of Interpretation. Philadelphia: University of Pennsylvania Press.

———. 1977. Towards an Oral Poetics. *New Literary History* 8: 507–17.

Thabane, Motlatsi, and Jeff Guy. 1983. The *Ma-rashea:* A Participant's Perspective. In *Town and Countryside in the Transvaal*, ed. Belinda Bozzoli. Johannesburg: Ravan.

Thoahlane, T. E. 1991. A Missing Link in Developing Phase 1A of the Lesotho Highlands Water Project. Ph.D. diss., Columbia Teachers' College.

Thompson, E. P. 1977. Folklore, Anthropology, and History. *Indian Historical Review* 3, no. 2: 240–66.

———. 1978. *The Poverty of Theory and Other Essays.* London: Merlin.

Tracey, Hugh. 1959. *Music of Africa.* Audio recordings. Roodepoort, Transvaal: International Library of African Music.

Turner, Victor W. 1967. *The Forest of Symbols.* Ithaca: Cornell University Press.

———. 1969. *The Ritual Process.* Chicago: Aldine.

Tyler, Stephen A. 1987. *The Unspeakable: Discourse, Dialogue, and Rhetoric in the Postmodern World.* Madison: University of Wisconsin Press.
Ulin, Robert. 1984. *Understanding Cultures.* Austin: University of Texas Press.
Vail, Leroy, and Landeg White. 1978. Plantation Protest: The History of a Mozambican Song. *Journal of Southern African Studies* 5, no. 1: 1–25.
———. 1983. Forms of Resistance: Songs and Perceptions of Power in Colonial Mozambique. *American Historical Review* 88, no. 4: 883–919.
———. 1991. *Power and the Praise Poem.* Charlottesville: University of Virginia Press.
Van Binsbergen, Wim, and Mathew Schoffeleers, eds. 1985. *Theoretical Explorations in African Religion.* London: Routledge and Kegan Paul.
Van Der Weil, A. C. A. 1977. *Migratory Wage Labour: Its Role in the Economy of Lesotho.* Mazenod, Lesotho: Mazenod Book Centre.
Van Drunen, Letitia. 1977. Lesotho Village Life and Migrant Labor. Ph.D. diss., University of Utrecht.
Van Onselen, Charles. 1982. *Studies in the Social and Economic History of the Witwatersrand, 1886–1914.* 2 New Nineveh. London: Longman.
Vansina, Jan. 1985. *Oral Tradition as History.* Madison: University of Wisconsin Press.
Wachsmann, Klaus, ed. 1971. *Essays on Music and History in Africa.* Evanston: Northwestern University Press.
Wainwright, A. T. 1979. The Praises of Xhosa Miners. M.A. thesis, University of the Witwatersrand.
Waterman, Christopher. 1990. *Juju.* Chicago: University of Chicago Press.
Wallman, Sandra. 1969. *Taking Out Hunger.* London: Athlone.
Webb, C. de B., and John B. Wright, eds. 1979. *The James Stuart Archive of Oral Evidence Relating to the History of the Zulu and Neighboring Peoples.* Durban: Killie Campbell Library.
Weisfelder, Richard. 1992. The Basotho Nation-State: What Legacy for the Future? *Journal of Modern African Studies* 19, no. 2: 221–56.
Wells, Robin. 1994. *An Introduction to the Music of the Basotho,* chap. 4. Morija, Lesotho: Morija Archives.
White, Landeg. 1982. Power and the Praise Poem. *Journal of Southern African Studies* 9, no. 1: 8–32.
Wilkinson, R. C. 1985. Migration in Lesotho. Ph.D. diss., Newcastle-upon-Tyne.
Williams, Raymond. 1972. *Drama in Performance.* Harmondsworth, England: Pelican.
———. 1976. *Keywords.* London: Fontana.
———. 1977. *Marxism and Literature.* London: Oxford University Press.
———. 1981. *Culture.* London: Fontana.
Wilson, Francis. 1972. *Migrant Labour in South Africa.* Johannesburg: SproCas.
Wolpe, H. 1972. Capitalism and Cheap Labour Power in South Africa: From Segregation to *Apartheid. Economy and Society* 1, no. 4: 425–56.

Index